MILTON AND
THE MAKING OF
*PARADISE LOST*

# Milton and
# the Making of
# *Paradise Lost*

WILLIAM POOLE

Harvard University Press

Cambridge, Massachusetts
London, England
2017

First printing

Library of Congress Cataloging-in-Publication Data
Names: Poole, William, 1977– author.
Title: Milton and the making of Paradise Lost / William Poole.
Description: Cambridge, Massachusetts : Harvard University Press, 2017. |
Includes bibliographical references and index.
Identifiers: LCCN 2017011997 | ISBN 9780674971073 (alk. paper)
Subjects: LCSH: Milton, John, 1608–1674—Biography. |
Milton, John, 1608–1674. Paradise lost—Criticism and interpretation.
Classification: LCC PR3581 .P64 2017 | DDC 821/.4 [B]—dc23
LC record available at https://lccn.loc.gov/2017011997

For Zoe

I am now to examine *Paradise Lost,* a poem which, considered with respect to design, may claim the first place, and with respect to performance the second, among the productions of the human mind.

SAMUEL JOHNSON

A Reader of *Milton* must be Always upon Duty; he is Surrounded with Sense, it rises in every Line, every Word is to the Purpose; There are no Lazy Intervals, All has been Consider'd, and Demands, and Merits Observation.

JONATHAN RICHARDSON

# Contents

# Preface and
# Acknowledgments

This book is an accessible introduction to and interpretation of the writing of the greatest single poem in the English language, John Milton's epic *Paradise Lost* (1667, second edition 1674). In offering an account of the making of *Paradise Lost*, this book is partly biographical and partly critical. Those interested predominantly in history may consider this something of a "stealth" biography, and may accordingly regret that I spend comparatively little time addressing, say, Milton's public, political life as an employee of successive interregnum regimes. On the other hand, those who seek a complete "reading" of Milton's poetry may miss a sustained analysis of, say, *Samson Agonistes* or *Paradise Regained*. I can only hope that the biography-of-a-poem hybrid that I have attempted possesses its own kind of coherence, and indeed that my manner of tying biographical concerns so closely to literary production will, after all, help to illuminate what an extraordinary achievement Milton's *Paradise Lost* is. I have also essayed in several chapters and an appendix to provide what are in effect reference guides to certain topics, notably Milton's known syllabus as a teacher, his theology, the evolution of his dramatic drafts, and the intricacies of the publication process of *Paradise Lost*. Some of these are rather technical, but then Milton was a technical man.

The particular focus of this study is on Milton as a reader and scholar, and indeed on how much of this scholarship was provoked and enhanced by his occupation as a teacher. To this extent my approach is, in Part 1, "Milton," more scholarly than critical, but Mercury can only speak with authority when Minerva speaks with him. Nevertheless, Part 2, "Paradise Lost," I hope, becomes increasingly critical as I lead the reader into some of the complexities of Paradise Lost's internal construction and interpretation. For me Milton is above all a late, perhaps even a belated, humanist, but one with pronounced Hellenistic (he would perhaps have said "Alexandrian") tastes, and a scholar who, sensitive to the times, and led on by his own massive self-esteem—a compound seemingly coined by Milton himself—drew some markedly radical conclusions from his reading. I have also tried to deal with the literary impact of some practical problems for Milton, most profoundly the total blindness to which he succumbed in 1652. That, to me, is the emotional core of this book. Conversely, I have only tangentially engaged with the politics of Paradise Lost, a notoriously inconclusive venture, not because I deny the political dimension of this poem or indeed of Milton's life as a poet, but simply because it has been done to death and it is time now to vary our critical accents. For the same reason I have tried to deviate from some of the more well-trod routes up the Miltonic mountain, stepping round Milton's Maske and his pastoral elegy "Lycidas," and providing instead a slightly more unusual route through his shorter poems.

Finally, it may be objected that to treat Milton's intellectual development as preparation for his great epic is Procrustean, Whiggish, and slavishly influenced by how Milton himself directed us to appraise his development. To this I answer that were this truly a biography, these criticisms would hit home. But my intention is to explain the genesis of a poem and how its writer came to be in a position to write it. I start and conclude this project, that is to say, with a conviction that the poem is paramount, and if I have managed to persuade readers not so well acquainted with Paradise Lost that it would be a good thing to become more so, I shall have succeeded. In short, I have tried hard not to speak solely to the community of experts.

This book was written in the summer vacation of 2016, but it is informed by some longer-term research, especially for my forthcoming editions of Milton's commonplace book and that section of the Trinity College manuscript in which Milton noted down dozens of ideas for prospective dramas. I have also relied on the research done for a few previous publications of my own; in particular the section on Milton's theology revisits themes developed in an earlier piece on "Milton's Theology."

As befits this kind of book, I have—with mixed success—tried to curb my references, although I have been free with bibliographical information in the chapters closest to reference guides. I am painfully aware that the more general the book on the more major the writer, the more one ends up re-peating one's more talented colleagues, often unawares. I would, however, like to acknowledge here the debt all writers on *Paradise Lost* continue to owe to Alastair Fowler's superb annotations for his Longman edition. Over the last several years, I have been deeply influenced by my friend Nicholas McDowell's ability to get Miltonic poetry and biography talking to one an-other, and I would also like to express my admiration for the criticism of John Leonard, David Quint, and John Rumrich. Rumrich in particular has done me several good turns now. I have relied heavily on the biographical tradition, most recently and notably Gordon Campbell and Tom Corns's *John Milton: Life, Work, and Thought* (2008), a work of great acumen, although I prefer Jeffrey Miller's recent restatement of the young Milton's religio-political milieu as that of a "conformable puritan."

Six friendly experts read parts or all of this manuscript at short notice. Thus I am deeply indebted for comments furnished by Gordon Campbell, Tom Corns, Edward Jones, and Nigel Smith; and I am especially fortunate to have had the whole text poked and prodded in almost medical detail by Zoe Hawkins and Jeffrey Miller. My readers for Harvard University Press produced unusually useful reports, for which I am also most grateful. Among the publishers, Mark Richards first suggested the project, and at Harvard, I thank my sympathetic editor, John Kulka, for allowing me to write this book when I had promised him a different one.

MILTON AND
THE MAKING OF
*PARADISE LOST*

# PART ONE

## Milton

# 1

## The Undertaking

I N THE WINTER of 1641–1642 an obscure London schoolmaster with his eyes on eternity was embroiled in a pamphlet war. The skirmish turned on a question of church discipline, or who ought to officiate in churches and what they should be called. On the one side, "two bishops of superior rank," as the private schoolmaster later recalled, were affirming that their episcopal order and office were biblical and hence divine in origin; on the other, "some eminent ministers" argued rather that bishops were not biblical and hence not divine, and that they and their office ought therefore to be abolished.

The young schoolmaster weighed in on the side of the "eminent ministers," with, as he later congratulated himself, decisive effect: he "bore aid to the ministers," until then "scarcely able to withstand the eloquence" of their opponents—"and from that time if anyone replied, I stepped in."[1]

This schoolmaster was John Milton (1608–1674), a man remembered today chiefly as a poet and a political writer, the author of *Paradise Lost*, *Samson Agonistes*, and *Paradise Regained*, the advocate of the right to divorce for reasons other than adultery, to a free press, and to depose and even execute tyrannical kings. At the time of this pamphlet war, however, he was merely a promising youngish scholar who had nevertheless rejected or avoided careers in the academe and the church, and who, after an inspiring literary tour of Italy in his thirties, had set up as a private schoolmaster back in London. Armed conflict had broken out in the summer of 1639 between the English and the Scots; the Short and then Long Parliaments were called in London in April and November of 1640 respectively; 1641 would see the outbreak of rebellion in Ireland; and the next year civil war itself finally descended on England.

Milton's little pamphlet war might at first strike modern readers as rather antiquarian, turning as it did on the equivalence or otherwise of two Greek words in the text of the New Testament—*episcopos* (bishop) and *presbuteros* (elder). One camp (termed "Presbyterians") argued that these words signified one and the same thing; the other (termed "Episcopalians") that they were distinct, *episcopoi* referring to members of a separate and senior rank from the *presbuteroi*. The stance that one took on this issue was, however, of fundamental importance for the larger political climate of the country. For if the order of bishops had no divine authority, as the Presbyterians argued, then bishops themselves, who had achieved considerable political power in the state, ought perhaps to have that power removed from them. And if priests, at least of an episcopal persuasion, no longer possessed that power, then perhaps many of the problems experienced by the state—which Milton and his allies blamed on the bishops and their priests—could be solved.

In fact, the bishops were already losing the political fight, and Milton and his party were snapping at the heels of a falling regime. Milton himself chose not to sign his initial contributions to this skirmish; they appeared anonymously, something a little at odds with his later presentation of himself as the great rescuing hero of the moment. But with his last two pamphlets, probably because Milton's onslaughts had provoked reprisals, Milton's self-estimation changed. Milton signed his new publications with his own name, stepping out of the shadow of those he had been defending and into a light all of his own.

Now, Milton found it expedient to tell his reader all about himself. Within these prose pamphlets ostensibly about church politics, Milton, who was not even a clergyman, gave his own personal history at length, insisting that he was and remained a pious and virginal scholar, one who had but interrupted "the full circle of my private studies" to aid slighted truth, one forced, for a brief season, to try his "left hand" at prose, a reluctant champion. For the schoolmaster was really a poet, one who had been lauded and applauded, so he advertised, even in "the private academies of Italy"; and poetry was his destiny: "I began thus farre to assent both to them [his Italian friends] and divers of my friends here at home, and not lesse to an inward prompting which now grew daily upon me, that by labour and intent study (which I take to be my portion in this life) joyn'd with the strong propensity of nature, I might perhaps leave something so written to aftertimes, as they should not willingly let it die."[2] "Something so written to aftertimes"—it is an extraordinary outburst. Pamphlet writers often went for each other's reputations but rarely did they bother to respond with such self-defensive, self-aggrandizing responses.

Milton had already offered some hints of his peculiar ambition at the end of his first, anonymous pamphlet against the bishops, where in an apocalyptic fantasy he had imagined himself amid a choir of the just, spectating the damned, singing "high *strains* in new and lofty *Measures*"—and these, Milton was clear, were his own specific, poetical strains and measures, not merely those of the choir around him.[3] This kind of thing was bound to provoke a response, and after Milton had started publishing under his own name, one of the episcopal party hit back hard. Milton was branded as a man who "spent his youth, in loytering, bezelling, and harlotting," who had been "vomited out" of the university and onto the streets of London, where he was to be found in "Play-Houses" and "Bordelli."[4] Milton's response to this unsigned attack was, again, arresting. He rehearsed once more the history of his reading habits and his personal purity. He had indeed attended comedies as a student, but only to laugh in scorn, he uneasily protested; and, approaching his mid-thirties, he claimed he was still a virgin.[5]

Readers of Milton have always cherished these autobiographical declarations; there are no major writers in English before him who have left us this kind of evidence. We can forget, however, how astonishingly egotistical, incongruous, even crass these digressions must have sounded to Milton's first readers—if, indeed, they followed such skirmishes closely and if they were as interested in Milton the man as he assumed they must be. For Milton was not merely clearing his own name but making a public declaration of intent: he would write the major poem of his age. It is an astounding undertaking, all the more so because the man who made it could not have been known to more than a handful of his readers—he was not a politician, or a man of wealth or status, or even an established cleric or academic. Who was this astonishingly confident, if touchy, private scholar?

Eleven years later John Milton had gone completely blind. Fifteen years later, in late 1667, appeared the work he had here obscurely pledged, the epic poem *Paradise Lost*. It is an extraordinary promise, with two and a half decades and total loss of sight separating the undertaking from its fulfillment. And yet fulfilled it was.

Nor is this a confidence that Milton kept out of his own poem. Indeed *Paradise Lost*, if anything, claims a centrality beyond mere national literature. Milton declared that his poem performed "Things unattempted yet in Prose and Rhime" (*PL* 1.16).[6] Later he cast a curled lip on previous epics, *all* previous epics: mere "tedious havoc of fabl'd Knights / In Battels feign'd" (*PL* 9.30–31). He, in contrast, would champion a new kind of heroism, a Christian heroism, to be revealed, implicitly at first and then explicitly, through his epic narration of what were actual events for Milton: the Rebellion of Satan in Heaven; the subsequent angelic war; the Creation of the visible universe; Adam and Eve in Eden; God's Prohibition of the Tree of the Knowledge of Good and Evil; the Temptation of Adam and Eve by Satan in the serpent; their Fall and Expulsion; and the subsequent Redemption of fallen mankind through the sacrifice of God's Son on a cross. Nor would this be a simple narrative: Milton sought to "justifie the wayes of God to men" (*PL* 1.26), to render a theologically coherent account of the traditional Christian interpretation of these historical events. He was, in short, offering a narrative solution to the "problem of evil": if God is good, whence evil? Previous epics had abounded with gods or God; but the fundamental theology of how the divine related to the human had been simply assumed by most prior writers. Milton would not assume it; he would justify it.

Milton's justification is examined and assessed later in this book, but a summary may be given here, as Milton's solution to this problem underpinned his entire ethical existence. His solution was that adopted by many prior and most subsequent systems of theistic belief: the free-will defense. God created humans free, and their sin is their own fault. This was not, however, an uncontroversial view in Milton's age, where the academic theology of his youth had been dominated by Calvinism, which taught that God had predestined all people to salvation or damnation, and that free will, at least in the theological sense of self-determination of one's own salvation, was illusory. Because he disagreed with this, Milton therefore made his poetic God present his own case himself, an extraordinarily bold move, paralleled only by Milton's equal and opposite audacity in allowing Satan his own eloquent, blasphemous voice.

How could Milton be so sure of his achievement and indeed of the safety of such an achievement? The narrator of *Paradise Lost*—a being presented by Milton as indistinguishable in biography and authority from Milton himself—tells us this is a poem not written by a man with his eyes open at his desk in the day, but delivered to a blind man at night, in bed, asleep, by a visitor who "dictates to me slumbring, or inspires / Easie my unpremeditated Verse" (9.23–24). At the halfway point in the epic this being is tactfully described as female, a classical muse, indeed the muse of astronomy, Urania (7.1), often represented in the period holding a celestial globe. To this extent Milton's nightly visitation is a poetic device. But Milton's initial invocation had been to a genuinely divine being, described in terms that imply for the Christian reader the Holy Ghost itself:

> Thou from the first
> Wast present, and with mighty wings outspread
> Dove-like satst brooding on the vast Abyss
> And mad'st it pregnant (*PL* 1.19–22)

This invocation is quite sincere—Milton called for, and hoped he had obtained, divine assistance. This tense balance, even compromise, between the classical and the sacred is fundamental to Milton's project: his divine intentions nevertheless work through the stories of pagan classicism; and the relation between these two forces is what is most interesting about Milton's poetics.

A connoisseur of new poetry in 1667 picking up this work in one of several London bookshops retailing *Paradise Lost* would have several points of comparison for this poem, but none both recent and strong. The long but unfinished late Elizabethan epic of Edmund Spenser, *The Faerie Queene*, remained an iconic achievement, but it was a distinctly antique book, and had not been republished since 1617. Spenser had continued a comparatively well-established, Italianate approach to Christian epic by writing moralized chivalric romance. Moreover *The Faerie Queene* was an allegory, whereas *Paradise Lost* retold biblical events, regarded as literally true, whatever subsidiary allegorical meanings they might also possess.

A closer comparison, therefore, was the biblical poetry of the Huguenot courtier and nobleman Guillaume de Saluste, sieur Du Bartas, whose *La Sepmaine* (The Week, 1578) in particular provoked a wave of imitations and translations across Protestant Europe. This initial work—Du Bartas was to follow it with *La Seconde Semaine* (The Second Week, first instalment in 1584), an incomplete attempt to bring his poem up to the end of the world— poeticized the week of divine creation, day by day, a conscious revival of the hexameral exegesis and indeed heroic poetry of the early Christians. In England, where Du Bartas found a readership even in his original French, dozens of partial translations appeared, most influentially those of the merchant and poet Josuah Sylvester, published between 1592 and 1608, the year of Milton's birth. (His main English retailer, indeed, was the printer Humfrey Lownes, whose print house was "at the signe of the Starre" on Bread Street, the street in which Milton was born and grew up.) This translation was still felt to be worth republishing in full in 1641.

Du Bartas was one of those rare modern vernacular poets deemed significant enough to merit a line-by-line commentary, that of the Frenchman Simon Goulart, a serious Protestant theologian and scholar; and Goulart's commentary, which was often published in English to accompany Du Bartas's poem, also earned a separate edition (first edition, 1621, several subsequent reissues). Biblical paraphrase in the Bartasian mode, applied to various periods of biblical history, became very fashionable in the Jacobean age. English examples include Samuel Daniel's short *Moyses in a Map of his Miracles* (1604), and William Alexander's long *Doomes-Day* (1614).[7] Indeed Du Bartas's work was close enough to biblical commentary that it could in effect be converted back into it, something achieved by the clergyman John Swan with his popular *Speculum mundi* (1635, five editions to 1698), a handy encyclopedia divided up into the days of creation and studded for ornament with excerpts from Sylvester's translation.

A contemporary reader might easily liken *Paradise Lost* to Du Bartas's *Divine Weeks and Works,* as it was known in English. A very attentive reader might even spot some significant debts and allusions, not least to Milton's Urania herself, who had earlier been Du Bartas's "heavenly muse," likewise appearing to him in a vision to direct his poetic destiny:

I am VRANIA (then a-loud said she)
Who humane-kinde aboue the *Poles* transport,
Teaching their hands to touch, and eyes to see
All th'enter-course of the *Celestiall Court.*[8]

Here and there Milton audibly improves and compresses Sylvester's translation, picking out pertinent words and jettisoning the rest: for instance, Milton's phrase "in his sun-bright chariot sat" (*PL* 6.10) brusquely pares down Sylvester's "As now the *sun,* circling about the ball, / (The Light's *bright chariot,*) doth enlighten all."[9] In one place Milton even transfers unaltered an entire line from the *Divine Weeks* into *Paradise Lost:* "Immutable, immortal, infinite."[10] Such ringing, line-length triplets, tethered to their negative prefixes, would later be held to be one of the hallmarks of the specifically Miltonic style:

Unrespited, unpitied, unrepreevd.

. . .

Unshak'n, unseduc'd, unterrifi'd.

. . .

Unpractis'd, unprepar'd, and still to seek. (*PL* 2.185, 5.899,
8.197)[11]

Yet any Restoration connoisseur of poetry would regard Sylvester's Du Bartas as extremely dated. Opened at random, *Paradise Lost* certainly might feel a little old fashioned, with its feet firmly in biblical paraphrase, but it would take only a few moments of browsing to reveal some exciting, even disturbing differences. First, very unusually, Milton's poem does not rhyme. He wrote in blank verse, something more obviously associated at the time with the genre of tragedy.[12] Second, Milton's project was vastly more ambitious than mere hexameral poetry, and Milton in effect dispatched the hexameron itself in a single book of his poem, the seventh. Hexameral poetry, moreover, had tended to distinguish sharply the poetry of God's Creation from the tragedy of man's Fall. It was a fairly safe and pious exercise to gloss the Six Days of Creation in meter, packing out the verse with contemporary natural philosophy—discussions of the sea, the land, and the flora belong to the Third Day, for instance, while the Fourth Day provided opportunity for explaining the motions of the heavenly bodies.

But dramatizing the Fall, be it in its angelic or human phases, or in both, was a quite different enterprise, and those who dared approach this topic therefore usually chose the genre of drama. After all, whereas God intones the Creation as a series of ghostly commands ("Let there be light"), Adam and Eve and the Serpent move about Eden, a physical place, and actually talk to one another ("And he said unto the woman, Yea, hath God said, Ye shall not eat of every tree of the garden?"). A good example of the poetic nervousness this section of the Bible could induce is Du Bartas himself, who in fact did address the Fall, but only in the *Seconde Semaine.* There he hurried the reader from the pre- to the postlapsarian world in as few lines as he could, covering over the actual events with a blanket of similes and disallowing any dialogue between Adam and Eve.[13]

Milton, who filled entire books with lengthy conversations between Adam, Eve, and the Serpent, could not be more different. In effect, Milton took the older tradition of the poem of biblical Creation, and set it, like a jewel held in calipers, inside a larger narrative of the human Fall in Eden—and set that too inside the precosmic disaster of the angelic fall, in the aftermath of which *Paradise Lost* opens. He then placed at the end of his poem, this time following Du Bartas's *Seconde Semaine,* a prophetic history of the events separating the Fall and Expulsion from the Second Coming and Last Judgment. And so *Paradise Lost* is, in brief, a double fall epic with a creation epic embedded inside it, and a final visionary appendix bringing the poem to the end of human time—the first divine comedy, set within angelic and human tragedies, and then crowned with the final divine comedy, ending in salvation, at least for the just.

This was something indeed more audacious than had hitherto been attempted. Moreover, the poet or his printer seemed unusually sure that the result was important enough that the reader would wish to be able to refer back to the text with exactness, and to communicate about this remarkable poem accurately with others. To that end the printer inserted line numbers down the side of the poem, in tens, a practice unwitnessed outside the editions of the Greek and Latin classics prepared for schoolboys and scholars.[14] In this quietly assured way, right from the first *Paradise Lost* announced itself to its readers as, quite literally, a classic.

This book traces the making of that classic in three phases. First, Chapters 1–13 examine the biographical processes that led to, and accompanied, the composition of *Paradise Lost*. Next, Chapters 14–22 present the poem itself—its structure, its genre, its content, its purpose, its method, and what kind of reader it demands. Finally, as a coda I examine how the poem was turned into a classic not simply by its author, who can only hope for such reception, but by its readers, who alone have the power, and the continued responsibility, to greet the poem on these terms.

# 2

## School and the Gils

MILTON'S FACILITY AND aesthetic as a writer flowed from his education, first as a pupil and then as a teacher. His early family life was happy, and his father, also named John, was a successful scrivener with a serious side interest in performing and composing music. He initially arranged for the young Milton to be taught privately at his London home by language tutors and by a hot protestant called Thomas Young, who hailed from Perthshire, via the University of St Andrews. We know little about this first educational relationship other than that Young and Milton later maintained a Latin correspondence-with-gifts, the teacher sending his former pupil a Hebrew bible, and the former pupil reciprocating with a copy of the new edition of Thomas Cranmer's *Reformatio legum ecclesiasticarum* (Reformation of Ecclesiastical Laws), the Edwardian legal blueprint for an international protestant reformation.[1] This may neatly characterize the shared cultural assumptions of the two at the time—Bible and Reform, "ev'n to the reforming of Reformation it self," as Milton later wrote.[2]

Young was what was termed a "conformable puritan," that is someone who sought further reformation but from within the church, and this probably best describes Milton's own attitudes as a young man. Milton addressed a Latin poem to Young in which he recalls with delight the pagan literature they read together, but also, perhaps, regrets that Young has felt the need to carry his ministry abroad.[3] Young may have been the one who introduced Milton to the world of polemical prose, as Milton's first pamphlets were written on behalf of a five-man literary dreadnought calling itself "Smectymnuus" (after their initials, T[homas] Y[oung] being the "ty"). Young and Milton's friendship does not seem to have survived the turbulent 1640s, as the latter grew more radical than the former.

We can be slightly more confident about Milton's formal schooling, for even though the Fire of 1666 removed most of the primary evidence, the school Milton attended, St Paul's, was an institution prominent enough to have left long grooves in the historical record. The school was in this period presided over by the formidable figures of Alexander Gil ("the Elder," 1565–1635) and subsequently his son, also Alexander ("the Younger," 1596/7–1642?), from 1609 to 1639, when the younger Gil was finally sacked for drunkenness and misconduct.[4]

The earliest detailed curriculum we have for the school dates only from the last three decades of the seventeenth century, but the course reported is unlikely to have evolved radically, and from this document we can get a reasonably clear sense of Milton's schooling.[5] At this point the school was divided into four lower and four upper forms. Lower school was devoted solely to Latin, getting as far as Ovid for poetry and Justinus for history. Versification into Latin took for its sources Proverbs, Psalms, or "a story in Heathen Gods"; short prose composition or "themes" on moral and divine subjects were also produced. In the upper school, Greek, especially New Testament Greek, was studied, with Hebrew in the final form, specifically "A Part in [the] Hebrew Psalter or Grammar." Latin poetry included Virgil and Martial, then Horace, Juvenal, and Persius; oratory was studied in Cicero, and history in Sallust. More advanced Greek was pursued among the poets in Homer, Aratus, and possibly Dionysius Periegetes; for oratory there was Demosthenes; and, for mythography, the *Library* of Apollodorus.

Milton was in adulthood critical of elements of his formal education. For instance, he called it "a preposterous exaction" to force "the empty wits of children to compose Theams, verses, and Orations, which are the acts of ripest judgement and the finall work of a head fill'd by long reading, and observing, with elegant maxims, and copious invention."[6] Although we do not know for sure when Milton entered St Paul's, this is good circumstantial evidence that he himself had experienced this kind of education. And almost all of the study specified above, both in reading and in generating verses and themes from this reading, contributed visibly to Milton's own achievement. His earliest surviving poetry consists of versifications and themes as above.[7] Ovid is a constant presence throughout his poetry, as an author both absorbed and transformed. Sallust was the man whom Milton in adulthood described as "the historian I prefer before any other Latin writer,"[8] Virgil and Homer structured his epic writing. And among the more complex Greeks it is intriguing to see already present in Milton's early education his favored geographical and astronomical poets, Dionysius and Aratus, as well as the compendium that stands behind a good deal of Milton's (and everyone else's) mythological references, the indispensable *Library* of Apollodorus. We will later see to what profound uses the adult Milton put these texts.

Being under the regime at St Paul's was not, however, necessarily a pleasant experience. Both the Gils were serious "firkers" or beaters of boys. Fractious and nepotistic, they argued with colleagues, and argued with one another. If Milton attended the junior half of the school, the man responsible for drilling him in the classical tongues was the undermaster William Sounds. Poor Sounds was professionally bullied by Gil the Elder, who openly wished to force him out in favor of one of his own sons. Gil proved unable to do so, and instead denounced Sounds as not up to the job of teaching Greek; Sounds was rebuked by the school's governors, the Mercers, and he confessed his Greek was a bit rusty.[9] We can only speculate what Milton made of all of this, but he cannot have been unaware of tensions in the school, and one wonders where John Aubrey and Andrew Marvell, both later acquaintances of Milton and not themselves Paulines, obtained their various stories about cruelty and mismanagement in the school.

Nevertheless Gil the Elder was a formidable scholar, and as the sole instructor of the upper four forms of the school, he had a pervasive influence on Milton's daily life for a number of years. Gil had himself been appointed to his post under a royal sign-manual, in which it was claimed that he was one of the translators working on what would be published in 1611 as King James's Authorized Version of the Bible.[10] This is a tantalizing and otherwise uncorroborated claim, but we might note that in his will Gil left to his wife a set of specific books, including no fewer than seventeen volumes of learned bibles and biblical aids, among them the valuable Antwerp Polyglot, several other Greek and Hebrew bibles, and a Hebrew concordance.[11] Gil's biblical Hebrew was real, and he passed it on to Milton.

If Gil's general influence as a teacher on Milton is undoubted but indefinite, the specific influence of his published writings on Milton poses a different kind of problem: we have tangible texts, but of debatable influence. First, in 1621, Gil published a revised edition of his *Logonomia Anglica* (first edition, 1619), probably just after Milton had entered his school. This was partly a polemic on spelling reform and partly a treatise on English and its development as a language. Gil, who promoted literary examples from recent English poets, proved himself a Saxon chauvinist, deprecating Chaucer, for instance—as an "infausto omine" (unlucky omen)—for introducing Frenchified and Latinizing terms into what had been hitherto, Gil claimed, an unadulterated tongue.[12] Gil emphasized that the spelling of English ought to follow the sound, although he allowed exceptions to his rule, specifically where orthography expresses derivation, a difference of meaning, usage, or dialect.

It has often been remarked that this (admittedly loose) rule—spell to the sound, unless there are good reasons or customs against it—can be traced in Milton's own practice, albeit in a slightly softened form. Milton's preferred spellings, and especially his minute adjustments to the orthography of the manuscript of the first book of *Paradise Lost,* show sensitivities in line with Gil's rules. Milton did not like the etymological spelling "subtle," for instance, preferring "suttle," as had Gil ("sutl" in Gil). He also favored the aural spellings of "hunderd" for "hundred" and "parlament" for "parliament." Gil's chapter on the syllable, as Helen Darbishire first noted, commented that in English a consonant without a vowel might stand for a syllable where a liquid consonant follows a mute consonant, for instance after the mutes "d" and "p." Gil gives as examples "bidden" and "open," which may, he claims, legitimately be spelled "biddn" and "opn," because we do not say "bid-den" and "op-en." It is fortunate that the manuscript for the first book of *Paradise Lost* survives. In it Milton, otherwise inexplicably, instructed his amanuensis to correct "forbidden" and "open" to "forbidd'n" and "op'n."[13] Poetically, Milton also believed in adjusting orthography to indicate stress, especially where metrical position did not already do so, and so he distinguished between "their" and "thir," "hee" and "he," "wee" and "we" (stressed versus unstressed). He felt strongly enough about this to insist among the printed errata he added to the first edition of *Paradise Lost* the change from "we" to "wee" at *Paradise Lost* 2.414 ("All circumspection, and we[e] now no less"), to point up a metrical heterodyne—an enforcement of poetic spelling unique to Milton among published poets of the period, and surely a legacy of his education.

A more numinous influence on Milton, however, was Gil's magnum opus, his *Sacred Philosophie of the Holy Scripture*, a quasi-philosophical commentary on the Apostles' Creed, published in 1635 when Gil was, as he states, "a dying man." The *Sacred Philosophie*, which Gil had been assembling since at least 1601 and drafting in earnest since 1625, was licensed and printed in early 1635. Gil died later that year, and the immediate promotion of his book was largely the work of Gil's son Alexander, who carpet-bombed almost every single Oxford (but no Cambridge) library with copies. (They are almost all still there on the shelves.) Milton's last surviving letter to the younger Gil dates from December 1634, in which Milton tells Gil to expect him on Monday, "among the booksellers." As they browsed the bookstalls of St Paul's together, surely Gil told Milton that his dying father's labor of over three decades was now complete, either at or on its way to the licenser, and about to enter production.[14]

*The Sacred Philosophie* is notable for its rationalist, even tolerationist hue. For instance, when addressing the *descensus* clause in the Creed ("He descended into Hell"), an article of particular theological sensitivity within the English church, Gil commenced his remarks by recognizing that "different interpretations" were possible, and that there was no point crying "heresie or schisme," "so long as the substance of it is granted."[15] Calvinistic theologians habitually interpreted this article as metaphorical: understood literally, it seemed too close to the popish story of Christ's "Harrowing of Hell," or the triumphant descent of Christ into Hell between the Crucifixion and the Resurrection, when Christ brought salvation to the righteous who had died since the beginning of the world but before Christ's own time. Gil himself, in what was becoming the Anglican interpretation, upheld the literal truth of the article, as did Roman Catholics; interestingly, he backed this up with a natural-philosophical discussion on the hollowness of the Earth. In this account, natural, even "chymical," philosophy supplied a physical mechanism for theological doctrine—the damned may indeed be literally under our feet.[16]

This commitment to finding rational support for revelation powered Gil's entire book. For him God and his ways were open to rational inquiry:

"is not reason the Scripture of God, which hee hath written in every mans heart?" God may be infinite, but he is not therefore incomprehensible: "I confesse that humane reason turning it selfe to behold the divine truthes, is as the eye of a Bat to looke on the Sunne. But yet the eternall and infinite truthes are so apprehended by mans finite understanding, as the light of the Sunne is by the eye, that is verely and indeed the same light, and no other."[17] Or as Milton expressed it a generation later in *Samson Agonistes:* "Just are the ways of God, / And justifiable to Men" (293–94). Gil therefore located his book in the tradition not of biblical commentary but of "natural theology," a genre traditionally performed with as little recourse to scripture as possible and in the register of debate against pagan objection. Gil looked back, explicitly, to Thomas Aquinas's *Summa contra Gentiles,* Raymond of Sebunde's *Theologia Naturalis,* and Girolamo Savonarola's *Triumphus Crucis.* Although previous commentators have acknowledged Gil's rationalism in this work, they have perhaps not appreciated how problematic, even gauche this may have looked in the increasingly tense religious climate of the 1630s, where overemphasis on the power of human reason courted the accusation of Socinianism, of method if not of doctrine. ("Socinianism" was the name of a Christian heresy frequently faulted for being too fond of logical method, often in conflict with what were felt by its detractors to be matters of faith.) And indeed Gil's *Sacred Philosophie,* half a lifetime in the making, fell stillborn from the press, exciting barely a murmur. As a document of rationalism it was perhaps too soon overtaken by William Chillingworth's classic *The Religion of Protestants a Safe Way to Salvation* (Oxford, 1638), which introduced to English thinking the notion of "moral certainty." This was a work that Chillingworth's bitter enemy, the deeply unlovely Presbyterian Francis Cheynell, cast into its author's open grave, declaiming "get thee gone, thou corrupt rotten booke . . . get thee gone into the place of rottennesse, that thou maiest rot with thy Author, and see corruption."[18] No one threw Gil's book into his grave; indeed hardly anyone seems to have picked it up at all.

Milton is a plausible exception. Gil, for instance, emphasized that the earliest Christian apologists knew that they had to reason philosophically and not simply appeal to scripture, for the authority of scripture was precisely the question under debate. He remarked that St Paul had quoted the pagan poet Aratus; and that the last pagan emperor, Julian the Apostate, in order to render the hated Christians intellectually powerless, had banned them from teaching the liberal arts.[19] Gil's linked citation of both these anecdotes is significant, because Milton, in his defense in *Areopagitica* (1644) of the Christian use of pagan literature and learning, likewise linked them:

> *Paul* especially . . . thought it no defilement to insert into holy Scripture the sentences of three Greek Poets, and one of them a Tragedian, the question was, notwithstanding sometimes controverted among the Primitive Doctors, but with great odds on that side which affirm'd it both lawfull and profitable, as was then evidently perceiv'd when *Julian* the Apostat, and suttlest enemy to our faith, made a decree forbidding Christians the study of heathen learning: for, said he, they wound us with our own weapons, and with our owne arts and sciences they overcome us.

Milton then went on to recall how two Christians, the Apollinares, father and son, sought to evade Julian's edict by translating scripture into classical genres: "the two *Apollinarii* were fain as a man may say, to coin all the seven liberall Sciences out of the Bible, reducing it into divers forms of Orations, Poems, Dialogues, ev'n to the calculating of a new Christian grammar."[20] The ultimate source for both men's accounts is the church historian Socrates Scholasticus:

> For the former, as a grammarian, composed a grammar consistent with the Christian faith: he also translated the Books of Moses into heroic verse; and paraphrased all the historical books of the Old Testament, putting them partly into dactylic measure, and partly reducing them to the form of dramatic tragedy. He purposely employed all kinds of verse, that no form of expression peculiar to the Greek language might be unknown or unheard of among Christians. The younger Apollinaris, who was well trained in eloquence, expounded the gospels and apostolic doctrines in the way of dialogue, as Plato among the Greeks had done.[21]

This Christian strategy of adaptation to and of the pagan intellectual tradition—we might call this strategy "Apollinarian"—was therefore not just a philosophical but a literary enterprise. This should not be mistaken for rapprochement, however. Underneath lurked a more hostile resolution, that the Christian recapture of pagan genres must conclude in the deletion of the pagan deities, even as they flee crying. Milton's "Ode on the Morning of Christ's Nativity" expressed this darker view with notable ambivalence:

> The parting Genius is with sighing sent,
> With flowre-inwov'n tresses torn
> The Nimphs in twilight shade of tangled thickets mourn.[22]

Gil the Elder was a linguist and a theologian. His son Alexander, however, who acquired the theological degrees his father lacked, was firmly a poet. It is customary to ask which English poets influenced Milton, and it is customary to assume that this is to ask what English poetry influenced Milton. Gil the Younger, however, wrote almost solely in Latin. Gil, who also taught in St Paul's—as under-usher from 1622, so he will not have taught (or beaten) Milton, who was by then in the upper forms—composed poems of considerable technical poise, but entirely of an occasional nature. He collected and published these in 1632, in a volume entitled *Parerga*. This appeared with a Virgilian quotation on its title page insinuating the poet's vocational uncertainty—"me quoque dicunt / Vatem pastores, sed non ego credulus illis" (The shepherds say that I am a poet, but I don't believe them), spoken in Virgil's ninth eclogue by one Lycidas.[23] This was a tactic Milton would imitate on several occasions—for instance, in the epigram to the first printing of *A Maske* (1637): "Eheu, quid volui misero mihi? floribus Austrum / Perditus" (Alas, what have I wished upon my wretched self? I have let the south wind upon my flowers), from Virgil's second eclogue.[24] Inside Gil's volume, we find poems on the death of a bishop, on the poet's father, even anti-Catholic epyllia. Milton wrote poems of these precise kinds too, although Gil's little volume was perforce of a quite different political complexion. Milton and Gil swapped poems, the younger man declaring the elder to be "the shrewdest judge of poetry, and the most honest judge of mine."[25]

But in late 1628 Gil proposed an unwise toast in Trinity College, Oxford, to the assassin of the Duke of Buckingham, and, overheard by the young William Chillingworth—he whom we encountered above being abused in his grave—the schoolmaster paid a heavy price.[26] Chillingworth, who may have had an animus against Gil anyway, fled murmuring to London, and informed his godfather William Laud, then Bishop of London. Gil, who was in holy orders by this point, was personally examined by Laud, and although, after the intercession of his father, he escaped having both his ears sheared off, he was fined heavily and imprisoned. The scandal was widely discussed, including by Joseph Mede, a fellow of Milton's college in Cambridge, Christ's College, who sent reports to a rural correspondent.[27] That Chillingworth was the snitch in Trinity was claimed by his fellow collegian "Deodat"—that is, Charles Diodati, Milton's best friend.[28] Gil may have acted foolishly, but Milton now had an admired friend in jail and disgrace for some hasty words in a college bar.[29] Gil's 1632 volume of poems, appearing after his release from prison, is therefore an expiatory publication, dedicated to Charles I, royalist and loyalist to a pitch that is cringing, and Milton surely cringed too. It is also at least partially a volume of prison poetry, as some of it was composed during Gil's period of incarceration in the Fleet.[30] Nor did Gil restrict his prison poetry to Latin: there survives a miserable little birthday poem from Gil to Charles I in English, imploring him for release: "A prison is a wombe whence onely you / Have power to bid bad men be borne anew."[31]

After Gil's disgrace, Milton wrote to him, encouraging him not to give up poetry—"if you have broken your promises to yourself, I praise your inconstancy"—and tactfully looking forward to the day when *res nostræ,* "our affairs," might at last become more fortunate, when Gil's *gratulatrices musas,* or "thanks-giving muses," might be heard once more.[32] Milton was responding to a poem Gil had sent him, his epyllion "In Sylvam-Ducis," an impressive hexameter piece on a recent siege, and Milton, perhaps just after Gil's release, was able to send in return his first actual publication, some printed Latin verses prepared for an official occasion at Cambridge, where Milton was now studying. (No copy of Milton's little edition has ever been recovered, but there is in Trinity College Cambridge a manuscript of Gil's poem which may well be the one Milton received.)[33] Later Gil sent Milton some hendecasyllables for the wedding of a female acquaintance, and to these Milton riposted with an ode, his one and only mature attempt at Greek verse composition, a translation of Psalm 114 "according to the rules of Greek heroic poetry."[34]

Gil's "Sylva Ducis" was one of the two poems of which he was most proud. As he advertised to the reader of his *Parerga:* "And if browsing through this farrago you should chance across some slight pieces, when indeed you come to the 'Sylva-Ducis,' or the 'Gesta Gustavi Magni,' it is in those that I should wish to be imitated, than to be criticised for the rest." Indeed, he

linked together the two poems, written perhaps in 1630 and 1631, respectively, by recalling the former in heroic diction in the opening lines of the
latter—"Arma priùs cecini" (Formerly I sang of arms)—on the deeds of
the Protestant hero, the Swedish king Gustavus Adolphus, who was unfortunately to fall in battle in 1632.[35]

When Gil sent the "Sylva-Ducis" to Milton, the younger poet was all
praise: "Poetry altogether grand, and everywhere truly redolent of poetical
majesty and Virgilian character."[36] "Sylva-Ducis" took as its subject a major
event in the continuing struggle of the Thirty Years' War, the siege of the
Brabantine city 's-Hertogenbosch (in French "Bois-le-Duc"; in Latin "Sylva
Ducis"). It was invested by Frederik Hendrik, Prince of Orange, in 1629, and
capitulated in September after three months' siege; four English regiments
were present. This was celebrated as a great victory for the States General
and the Protestant cause, and was a symbolic and strategic blow to the
Habsburg interest. An official account in Latin by the renowned humanist
scholar and poet Daniel Heinsius was commissioned officially, and published
by the Elzeviers at Leiden in 1631. The siege of "Shertoken-Busse" was the
subject of at least six English pamphlets, all struggling with the unfamiliarly
articulated name; one or more of these must have been used by Gil.[37]

It is also a reminder that Milton's whole life was overshadowed by warfare, and that the English Civil War took place in the wings of a much larger
conflict that had been raging across the continent since 1618. Critics often
debate how much of the actual fighting of the English Civil War marks Milton's *Paradise Lost,* but we should preface that discussion by noting that the
conflict of the Thirty Years' War certainly marked Milton's earlier poetry—
for instance, his elegy on Lancelot Andrewes, in which he alluded to the loss
of English forces at the siege of Breda in 1625, a siege Gil had also recalled
in his poem.[38] "Really, I don't know whether I ought to be more grateful to
Henry of Nassau for the capture of the city, or for your verses," Milton
bubbled.[39]

Gil's siege poem is notable because it adapts heroic diction to modern
warfare, specifically the invention of cannon:

> At Princeps operi intentus, rapidúsque moræque
> Impatiens, magnâ junctis cum viribus arte,
> Acrior insurgit, quasque ærea machina fundit
> Glandibus hostiles animos & moenia frangit.[40]

[But the Prince, intent on his work, speedy, and of delay
Impatient, with great craft and strength combined,
Fiercer, gathers force, and the brazen engine hurls missiles
    upon any
Hostile souls, and smashes in the walls.]

Gil, in a long classical negative simile, recalls, rather conventionally, Virgil's
Salmoneus with his shaking lamps, Athena smashing the ship of Ajax, Jupiter himself with his triple-forked spear—yet none of these come near "Ig-
nivoma *Henrici* quantum tormenta minantur, / Dejiciuntque altos explosa
tonitrua montes" (the fire-spewing machines of Henry, / Hurling thundering
explosions upon the high hills). And to his cannon, Henry joined mines:

> nunc ima petit, multáque fodinâ
> Callidus aggreditur, pyrióque trementia nitro
> Fundamenta quatit: magno convulsa fragore
> Mœnia dissiliunt.[41]

[now he seeks the lowest parts, and, crafty,
He advances through many mines, and with fiery nitre
Shakes the trembling foundations; with a mighty crash,
    convulsed,
The walls burst asunder.]

This verse reminds us that early modern battle poetry had to find ways of
accommodating the new technologies of warfare, notably gunpowder. Perhaps the greatest spike of such poetry in the period is be found in the many
neo-Latin battle poems inspired by the greatest sea-battle since antiquity, that
of Lepanto, in 1571.[42] But the terrors of such technology raised rebuke, too:

> But he that first did finde
> That Diuelish enemie to all Mankinde,
> *Pouder,* the *Gun* and *Bombard;* his great'st fame
> Is, That to future Times he left no Name.[43]

Gil, indeed, had a taste for poetry on the major sieges of the all-engulfing
war on the continent: he later wrote comparable poems to his "Sylva-Ducis":

first on the Siege of Maastricht (1632), and then on the Siege of Schenken-schans (1635–1636), although these only circulated in manuscript.[44]

Milton himself had already tried his hand at gunpowder poems, in a set of five epigrams and a longer epyllion on the Gunpowder Plot, all possibly written as Cambridge tutorial exercises in 1626 for the anniversary of the plot. But in this early poetry he was actually somewhat averse to modernist remark—gunpowder is usually periphrastically described, and Fawkes is mentioned by name only once, in Milton's first epigram, and without the usual tortuous wordplay on the name common to other poems on this theme.[45] Milton's taste remained rather for the complex classical allusion. We now appreciate that Milton's gunpowder epyllion was written in a tradition of such poems, and whereas some of the Latin poets writing comfortably after the event tried to put back into their narratives some historical accuracy, Milton opted for the reverse tendency—"a distillation of the tradition's mythological component."[46]

Such distillation can in fact be extremely subtle. When thinking of thunder-bearers in his own Fifth of November poem, for instance, Milton invoked neither some modern incendiary, nor the classic Jupiter, god of day-time thunder, but, very unusually, Summanus, the ancient Roman deity of specifically nocturnal thunder.[47] He was, as Pliny the Elder reported, one of the two gods of thunder the Romans retained from the original nine thunder gods of the Etruscans, and Jupiter's shadowy counterpart.[48] But Milton probably recalled Summanus too from the church father St Augustine's City of God, where he is introduced as an example of a deity once afforded greater honors than even Jupiter, but who is now so forgotten that no one remembers his name.[49] A passage in Ovid confirmed Augustine's sense of the obsolescence of this pagan false god, where a certain temple was said to have once been dedicated to Summanus, "whoever he is" (reddita, quisquis is est, Summano templa feruntur).[50] In short, where Gil would later use his war poetry to modernize and to particularize, Milton generalized, excavating myth, even suggesting, through his subtle choice of this outdated deity, how flimsy the pagan (and indeed, in these poems, Roman Catholic) traditions were. Milton, in short, used occasional poetry to meditate on some more general and abstract issues.

Gil, then, undoubtedly impressed Milton, and it is important to recognize that Gil and his poetry represent the kind of versification that Milton would most frequently have encountered as a young poet amid many other young poets. Yet the comparison introduced here serves also to underline a disjunction. Milton, unlike the younger Gil, was inclined to avoid occasional poetry as far as he could, or at least to co-opt it for less occasional purposes. His later examples, sonnets on the Piedmontese massacre, or for his familiar friends or approved political superiors, are, even as they are more personal in origin, altogether more publicly engaged, and often turn away at their conclusion from the occasion that prompted them and toward some broader, deeper literary world. For instance at the close of Milton's sonnet for the composer Henry Lawes, he writes:

> *Dante* shall give Fame leave to set thee higher
> Then his *Casella* whom he woo'd to sing
> Met in the milder shades of Purgatory.

This is a poetics quite removed from the traditional art of the occasional, where literary technicians of uncertain allegiance fuss over their subjects with uncertain sincerity. Milton remained committed to mythographic exploration in his poetry, probing the traditions of the ancients, finding in their weaknesses his own Apollinarian strengths. Although it provided the young Milton with something and someone to emulate, Gil's technically accomplished poetry, despite its justified reputation at the time, was simply not as profound in its range and depth of allusion or ambition.

# 3

## An Anxious Young Man

A FTER HIS SCHOOLING among the Gils, Milton attended the University of Cambridge from 1625 to 1631, a period in which the academic population numbered perhaps around three thousand men and boys.[1] These people lived together in corporate communities larger than any other comparable collectives in the country at that time, and the sense of competition between students must have been overwhelming. This is one reason why we can believe the otherwise extraordinary anecdotes from the period of scholarly labor, especially among the puritans: Edmund Calamy of Pembroke Hall was said to have studied sixteen hours a day; Joseph Truman of Clare Hall allowed himself only three hours sleep a night; William Bridge of Emmanuel rose at four in the morning every day, and so on.[2] These people were all professional, competitive readers, as the academic voltage they could generate from such reading might easily lead to success or otherwise for their futures. It was also an environment of complex hierarchies, rituals, and close homosociality, with very few places to hide if you were upset or unpopular.

Milton had grown up around the London book trade centered on St Paul's Cathedral, and in a new town he would have been quick to appraise the bookshops. Cambridge, home to so many scholars, had a busy first- and secondhand trade in books, probably the third largest in the country, clustered around Great St Mary's, the university church, in the center of the town. Even if Cambridge's actual printing was puny compared to what London offered, some of the more adventurous publications of the Cambridge press while Milton was a student would have caught his eye—for instance, the Latin translation of Paolo Sarpi on the Venetian Interdict of 1606–1607 (1626) by Sarpi's English champion, William Bedell; Phineas Fletcher's Gunpowder Plot poem the *Locustæ* (1627); and, most influentially, the *Clavis Apocalyptica* (1627) by the famous Joseph Mede of Christ's, Milton's own college.[3] It is inconceivable that Milton did not read at least the last of these books, and the presence of Fletcher in this list hints at what was quickly becoming a surprising strength of the Cambridge academic press—its poetry. As we saw, Milton was able to enclose some "printed" verses of his own in a 1628 letter to Alexander Gil, and so he himself probably transacted personally with the university's licensed printers, the academic brothers Thomas and John Buck, at their print house, the Angel, on the north side of the marketplace, next to Great St Mary's.[4]

Milton was admitted to Christ's College at the age of sixteen, perhaps just a little younger than the average freshman at the time. The college, founded in 1505, was by Milton's time the third largest by number in the university, comprehending around a dozen fellows and one hundred and fifty undergraduates, who all lodged in the college, up to three a room. The Elizabethan college had been at the hotter end of the Protestant spectrum, boasting such Calvinist heavyweights as William Perkins (1558–1602) and Andrew Willett (1561/2–1621), whose works dominated Cambridge's press, and George Downame (d. 1634), professor of logic, who, in advance of becoming a bishop like his father before him, demonstrated that the pope was the antichrist. But early on in the reign of King James VI and I, the college boat was rocked by the king's controversial imposition on the college of a royal chaplain as its head in 1610: "Woe is me for Christ's College," Samuel Ward of neighboring Sidney Sussex lamented. This chaplain, Valentine Cary, scandalized the puritan godly, and his appointment demonstrated to the dons that the king meant to pacify the university at large. The college's most famous theologian, William Ames, on one of whose works Milton would later model his own *De doctrina Christiana,* soon abandoned the college for a life of exile on the continent. By Milton's time the college could no longer be characterized as puritan in any factional sense; Cary's successor, Thomas Bainbridge, head of house in Milton's time, remodeled the college chapel along Laudian lines and even managed to get an organ installed, albeit after Milton's departure.[5]

The great scholar of the college in Milton's period was Joseph Mede, the famous exponent of the biblical Apocalypse and a man who apparently had difficulty pronouncing the letter "r"; he had been a fellow for over a decade by the time Milton arrived. Mede was the most prominent English millenarian of his day. A millenarian is someone who investigated, and believed in, the biblical promise of an imminent religious transformation in this world, ushering in a thousand-year period of grace, often presided over by Christ in person, followed by a final conflagration. As Mede's most recent biographer has demonstrated, millenarianism in and of itself "did not necessitate extreme political or social activism," and although some radicals were millenarians, not all millenarians were radicals.[6] Indeed, Mede was first and foremost a biblical critic, and one who thought that the book of Revelation contained exact if encoded historical information, referring to identifiable episodes spanning historical time from John the Divine to the present day and beyond. The seven vials of wrath of Revelation 16, poured out on the earth by seven angels, for instance, may be decoded in order as: (1) the coming of the religious reformers the Waldenisans, (2) the Reformation itself, (3) the Elizabethan religious and military victory over Spain, (4) the Swedish king, Gustavus Adolphus, "now at length come from the *North*" to bring the Thirty Years' War to a successful Protestant conclusion, (5) the imminent destruction of the wicked church of Rome, (6) the conversion of the Jews, and finally (7) the conquering throughout the world of Satan and his forces, in their various forms of fornication, idolatry, and tyranny.[7] Arminianism, that tendency within Protestantism that favored a theology of free will and, in its dominant English form, more ceremony in worship than stricter Protestants could approve, was the defining controversy of the day; and Mede was at least sympathetic theologically, and more than sympathetic ceremonially, toward the movement. Yet he hated Rome and was again quite clear exactly who the antichrist was.[8] He was also the college's Greek lecturer and one of its major undergraduate tutors: his surviving account books for his pupils and his newsletters to friends provide us with unique records of Cambridge life in the period.[9] Within the fellowship he was friends with John Alsop, a fellow from 1623, who seems to have served as the college librarian, eventually donating several dozen folios on the early history of each European state to the library. Mede's own *Clavis* shows considerable learning in this area, and Milton would in time apply himself to such study too. Alsop is often supposed to have been the editor of the *Justa Edwardo King Naufrago* (1637), to which Milton contributed "Lycidas" in memory of the drowned don Edward King; Alsop was King's executor and was directed by King's will to take whatever books he wished from the deceased scholar's library.[10] Later, Alsop, who was also Mede's executor and preached his funeral sermon, became a chaplain to Archbishop Laud, fled to France, met Descartes, and is said to have sparked interest in Cartesianism in Cambridge and hence in English intellectual culture in general by putting the controversial philosopher Henry More of Christ's in touch with the French philosopher.[11]

Mede was also thick with Milton's first tutor, William Chappell; in November 1615 the two dons were disciplined for "skoffing at the Dean" together in hall. Chappell, who was the college's Hebrew lecturer, was again theologically Arminian and would become one of Laud's men in Ireland, where he clashed with Archbishop James Ussher. The bookish but inert Michael Honywood was a fellow from 1618 until he abandoned the college for the Low Countries in the civil war; this quiet Royalist's enormous library is now in Lincoln Cathedral. Milton just missed the man destined to become the greatest Hebraist of his age, John Lightfoot, also a pupil of Chappell. Lightfoot's biblical exegesis elucidated the Jewish origins of many early Christian practices, and when we encounter, for instance, swinging censers of incense in Milton's Heaven, we are in the presence not of any Anglican sympathy but of Lightfoot on the Jewish Temple.[12] As for literary figures, Christ's numbered among its Jacobean alumni the poet Francis Quarles (BA 1609), and later William Hawkins (MA 1626), a poet in English and Latin, the friend and translator, too, of Milton's friend Alexander Gil the Younger. Hawkins and Gil addressed poems to one another, and Gil may well have pointed out Milton to Hawkins.

One prominent litterateur who actually overlapped with Milton in college was the future Cavalier poet John Cleveland. Four and a half years younger than Milton, he arrived in 1627 as a fifteen-year-old. Cleveland soon shot to fame as an aggressively courtly, subsequently cavalier, poet with an equally aggressive, immediately identifiable style. Cleveland only had one poetic trick, however—the merely startling comparison—and what generated a reputation fast also caused it to fade with equal celerity. Months after *Paradise Lost* first appeared, John Dryden appraised and dismissed Cleveland and "Clevelandism": "he gives us many times a hard nut to break our teeth, without a kernel for our pains." Such a style struck Dryden as merely a cheapening of the technique of metaphysical Donne: "the one [Donne] gives us deep thoughts in common language, though rough cadence; the other [Cleveland] gives us common thoughts in abstruse words."[13] Other than a few tiny splashes in his student versifying, Milton steered clear of Cleveland's noisy tricks, and indeed, with a few exceptions he piloted around the entire metaphysical continent.

We do not know how much contact Milton had with the literary scenes of other colleges, but given Milton's sensitivity to competition, he may have preened a little at the thought of yet another precocious young talent, this time Thomas Randolph at Trinity. Randolph was in academic terms exactly a year senior to Milton (BA 1628; MA 1631). He was a rising star in both Latin and English, and an especially successful writer of academic drama. Milton's later sneers at academic comedy may therefore have had quite precise targets. It has been proposed that Milton was recalling Edmund Stubbe's Latin *Fraus Honesta* (1616, revived 1629, printed 1632), but it is plausible that Milton had in his sights academic plays by Randolph and the puritan-bashing Peter Hausted too.[14] Randolph also presided as "father" of a "salting" in his college in 1627, a student rite of passage which Milton too would direct in his own college the year after Randolph; Cleveland also performed this office.[15]

Milton would not easily shake Randolph free: the letter from the ambassador and literary doyen Henry Wotton printed in Milton's 1645 *Poems* before the Ludlow *Maske* reveals that Wotton had first encountered Milton's masque "in the very close of the late *R*'s Poems, Printed at *Oxford,* wherunto it was added (as I now suppose) that the Accessory might help out the Principal, according to the Art of *Stationers.*"[16] This "R" can only be Randolph, for he had just died, and indeed his *Poems* were printed at Oxford; and Wotton's elegant joke on the "Principal," the person who actually commits a crime, and the "Accessory," the person who merely assists, nevertheless subtly reinforces the sense that Randolph, at least when Wotton was writing, was the dominant literary figure.

Milton came to snub his university ("Which . . . I never greatly admir'd").[17] But he was careful to state in his later autobiographical comments how admired he himself had been as a student. This was not quite, or certainly not always, true. Milton quarreled with his first tutor, the redoubtable Chappell, and was transferred in Michaelmas 1627 to the care of the milder Nathanael Tovey, who a few years later would also briefly take on Milton's younger brother Christopher. The tutor-pupil relationship was very close in this period, with the tutor reading to his students, directing their studies, looking after their money, and in some cases housing them in his own rooms.[18]

If Chappell and Tovey were anything like Mede, Milton's education for the BA would have been structured around simple Aristotelian textbooks, such as those of the Dutch philosopher Franco Burgersdijk and the German systematician Bartholomäus Keckermann. The dominant subject here was logic, the study of which in theory dominated Milton's two middle years of undergraduate work, as rhetoric did his first, and natural and moral philosophy his fourth. Milton himself would later compose a short textbook in Ramist logic, based on that of a former fellow of Christ's, George Downame, but also explicitly bearing the mark of Keckermann.[19]

Mede's accounts show that he used Keckermann textbooks in logic, ethics, physics, and metaphysics, and Keckermann's approach emphasized the methodical division of each academic subject into subdivisions, the further division of those subdivisions, and so on. It was a severely logical way of organizing knowledge, and it offered as one byproduct a ready-made way of dividing up and maintaining commonplace books. Moral philosophy, for instance, is divided into "general" versus "special" branches; the general branch deals with ethics, or ideas in the abstract (for example, moral evil, the good man, and so forth); the special branch is subdivided into two further branches, one dealing with "economics" or the moral philosophy of the household (marriage, education, etc.), the other with "politics" or the moral philosophy of the state (parliament, the tyrant, etc.).[20] How deeply this way of thinking influenced Milton can be seen simply by picking up his own surviving commonplace book, which is divided into roughly two halves, the first marked in his hand "ethical," and the second subdivided into "economic" and "political" indexes. That Milton drew up his commonplace book (therefore strictly speaking his commonplace book in moral philosophy) in this manner long after he had finished his undergraduate degrees is a sign of how thoroughly his educational experience had marked his patterns of thought.

Glimpses of Milton's intellectual and personal experiences under the Cambridge system are provided by his academic *prolusiones* (openings), seven of which were printed as a pendant, indeed as an unplanned afterthought,[21] to Milton's 1674 *Epistolae familiares*.[22] This student writing is a mixed bag of more or less compulsory forms: "exercises," the scripted openings of what then turned into improvisatory duels or "disputations" in college or in the higher arena of the university schools; "act verses," summarizing theses to be defended, again *viva voce*, by all university graduands; and "declamations," or orations on set themes. Milton preserved examples of all three.[23] Indeed it has been established that his two surviving sets of "act verses" were written to be performed by one of the fellows, John Forster, on the occasion of the visit of the Earl of Holland and the French ambassador in 1629.[24] (The young Cleveland, in an interesting contrast, had been selected by the college to compose and deliver in person the Latin speech of welcome to the earl.) This is a fascinating example of Milton ghostwriting for his seniors, and since we know he had been commissioned before this, he must have been recognized by his seniors as a reliable jobbing versifier. Milton also kept bits of his script of a longer, more festive oration, delivered in the college, in the vacation, at a salting. These aforementioned student-led rites of passage featured a "father" presiding over a heavy-drinking initiation ceremony in which he introduced the younger boys to the student body. This last speech is especially interesting as it shows Milton transitioning from Latin into English—a moment that must have been striking in the performance itself, which for once shows Milton in a position of collegial authority, as the appointed "father" of the salting, addressing his freshmen "sons" in Latin and punning on their names.

It is little surprise Milton preserved this last text, a testament of perhaps the high point of his college popularity. The interest of such performances lies partially in what they reveal about the sociality, indeed the homosociality, of the early modern college, and about Milton's sometimes uneasy relations with his contemporaries. It is in this salting text, for instance, that he admits that he had formerly been unpopular with some of his contemporaries "because of disagreements concerning our studies"—a rather high-minded point of dispute.[25] Milton was certainly critical in another prolusion of the quality of teaching at Cambridge: logic poorly taught, metaphysics a "Lernian bog," natural philosophy afflicted with "monkish disease," mathematics declining into rhetoric, and law conducted in a language that Milton could only call "American."[26] Milton's attacks may be trendily Baconian, but dons do not like to be told that they are bad teachers, and several passages in the *prolusiones* imply that Milton annoyed at least some of his fellow students.

In his salting speech he also reveals to us his college nickname, Domina (the Lady). This is an uneasy passage, partially shrouded in Greek, in which Milton alludes to the tale of Caenis, the woman raped by Neptune and then turned, at her request, into a man, Caeneus.[27]

These Latin exercises also tell us what literature Milton proposed as common reference points between himself and his auditors. They are invited to appreciate some complicated allusions (such as "in the Neronian sense of the word").[28] Knowledge is assumed of Greek proverbs, and some of the more obscure corners of classical poetry—for instance, the Orphic Hymn to the Dawn. Notably, for his declamation in college on whether day or night is the more excellent, Milton steeped his text in pagan cosmogony, from Orphic sources and from the *Theogony* of Hesiod, in an interesting portent of things to come. As Milton explains, Chaos, also known as Demogorgon, begat Earth, who begat Night; or perhaps, as Milton comments, Night, with Erebus, came directly from Chaos, as Hesiod says. Night, understood as female, was then pursued by the shepherd Phanes, but fled to the incestuous embrace of her brother Erebus, "a husband who was certainly very like herself." Quoting Hesiod again, Milton says that to this couple were born Aether and Day.[29] This passage shows that Milton had been reading the opening chapters of Boccaccio's *De genealogia deorum,* a key reference text in the period, in which the genealogies of the classical Gods are described in fifteen books. It was also the seminal account for the view (derived from a now lost work on mythography by, so Boccaccio claimed, one Theodontius) that all the gods came from Demogorgon.[30] Much of this would resurface later in Milton's life, restructured, in *Paradise Lost,* where we encounter Chaos, with Night now as his consort and Demogorgon as a separate being (2.959–67), and the incestuous coupling of Satan with his "perfect image" Sin (2.764).

Milton's longest exercise and quite possibly his degree piece, his declamation "in defense of learning," was delivered in the chapel, Milton wearing his statutory surplice. This also identifies Milton as a poet, and one who in the summer vacation just passed has spent his time napping under village elms and receiving the muses in his *sacros somnos* or holy slumbers, just like Hesiod before him, or Endymion in his nightly encounters with the moon.[31] This idea evidently stuck with Milton, for when, a few years later, he wrote to an unidentified correspondent to apologize for his lack of productivity, he returned to Endymion as a symbol of his own studious retirement: "as you said, that too much love of learning is in fault, & that I have given up my selfe to dreame away my yeares in the armes of studious retirement, like Endymion w^{th} the Moone, as the tale of Latmus goes."[32] Milton's studious retirement, in short, involved both scholarship and poetry.

The *prolusiones* represent Milton's compulsory writing for his degree. Some of the poetry he produced as a student may also have been compulsory, on the deaths of prominent university figures, for instance, and on the Gunpowder Plot, which, as we saw, first gave Milton the chance to experiment with epic form in miniature. This poetry is carefully innocent of any political engagement beyond a kind of passive acquiescence: Milton clearly had no scruples at this stage about writing institutional pieces, and his string of poems on the Nativity, Circumcision, and Passion of Jesus Christ show a young man comfortable with a kind of fashionable (but not necessarily Laudian) devotional poetry that is almost baroque in its effect.[33] It is important to concede that the radical Milton of the 1640s nevertheless saw no difficulty in publishing all these pieces in his first collection of poems, in 1645. Milton evidently remained proud of his student literary progress.

Nevertheless there were shocks and shocking things in Milton's Cambridge too. Quite apart from the constant physical threat of plague, there were pressures on intellectual life, especially when academics were deemed to have approached a little too close to political free speech. One such event in particular, albeit before Milton arrived at Cambridge, has resonance for Milton's later thought. In 1622, following a rash Palm Sunday sermon in Oxford by one William Knight of Broadgates Hall, the biblical commentary on Paul's Epistle to the Romans (1613) by the German Reformed divine David Pareus (1548–1622) had been consigned to the flames publicly in London and at the two universities; book burnings were relatively infrequent in the period, and this one is all the more notable for it.[34] Pareus was condemned for several propositions: that the clergy could excommunicate their magistrates and rulers; that subjects in positions of power might take up arms against a tyrant; and that private subjects might defend themselves against attacks by a tyrant on their persons and property. Later, Milton would uphold several of the propositions for which the German's book had suffered, and he himself would enlist "the grave authority of Pareus," excerpting Pareus on Romans 13 in his list of Protestant precedents in *The Tenure of Kings and Magistrates*.[35]

The political signals around such proscriptions could be complex, however. In 1628 some excessively groveling sermons by the royal chaplain Roger Maynwaring were combusted, again in the capital and at both universities. The oleaginous Maynwaring had claimed that kings, higher than angels, might even be said to participate in God's essence; and that parliaments in no sense empowered kings, but were simply instruments for imposing the regal will. Maynwaring's doctrine, in the eyes of Parliament, threatened "the rights and liberties of subjects," and in an ominous skirmish Maynwaring was severely disciplined, with the reluctant but temporary acquiescence of the monarch. He was imprisoned, fined, suspended, and barred from both sacred and secular office, but to no lasting effect, as Charles pardoned him within a month of his condemnation, and in 1636 Maynwaring was consecrated Bishop of St David's.[36]

Yet the overall drift of political authority became obvious to Milton at Cambridge in more direct, even personal ways. In 1627 Fulke Greville, Lord Brooke, appointed the Dutch scholar Isaac Dorislaus to the lectureship in history he had just established at Cambridge, but to disastrous effect. Dorislaus lectured on Tacitus, specifically passages concerned with deposing tyrants in ancient Rome, on "the Power of the People under the Kings," on the replacement of the monarchical by the consular system—and on modern parallels. He was himself swiftly deposed from his lectureship. The vice chancellor was called on to investigate, and the vice chancellor at that point was Thomas Bainbridge, Master of Milton's college.[37] Opinions differed on how subversive Dorislaus had really been, and the fact that Cambridge split along party lines was the real key to the event: Calvinist academics were in favor of their Leiden-educated coreligionist, Arminian ceremonialists against. The latter party, on appeal to the king, prevailed.[38] Brooke was murdered in 1628, shortly after the assassination of the Duke of Buckingham. Dorislaus himself would be stabbed to death in a revenge hit by Royalists abroad in 1649; he faced his killers with folded arms.[39] In time, Milton would work in government with Dorislaus's son, also Isaac, who specialized in tampering with mail.[40] We cannot know if the young Milton attended the elder Dorislaus's notorious lectures, but he can scarcely have remained innocent of the controversy they ignited in claustrophobic Cambridge. It was against this backdrop that in 1628 Milton heard the news of Gil's punishment for toasting the assassin John Felton.

# 4

## Ambitions

THE ANTIQUARY JOHN AUBREY famously recorded that at the age of ten Milton "was then a Poet," and Milton's brother Christopher confirmed for Aubrey that as a schoolboy Milton "composed many Copies of verses, which might well become a riper age."[1] Alongside these signs of precocity we must place Milton's equally signal excuses of not yet being ready to perform. We encounter this reticence at every stage of Milton's career, from his student poetry, to the "forc'd fingers rude" at the opening of "Lycidas," to Milton's self-rallying sonnets on his blindness, and even retrospectively in his acknowledgment in *Paradise Lost* itself of his "long choosing, and beginning late" (9.26). We find exactly the same sentiments in Milton's youthful correspondence: in one letter, his Pegasus is as yet barely able to fly; in another, writing explicitly of his priestly vocation, but implicitly of his life as a writer, he bemoans the "reciprocal contradiction of ebbing and flowing at once."[2]

This ebb-and-flow dynamic—that of the prodigy unready to perform, or whose performances are really practices—is fundamental to Milton's self-conception as a poet. This is perhaps not uncommon for writers. But it is also fundamental to Milton's presentation of himself as a poet, and that, for his time, is the more unusual, even egotistical, attitude.

These tidal positions not only accompany but also generate Milton's poetry, for instance his sonnet on his twenty-third birthday, "How soon hath Time, the subtle thief of youth," in which he poetically complains about his lack of poetic progress: "My hasting days fly on with full career, / But my late spring no bud or blossom shew'th." This sonnet is a version of the traditional *dies natalis* poem, typically presented as a cheery birthday present to a friend. Milton's example, however, is self-addressed, consolatory, and with a fascinatingly weak, passive sestet, unable to allay the doubts rehearsed in the octave, and concluding with a conditional in its penultimate line "All is, *if* I have grace to use it so." It is, and deliberately so, neither a very confident nor indeed a very happy birthday poem. It is intriguing, therefore, that Milton chose to enclose it in the letter, discussed in Chapter 3, in which he apologizes to his unidentified correspondent for his seeming lack of direction.[3]

The birthday sonnet, addressing Milton's underachievement to date, was written at the same time, and may be read in tandem with a seemingly rather different poem, indeed Milton's first widely available poem. This is "On Shakespear," the crucial transitional text of Milton's early development. It tackles exactly the same problem as the birthday sonnet but from the other end, as it were—the preempting achievements of one's rivals, those whom the birthday sonnet had called the "more timely-happy spirits." "On Shakespear" was prefixed to a famous book, the *Comedies, Histories, and Tragedies of Mr. William Shakespeare,* in the edition known as the "Second Folio," published in 1632. How the young Milton came to be asked to contribute this, one of three new poems added to the new edition of Shakespeare's plays, is a puzzle, but he had evidently composed the poem a few years before publication, as when he republished it in his own 1645 *Poems* he dated it to 1630. Unlike many of the other writers of such verses, Milton was far too young to have known Shakespeare in person; and despite the seemingly affectionate "my *Shakespear*" of its opening, Milton's poem is not a heartfelt commemoration of a colleague or a friend but in its heart a colder literary appraisal.

Several striking observations about how this publication came to pass have been made by Gordon Campbell.[4] First, an earlier poem is to be found incised on a funeral monument to three members of the Stanley family in the church of St Bartholomew in Tong, Shropshire, dating from perhaps

1602 or 1603, and it appears to be the ultimate source for some phrases and rhymes of Milton's poem. Moreover, this inscriptional poem circulated quite widely in manuscript. And finally the text of this incised poem was attributed by several of Milton's contemporaries, including the antiquary Sir William Dugdale, to Shakespeare himself. This means that Milton probably believed that he was paying Shakespeare the compliment of complex imitation—writing an elegy *on* Shakespeare out of an elegy *by* Shakespeare. But regardless of whether the Tong connection is sound, Milton was likely to have known that he was also writing a poem within a genre already inhabited by juxtapositions of fame and graves, of whether reputations live on in poems or in monuments, in words or in things. This kind of poem was rooted in one of the most famous of Horace's odes, the final of the third book, with its "Exegi monumentum aere perennius / regalique situ pyramidum altius" (I have raised a monument [i.e., my poetry] more permanent than bronze, / And higher than the royal foundation of the pyramids).[5] Indeed, if Milton read Shakespeare's sonnets, not printed in the Folio, he would immediately have recognized Shakespeare's obsession with this ebb-and-flow dynamic too. Sonnet 60, for instance, starts with the eroding waves of time ("Like as the waves make towards the pebbled shore, / So do our minutes hasten to their end"), and ends on a hope that art may render permanent what life cannot ("And yet to times in hope my verse shall stand, / Praising thy worth, despite his cruel hand").

Campbell makes a final, virtuosic remark on Shakespeare and the youth of Milton. Milton's father, the scrivener and composer, is named in certain legal documents as a trustee of the Blackfriars Theatre, Shakespeare's theater. Now it was once suspected that Milton Senior frowned on Milton's poetic aspirations, and that this poem first appeared anonymously for that reason.[6] But if Milton Senior acted in some legal capacity for the theater, he may rather have been the catalyst than the obstruction here, and Campbell further notes that one of the other new anonymous poems for the Second Folio was signed "J. M. S."—John Milton Senior?

On a first reading, John Milton Junior's deceptively simple poem of eight heroic couplets might almost pass muster as an unexceptionable piece of Caroline exaggeration:

> On Shakespear. 1630.
> What needs my *Shakespear* for his honour'd Bones,
> The labour of an age in piled Stones,

Or that his hallow'd reliques should be hid
Under a Star-ypointing *Pyramid?*
Dear son of memory, great heir of Fame,
What need'st thou such weak witnes of thy name?
Thou in our wonder and astonishment
Hast built thy self a live-long Monument.
For whilst to th'shame of slow-endeavouring art,
Thy easie numbers flow, and that each heart
Hath from the leaves of thy unvalu'd Book,
Those Delphick lines with deep impression took,
Then thou our fancy of it self bereaving,
Dost make us Marble with too much conceaving;
And so Sepulcher'd in such pomp dost lie,
That Kings for such a Tomb would wish to die.[7]

This is as close to poetry in the dialect of John Donne and his school as Milton ever ventured, and even then it is more introverted and restrained in its "metaphysics." The poem asks whether "my" Shakespeare needs a physical tomb, and answers that such a tomb is not needed, because one has already been supplied by Shakespeare himself. This is the conceit (that is, concept, from the Italian *concetto*) of the poem, and it is rephrased, with variations, at the level of the couplet, from the first to the last. This is why the poem has a clear relation to the metaphysical style. But the first ripple in the poem's fabric is that this promised sepulcher is not to be found in Shakespeare's works—the book to which this poem is prefaced—but "in our wonder and astonishment." The (great) writer lives on not in the dead letter but in his reception, in the living spirit of interpretation.

At this point in the poem, however, it is claimed that Shakespeare prompts in his interpreters not amiable appreciation but the stronger, more alarming emotion of "shame"—at least in the other writers turning in Shakespeare's wake, with their "slow-endeavouring art," struggling to match the "easy numbers" of the child of nature. "Delphick," too, continues the dislocation of Shakespeare from the world of real writers: Apollo's oracle at Delphi was a quasi-divine figure, an old woman known as the Pythia, and her predictions were wrapped in riddles, hard to understand. For Shakespeare to be "Delphick" subtly undermines his achievement as a human, for the Pythia was not really speaking at all, merely Apollo through her. Some mythographers placed her origins before the Trojan War, and claimed that Homer himself had inserted her prophetic verses into his epics.[8]

Perhaps the most crafted couplet in the poem, however, is the penultimate one: "Then thou, our fancy of itself bereaving, / Dost make us marble with too much conceiving." Milton here employs slight hyperbaton, the unsettling of normal word order, in order to assure a rhyme on "bereaving" / "conceaving," a death / life juxtaposition at the heart of both this poem and the tradition in which it lies. If we straighten out the syntax, Shakespeare is "bereaving" (taking away) "our fancy," somewhat mysteriously, "of itself." ("Fancy" is the early modern faculty of creativity, so here, imagination is severed from imagination itself—as if the loss is felt, like mental amputation.) Shakespeare, in fact, turns his competitors into "Marble," a sentiment subtly prepared by the poem's earlier word, "astonishment" (note the conventional "marble" / "marvel" pun too). This was associated by false etymology with "stone," and we can compare Milton's own "Forget thyself to marble" in "Il Penseroso."[9] Shakespeare's legacy, then, is not life-giving writing but the paralyzing present of writer's block—literary posterity *is* Shakespeare's tomb, a wilderness of impeded writers, leaning at angles about a disused graveyard. Kings may indeed wish for such a tomb, but it is clearly bad news for the aspiring young poet.

Milton's first prominent printed poem, then, envisages the world of writing as one of not collaboration but competition. It is a world in which great writers paralyze rather than inspire those who come after them. If this is praise, it is backhanded praise, perhaps rendered acceptable by its air of tactical deference and its conventionally obsequious conclusion—this is all recognizable "metaphysics." There is however a way out of this predicament, a hidden possibility in the grammar of the penultimate couplet. "With too much conceiving" is, we initially assume, grammatically attached to "Thou," the sense being "Thou, Shakespeare, with thy too much conceiving," in the sense of thinking, creating, giving birth. But, delayed as this phrase is until the end of the couplet, we might also attach it grammatically to "us," and now "we" turn into marble because of *our own* "too much conceiving." In short, we are worrying too much. If we read the poem on the former grammar, Shakespeare is hard to escape; but if we read the poem on the latter grammar, Shakespeare must be escaped. Shakespeare only petrifies those who let him petrify them. There are here two poems living within one grid of words, and the second poem is more iconoclastic than the first.

It might indeed be suspected that the poem is not really about Shakespeare at all. Although Milton evidently appreciated Shakespeare and openly allowed his influence into works such as *A Maske,* and perhaps more covertly elsewhere, Shakespeare was not a competitor in Milton's eyes. Shakespeare wrote popular and insular drama for a fee-paying public, whereas Milton thought as a polyglot European, as a late humanist, and wished both to root and to be praised for rooting his work in European, late humanist traditions.[10] Thus even in Milton's poem on Shakespeare we can detect that Milton is already setting up Shakespeare as a thing of nature, different not in degree but in kind from the sons of art. This reclassification is, as many subsequent writers have realized, a coping mechanism. Milton was to elaborate on it in "L'Allegro":

> Then to the well-trod stage anon,
> If *Jonsons* learned Sock be on,
> Or sweetest *Shakespear* fancies childe,
> Warble his native Wood-notes wilde (131–34)

Here Jonson is the learned one whereas Shakespeare is the natural, if a natural who is rendered a little too rustic, a little too "wilde." The contrast between Jonson and Shakespeare as "art" versus "nature" was therefore current barely half a generation after Shakespeare's death, and while Jonson was still alive. Indeed, Milton took and developed the distinction from Jonson himself, specifically from the poem he set before Shakespeare's Folio. Milton's poem is in effect commentary on Jonson's lines:

> Thou art a Moniment, without a tombe,
> And art alive still, while thy Booke doth live,
> And we have wits to read, and praise to give.[11]

Jonson too wrote of "my" Shakespeare, but he in fact stepped back, a little too noisily perhaps, from giving Shakespeare entirely over to nature when he qualified: "Yet must I not give Nature all: thy art, / My gentle Shakespeare, must enjoy a part." Milton, conversely, reaffirms the divide. This misleading and condescending distinction between the fanciful Shakespeare and his learned observers bequeathed to literary history a distortion, the effects of which still trouble us today.

Milton rarely acknowledged other English poets and writers by name. Exceptions are "our renowned," even "our learned *Chaucer*," and "our old poet *Gower*," but when he came to speak of these poets in print, he gestured to them chiefly for their alleged proto-Protestantism.[12] Of the recent dead, Edmund Spenser received honorable mention in *Areopagitica*—"our sage and serious Poet *Spencer*"—and Milton deployed Spenser's man of iron, Talus, in *Eikonoklastes*.[13] Milton also admired Sir Philip Sidney's *Arcadia*, which he read for its moral lessons, noting appreciatively in his commonplace book passages against suicide, toasts, a corrupt oligarchy, and women sleeping their way to the top. But he hypocritically retracted this admiration ("no serious Book, but . . . the vaine amatorious Poem of Sir Philip Sidneys") when it became expedient later in his career to denounce Charles I for apparently plagiarizing from Sidney some of his own preexecution prayers.[14] It was the same with contemporary scholars, theologians, politicians, and even sects—Milton usually did not like naming contemporaries, because it pinned him to a grubby present and to an insular horizon. Only a handful of revered politicians and personal friends would ever see their names uttered by Milton in any artistic statement he wished to be permanent, and these were in a type of sonnet Milton developed for the purpose.

It was completely different with continental poets and writers, although "continental" for Milton usually contracted to "Italian." Dante, Petrarch, and Ariosto—again as alleged witnesses to pre-Reformation discontent with Romish popery—all make an appearance in Milton's first published prose work, *Of Reformation* (1641). Galileo himself makes a heroic entrance in *Areopagitica* (1644), and is later awarded two mentions in *Paradise Lost*, first as the *"Tuscan* Artist," and then by name, *"Galileo,"* albeit in interestingly ambiguous passages (1.288; 5.262). No other contemporary of Milton is honored by name in his epic. In contrast, Milton was extremely wary of French literary culture, and he all but ignored the more northern nations.

It is unsurprising therefore that as a young man the ambitious Milton had resolved to visit Italy itself. Milton prepared for his trip by intensive study of Italian history and literature. He worked up his spoken Italian to fluency, perhaps with his friend Charles Diodati and his family, or at the Italian Church in London, around which the community of Italian-speaking Protestants gathered. Of course he read a great deal of poetry, most intensively Dante and Petrarch, but also Tasso's *La Gerusalemme Liberata,* Ariosto's *Orlando*

*Furioso*, and Boiardo's *Orlando Inamorato* (in the *rifacimento* of Berni or the subsequent *rimaneggiamento* of Domenichi).[15] He had long owned copies of the sixteenth-century Florentine poets Giovanni Della Casa and Benedetto Varchi, exact contemporaries of one another; Della Casa in particular had already supplied Milton with both the model and the motivation for the strange new music of the *canzone*-style "Lycidas." Italian poetry was accompanied by Italian literary theory: it was probably at this time that Milton studied Jacopo Mazzoni on Dante, Torquato Tasso on epic poetry, and Castelvetro's Italian gloss-commentary on Aristotle's *Poetics*, three works he would later recommend for his ideal academy in his tract *Of Education* (1644).[16] For historiography he read the huge history of Florence by the fourteenth-century writer Villani, whose work contained the first biography of Dante; he later used this book to teach Italian to his nephews. Milton also wrote to his friend Charles Diodati to ask for a copy of a particular history of Venice.[17] Italian national history was acquired from the Latin works of Carlo Sigonio, a particularly impressive author, whose two large folios *De Regno Italiae* (1574) and *De Occidentali Imperio* (1578) covered the thousand years separating the third from the thirteenth centuries. Sigonio had experienced significant trouble getting these works published: the volume covering the later period had initially been suppressed; and the volume covering the earlier period only appeared after Sigonio grudgingly upheld the authenticity of the Donation of Constantine, which he had initially refused to declare genuine. Milton himself would also later treat the Donation of Constantine—whereby Constantine the Great had apparently handed over to Pope Sylvester authority over the Roman West—as authentic, an almost inexplicable error for a Protestant polemicist.[18]

Milton, as hinted, also had an interest in literary biography, and the biographies he read shaped his own ambitions. Like all schoolboys, he knew Donatus's *Vita Virgilii* and perhaps some of the other ancient lives of Virgil, and it has been suggested that Milton's student sobriquet "The Lady" is an allusion to Virgil's nickname Parthenias, (Virgin), given to him when he was a student at Naples, a conjecture strengthened by Milton's repeated early assertions of his own chastity.[19] In the 1630s Milton appears to have studied the lives of the later Italian poets too. He acquired from some secondhand stall in London a copy of Giovanni Boccaccio's *Life of Dante* (Rome, 1544); this uncommon little book had once been owned by none other than Sir Thomas Bodley, founder of the Oxford library that bears his name. Milton

proceeded to collate this book against the only other available edition of Boccaccio's biography, a doubly remarkable feat as both editions were exceptionally rare in northern Europe. His notes show that he worked out that
the other, later edition of this biography had been censored in order to rid
it of a passage, ironically, on the posthumous censorship of Dante.[20] Milton
was one of the earliest Englishmen to pay any attention to this work, and
that he sniffed out the problem of censorship in its textual history is an indication of just how intently and intensely Milton studied his books, and
how interested he was in the topic of censorship itself. In *Areopagitica* (1644),
his celebrated defense of a free press—though not free, however, for Roman
Catholics—Milton would even reproduce from copies in his possession examples of Catholic imprimaturs.[21]

Boccaccio's *Life of Dante*, itself heavily influenced by Donatus's life of
Virgil, from which several patterns are repeated, is concerned above all with
the poetic vocation itself and how the poet should conduct his life. For the
poet, the virtues of scholarship are emphasized, as well as dietary and sexual
temperance. But Boccaccio brought to his biography of Dante some new
preoccupations, namely the tension between Latin and the vernacular as
the proper language of poetry; the problem of the divine poet as treading
close to blasphemy; the difficulty of deciding whether the poet should
engage with or disengage from public, political life; and whether the love
of which a poet must write should be human or divine love. These were all
to prove central concerns for Milton too.

Milton also read the Italian biographies of Ariosto, or perhaps just Sir
John Harington's confection of these for his "Life of Ariosto," written to accompany Harington's famous 1591 verse translation of *Orlando Furioso*. We
know this because Milton appealed to the example of Ariosto when defending his choice to write his most ambitious poetry in the vernacular:
"I apply'd my selfe to that resolution which *Ariosto* follow'd against the per-
swasions of *Bembo*, to fix all the industry and art I could unite to the adorning
of my native tongue."[22] In fact the original passage includes a balder statement of ambition, suppressed by Milton: "His answere [to Bembo] was, that
he had rather be one of the principal & chiefe Thuscan writers, then scarce
the second or third among the Latines: adding, that he found his humor (his
Genius as he called it) best inclining to it."[23] Milton would also have pondered Ariosto's distaste for a career in law, into which Ariosto had initially
been pressed by his father. Ovid had made the same complaint, in his poem

on poetical immortality, and so had Petrarch, in a passage later copied out by Milton. This biographical topos gives point to Milton's thanks to his musical father in his Latin poem "Ad patrem" for not pushing him into law, especially given Milton's rejection of a clerical career.[24] The life of Ariosto contained a further trope for the budding poet: poetic inspiration happens before other people arise, often in the middle of the night. Thus Ariosto was said to get up spontaneously at one or two in the morning and call for ink and paper—"an early riser," as Harington's side note read.[25]

Milton's preparation paid off.[26] In Italy he was greeted as admirably conversable for an Englishman, in both Latin and Italian. He managed to gain introductions to several prominent cultural figures, and at least one highly controversial personage, namely Galileo himself, then under house arrest. Milton was introduced to Galileo either by Élie Diodati, Galileo's translator and the relative of Milton's best friend Charles Diodati, or by Milton's friend Carlo Dati, who had been taught by him, or by Galileo's son Vincenzo, whom Dati included among a list of friends greeting Milton in one of his later letters to the English poet. Milton famously recalled his meeting with Galileo in a passage in *Areopagitica*, and there is no reason to disbelieve his account. Milton also attended musical performances; startled by his first experience of a proper professional female singer, he wrote a string of epigrams on Leonora Baroni. In his second poem to her he gracefully alluded to the biography of Tasso, imprisoned for his love of another Leonora; this detail he had surely found in the first biography of Tasso, written by the nobleman Giovanni Battista Manso.[27]

Milton's most important Italian discovery, however, was the literary academies, especially the Florentine ones, and he possessed the fluency, the talent, and the credentials to participate in these learned symposia. In Florence he seems to have attended meetings of the Svogliati (The Will-less) and the Apatisti (The Unruffled). He certainly performed some of his poems before the former, as the Sovgliati recorded this in their proceedings; and he was even named in a list of the Apatisti's members.[28] It was most unusual for an English visitor to become so involved in and accepted by what were in effect exclusive literary salons, and Milton's (Latin) poems were evidently admired. He received the dedication of a sonnet cycle of fifty equivocal, rustic sonnets, "La Tina," by Antonio Malatesti, the sole surviving manuscript of which has only very recently come to light.[29] Milton later recalled his Italian academician friends in the *Defensio secunda* (1654) with nostalgic, defiant pride, and although many biographers have suspected Milton of exaggerating his bonds with these men, the archives of the academies bear out his claims, and it is hard to produce any other comparable foreign figure who, notwithstanding the obvious confessional divide, managed to pass so confidently into such intimacy with the academicians.

Milton collected testimonials, mostly poetic, from several of these men, and he was so proud of these tributes that he printed them before his Latin poems when he came to publish them several years later as the second half of his 1645 *Poems*. And indeed they were rather special: no other book from the fashionable atelier of Milton's publisher, Humphrey Moseley, boasts such cosmopolitan trappings. The list was headed by Giovanni Battista Manso, Marchese di Villalago, "a man of noble rank and authority, to whom Torquato Tasso, the famous Italian poet, wrote his book on friendship," as Milton proudly wrote of him in the *Defensio secunda;* Manso, also the patron of Marino, had even been named in a list of worthies in Tasso's *Gerusalemme Conquistata*.[30] Manso, now in his seventies, produced one elegiac couplet for Milton; Milton sycophantically responded with one hundred hexameters.

Manso's testimonial nevertheless turned on a slight dig at Milton's membership of a heretic church: "Ut mens, forma, decor, facies, mos, si pietas sic, / Non Anglus, verùm herclè Angelus ipse fores" (If only your faith were as your mind, body, grace, face, fashion, / You should have been no Angle but, assuredly, a very Angel).[31] Milton's inclusion of the couplet at the head of his little collection of such salutations brings into implied existence alongside it his own commentary. He was charming, he was clever, he was admired; but, it is implied, in a city where many Englishmen went about under false names, Milton obfuscated neither himself nor his religion.

Manso's couplet is then followed in Milton's collection of testimonia by further epigrams. Giovanni Salzilli, one of the Roman academy of the Fantastici, using the old association of poets with their local rivers hailed Milton as a poet crowned with the triple crown of Greek, Latin, and Tuscan:

> Cede Meles, cedat depressa Mincius urna;
>> Sebetus Tassum desinat usque loqui;
> At Thamesis victor cunctis ferat altior undas
>> Nam per te Milto par tribus unus erit.[32]

[Yield, Meles, and let yield Mincius with urn sunk down,
 Let Sebetus stop talking always of Tasso;
But let the Thames bear its waves higher than the rest,
 For through you, Milton, that one shall equal those three.]

And, in a couplet Dryden would later imitate in his own epigram on Milton, set below the portrait of Milton in Jacob Tonson's 1688 illustrated edition of *Paradise Lost,* the mysterious Selvaggi said that Milton, an Englishman, equalled Homer and Virgil.[33] The Florentine Antonio Francini, one of the Apatisti, addressed an ode in Italian to the "Nobile [!—what had Milton been claiming?] Inglese," in which he picked out for particular praise Milton's facility with languages:

Ch'Ode oltr'all Anglia il suo piu degno Idioma
Spagna, Francia, Toscana, e Grecia e Roma.[34]

[{For from your lips} not only England, but Spain, France,
Tuscany, Greece, Rome, hear each her most dignified speech.]

Another of the Apatisti, the young scholar Carlo Dati, in a display letter, called Milton the "Polyglottus," "in whose mouth languages now lost are . . . revived"; Dati and Milton struck up a friendship that long survived Milton's return home.

These are typical exaggerations—the shorter the epigram, the taller the praise—and it has sometimes been wondered how Milton managed to solicit precisely this kind of hyperbole. I suspect that Milton, following the common custom, kept an *album amicorum* on his travels, a little pocket book which the traveler would ask notable figures to inscribe with short couplets or mottos, or even more extended salutations exactly in the manner of the Dati address. Milton himself signed several later in life, even after he was blind. It is a great tragedy his own *album amicorum* seems not to have survived.

Whatever the origin of Milton's testimonials, they all imply one crucial fact: Milton presented himself to the Italian academicians as an epic poet, even though he was one as yet without an epic poem. In his poem to Manso, Milton famously explained the kind of poem he had in mind: commenting, with a hopeful exaggeration of the available sources, that the ancient British druids were also epic poets, he went on to envisage his own Arthurian (pro-British, anti-Saxon) epic:

> O mihi si mea sors talem concedat amicum
> Phoebaeos decorasse viros qui tam bene norit,
> Si quando indigenas revocabo in carmina reges,
> Arturumque etiam sub terris bella moventem,
> Aut dicam invictae sociali foedere mensae,
> Magnanimos heroas, et (O modo spiritus ad sit)
> Frangam Saxonicas Britonum sub Marte phalanges.[35]

> [O let it be my lot to have such a friend,
> Who shall have known so well how to have graced the men
>     of Phoebus,
> If I shall someday recall into poetry the kings of my land,
> Even Arthur, urging wars under the earth,
> Or shall I say of the great-souled heroes, in the pact
> Invincible of the round table, and (O, only grant me
>     inspiration!)
> I shall smash the Saxon phalanxes under the Mars of the
>     British.]

Rather disconcertingly, Milton concluded his poem to Manso by imagining himself, Milton, dead, applauding with a bright red face his own achievements: "Ridens purpureo suffundar lumine vultus / Et simul aethereo plaudam mihi laetus Olympo" (Laughing, my face suffused with a purple glow, on ethereal Olympus, happy, I shall applaud myself).[36] We do not know what Manso made of this extraordinary egotism. It is also noteworthy how strongly Milton must have emphasized, amid all his impressive polyglottism, his Englishness. For every single poem to him mentions it upfront: "Anglum," "Anglum," "Anglia," "Inglese," and finally "Londiniensi."

In terms of Milton's development, however, what he heard was perhaps more important than what he performed. It is particularly suggestive that at least one of the sessions of the Svogliati in Florence which we know Milton attended featured a recitation by Milton in the midst of several other interesting activities:

A di 24 Mar. [1629]

Furon recitate oltre un elogio et un sonneto dal signor
 Cavalcanti diverse poesie Toscane delli signori Bartolommei, Buommatei e Doni, che lesse una scena della
 sua Tragedia, e diversi poesi latine del Signor Miltonio e un
 epigrama dal signor Girolami.[37]

[On 24 March 1629:

There were recited, besides a eulogy and a sonnet of
 Mr. Cavalcanti, various Tuscan poems of the Messrs.
 Bartolommei, Buonmattei, and Doni, who read a scene
 from his Tragedy, and various Latin poems of Mr. Milton,
 and an epigram of Mr. Girolami.]

So of the six recorded performances at this symposium, some were in Tuscan
(the dialect of Tuscany, already emerging as the dominant literary language)
and some in Latin. Milton, moreover, read out more than one of his poems;
and Doni read out a scene from a new tragedy. These were readings like
those reported in classical times by Pliny the Younger, where all sorts of
literary compositions were performed by their authors, including orations,
history, tragedy, and lyric.[38] Doni and his tragedy are of particular interest,
because when Milton returned to England he set about writing down ideas
for tragedies of his own, including on the Fall of Man, and out of these grew
some of the verse of *Paradise Lost*. Of the many causes that fed into the epic,
one of them, therefore, may well have been this experience of participating
in a literary symposium, the like of which England did not possess.

# 5

# Milton's Syllabus

AFTER HE RETURNED from Italy in the summer of 1639, Milton set up as a private teacher, and his home doubled as his school. Edward and John Phillips, Milton's nephews by his sister Anne, moved in, and became his pupils. Others may have lodged with Milton too, especially after he transferred to a bigger house in Aldersgate Street. We know only some of the names of Milton's pupils, but several were of a rank and wealth that suggest a high level of trust and presumably of remuneration. Over the 1640s, these included the aristocrats Richard Barry, who became second Earl of Barrymore in late 1642, Thomas, later Sir Thomas, Gardiner of Essex, and Richard Jones, son of the boorish first Viscount Ranelagh and his literary wife, Lady Katherine Boyle, herself sister to the famous chemist and philosopher Robert Boyle.[1] Milton was no impoverished graduate eking out an existence as a pedagogue but a self-sufficient intellectual already with a private income, experimenting on the well-to-do in his educational laboratory.

Edward Phillips, who was only ten when he became his uncle's pupil, told the antiquary John Aubrey that Milton rendered both Phillips boys fluent in Latin in one year flat. And in three years, he had led them through "the best of Latin & Greec poetts," whom Phillips recalled in detail.[2] Aubrey must then have quizzed Edward about these claims, as he returned to this account to add further snippets of information. Which authors were you taught first?, Aubrey enquired. Cato, Varro, and Columella, were the slightly surprising answers—the three Latin writers *de re rustica,* on agriculture (Phillips would later add the fourth, Palladius, to this list). Aubrey, who was himself an enthusiast of the more practical aspects of mathematical and astronomical education, also asked whether such study under Milton was all just books.[3] No, Edward replied, "and with him [the Greek astronomical poet Aratus] the use of the Globes." A further comment prompted Aubrey to add in the margin "and some Rudiments of Arithmetique and Geometry." Was he "severe"? Yes, Edward admitted, but "most familiar and free in his conversation" to those who had been his pupils. What about music? "He made his Nephews Songsters, and sing from the time they were with him."[4]

Edward Phillips eventually published his own biography of Milton as a preface to his translation of his uncle's *Letters of State* (1694). In it he reprised the same information, with considerable material not picked up by Aubrey. Yet the two accounts of what authors were studied cohere, and with them we can compare Milton's own prescriptive remarks in his tract *Of Education* (1644), in which he laid out what might seem an impossibly ambitious curriculum were it not that Phillips confirmed enough of it to suggest that it was grounded in practice.

*Of Education* was commissioned by the London-based intelligencer and educational reformer Samuel Hartlib, to whom it is addressed as a letter. Yet it is in many aspects quite out of kilter with the Hartlibians, who were pursuing educational reform along a far more radical trajectory than Milton could ever have traveled. Milton was evidently solicited for a tract on the subject of education, and this must be because he had been made known to Hartlib as a brilliant graduate of independent means, who had set up as a private teacher out of genuine interest in the problem of education. Nevertheless, as has been excellently demonstrated by Timothy Raylor, Milton was in fact proposing an intellectually unstable amalgam. On the one hand, his ideal school looked like a modernizing French-style academy for aristocratic youth, but on the other hand his ideal pupils were nourished on what in context was a reactionary, textual diet of traditional authors—some indeed of a level of obscurity that even a university graduate might be forgiven for not having heard of, let alone read, them.[5]

Now it might be objected that in recalling his experiences as a pupil Edward Phillips was reinforcing his memories from his own reading of his uncle's *Of Education*. But in fact his published writing is formidably learned in ancient and modern authors and languages in just the manner of his uncle's precepts, and thus he may be allowed to corroborate his own testimony. Even if this was a viable curriculum, however, it was a punishing one: if we compare, say, the Cambridge don Richard Holdsworth's "Directions for a Student in the Universitie," prepared for Milton's student contemporaries, it would have seemed preposterously elementary for a pupil who had passed through Milton's hands—Holdsworth's students stick to little systems and Latin authors, only stumbling into the Greek of Demosthenes and Homer at the end of their degree.[6] Milton advertised, and rendered, a superior service.

It is worth taking some time to reconstruct the teaching and learning of Milton's classroom, and in the appendix to this book I have laid out in parallel columns the authors taught by Milton as recorded by Phillips in his life of Milton, by Phillips as he was interviewed by Aubrey, and then finally by Milton as he laid out his ideal curriculum in *Of Education*. Milton's own list is, inevitably, somewhat longer, as it describes an elasticated ideal, but the three display such core similarities that we can use them together to get a fairly good picture of what Milton did as a teacher. An understanding of Milton's syllabus is fundamental to his own literary art because, as Phillips said, teaching this curriculum made Milton himself reengage with the authors he considered to be the most important: *dum docent discunt,* we learn by teaching.[7]

Milton, like any other schoolmaster of the time, taught his pupils not only to read but also to speak Latin. But ever the Italophile, and quite out of keeping with the prevailing practice in the northern climes, Milton insisted that his students pronounce Latin "as near as may be to the Italian, especially in the vowels." Although complaints about the English manner of pronouncing Latin were common, Milton's extreme Italianism was eccentric; a generation or so earlier, when Giordano Bruno had visited Oxford, he was jeered at by the dons for uttering words like *"chentrum & chirculus & chircumferenchia"*—Englishmen pronounced their Latin C's hard and not as affricates.[8]

Milton's pupils commenced serious study in Latin, as we saw, with the *authores de re rustica,* an austere and earthy start, "an occasion of inciting and inabling them hereafter to improve the tillage of their country, to recover the bad soil, and to remedy the wast that is made of good: for this was one of Hercules praises," as Milton himself admonished.[9] Milton's obvious moralism of "good" and "bad soil" is also the authentic accent of the rustic authors; Cato, for instance, opened his text with, respectively, applause, distaste, and denunciation for the farmer, the trader, and the usurer. This view would be carried across into Milton's own severely "georgic" approach to gardening in *Paradise Lost:* man was not placed in Eden to relax. Such reading may have been followed immediately by the eight books of Celsus on medicine, for not only does he appear next in the lists of both Phillips and Milton, but the *De re medica* commences as a continuation and complement to the *res agricultura:* "Ut alimenta sanis corporibus Agricultura sic sanitatem aegris Medicina promittit" (As Agriculture gives food to healthy bodies, so Medicine gives health to sick bodies).[10] Milton's medical understanding of his own eventual blindness may have rested on Celsus.

A similar kind of approach to Greek was adopted too, Milton recommending in *Of Education* "all the historical physiology of Aristotle and Theophrastus," meaning by this Aristotle's *History of Animals* and Theophrastus's *History of Plants.* (It is possible that this general phrase included Aristotle's *Generation of Animals* and *Parts of Animals* too.) Phillips does not recall this stage, but he did remember reading the second- and third-century military strategists Polyaenus and Aelian, alongside the much earlier classics of the fourth-century BC soldier and historian Xenophon, namely his *Anabasis,* on the Ten Thousand stranded in Persia and their famous march to the sea, and his *Cyropedia,* an essay on the qualities of the ideal ruler, widely used in Renaissance classrooms.[11] Milton's manner of listing in *Of Education* shows that he considered all these books to be part of a student's training in moral philosophy. Some of Milton's texts were, as suggested, very obscure: among his moral philosophical authors he added "the Locrian remnants," that is to say (pseudo-)Timaeus of Locri's *On the Soul of the World and of Nature,* a short Platonic text still accepted in Milton's time as really by that Timaeus who lent his name, and perhaps his philosophy, to Plato's dialogue of that title.[12] And, in a premonition of how searching Milton's own study of classical astronomy would prove to be, he recommended as an introductory textbook the *Isagoge* of Geminus, a mathematician of the first century BC; this was in scholarly terms a recent rediscovery, the *editio princeps,* which Milton almost certainly used, having appeared only in 1590.[13] A classroom containing both Timaeus of Locri and Geminus was indeed a school of rather advanced study.

Back in Latin, notable prose texts in specialist areas both recommended by Milton and recalled by Phillips include "a great part of" Pliny the Elder's vast *Natural History;* the Roman strategist Frontinus, from whom Milton himself took notes;[14] and Vitruvius, the first-century BC Roman architect and engineer, whose *On Architecture* is important not just for its strictly architectural content but for its descriptions of ancient machines of all kinds. These are important inclusions because they show that Milton's thought fully embraced the more scientific side of education, specifically natural philosophy, the quadrivial arts, and, as Phillips confirmed to Aubrey, the practical use of globes and maps. Milton's own comment on cartography here is revealing, as he wished maps to be studied "first with the old names, and then with the new," so he himself must have profited from comparing the classical geographers with the accounts of the more recent voyages of discovery. Milton also recommended for study quite early on in his syllabus "any compendious method of natural philosophy," and he evidently equipped students with basic skills in arithmetic, geometry, and even trigonometry.[15]

One area that does not seem to have left any trace in Milton's teaching is the so-called new science, that complex of modernizing ideas and practices we might associate with thinkers such as Francis Bacon, William Harvey, or René Descartes. This has come as a disappointment to some later scholars of Milton, who would prefer their poets to be leaning into the future. Yet turning to Milton's prescriptions in *Of Education* we learn that he would bolster natural philosophy not with any neoteric works but with Seneca's *Natural Questions;* likewise geographical study was to be grounded in the earliest Roman geographers, Pomponius Mela and Solinus.[16] 1644, the year of *Of Education,* was also the year in which on the continent Descartes published his influential *Principia Philosophiæ,* which proposed, hypothetically, a cosmic physics based on swirling vortices of particulate matter; this hypothesis, which had a brief vogue in English philosophy, did not even touch *Paradise Lost,* which, as we shall see, poetically combined the older matter theory of four elements with an Epicurean interest in shaped atoms. Milton later claimed that when on a reading retreat in the country in the 1630s he would now and then travel to London "for learning something new in mathematics or in music, in which I at that time delighted."[17] This may well have been so, but it had little impact on his surviving writing, and there is no evidence in any version of his syllabus that he taught any of the *novatores,* despite his obvious later interest in his epic in the claims of Galileo, an interest he shared with any other literate person.

Turning to the modern languages, it is interesting that here we can detect a slight divergence between what Phillips really remembered and what Milton ideally recommended. For Milton, still deeply enamored of his Italian experience, that literary language was the one absolutely necessary modern tongue, and in *Of Education* he recommended Italian comedy as light reading for his pupils. But Phillips recalled something altogether more typical of Milton's strategy of combining factual learning with language practice: Phillips learned his Italian by reading historical writing, specifically Giovanni Villani, the fourteenth-century Florentine banker and historian, from whose *Croniche* Milton himself took notes at this time.[18] In contrast, Milton disliked French culture ("the monsieurs of Paris," as he snorted) intensely, and so it is ironic, as hinted above, that the chief, if implicit and resisted, model of the more active side of *Of Education* was in fact the upwardly mobile French academy. And so it is that Milton in *Of Education* passes over French as a language in silence, despite the fact that he clearly knew it and taught it. For Phillips records that as a pupil he read Pierre Davity's geographical work *Les Estats, empires, et principautez du monde* (1613, many subsequent editions) to gain proficiency in the language. This popular work took as its inspiration the Italian Giovanni Botero's seminal *Relazioni Universali* (published in expanding editions from 1591 and translated into English in 1603), essays on political geography.[19] This political emphasis was carried over by Davity into his French work, and an impression of this text's preoccupations can be quickly gained from the fixed headings under which each autonomous state, from Great Britain, to Japan in the East, to the thirty-odd states of the "Nouveau Monde' in the West, is treated—"Sommaire" (geographical boundaries and subdivisions), "Qualité," "Moeurs Anciennes," "Moeurs de ce temps," "Richesses," "Forces," "Gouvernement," "Religion," and "Rois" (or "Ducs," etc., as appropriate). The reason this is relevant to Milton's own writing is that it is a work packed with suggestive cultural details: the Chinese, for instance, "vsent au plat païs d'vne espece de chariots à vent & à voile" (employ on level ground a kind of wind-and-sail powered chariot). This detail would turn up in *Paradise Lost:* compare the close phrasing of Milton's "Sericana, where Chineses drive / With sails and wind their cany waggons light" (3.438–39).[20] Milton himself was a completely fluent reader of French, crunching through several huge historical folios in the language in the 1640s; Davity alone is a fat quarto of almost fifteen hundred pages.

Milton's own expanded account in *Of Education* shows us how he hoped that his ideal education would go beyond what he was managing to do with his small cohort, not least because Milton's ideal academy "should be at once both school and university." Thus he included the *trivium* of logic, rhetoric, and poetics, albeit now reoriented, with logic firmly relegated to the role of a supporting art to rhetoric—it had been quite otherwise in Milton's own Cambridge education, where the curricular emphasis had been on logic—and rhetoric giving way to poetics, delayed until late in the curriculum, when the pupil was ready. Rhetoric was studied in "Plato, Aristotle, Phalereus, Cicero, Hermogenes, Longinus,"[21] conventional sources. By "poetics" Milton meant the theory of poetry, as encountered in Aristotle and Horace, but here he more unusually augmented these again conventional starting points with the works of the three sixteenth-century Italian theorists Castelvetro, Tasso, and Mazzoni, as we have seen. This last prescription is especially helpful for any literary assessment of Milton, as it shows that he indeed studied the Italian theorists, and of these Tasso would prove to be a fundamental theoretical reference point for Milton's own evolving ideas on epic.

Finally, although Milton only promised to bring his ideal students to the equivalent of the MA—the conclusion of undergraduate study as it was structured at the time—he evidently considered that an introduction to the higher, graduate disciplines of law, medicine, and theology was desirable. Law was to be encountered in the texts of Justinian, possibly just the *Institutes*, the shortest part of the Corpus Juris Civilis, explicitly framed as a first textbook in Roman law.[22] Medicine, as we saw, had probably already been encountered in the *De re medica* of Celsus. *Of Education*, a tract replete with military metaphors, was written in the midst of the first civil war, and a Parliamentary accent might be discerned in Milton's insistence that the civil law of the academe had to be supplemented with the common law: his ideal pupils would study "the Saxon and common laws of England, and the statutes." Likewise Milton's "physick" was to be practical as well as theoretical: his students should "know the tempers, the humours, the seasons, and how to manage a crudity." But of all of this ambitious stuff, Phillips recalled only the classical Celsus.

Finally, this was to be a rather active education. Milton envisaged guest lectures by "Hunters, fowlers, Fishermen, Shepherds, Gardeners, *Apothecaries . . . Architects,* Engineers, Mariners, *Anatomists*"; and as for "Their Exercise," Milton's well-to-do young men were to practice swordsmanship, wrestling, music, and military maneuvers, and to embark on school expeditions to all parts of the country, even onto the high seas. This is all terribly virtuous: these athletic, sober intellectuals were to be the nation's future leaders. Indeed, Milton writes in the tones less of a Thomas Arnold than of a Christian Cato: his proposed system would "bring into fashion again those old admired vertues and excellencies, with farre more advantage now in this puritie of Christian knowledge."[23] And amid all this virtuous bustle, there is still a connection to remote Paradise, its loss, and perhaps its partial recapture through education: "The end then of learning is to repair the ruins of our first parents by regaining to know God aright."[24]

Sundays, therefore, were devoted to Bible study. Milton's emphasis was on linguistic competence rather than any profound drudging in patristic or controversial theology, work for specialists. Phillips recalled study of the Pentateuch in Hebrew and the New Testament in Greek, tasks Milton himself had performed at St Paul's, and "a good entrance into" the biblical paraphrases or *targumim* in Aramaic, as well as some of the Gospel of Matthew in Syriac.[25] It is tempting to think that the more basic Hebrew work was on the psalms; for this specifically was what Milton had done at St Paul's, and in 1648 he would himself produce a burst of literal verse translations of the psalms from Hebrew, another poetic output that may have been at least partially prompted by his role as a teacher.[26] This was all resolutely philological work: Milton aimed to establish the meaning of the biblical text for his students by comparing it in all its oldest versions, and he showed little interest as a teacher or a scholar in the broader activity of "Christian Hebraism" so in vogue at the time. His only strictly theological instruction seems to have been his dictation on Sundays, after group study of a chapter of the Greek New Testament, of a "perfect System of Divinity," the tract that would in time metamorphose into Milton's own vast work of systematic theology, the *De doctrina Christiana*.

This was already an impressively fleshed-out education, but the bones and nerves of Milton's syllabus, of course, were literary, specifically the texts of the Greeks and the Romans, and overwhelmingly the poetic ones. That is what Phillips remembered above everything else: "y^e best of Latin & Greec Poets." Here the emphasis was on big, philosophical poems, and it is striking that, just as there is no Lucian nor even any Pindar among the Greek authors, among the Latins there is no mention of, say, Ovid, or any of the satirists or love poets, only the tiniest hint of Horace, and, interestingly, no

Lucan. Instead we have Lucretius and Manilius, perhaps Virgil's *Georgics*—the austere poetry of natural philosophy, political theory, astrology, and agriculture.

This is equally true for the Greeks, where the reading in Greek heroic poetry was heavy, perhaps literally so,[27] and started with the poems of the legendary Orpheus.[28] Some of this was rather specialist, for instance the didactic works of Oppian, the poet of fishing (the *Halieutica*) and hunting (the *Cynegetica*), said to have been awarded a gold stater by the emperor Marcus Aurelius for every single verse;[29] likewise Nicander, whose surviving poetic works, the *Theriaca* and the *Alexipharmaca,* took as their respective subjects venomous animals (especially snakes and how they move, a passage that may have aided Milton's descriptions in *Paradise Lost*)[30] and poisons and their antidotes.[31] Among the major poets, there is the ubiquitous third-century BC founder of bucolic poetry, Theocritus. Hesiod is also prominent, and Milton's age generally considered Hesiod to be more ancient than Homer, with the implication that the most primal kind of poetry was therefore cosmogonic (*Theogony*) and georgic (*Works and Days*) in genre. This exact use of Hesiod, as we have seen, is already apparent in Milton's student exercises, the *prolusiones,* where Hesiod on the generation of the gods was encountered, and Hesiod's *Theogony* would come to underpin Milton's Chaos and Hell in *Paradise Lost*.[32] Mythology was pursued not just in Hesiod and Homer but also in the masterpiece of Hellenistic epic, the *Argonautica* and its scholia,[33] and in the *Posthomerica* of Quintus Smyrnaeus (still called "Calaber" by Phillips, an obsolete form by his time and presumably reflecting his uncle's custom),[34] the fourth-century AD hexameter poet who filled in the period falling between the end of the *Iliad* and end of the Trojan War. It was well-known that the ancient cyclic poets had covered the entire cycle of the Trojan War, as well as other subjects; Quintus, it was hoped, provided late but possibly authentic testimony concerning what some of these lost ancient epics had contained. Milton would later quote the *Posthomerica* against perhaps his greatest polemical enemy, the French scholar Claudius Salmasius, to good effect.[35]

In terms of Milton's own ascertainable reading, to these Homeric epiphenomena we might add the *Alexandra* of Lycophron, an older work, of the third century BC, in which Cassandra, daughter of Priam ("Alexandra" is Cassandra's alternative name), prophesies the fortunes of both Trojan and Greek heroes. This excruciatingly difficult poem ("τὸ σκοτεινὸν ποίημα"—the dark poem) in iambic trimeter was really a vehicle for its Hellenistic author to demonstrate his knowledge of the intricacies of surrounding myths and his penchant for archaic, coined, and compounded words; but it was a popular obstacle course for ambitious early modern scholars and their pupils, who had, merely at the level of vocabulary, to wrestle with around five hundred *hapax legomena,* or words occurring only once.[36] In 1634 Milton bought a copy of Paulus Stephanus's 1601 edition of this work, accompanied by the Byzantine scholia attributed to Isaac Tzetzes, for the high price of thirteen shillings, and covered it with his annotations.[37] Then there is the first-century AD Greek orator Dio Chrysostom's paradoxical oration "On Troy Not Captured"—not only was this published alongside Quintus in the best edition available to Milton, but in 1636 Milton himself purchased, this time for the even higher price of eighteen shillings, a complete copy of Dio Chrysostom.[38]

Milton's interest in mythography extended to astronomical myths, in the form of Aratus's *Phainomena* and *Diosemeia,* Greek didactic astronomical poems of the early third century BC, two connected works on the constellations and on weather signs. Milton, like many of his contemporaries, was particularly impressed with Aratus, because St Paul had paid him the honor of quotation (Acts 17:28), and so Scripture contained a fragment, one of three such quotations by Paul, of a pagan poet. And once again, we have Milton's annotated copy of this text, acquired in 1631, in the 1559 Paris edition.[39] Across its title page Milton has written Ovid's admiring "cum sole, et lunâ semper Aratus erit"—"Together with the sun and the moon, Aratus shall last forever." It is significant that this quotation comes from Ovid's poem on poetic fame; Milton's annotation therefore transfers that dream from Ovid to himself.[40] Milton also underlined the Pauline passage in his copy, and in *Areopagitica* he made much of the Apostle's assimilation of pagan wisdom, for Paul's quotation of Aratus, Epimenides (Titus 1:12), and Euripides (1 Cor. 15:33) supplied Milton with unassailable precedents for the Christian recapture, rather than rejection, of pagan literary spoils.[41]

As for Dionysius Periegetes, this second-century AD Alexandrian geographical poet provided a periegesis, or description, of the known world in just under twelve hundred verses.[42] Because his poem was factual, rationally organized, and of a manageable length, it was a staple of many classrooms before and beyond that of Milton.[43] It is therefore not surprising that the periegesis spawned several English poetic imitations smelling very much of the schoolroom or tutorial.[44] The technique the periegesis bequeathed to poetry was the geographical catalogue, thick with exotic place names, wrapped in their anthropological or mythical associations. It is here, perhaps, that we can find a prompt for the geographical sweep and range of *Paradise Lost*. What the most recent editor of Dionysius writes of his vision might be said of Milton's too: "He is sufficiently distanced from his subject to be able to sweep from one very large landscape feature to another, whether we are to imagine him looking down from a height or contemplating a map."[45] Milton's atlases may indeed have provided the detail,[46] but Dionysius provided the model for passages such as:

> from the destind Walls
> Of Cambalu, seat of Cathaian Can
> And Samarchand by Oxus, Temirs Throne,
> To *Paquin* of *Sinæan* Kings, and thence
> To *Agra* and *Lahor* of great *Mogul*
> Down to the golden *Chersonese,* or where
> The *Persian* in *Ecbatan* sate, or since
> In Hispahan, or where the Russian Ksar
> In *Mosco,* or the Sultan in *Bizance,*
> *Turchestan*-born; nor could his eye not ken
> Th'Empire of *Negus* to his utmost Port
> *Ercoco* and the less *Maritim* Kings
> Mombaza, and Quiloa, and Melind,
> And *Sofala* thought *Ophir,* to the Realme
> Of *Congo,* and *Angola* fardest South;
> Or thence from *Niger* Flood to *Atlas* Mount
> The Kingdoms of *Almansor, Fez* and *Sus,*
> *Marocco* and *Algiers,* and *Tremisen* (11.387–404)

The geographical sweep is of course broader than that of Dionysius, but note Milton's retained medievalisms, especially his separation of Cathay and Cambalu (i.e., Khanbaliq) from Sina and Paquin (i.e., Peking). The former pair is from Marco Polo in the time of Kublai Khan, the latter from more recent travelers to the Middle Kingdom, but both of course referring to the same country and the same capital, modern China and modern Beijing, just encountered in these lines at two different points in their history. Milton therefore appears to have believed that "Cathay" was a separate country to the north of China, and although the best modern authorities and maps had long since exposed this confusion, it made literary sense. For "Cathay" had already worked itself into the epic imagination, notably through Boiardo's *Orlando Innamorato,* where the heroine Angelica is the daughter of the king of Cathay—what was geographically dated nevertheless retained a certain literary appropriateness.[47]

Milton originally intended *Paradise Lost* as a drama, and as a teacher Milton's definition of poetry included drama in Greek, Latin, and Italian, and among the Greeks, especially the tragedies of Sophocles and Euripides. A chance survival from Milton's library once again reinforces Milton's philological precision: his Euripides, in two volumes, is covered in annotations, many by hands later than Milton's, but the Miltonic marks appear to have been made in different phases, some closer to when he acquired the book, in the 1630s, and some probably from the 1640s, when he found himself teaching the plays and plausibly returned to his own copy as a result. Milton's marks mainly correct typographical errors and the like, but he was extremely sensitive to meter, proposing emendations based solely on metrical principles; he also read for dramatic coherence, for instance reassigning several speeches from the Chorus to Adrastus in the *Suppliants.* Half a dozen or so of Milton's corrections have been accepted into the editorial tradition of Euripides.[48]

Another if oblique resource for eavesdropping on Milton's thinking about tragedy is an essay published in 1669 by Edward Phillips, "De carmine dramatico poetarum veterum" (On the Dramatic Poetry of the Ancient Poets), which he appended to his edition of a popular poetic manual.[49] As Phillips endured no significant education other than what his uncle had provided, it is quite likely that what he wrote he had been taught by Milton. His focus, interestingly, is formal, almost exclusively devoted to questions and examples of genre and metrics. There are three types of versification, he explains: *stichica, systematica,* and *mixta,* of which the first consists of many lines of the same structure (e.g., hexameter poems), the second of regular combinations of dissimilar lines (e.g., elegiac couplets), and the final a combination of these methods, of which Phillips considers drama to be the major expression. Thus dialogue is usually set in a given "stichic" meter (trimeter, anapaestic, trochaic), but choruses are best suited, as are odes, to "systemic" forms of differing lines. Phillips then follows the Euripidean scholar Gulielmus

Canter—his commentary was printed in the edition of Euripides owned and annotated by Milton—in dividing the tragic chorus into five parts. A worked example of the first three in series (*strophe,* the chorus walking from the left to the right, accompanied by the pipes; *antistrophe,* the chorus walking back, likewise; and *epode,* the chorus standing in one place, singing to the accompanying pipes) is supplied from Euripides's *Hecuba;* the last two (*systema* and *antisystema,* following a given *strophe* and *antistrophe* respectively) are then illustrated with another worked example from Euripides, this time from *Orestes.* Phillips next enumerates several complex subvariations before turning to the choric odes of comedy, where—this time following the theories of Nicodemus Frischlinus[50]—such odes are divided into six parts. This is followed by a parallel analysis of the Latin dramatists, again focused overwhelmingly on the metrico-formal properties of the varying types of chorus.

Behind Phillips's exposition we can hear Milton speaking too, especially when we compare this passage with Milton's own remarks on the meters proper to ode and tragic chorus, accompanying his own "Ad Ioannem Rousium" and *Samson Agonistes,* the latter repeating a distinction set up in the former between the strophe-antistrophe-epode structure, and the *apolelumenon* or "freed' chorus, which latter, monostrophic form Milton prefers for the choruses of *Samson,* as no longer "fram'd only for the Music" as in ancient drama.[51] Analysis of Milton's own Latin meters shows him to have been extraordinarily subtle: his Latin *scazontes* to the ailing Salzilli, for instance, open on an allusion to the limping god Vulcan, and thus employ throughout the "limping' meter of the choliamb (literally "lame iamb"), suited too to the recipient's illness. Milton's own "Ad Ioannem Rousium" follows the strophe-antistrophe-epode structure, but with the individual lines made up of audacious combinations of aeolic, iambic, and dactylic measures.[52] This latter poem in turn supplies us with a precedent, from within Milton's own (Latin) poetry, for the (English) metrical experimentalism of the late *Samson Agonistes.*

What kind of a curriculum was this in poetic terms? It is tempting to call it, if anachronistically, "Hellenistic," with its Alexandrian emphasis on philology, poetics, and science, often intertwined in a fashion that recognizes no boundaries between what we would regard as the aesthetic and the technical, seeking reciprocally the one in the other.[53] I shall return to this suggestion in Chapter 16. Thinking about Milton's specifically poetic project, a more contemporary reference point is perhaps J. C. Scaliger's *Poetics* (1561), the most influential early modern *summa* of its kind. Scaliger opened his treatise by defining, conventionally, the end of poetry as to give instruction in pleasurable form through the art of imitation.[54] He then proposed several ways of dividing up poetry. His most basic analytic distinction was to subdivide by inspiration, age, and subject. Poets can be inspired by birth, by divine intervention, or by wine (Scaliger is perhaps somewhat arch in this section). As for the ages of poets, there are three: the pristine, where poetry was an entirely rude art, lost in the mists of time, save the name of its inventor, Apollo; then there is a period where poetry is used to express divine mysteries, Orpheus being a poet of this period; then there is the age of Homer and Hesiod. Although Scaliger is not explicit, his division, I suspect, is an allusion to the famous three-fold distinction of elapsed time, as proposed by the Latin scholar Varro, into "uncertain," "mythic," and "historical" periods.[55]

Scaliger's last and most useful distinction is by subject. First there are the religious poets. Then there are the philosophical poets, who may themselves be divided into the natural philosophers (including Aratus, Nicander, and Lucretius), and the moral philosophers, who write of political or economical (i.e., household) spheres, or of "common" moral philosophy, that is ethics. (Recall that this conventional subdivision of moral philosophy into a general, "ethical" part and two specialized practical divisions treating *politica* and *oeconomia* was the method Milton followed when subdividing his own commonplace book.) Finally, there is a third class of poets, whom Scaliger says he will treat in their own chapters; and as the rest of his first book is divided by genre (pastoral, comedy, tragedy, satire, and so forth), we may infer that this is what he means—poetry specifically as performing a given literary genre. So for Scaliger, poetry can be classified by inspiration, evolution, or by its subjects, and these can be religious, philosophical, or dictated by literary genre.[56] Indeed these genres too have a history relative to one another, pastoral being the most ancient type of poetry, followed by comedy, out of which was generated tragedy.

Scaliger's humanistic methods and conclusions are typical of the period—taxonomize and moralize; delight and instruct—but they are helpful in explaining why Milton's poetic curriculum included a great deal of technical, didactic poetry (e.g., Aratus, Dionysius, Oppian, Nicander). This was the "natural philosophical" wing of poetry, and it taught the scientific side of knowledge in its various guises of astronomy, geography, and agriculture, embracing hunting and even the knowledge of harmful animals and substances. This renaissance conception of poetry as overlapping with what we might think of as medical, scientific, and technological instruction was to dwindle as the seventeenth century progressed,[57] but Milton remained thoroughly humanist in this as in so many other respects—for him poetry, as in the Hellenistic aesthetic to which he paid homage, was still a legitimate vehicle for knowledge.

Milton's syllabus both as it was taught and as Milton theorized it was resolutely humanistic, and he evidently considered that an institution based on his plans would comprehend, rather than complement, the education already offered by both schools and especially universities, at least in terms of the undergraduate arts degree.[58] Milton, in short, offered and demanded a kind of hyperactive humanism rather than anything educationally iconoclastic.

What was iconoclastic was Milton's conviction that his boarding school for noble young men, if widely adopted, would render the universities, at least as undergraduate institutions, obsolete. Ironically, a not dissimilar scheme was promoted by the poet Abraham Cowley in the early Restoration. Cowley proposed a "Philosophical College," to be located on a riverside near London, and supporting a school. The "Philosophical College" itself overlapped with, but went much further than, Milton's plans in *Of Education,* as it functioned as a kind of advanced scientific institute supporting a grammar school in its midst. But looking solely at Cowley's school curriculum, it closely resembles Milton's, and indeed, Milton and Cowley's schemes were grouped together and implicitly dismissed by one later critic as comparable examples of utopian folly.[59] Cowley, like Milton, wished to combine the useful and the educational, but using traditional texts—and so commenced likewise with the *authores de re rustica;* followed by Pliny and Celsus; Manilius; then Nicander and Oppian; Aristotle and Theophrastus for medicine; Cicero and Quintilian for rhetoric, with Aristotle, Hermogenes, and Longinus in Greek; Terence and Plautus for drama; then "the understanding of the Globes, and the principles of Geometry and Astronomy."[60] Cowley's curriculum is not an exact copy of Milton's, but it is eerily close; and the match shows how both were working within an established series of texts, hoping to innovate on its edges rather than supplant it entirely.

There is, however, an interesting silence in Milton's syllabus, and one that is at odds with his own reading as we can reconstruct it. This can be isolated by considering another of Milton's literary projects, albeit one only partially and problematically visible today. For on top of all of the sheer graft detailed above, we learn from Edward Phillips—a final surprise—that Milton started compiling Latin and Greek thesauruses on the model of Robert Stephanus's great *Thesaurus linguae latinae* (1532) and his son Henri's *Thesaurus linguae graecae* (1572). It is a sign of Milton's extraordinary work ethic that he resolved to convert some of the necessary energy expended on the teaching of classical texts into some profitable byproduct. And he carried out his resolution: although we know nothing of his efforts in Greek, Milton's manuscript Latin dictionary was acquired after his death by lexicographers revising Adam Littleton's popular Latin dictionary.[61] When that revision appeared in 1693, it was advertised as augmented by Milton's manuscript, a three-volume compendium arranged alphabetically.[62] Unfortunately it is difficult now to divine which entries are indebted to Miltonic effort.[63] But, thankfully, the preface to this edition of Littleton lists the eighteen Latin authors Milton atomized, and these act as yet another confirmation of Milton's syllabus—he really did plough through all four *authores de re rustica*, Cicero, the poets Lucretius, Virgil, Horace, Ovid, and Manilius (note now the admission of Ovid), the physician Celsus, and the playwrights Plautus and Terence. What is of especial interest is that Milton's dictionary also contained words drawn from the historians Livy, Caesar, Sallust, Quintus Curtius, and Justinus. Now Milton cited Livy frequently in his prose writings; everyone read Caesar; Justinus and Sallust (the latter particularly prized by Milton) were St Paul's authors; and Quintus Curtius Rufus was the standard Latin source for the doings of Alexander the Great. Milton himself in his private reading drive of the 1630s and 1640s could also be described as following an essentially historical curriculum.[64] So it is all the more striking that *none* of these five historians will be found in any of the three parallel lists in the appendix. Indeed, the only mention of historiography as a specific field of study Milton makes in *Of Education* is "Church History ancient and modern," as part of Sunday study.[65] This points again to the interesting conclusion that Milton prioritized poetry, even as he was quietly assembling a lexicon from sources including some voluminous historical works. So if Milton's teaching was humanist, it emphasized poetry at the expense of history; and when Milton theorized his ideal academy, he once again all but dispensed with the formal study of history. In the midst of such a heavy banquet, this particularly dietary exclusion is remarkable. Why was this?

One answer is that Milton knew how important and how dangerous historiography could be. In *Of Education* he showed himself to be very interested in the best sequencing of education—he advocated delaying some aspects of education, especially literary composition, to the time of "ripest judgement"; he placed the (usually propaedeutic) trivial arts right at the end of his curriculum; and he laid great emphasis on moral indoctrination as again something not to be handled prematurely. It is consistent with this ethical seriousness that Milton quietly moved the historians to the edge of the classroom. This was not out of any underestimation of their power and pertinence; quite the opposite. We might remember, in this connection, that John Aubrey blamed Milton's republicanism on, precisely, too much reading of "Livy and the Roman authors."[66]

Was this punishing program successful? The evidence is that it was. Not only did Edward Phillips recall his home schooling with some pride, celebrating his uncle's importance as a teacher, but it gave him and his brother a solid humanistic training everywhere evident in their own published works, even if today we tend to find the brothers less talented, less original, less interesting, than their uncle. Yet such an education cannot have been altogether welcomed by boys under the age of fifteen. Recall again Phillips's response to Aubrey's question on whether Milton was "severe." Yes, Phillips had replied—but "familiar and free" to those who *had* been his pupils. In the classroom itself there may have been more of the birch than Milton or the Phillips brothers cared either to recall or commend. At St Paul's, the Gils had been firkers; Milton, according to Aubrey, in one of the incurably sore thumbs of Miltonic biography, was "whipt" by one of his tutors at Cambridge, an incident, if it happened, perhaps connected with Milton's inferred rustication for a period; and Milton's young wife Mary Powell found her new life with her schoolmaster husband distressing, because she "oftentimes heard his Nephews, beaten, and cry."[67] The circuit of the classics, from Aelian to Xenophon, with three ancient Near Eastern and two modern European languages on top of the standard Latin and Greek, as well as arithmetic, geometry, astronomy, music, geography, natural history, natural and moral philosophy, logic, rhetoric, and poetics—all this for boys "from Ten to Fifteen or Sixteen Years of Age"![68] It must have come at some cost.

# 6

## Securing a Reputation

A s  w e  s a w  in Chapter 5, Milton's career as a private teacher was run out of his own home, and at least a few of his pupils lodged with him. Milton may have found this extended household hard to manage. His first marriage collapsed almost immediately after its consummation, and he and his wife lived apart for almost three years between mid-1642 and mid-1645. Among other activities, Milton consoled himself by writing tracts on how marriage was dissoluble anyway, some of the earliest published arguments in favor of divorce on the grounds of mental incompatibility. These tracts almost wrecked Milton's reputation, and they cannot have delighted either his relatives or his in-laws either, especially when they came to the attention of Parliament. By the mid-1640s, then, Milton was almost a prominent and certainly a notorious man: a private schoolmaster who was also the author of a dozen tracts on, variously, episcopal power, education, the press, and divorce. He had been attacked in print for his views on bishops and divorce; questions had been asked in high places. He had not joined any of the expected professions of a postgraduate: he was not a lawyer; he was not a physician; he had not taken and showed no sign of taking holy orders.

Milton would later come to terms with his reputation as a writer of powerful prose, but in this period he was distinctly worried that his activities as a polemicist were threatening to overwhelm his identity as a poet, which had looked so strong when he was in Italy. So he sought to recapture, secure, and publicize this aspect of his ambition, and this chapter examines three strategies by which he did so. First, perhaps fed up with the opprobrium being heaped on him for, especially, his divorce writings, he decided to collect and publish his poems. Second, he rekindled his friendship with the composer Henry Lawes, who was somewhat of a Royalist cultural icon. Third, he made steps to deposit copies of both his poetry and his prose in the most future-proofed institution then available: the Bodleian Library at Oxford.

Milton's friend the London bookseller George Thomason spent twenty-one years from 1640 collecting every new book, pamphlet, and newspaper he could find, eventually amassing over 22,000 items. Thomason tried to acquire items as soon as they were available, and his inked dating on each item can tell us a great deal about when various books or pamphlets in this period were actually published. His copy of Milton's *Poems* is marked January 2, 1646, which raises the possibility that the volume, which bears the date "1645," was in fact published very late in that year—so late, in fact, that we may well suspect that something happened to hold up the final passage of the completed items from printer to bookshop. It was common if sharp practice for books published in late 1645, say, to bear an anticipatory date of 1646; but the other way around usually signals some unforeseen delay. We shall return to what that might have been.

Why Milton chose to collect and publish a volume of poems at this exact time has been much debated, but somehow Milton got himself taken on by the publisher Humphrey Moseley.[1] Moseley, a rising man, in the process of becoming the *arbiter elegantiæ* of refined poetry, had just managed to acquire and republish Edmund Waller's poems, and his list would in a few years include most of the major living poets and not a few of the dead. His literary atelier featured poets lining up in a neat Caroline, courtly tradition. In short, "Moseley's list" was a Royalist protest, albeit one muted enough not to pose serious political threat, "trading in genres which counseled a life of reflection, retreat, and political quietude to their well-heeled readers."[2] Given Milton's half-decade of furious pamphleteering, his willingness to appear as a Moseley poet—albeit rather early on in Moseley's development of his list— nevertheless requires some explanation. How he came to Moseley's attention, or at least how Moseley was persuaded to consider him, is perhaps not so difficult: many of the Moseley poets past and future had their lyrics set to music by Henry Lawes, including Waller. Lawes and Milton had collaborated in the 1630s on two aristocratic entertainments—the "Arcades" and the *Maske* subsequently known as *Comus*—and Lawes may easily have pointed out the poet to the publisher. Moseley was proprietorial: he, not Milton, wrote the preface to the resulting volume, reporting to the cultured reader, fresh from his Waller, that he had now signed this new pastoral player John Milton, "as true a Birth, as the Muses have brought forth since our famous *Spencer* wrote," a pointer toward the English tradition against which Milton's poems might most obviously be read.[3]

Milton's individual "1645" poems are indeed almost all Caroline products, even if the meaning of the volume as a whole is colored by its appearance toward the end of the first civil war. The most recent pieces are the sonnets to Lady Margaret Lee, to an unknown "Lady," and to the "Captain or Colonel." A reader might catch the potentially Parliamentarian tone of the first (for, addressed to the wife of a Parliamentarian, it laments the "sad breaking" of Charles I's third Parliament of 1628–1629, dissolved abruptly and replaced by the Personal Rule), and the last takes place in some undefined but clearly recent time of war. But the next most recent poem was the Latin "Epitaphium Damonis" in memory of Charles Diodati, written in 1639, and so the whole volume contained only a flicker of poetry from the warzone of the 1640s.

Granted, Milton did write a new headnote for the republished "Lycidas," in which he boasted that the initial poem (written 1637) "foretels" the fall of the bishops (abolished 1641).[4] This is willful misreading: the attack on clerical abuse in "Lycidas" is voiced not by some righteous Presbyterian elder but by St Peter himself, wearing his miter, and complaining about greedy priests. "Lycidas," in other words, laments clerical abuse, but it does so from within the church.[5] Milton now unconvincingly glossed his elegy retrospectively as an attack on the episcopal order itself. This is enough to show that Milton at least felt a little awkward about the possibility that readers might find this poetical Milton too different from the man they vaguely knew as a political pamphleteer. But clearly Milton wanted to have it both ways, for the 1645 *Poems* contains little that would have barred Milton from playing for Moseley's side: there are devotional poems, elegant occasional pieces on music and on time, elegies for dead marchionesses and bishops, by turns hearty and somber student poems, sonnets in English and Italian, an "entertainment" for a countess dowager, and a "masque" for an earl. The Latin half of Milton's volume—no other Moseley poet managed this—was particularly impressive, with all its commendatory poems in two languages signed by grand-sounding Italian academicians, and then divided into *elegiæ* and *sylvæ* ("elegiacs," and then "miscellanies"). One could be forgiven for mistaking this poet for a courtier.

But Milton was not a courtier, and we must find some way of explaining what he was doing. One answer is that although we tend to look at figures in the past and detect them moving against an often implicitly static background (and thus are tempted to write sentences such as, say, "Milton drifted further and further to the radical end of the political spectrum"), the figures themselves may not have experienced or explained their lives in this way. Milton, indeed, may not have considered himself to have "moved" much at all. In writing against the bishops he had realized that he (had always) believed people ought to work out their own forms of worship; experiencing disaster in marriage he realized that he (had always) thought that people had misunderstood Christ's briefing on the topic; and as he had indeed always been a poet, perhaps he need not be too ashamed about what he had written when and for whom. Nor did upwardly mobile Milton at any point of his life seek to attack aristocracy as such. After all, for many people, perhaps including Milton, the civil war was best defined and defended as the traditional hierarchies of the land reaffirming certain political rights and freedoms which they believed had been temporarily infringed by an ill-advised king and his tiny inner cabal. There was no real tension, then, between Milton the campaigner for certain kinds of liberty and Milton the poet, by appointment to duchesses and earls.

This, though, is only partly convincing. Doubtless Milton wished to believe in this formulation in some sense, for it is troublesome to think that one has changed one's mind. But some of the disparities remain glaring, especially for a man who had already made several statements in his prose about the purity of the poet and the poet's vocation. What, we might ask Milton, about that Marchioness of Winchester, an elegy for whom he included in his 1645 volume? She was a Roman Catholic.[6] So were all those Italians who had written their poems in praise of the young Englishman. And these were only the more extreme elements of a volume that, at first and at last, does not read like the poetry of a man whom even Milton's former Presbyterian allies now considered to be a dangerous radical.

For many years literary historians and critics dealt with this problem by a combination of excusing juvenilia as juvenilia and then nevertheless seeking in that same juvenilia signs of an implicit radicalism. The problem is that almost every radical element of the volume can be paralleled in non-radical poems by nonradical poets, as Campbell and Corns's revisionist 2008 biography of Milton so trenchantly demonstrates, and so we are seemingly left where we were. But it may be that the implied binary, where someone is either a radical puritan or an Arminian ceremonialist, is too stark. Jeffrey Alan Miller proposes a more subtle way of describing the religiopolitical choices of Milton's youth. "Milton the conformable puritan" is his suggestion, based on what we know of the preachers with whom he and his family associated. The strength of Miller's middle category, which was widely recognized in Milton's time, is that it can explain some of the poetry too. A conformable puritan can write an elegy for a scholar-bishop and yet be far from thereby endorsing Laudian reform.[7] (Milton may also simply have admired the individuals more than their office.) Powerful and persuasive as this is for describing the young Milton and his religious and poetic choices, however, it necessarily loses its explanatory power in the 1640s, because the episcopal church was itself dismantled in those years and Milton helped dismantle it. As the religiopolitical landscape became increasingly polarized, the middling category of "conformable puritan" was starved into extinction.

A way to make sense of Milton's poetic strategy in the revolutionary 1640s has been developed in recent years by, especially, Nicholas McDowell.[8] McDowell too concedes that the 1645 volume does not make sense if we start from what we think we know about Milton's politics and then insist on making the poetry conform to that. But rather than seeing Milton as trying to convince himself that a great poet awards continuity and coherence to his own work simply by virtue of being great, McDowell has developed a more politically sensitive solution.

In 1645 Milton, in brief, was fed up with and embarrassed by his own former party. He had fought like a champion for a political and ecclesiastical tendency that had not deserved his help. The Presbyterian ascendancy had turned out to be culturally philistine, and as soon as Milton started going it alone—for instance his tracts on divorce or on a free press (the latter perhaps catalyzed by his difficult experience with the former?)—that same ascendancy turned on him. Worse, the cultural and literary world with which

Milton had associated in the 1630s now seemed distressingly remote, with the wall of the Presbyterians standing between them. In order to reconnect with this world and with his own vocation he had to find a way under that wall, to make some statement reaffirming his earlier identity, and the 1645 *Poems* is that statement.

This is a much more satisfying way of making sense of the Roundhead politician with his distinctly Cavalier poetry. Milton was not just trying to reconnect with himself but with others too. We need not interpret this as an entirely successful or coherent attempt, of course: the headnote to "Lycidas" discussed above displays one such wobble in Milton's self-presentation. His Latin verse rejection of his elegies as the overheated products of youth may be another, although we should be careful to recognize that this is more Milton presenting himself as a poet who works, like the classical poet, through stages and genres. Perhaps Milton allowed his pride in his earlier poems to outweigh too much precision when it came to making a selection broad and deep enough to fill a volume. We can be grateful for this: if Milton had been more rigorous, we would not have many of his early poems.

Was Milton's plan to relaunch himself successful?[9] He must at least have convinced Moseley that he was the right kind of poet for Moseley's business. Moseley agreed; and as the usual adornment for one of his volumes, he commissioned an engraving of Milton. It shows Milton in a roundel, encircled by the muses Erato (love poetry), Clio (history), Urania (astronomy), and Melpomene (tragedy)—with the exception of Erato, entirely the wrong grouping of muses for this volume. Milton himself is wearing what are probably his MA robes, and an inscription informs us that this (alas insultingly haggard) man is the poet at the age of twenty-one ("Viges: pri:," for *vigesimo primo*). The engraving was executed by the man who had a virtual monopoly for such commissions at the time, William Marshall, but it was a terrible likeness, especially when we ponder how often Milton stressed his unusually youthful appearance. (Compare, for instance, his earlier self-description in his birthday sonnet: "Perhaps my semblance might deceive the truth / That I to manhood am arriv'd so near.") Milton evidently saw the result before publication and hated it.

This brings us back to the apparent delay in the appearance of the volume. Milton was not able to have the engraving removed from the volume, as it would have cost Moseley good money, and Moseley wanted his connoisseurs' volumes to look the part. But Milton did persuade Marshall to append to his engraving some Greek verses, and this must have delayed things at least a little. These verses, willingly engraved by Marshall, do not celebrate the poet, however, but attack Marshall himself, who evidently was none the wiser. That Milton was content to graffiti his own volume of poems, so carefully launched amid such difficult times, is an indication of just how incensed Milton was—and also, perhaps, that despite his ambition, he was not without a sense of humor, grim though this indelible joke was.

Ἀμαθεῖ γεγράφθαι χειρὶ τήνδε μὲν εἰκόνα
Φαίης τάχ᾿ ἄν, πρὸς εἶδος αὐτοφυὲς βλέπων.
Τὸν δ᾿ ἐκτυπωτὸν οὐκ ἐπιγνόντες φίλοι
Γελᾶτε φαύλου δυσμίμημα ζωγράφου.

[That this picture was done by a stupid hand, / You might say, when you looked at the self-grown form. / Since you do not recognize the character, friends, / Deride this dreadful picture by a paltry portraitist.]

The poem, even in its anger, shows Milton splitting his readership into two. There are those who cannot tell the difference between representations and things seen (*eikon* v. *eidos*), who cannot draw good *ektupoi* or "characters" (and Marshall even misengraved that word), and those, Milton's *philoi*, his "friends," who can. Of course, the latter group also reads Greek.

Milton was not a clubbable man, and although he wrote occasional poetry of a kind the clubbable wrote, he often tried to efface this on publication. When he first published his sonnets in the 1645 *Poems*, for instance, he simply numbered them "I" to "X," stripping them of their individual titles and presenting them instead as a disembodied series, bearing relation more to one another than to the external events that once prompted them.

This process of dematerialization can be observed by tracking how the title of the famous sonnet "Captain or Colonel, or Knight in Arms" changed over time. In his manuscript poetical notebook, Milton first called this poem "On his dore when yᵉ Citty expected an assault." He then toned this back to "When the assault was intended to yᵉ Citty." The date "1642" was also effaced, so that the poem's origin as a physical as well as a poetic act, among the opening moves of the first civil war, is now at best implicit. By his published poems, "Captain or Colonel" has become just "VIII."[10]

Milton did not like to look as if he moved and had his being in the common, occasional, embodied element of other poets. This was not, however, an impression he could uniformly maintain. With the luminous exception of the great pastoral elegy "Lycidas," Milton is, indeed, markedly absent from the many volumes of student verse published in the period; but several of his published poems cannot easily deny that they were occasioned by the death of this bishop or that marchioness. In fact there are slight hints that several of Milton's early poems circulated in manuscript form, albeit modestly. There survives, for instance, a variant text of Milton's "Of Time" in a manuscript associated with the antiquary and collector Elias Ashmole—incidentally sometime an employer of Edward Phillips as a scribe—in which the poem appears under the title "Vpon a Clocke Case, or Dyall," a smoking gun that this text circulated independently of, and presumably before, the printed version, in the period of its existence when it was indeed, as Milton initially titled it, "set on a clock case."[11] His epitaph on the Marchioness of Winchester again occurs in a manuscript in which it is described as by John Milton "of Christs College Cambridge," marking it therefore as a student piece, and circulated as such.[12] A few texts of his poems on Cambridge's carrier, Thomas Hobson, also circulated.[13] Nevertheless, although we can add the odd further example to this list, it is noticeable that for such an ambitious and talented poet in an age of many other ambitious and talented poets, all busily copying, collecting, and imitating one another's poems, Milton maintained a slightly haughty separation from the busy economy of manuscript circulation. As a poet, he was a peninsula.

One seeming exception to this rule is Milton's poem on the composer Henry Lawes. Granted, Milton did subject this text to some of his usual dematerializations and alienations, for in his second manuscript draft of the sonnet Milton dropped the date "Feb. 9. 1645" (i.e., 1646) originally attached to the first draft—and, more worryingly, he cancelled the phrase "my friend."[14] Lawes printed the poem as addressed to "my friend" in his collection of his and his brother's *Choice Psalmes* (London, 1648), but when Milton came to publish it, finally, in his own 1673 *Poems*, "my friend" was gone again. That Lawes could preserve the more personal reading shows that Milton actually sent him the original poem as a present, just as Milton's earlier elegy for Thomas Young and his later sonnet to Sir Henry Vane were also passed as gifts enclosed in letters.[15] Nevertheless, in all texts of his poem Milton in his first line calls Lawes "Harry," a pally hello quite at odds with Milton's usual detachment. The poem is unusual, and indeed it operates on an important fault line in both Milton's artistic allegiances and his poetic behavior. This is the text as Lawes printed it:

> To my Friend Mr. *Henry Lawes.*
> *Harry,* whose tunefull and well measur'd song
>     First taught our English Music how to span
>     Words with just note and accent, not to scan
>     With *Midas* eares, committing short and long,
> Thy worth and skill exempts thee from the throng,
>     With praise enough for Envie to look wan:
>     To after age thou shalt be writ the man
>     That with smooth Aire couldst humour best our tongue.
> Thou honour'st Verse, and Verse must lend her wing
>     To honour thee, the Priest of *Phœbus* Quire,
>     That tun'st their happiest Lines in hymne or *story.
> *Dantè* shall give Fame leave to set thee higher
>     Then his *Casella,* whom he woo'd to sing,
>     Met in the milder shades of Purgatory.
>                     J. Milton.[16]
> *the story of Ariadne set by him in music

Henry Lawes (1596–1662) was one of the best-connected cultural icons of his time, especially among royalist circles. Lawes set to music the poems of most of the famous versifiers of the day; and they reciprocated by expressing their loyalty and friendship in poems on Lawes.[17] His brother William Lawes (1602–1645) was, or rather had been, another iconic composer, killed in action near Chester, at which disaster "Royalists sharpened their quills, adding to a brimming quiver outrage for mutilation of this harmless Orpheus."[18] This loss of a major composer to armed conflict had taken place barely four months before Milton wrote his own sonnet for Henry. Perhaps Milton was trying to rekindle, or reaffirm, an earlier friendship—one that had started with the Lawes-Milton collaborations in 1634 on *Arcades* and *A Maske,* and extended to Lawes's procuring of a passport for Milton's foreign travel in 1638. If their friendship was functioning at all by 1645 or 1646, it must have been in need of reaffirmation after William's untimely death; and Milton's problematic political trajectory cannot have gone unnoticed by the grieving brother. Yet equally, if Milton was trying to reassure an old friend that artistic friendships transcended mere party political lines, then he succeeded. For Lawes indeed published the poem from Milton to his "friend" in Lawes's *Choice Psalmes*, where it sits amid a clamorously royalist choir—the book was dedicated to the king, and two of Milton's three companions among the liminary poets address their poems to *both* brothers, lamenting the fall of William in what Henry termed "these unnaturall Warres."[19] It is an initially surreal context in which to find the bishop-hating divorcer Milton, and Lawes's publication of Milton's poem positions it in a context that may not, or no longer, have pleased its author.

A subtle reading of the poem has been proposed again by McDowell. McDowell is keenly alive to the political complexities of Milton's position as a man who, well before any armed conflict had broken out, had thrown in his lot with a religiopolitical confederacy now disastrously revealed to be both controlled by and infested with unlettered bigots. The Presbyterians had not brought peace but the sword; they had greeted Milton's own proud notions of freedom with cries of heresy; and all the while the literary laurels were being spirited away by the embattled royalists. Perhaps then Milton's poem to Lawes, most probably enclosed with a copy of Milton's own politically plurivocal 1645 *Poems,* was an olive branch not just to Lawes but to the literary milieu he represented. Or, in McDowell's words, had Milton decided to "look to the royalist literary community in the hope of an anticlerical alliance that would protect literate values against Presbyterian repression"?[20] This is a persuasive reading of a sonnet that exudes a "cavalier" ethic of friendship and yet excludes all mention of war or conflict in a volume, Lawes's *Choice Psalmes*, otherwise marked by the experience of defeat and the death of its coauthor. Some circumstantial evidence of reaffirmed friendship is provided here by a later Lawes publication, his 1653 *Ayres and Dialogues.* For here we find prefatory poems by not one but both Phillips brothers, and Edward refers to Lawes as his "Father in *Musick.*" Had Milton arranged for music lessons with Lawes for his nephews? Lawes, with no Chapel Royal left to employ him, relied on income from private tuition.[21]

Nevertheless, Milton's poem to Lawes also contains a subtle counterpoem to this implied narrative of rapprochement, as McDowell also elucidates. The closing reference to Dante is to that poet's encounter in the

*Purgatorio* with Casella, the Florentine composer and singer who had set some of Dante's own *canzoni*, the lyrics accompanying Dante's prose *Convivio*. At Dante's request, Casella plays him a song, indeed one of his settings of Dante.[22] If, in Milton's poem, Dante stands for Milton and Casella for Lawes, then the reference reminds both men of their past collaboration. It may even contain just the hint of an acknowledgment, after all, of the death of Henry's brother William, as Casella is of course encountered by Dante in Purgatory, whereas Henry, the recipient of the poem, is still very much alive. Dante, however, was a deeply symbolic figure for Milton himself, the poet who had manifested his suspicion of clericalism and who had warned against the political consequences of confounding sacred and secular powers. The allusion, therefore, subtly reaffirms Milton's own suspicions about the master values of royalist literary culture, even as he reopens dialogue with that culture. McDowell stabilizes this reading by noting that Dante's encounter with Casella in the *Purgatorio* is then interrupted by the shade of Cato the Younger, exhorting the penitents to hasten on toward the peak of Purgatory. (With Statius, Cato is one of only two pagans to be so honored by Dante with the promise of eventual salvation; we encounter him first in the previous canto, resplendent, "come'l sol fosse davante," "as if the sun were before him.")[23] Cato, as celebrated in prose and verse by Milton's prized authors Sallust and Lucan,[24] was the star republican Stoic and the implacable opponent of Caesar, even unto his iconic suicide at Utica. Does Cato's exhortation to move on sound silently in the open space following Milton's distracting conclusion, as Milton gazes back into "milder shades"?

Intertextuality, however, can lead one down ever more echoing pathways. If we push this implicit allusion to Cato, we might recall that Milton was particularly impressed by Sallust's account of Cato in the sixth chapter of *The Conspiracy of Catiline,* which concludes on a formal comparison between Cato and Caesar.[25] For Sallust, comparing the two foremost men of the age, Caesar was generous where Cato was upright; humane where Cato was austere; ready to relieve and pardon where Cato was reticent to court by gifts; a refuge for the unfortunate rather than a scourge for the wicked; and where Caesar wanted to be thought a good man, Cato wanted to be one. This is a finely balanced comparison, and if we want to wind it back into Milton's poem of friendship, the result is again ambiguous, but richly so— Milton's rapprochement with Lawes is tinged with reticence, but that reticence is itself qualified by an ever-so-slight acknowledgment that republican austerity can be a difficult mood for the poet, especially the amatory poet, present in the poem in the word "woo'd," as Dante "woo'd" Castella to sing. Truculent, unpoetic Cato refused to win people over with gifts; but here Milton tries to do exactly this, as he approaches an old friend by looking backward, to the great musico-poetic tradition they shared together, and specifically to the epic achievement of Dante.

Milton wanted his writings to endure, and so he saw to it that copies of his printed works were distributed to able readers and reliable libraries. An example of the former was the Royal Librarian, Patrick Young, to whom Milton sent a collection of ten of his prose tracts (i.e., everything except *Of Education*) at some point in the later 1640s. (We would like to know more about how these men knew one another, but the connection may have been Thomas Young, Milton's boyhood tutor, and possibly Patrick's kinsman.) This volume survives in Trinity College, Dublin, and the inscription in Milton's hand is still partially legible on the title page of the first item. It reads (I supply the damaged letters): "Ad doctissim[um] virum Patri[cium] Junium Joann[es] Miltonius hæc sua, unum in f[asci]culum conjecta mittit, paucis h[u]jusmodi lectori[bus] contentus." Which means: "To the most learned man Patrick Young John Milton sends these his writings, gathered together in one little volume, content with but few readers of this kind." The interest here is that Milton's inscription repeats a famous Horatian tag, *contentus paucis lectoribus*,[26] and it is one that he would later translate in *Paradise Lost* as "fit audience . . . though few" (7.31). Here, accompanying his prose, as in his later epic, Milton's Horatian allusion assumes that true readers are vastly outnumbered by the unlettered herd.

The same effect is produced by Milton's more complex presentations of both prose and poetry to the closest institution England had to a national library at the time—the Bodleian Library in Oxford. Indeed, in the decade following the publication of his 1645 *Poems,* Milton presented no fewer than seventeen of his books to the Bodleian, an extraordinary statistic for a man educated elsewhere and one who does not seem to have formalized any connection with Oxford University itself.[27] In fact Milton sent to the Bodleian a copy of every single one of his vendible publications up until 1656, the date of his last recorded donation. When Milton sent a collected volume of his tracts in 1646, it contained two items that Bodley's librarian, John Rouse, had only just bought for the library—and so the first two duplicates of Milton's works in the Bodleian came from Milton himself.[28]

Milton's most notable presentation to Oxford was a replacement copy of his 1645 *Poems,* accompanied by an ode in Latin for librarian Rouse, dated January 23, 1647, subtitled "de libro poematum amisso quem ille sibi denuo mitti postulabat, ut cum aliis nostris in Bibliotheca publica reponeret" (concerning the lost book of poems which he [Rouse] asked to be sent again to him, so that he could restore it to the public library alongside my other books). From this we can surmise that the original book had been sent in late 1646; there is no independent evidence of how and when Milton met Rouse. Milton had sent Rouse two volumes, then, verse and prose, his right and his left hands as he had once put it, and only one, the poetic volume, had miscarried. Milton suspected theft.

Milton's ode, although formally addressed by Milton to his book, refers to Rouse as the poet's "Docto . . . amico" (learned friend)—another friendship about which we know all too little!—and claims in the same line that Rouse had requested the first copy of the book, "jugiter obsecrante" (perpetually beseeching). Later, Milton's book is once more "dextri prece sollicitatus amici" (sought for by the entreaty of a favorable friend). The *aliis nostris* alluded to in Milton's subtitle were a collection of prose tracts previously sent to Rouse by Milton and bearing in his hand the inscription:

Doctissimo viro proboque librorum aestimatori Joanni
Rousio, Oxoniensis academiae Bibliothecario, gratum hoc sibi
fore testanti, Joannes Miltonius opuscula haec sua in Biblio-
thecam antiquissimam atque celeberrimam adsciscenda libens
tradit, tanquam in memoriae perpetuae Fanum, emeritamque,
uti sperat, invidiae calumniaeque vacationem; si Veritati,
Bonoque simul Eventui satis litatum sit.

[To the most learned and honest judge of books, John Rouse,
librarian to the University of Oxford, he averring that this will
be welcome to him: John Milton freely imparts these his little
works to be received into a most ancient and famous library,
like unto a temple of everlasting memory, and merited
immunity, as he hopes, from envy and calumny: if sufficient
favor be obtained from Truth, Goodness, as well as Fortune.]

Note here Milton's opposition of the most ancient library (it had in fact only opened in 1602), a temple of memory, to the world outside, full of *invidia* and *calumnia*. Given the horrified reception that had greeted particularly Milton's divorce tracts, we can hear even in this short Latin inscription the classic note of Miltonic defiance.

Milton's ode to Rouse has troubled some readers, because it is decidedly snobbish. But it is another crucial document for Milton's poetic development and intended by him as such, because in it Milton once again portrays himself as a man apart, linked to the literary giants of the past, and facing forward toward the judgment of posterity. His tone is aristocratic: he emphasizes how he is set apart from the common herd, a man "insons populi," or "innocent of the masses"; "humum vix tetigit pede," "his feet scarcely touch the ground"; he worries lest his lost book suffer "vili / Callo teréris institoris insulsi," "the vile thumbing of some stupid shopkeeper." Milton celebrates that its replacement will go to Oxford and eternity, placed among the "antiqua lumina," the "ancient lights" of the specifically Greek and Latin classics, away from the "lingua procax vulgi" or "licentious tongue of the common folk," and the "turba legentum prava," or "perverse mob of readers." There, Milton's writings may await the approbation of a "cordatior aetas," a future, finer age. This is not mere isolationism: Milton, writing just after the cessation of the first phase of the civil war, alludes to the horrors of war, but his response is nevertheless moralistic. For these are the times, he regrets, of "mollique luxu degener otium," of "idleness degenerate in effeminate luxury."

These tones have been desperately interpreted by some modern commentators as playful, perhaps because it is hard to square Milton the radical with this kind of language. We should not try to do so. Milton believed he was a man for but not of the people, and in the thick of the first civil war of the 1640s, as we have seen, he was nervous about his own artistic look.[29] His presentation of his writings to the Bodleian was part of the project to resecure his reputation.

Nevertheless, Milton's presentations in late 1646 to the Bodleian as "a temple of everlasting memory" are yet more complex. By sending both his prose and his poetry (books referred to as *fratres,* or "brothers," twice, in the poem), Milton was staking his claims both as a poet and as a prose writer; in reaffirming his poetry, he also sought to elevate his prose above the specific controversies that had provoked it. Yet this does not defuse the explosive ideas of particularly the divorce tracts: there is still an almost perverse defiance in presenting such materials to Bodley's librarian as classic objects seeking asylum from envious tongues. Milton's presentation inscription and poem in tandem bespeak a familiar combination of radical intellectualism and injured merit.

Milton's ode to Rouse, both the longest poem Milton wrote in the 1640s and his final Latin poem, has always engaged critics, especially on account of its innovative formal properties. I want to focus, finally, on simply the opening phrase of the poem, especially when we consider it in light of its original placing.

Following a classical custom familiar to anyone who has opened Catullus at the first page, Milton, as has been noted, addresses his poem to his own book: "Gemelle cultu simplici gaudens liber, / Fronde licet geminâ" (O twin book, rejoicing in a single dress, though with twinned leaf). The primary meaning of this difficult opening phrase is that this is a book of English followed by a book of Latin poems, published and bound as a bibliographical unity, "simplex." It has a "gemina frons," a "twin leaf," because it has two title pages, one for each part. But there are some secondary meanings in play here too. The first depends on a piece of bibliographical knowledge obscured by how Milton's presented texts are kept today.

Milton's poem was once pasted into the volume in question, but was subsequently removed. The earliest commentators on Milton had access to the volume when it was still complete, and, as the scholar and cleric Henry John Todd testified in the early nineteenth century, the ode to Rouse was originally placed not at the front of the volume, as we might expect, but halfway through, before the second *frons* or title-page leaf, so the opening is underscored by the physical positioning of the manuscript addition. If the book is *bifrons,* then the poem stands literally between the two *frondes,* casting its gaze backwards and forwards. This in turn may remind us of *Janus bifrons,* the deity of beginnings and transitions, of gates and doorways. Perhaps Milton's poem stands as the double-facing god in the midst of his first poetic volume. Second, the poem is itself on a folded leaf—originally, in order to read the poem, it had to be unfolded out of the book, and the unleafing of the poem in its two sections may also be alluded to here.

Perhaps most interesting, though, is that phrase "cultu simplici"—for what is a *simplex cultus?* I translated it above as "single dress," *simplex* being "single," and *cultus* external appearance, or clothing. Milton means primarily "one uniform binding," that is, one volume, but his wording is general enough to invite attention to more common meanings of these terms: *simplex* is usually simple, pure, plain, frank; and *cultus* is most commonly "religion," literally something honored, cultivated. At this level it is hard not to see Milton also advertising his poetic achievement as literally "pure religion" as well as "bound in one volume"—and he is presenting this book to a library which he called in his inscription to the companion volume of prose a *fanum,* a temple, as if the Bodleian were a church for texts.

Finally, there is a sense in which the book itself is a frank, plain, but not inelegant or cultureless offering: for both these little books, the one of poetry, the other of prose, still survive in their original binding; and, although one has been rebacked, it is obvious from not only the decoration but the presence of the same printer's waste in both volumes that Milton had these volumes bound before presenting them. (Furthermore as the poetic volume was a replacement, but is also in matching binding, this also proves that Milton had a number of such books bound at once, uniformly, for presentation; if he sent a copy to Lawes, it will have looked like this too.) And they are indeed elegantly understated—bound in plain calf, but with blind fillets tooled into the leather, and a discreet flash of gilding restricted to a simple, almost invisible roll on the edges of the boards. I propose, in short, that the physical appearance of Milton's presentation copies answers to the artistic tone of his presentation poem: austere in *cultus,* but showing a little gold around the cuffs. Perhaps this is an act of *simplex cultus* in different ways, then—a *simple* but *cultured* object; two poetic *guises* bound in *one;* and also an act of *pure religion.*

# 7

## Two Problematic Books

MILTON'S 1645 *POEMS* was not necessarily the book of a radical, and there are good reasons why Milton might want to appeal to what could be considered a Cavalier ethic. But by 1649 Milton was very certainly a radical, now in the strong sense of a man willing to attack the institution of monarchy itself, as it was understood at the time. He was one of the minority of English men and women who approved of the execution of Charles I, who had lost his head on the penultimate day of January. Milton very quickly assembled a book in defense of this act, *The Tenure of Kings and Magistrates,* and it probably won him a job, as not long after its publication he was appointed Secretary for Foreign Tongues to the Republican Council of State. Milton was the Council of State's documents man, sworn to secrecy as such, and salaried for his considerable pains at almost £300 *per annum.*[1] Compare the basic rate of a fellow of Christ's College, who in the period received by statute only 13s 4d a quarter, the same sum annually for clothing, and credit in hall of 12d a week for food and drink![2] His primary duty as Secretary for Foreign Tongues was as a translator and drafter, for both incoming and outgoing documents, and these involved him in some high-level international diplomacy: expressing, for instance, outrage at the murder by royalists of the diplomat Anthony Ascham and his translator in Madrid in 1650; attempting to claim almost unthinkable sums in damages from the Dutch East India Company; or protesting at the Duke of Savoy's persecution of the Protestants in his territories, a persecution that simultaneously moved this well-paid civil servant to a memorable sonnet.[3] Later in his career Milton was quite possibly asked to write an official history of the Cromwellian Protectorate, as this seems the only way to explain how he came to be in possession of an extensive dossier of suitable but sensitive state documents.[4]

Milton was from time to time ordered to carry out several other documentary jobs too: to "make some observations," to "examine," to "answer," to "confer with some printers or stationers," to "peruse," to "view and inventorie"—he was not a sedentary secretary, then, but a man tasked with assessing and answering, even seizing and scrutinizing the publications and papers of several persons of interest to the state. These included the Leveller John Lilburne and the indefatigable Presbyterian controversialist William Prynne, for the searching of whose chambers in Lincoln's Inn Milton was issued a warrant. Lilburne, for his part, nevertheless felt able to refer to Milton in a 1652 pamphlet as "valiant and learned"; but Prynne was an old ally turned enemy, and this must have been a satisfying moment for Milton.[5]

Milton also licensed books, and this had led some to criticize him for "taking the republican equivalent of the king's shilling."[6] For how could the man who had published *Areopagitica* accept such a role with a clear conscience? Matters may be more nuanced, however. Milton's friend and superior in government, John Bradshaw, managed to pass a Press Act on September 20, 1649 that in effect abolished the licensing of books, with the exception of works of political comment and newsbooks, a sensible precaution for a new administration. Milton admired John Bradshaw immensely, and it is telling that when the intelligencer Samuel Hartlib recorded in his diary that the effect of Bradshaw's Press Act was that "everybody may enter his book without licence," he credited this information to "Mr Milton," who must therefore have interpreted the act in precisely these terms for Hartlib, because these were the terms of which he approved.[7] Indeed, he may even have influenced Bradshaw himself; he had after all published on this very subject.[8] Milton granted a license to at least one work that the state itself held in the highest suspicion, further indication that he tried to remain as faithful as his job allowed him to the principles he had espoused in *Areopagitica.*

Milton, then, brought to his new job his literary skills of composition and analysis, and his most famous commissions from the state were his Latin defenses of the regicide, the *Defensio pro populo Anglicano* (1651), the *Pro populo Anglicano defensio secunda* (1654), and finally the *Pro se defensio* (1655). Indeed, the state paid for these works to be published and rewarded Milton for writing them. However, Milton encountered two other books in his job, both exceptionally controversial and both of relevance to Milton's larger intellectual and poetic development.

The most remarkable text Milton encountered officially was the Quran. The defective and doctored twelfth-century translation of the Quran into Latin by Robert of Ketton was a current enough text in the period of the printed book and was usually encountered in the various printings of the heavily polemicized edition of the Swiss scholar Theodore Bibliander (first edition, Basel, 1543). But inevitably this text circulated only among learned readers. The most recent translation of the Quran into a European vernacular was *L'Alcoran de Mahomet* (Paris, 1647), the work of the French orientalist André du Ryer, and a book that only made it into print against strong opposition from some of the *conseil de conscience.*[9] This was in turn pirated, and then translated into other vernaculars, including English, in which form it was published in London in 1649. The identity of the translator is somewhat controversial, but he was certainly not the man who signed the "needfull Caveat" placed at the end of the book, the tedious pedagogue Alexander Ross—who nevertheless managed to defend the reading of the Quran in terms occasionally reminiscent of Milton's *Areopagitica.*[10]

It is striking that the earliest days of Milton's appointment as Secretary for Foreign Tongues coincided exactly with the scandal of the English Quran. Milton was appointed to his new post on March 15, 1649. Four days later Colonel Anthony Weldon warned the House of Commons that a most dangerous and scandalous book had been let loose on the public. Soldiers were sent to seize the edition and arrest the printer. The next day, Milton commenced his official duties. His time was immediately occupied with drafting and circulating for approval letters for Hamburg, but he also had to compile reactions to a pamphlet called *Englands New Chains* by John Lilburne the Leveller, and he was ordered to write what were soon published as his *Observations* on the situation in Ireland. Meanwhile the Quran controversy came to a head: on March 21 the printer of the book was apprehended and the problem referred to the Council of State, the committee that Milton attended. On March 29, a subcommittee of three was ordered to examine the matter. The official licenser of divinity books, the venerable John Downame, and the bookseller of the Quran translation, John Stephenson, were summoned to explain themselves. Various other interviews took place, and eventually "Ross" (not Alexander but Thomas Ross, of likely but uncertain relation), who had been summoned for having passed the original manuscript to Stephenson, was dismissed on April 4 "with a monition not to meddle with things of that nature." So the first fortnight of Milton's exciting new job was punctuated by this controversy, which ended ambiguously, with the perpetrators warned, but the book itself somehow unsuppressed. Indeed, it was entered into the Stationers' Registers in late April and was in the hands of the purchasing public by early May.

Here a comparison is pertinent. Milton has left only slight evidence that he was interested in Jewish sources for any reasons beyond the light they might cast on the meaning of the original biblical text. He was momentarily attentive to what the learned scholars Selden and Schickard had to say about Jewish marriage and kingship, respectively, but his engagement with their (Latin) texts was slight and opportunistic. In this he differed from many professional Christian Hebraists, such as John Lightfoot of Christ's, who had realized that a broader cultural understanding of Judaism had to be attained before the business of fact-stripping for Christian purposes could effectively commence. This meant heavy work in nonbiblical Jewish sources. There were no Lightfoots for Islam, however, and Milton was quite typical in his lack of recognition of Islam as a legitimate category of belief. He no doubt assumed that it was a sect, a "later deformation" of Christianity, as most theologians of his time did, and, unlike Judaism, chronologically incapable of offering genuine theological insight.[11] Judaism was an ancient religion, instituted by God; Islam was a modern heresy, invented by a man. As Alexander Ross said in his "needful Caveat," the Quran was the "misshapen issue" of Mohammed's brain, through the midwifery of a "Jew" and a "Nestorian."[12] Nevertheless, the appearance of the vernacular Quran was sensational, and at least two elements of the Quran as it was available to Milton in Latin or English have relevance to his thought.

This first similarity was unnerving. For, like Milton, the Quran proposed strong arguments in favor of divorce, especially in the Surat al-Baqarah (the

famous "Cow" Surah; second—and indeed longest—in the Quran): "Divorce
the first and second time, ought to be performed with mildnesse, courtesie,
and good deeds; it is not lawfull for you to take anything from your wives. . . .
He that shall hath repudiated his wife thrice, shall not resume her, untill she
hath been married to another that hath divorced her: then they may returne
to each other, and marry againe without Sinne."[13] This was a view of divorce that had obvious similarities with both Jewish and Roman ideas; and
we know that in the mid-1640s Milton spent a good deal of time researching
what later (Byzantine) Roman law had said on the matter, perhaps in order
to confirm his belief that Roman law upheld, through natural law, divorce,
in the manner in which the ancient Jews had upheld the practice, but which
subsequent and popish canon law had obscured.[14] Perhaps Milton reflected
that Islamic law, as promulgated in the Quran, confirmed this view, rather
usefully at a date before the corruptions of canonists, and before the Byzantine revisions of the Roman codes. That the Turks were polygamists,
divorcers—even "familists"—was of course a commonplace of polemical
writing too, and we can hear it applied to Milton as late as Samuel Johnson's notorious remark on Milton's "Turkish contempt of females."[15]

Perhaps the most interesting Quranic resonance for Milton, however, is
the presence in the Quran of a Fall narrative. In the extremely corrupt text
of Bibliander, the *non serviam* in heaven comes from "Beltzebub," and Adam
and Eve fall from Paradise merely through a vague "diabolica suggestio."[16]
As the slightly more faithful 1649 English "translation," resting on du Ryer's
French translation from the Arabic, ran:

> He [God] taught Adam the names of all things, who discov-
> ered them to the Angels, to whom God said, Declare to me
> the names of all things that I have created, if you know them;
> they replied, Praise is due to thy Divine Majesty, we know
> nothing but what thou hast taught us, thou alone art knowing
> and wise. He said to Adam, Declare to them the names of all
> things that I have created. After he had taught them, God said,
> Did I not tell you, that I knew what is not, neither in Earth, or
> in Heaven: and that I understand whatever you make mani-
> fest, and whatever you keep most secret? Remember thou, that
> we said to the Angels, Humble yourselves before Adam; they
> all humbled themselves, except the Devil: He was already

proud, and in the number of the wicked. We said unto Adam, Dwell thou and thy wife in Paradise, and eat there what thou likest, but approach not that Tree, least thou be in the number of the unjust. The Devil made them to sin, and depart from the Grace in which they were; then we said to them, Descend you enemies one to another, you shall have a dwelling upon Earth, and goods wherewith to live for a time. Adam begged pardon for his fault of his Lord, he pardoned him, because he is gracious and merciful, and said, Descend, and go all of you out of Paradise; there shall hereafter come from you a guide from me.[17]

The Quranic text itself is considerably more complex, because the "Devil" reported twice above is actually two different beings in the original text, the first, "proud" one a Jinn, not an angel, and the second one alone—indeed called Satan—leading mankind astray.[18] What has happened is that the original text, which had already absorbed Christian elements (hence, for instance, the replacement of the serpent with a supernatural tempter), was then subjected through translation to a *second* layer of Christianized generalization, resulting in a narrative that resembled even more the Fall of Christian tradition. Having been separated out in the Quran itself, the proud one and the tempter, in translation, coalesced back into one being.

This intermingling is typical: consider, for example, the Cambridge Arabist William Bedwell's *Mohammedis Imposturæ* (London, 1615), a translation of what claimed to be an original Islamic dialogue but which was in fact a Christian forgery. This again repeated versions of the Quranic Fall both genuine and adulterated, for instance, respectively, the fall of certain angels "into the shape of Satan" for refusing to worship Adam, and the creation of Eve from out of Adam's side.[19] As far as Milton and most of his contemporaries were concerned, this was all just postbiblical distortion—the Quranic location above of Paradise in Heaven rather than on Earth had long before Milton been isolated as a blatant mistake—and yet it was distortion which subtly buttressed the narrative Milton would himself explore and expand in *Paradise Lost*. The Quran inherited the Christian notion that some conflict in heaven had caused an angelic being to corrupt the first human pair; what the texts available to Milton also show is how complex the cross-contamination of different textual traditions had become.

The other state controversy over a book involved Milton much more directly. On January 27, 1652, the Council of State issued a warrant for the seizure of the entire edition of a Latin text of the Racovian Catechism, the statement of faith of the Polish Socinians, an anti-Trinitarian church whose acute theologians were the terror of Christendom. Parliament summoned the printer William Dugard, and set up two committees to examine the matter. One considered the book itself; the other debated where the limits of toleration for a state church should be drawn.[20] The group investigating the printing of the catechism soon discovered that the work had been licensed by none other than Milton himself, who granted his imprimatur the day after Parliament had passed the Blasphemy Act (August 9, 1650), an ordinance that in fact signaled a considerable relaxation in the state's attitude to blasphemy. It has been shrewdly argued that Milton took this act as a green light for his license.[21] Milton was questioned, and in a move that would be surprising in a man other than Milton, apparently referred his accusers back to his own *Areopagitica,* saying "that he had published a little book on that subject, that people ought not to forbid any books."[22] It is difficult to think that the examining committee was conversant with this eight-year-old tract; yet no further action against Milton was taken. A few copies of the catechism were seized and burned, but this was not very effective, and an English translation soon appeared. The Racovian Catechism is an interesting book to place alongside Milton's own religious thinking, which shared some important similarities with this notorious heresy, as well as displaying some important differences. Milton, like the Socinians, was very keen on the use of reason in theology, and like the Socinians he thought that the doctrine of the Trinity was both irrational and unbiblical. But he was not prepared to follow every path laid open by the Racovian Catechism. Socinians, for instance, placed little store on the doctrine of original sin and were therefore keen to downplay the importance of the events in Eden; nothing could be further from Milton's own convictions.

# 8

## Systematic Theology

ALTHOUGH HE LEFT university before commencing the higher
theological degrees, Milton considered himself to be a legitimate
theologian, and all of his work in poetry or prose is instinct with an air
of theological authority. Indeed, Milton is a significant example of the rise of
the "lay theologian" in the period—thinkers who were deeply theological
in their mentality, but who, for various reasons, pursued their theology
outside the vocation of the church itself. Most pertinently for Milton, on
the radical spectrum we might think of the earliest Quaker attempts to
systematize their beliefs, for instance the Quaker pioneer Robert Barclay,
who wrote a systematic treatise based on Protestant models but contesting
the biblical principles on which such treatises had traditionally been founded.
Within natural and experimental philosophy, we might adduce Robert Boyle
or Isaac Newton, who both struggled to develop theories of matter and motion compatible with a providentialist, biblical universe. Milton partakes in
both these strands of "lay theology": his own theology is deeply involved
with questions of matter and of scripture, and, like most other such lay theologians, his conclusions are notably heterodox. And yet by the end of his

life Milton attended no organized church or gathered congregation of any kind: his theology was an expression of one man's belief, exercised alone. "Quo fideiussore? Ecclesia? Ego verò docente ipsa Ecclesia orthodoxa, rectè aliter instituor; Christum prius esse audiendum," he declaimed: "With whom as guarantor [should I reason]? The Church? But I, with the orthodox Church herself as teacher, am rightly instructed otherwise: that Christ should be listened to first."[1]

"Systematic theology" in Milton's age was a specific discipline, one directed toward assembling a coherent system of beliefs based on interconnected propositions, backed up by references to authoritative, that is to say biblical, texts. It appealed to Milton because it could be used to collect and test theological data extracted from the fundamentally literary genres of the Bible—historical and legal narratives, poems, letters, visions—but now reorganized into configurations better suited to the purpose of formulating theology. Systematics on this model would soon be challenged by John Locke, close kin to Milton in his sense of himself as a theologian without a church, who insisted that such decontextualized slicing and dicing of biblical books could lead only to artificial confirmations of the compiler's opinions. The original writers, he pointed out, had no concept of "chapter and verse," a later editorial intervention in the text of the Bible. (And what, for that matter, wondered Locke, are we to do without the letters written *to* Paul?) For Locke, it was debatable whether one genre of writing could simply be converted into another without distortion of the original meaning.[2] Actually, complaints about the use of systems were common even in their heyday, from the mid-sixteenth to the mid-seventeenth centuries, as scholars who had been brought up on *systemata* for everything from logic to the use of the globes conspired in age to agree that their youth had been thus wasted.

Nevertheless it was a pedagogical and academic necessity to have available such theological systems, especially in the confessionalized world following the Reformation, where the young had to be able to identify and defend their own particular church; and a general intellectual culture so steeped in the practice of commonplacing needed no patristic and medieval precedents—though there were many—to perpetuate the genre with gusto. Protestant scholasticism in the sixteenth century was founded on Calvin's own systematic *Institutes* ("Instructions" might be a better translation of the Latin *Institutiones*), and generated numerous other examples, small, large, and very large indeed, into the seventeenth and eighteenth centuries. Thus, when Milton needed serious artillery—for instance in the midst of the controversy provoked by his divorce tracts[3]—for systematics he consulted Johann Gerhard's massive *Loci Theologici,* a leviathan of a publication in nine volumes (Jena, 1610–1622); whereas for the more violent genre of polemical theology, he employed some version of Daniel Chamier's four-volume behemoth *Panstratia Catholica* (Geneva, 1626). For the purposes of teaching his nephews, however, and indeed for the construction of his own example of the genre, Milton turned to the shortest and most recent examples of systematics: the Calvinist William Ames's *Medulla sanctæ theologiæ bipertita* (Franeker, 1623; at least five editions to 1634, including London editions of 1629 and 1630), and the Basel theologian Johannes Wolleb's *Compendium theologiæ* (Amsterdam, 1626; at least five editions to 1647, including London and Cambridge imprints). These, unlike the tomes of Gerhard or Chamier, were typically pocket-size duodecimos, for student use. So when Milton himself snorted in one pamphlet at "the easie creek of a System or a Medulla" and in another at the use of "a topic folio, the gatherings and savings of a sober graduateship, a harmony and a catena, treading the constant round of certain common doctrinal heads," he was not being quite fair, for he himself had not only learned but taught by means of such aids.[4] In fact, the situation was yet more complex for Milton, because in the preface to *De doctrina* he took the unusual step of arguing that there were biblical injunctions to gather doctrine into systematic form. Indeed he even claimed that the early church had developed "some methodical course of instruction," and that Paul at Ephesus had effectively taught by means of a kind of *De doctrina,* several times over.[5] It is a very Miltonic Paul.

As a private teacher, Milton devoted Sundays to the study of the New Testament in Greek, and to dictating and discussing passages from Ames and Wolleb, as his nephew Edward recalled.[6] Thus commenced the treatise that would gradually metamorphose into Milton's own *De doctrina.*[7] At first Milton no doubt told his pupils to copy down the headings of, say, Wolleb's treatise into a fresh notebook. He would then read out and debate the scriptural "proof texts" for each theological notion with his pupils, and these would be added to the notebook, which would be augmented as more texts were encountered in Bible study. Milton does not seem to have professed recognizably heterodox views before the 1640s, and it is likely that his theological treatise started out as an unexceptionable document. As time went on, however, subsequent heterodox notions gradually accreted to, and usually effaced, prior readings; but this may mean that the text as we have it contains fossils from older strata of the text's development, and what look like surface inconsistencies are really depth transformations.

Milton's heterodoxy also explains why he pursued with increasing involvement what was in fact a rather belated activity. Very few contemporary theologians would have bothered to systematize their thought in this dated manner unless they were aware that what they had to say was so controversial that it had best appear in full armor, as it were. A fruitful comparison here might look beyond the tracts of an Ames or a Wolleb to the first Quaker attempt at systematics, Robert Barclay's *Theologiae verè Christianae apologia* of 1676, dedicated, audaciously, to Charles II, and published in English two years later. Milton's own treatise can be plotted on a line between Ames and Wolleb on the one hand, and Barclay on the other, and one fresh approach to *De doctrina* is to ask not only where it departs from its orthodox origins but how far toward the full Quaker radicalism it approaches, and where and why it refuses to do so. Although Barclay published his treatise, whereas Milton's remained in manuscript, it is a sign of Milton's courage that he clearly intended to promulgate his systematic theology in print and to be judged on the model he himself had advanced in *Areopagitica*. Political circumstances overtook him, however, and he was forced to lay that project aside. When his last amanuensis Daniel Skinner tried to print the work in Amsterdam in 1675, the manuscript was judged suspect by the eminent Dutch scholar, Philipp van Limborch, who had been commissioned by the publishers to provide an independent opinion; and, with added pressure from England's secretary of state for the Amsterdam press to desist, the manuscript was returned to England and impounded by the English government. That Barclay managed to publish his more extreme example of the genre in the same city the following year suggests that Skinner could have succeeded had he not blundered in how he went about it.[8] What a parallel universe of literary history we would be living in had he not failed!

Ames and Wolleb agreed that there were two parts to theology: faith or knowledge, and observance or cultivation—in other words, what we should believe, and how we should behave.[9] The Latin terms behind these ideas were usually translated in the period as "doctrine" and "discipline," and this is why they are so often found coupled in the period, especially in the texts of hotter Protestants, as, for instance, in the title of *The Doctrine and*

*Discipline of the Kirke of Scotland* (1641), or Milton's own alarming, almost paradoxical title *The Doctrine and Discipline of Divorce* (1643). What Milton thought about "discipline" is not a primary concern of this book, although it is important to grasp that Milton's emphasis on religious independence went hand in hand with his Independency, that is to say his rejection of a "Presbyterian" sense of rigid church discipline, in favor of an "Independent" understanding of church organization, where individual congregations decide on what manner of worship suits them best. What is of primary concern, however, is Milton's doctrine: his views on God, God's decrees, the Son of God, how creation took place, what angels are and how they behave, the creation of man, his fall, and the effects of that fall. By working through Milton's views on these topics as expressed in *De doctrina,* we can assemble a system which may be compared with Milton's actual practice in *Paradise Lost.*

The manner in which Milton composed and added to his *De doctrina* had the potential to accrete heterodox notions to prior, more orthodox readings. A good example of this is Milton's startling discussion of the nature of God and how humans might understand this.[10] Milton's source texts assure the reader that God in himself is unknowable to any but himself; he is knowable to us only insofar as he has revealed himself to us, and that "from behind" rather than "face to face"; and so scripture frequently employs "anthropopathy" or the ascription to God of human passions, whereas in himself, strictly speaking, God does not feel emotion.[11] If we turn to *De doctrina,* we can see a similar thread: God in himself is unknowable to humans; he has revealed himself to us through scripture, and that in such a manner as our human minds can grasp. At this point Milton ought to have continued with, roughly, "and so scripture frequently employs anthropopathy." But instead he reverses his source, stating that theologians do *not* need to use anthropopathy to understand God's statements about himself in scripture, because God has made sure that what is recorded of him in scripture is exactly, and only, how he wishes us to contemplate his being. So when God regrets (Genesis 6:6, Judges 2:18—these and subsequent examples are Milton's), or grieves (Genesis 6:6, Judges 10:16), or is refreshed (Exodus 31:17), or fears (32:27), "why should we be afraid to assign him what he assigned himself, so long as we believe that what is imperfect and feeble in us is most perfect and beautiful wherever assigned to God?'[12] This is a key moment for understanding not just Milton's theology but also his poetics. Milton had seen in his source texts—and it was an utterly conventional position—that the awkward moments in the Old Testament when God behaves more like a pagan god than the god of the theologians were routinely explained (away) by the commonplace that God is not "really" like that. Milton was not content with this. God is the author of scripture, and so he must intend us to contemplate him as he presents himself. What this contemplation in turn suggests is that God *does* possess emotions analogous to what we understand as emotions, but purged of their human imperfections. "Anthropopathy," insisted Milton, was in origin a device of the pagan grammarians to excuse the behavior of Jupiter; whereas the God of scripture neither asked for nor needed any such apology.

This is fundamental to Milton's depiction of God in his epic writing—the theory that underpins his practice. God in *Paradise Lost* cannot be regarded as having said exactly the things Milton makes him say. But, at least for Milton, the things he says have to be compatible with the God of scripture, even a God who smiles and laughs, who can be angry, repent of his anger, and then grieve; and Milton's God indeed does all these things (*PL* 5.718, a smile; 8.78, a laugh; 11.885–87, anger, repentance, grief). In the hands of a less serious writer, literary depiction of a deity might claim the refuge of anthropopathy—"of course God is not really so," a poet might assume. Milton is altogether bolder and more dangerous. His poetics relies on the expressibility of God in human terms, but he recognizes the danger of his project—'May I express thee unblam'd?" (*PL* 3.3). Milton's conclusion in his treatise is, however, in philosophic tension with his starting point: if God in himself is really unknowable, then how can we know him in the way Milton argues we can? What we can see here is both a genuine philosophical problem and an example of Milton's evolving thought. It also offers us one way of thinking about the status of *Paradise Lost* for Milton as itself a kind of experimental theology—Milton challenges himself to make sense of the God of scripture, not simply through theological theory but in narrative practice.

Such, then, is Milton's view of God. God's decrees were a controversial topic for Milton's contemporaries. The orthodox Reformed position was that God, before he created the world, had decreed all individuals to salvation ("the elect") or to damnation ("the reprobate"). Milton could not accept this. Instead, he argued that God offered the chance of salvation to all, and that they were free to refuse it. In theological language, election for Milton is general and resistible as opposed to particular and irresistible. As Milton said, "no one is predestined or chosen inasmuch as he is Peter or John, but insofar as he believes and perseveres in believing."[13] In the same fashion the wicked also exercise free will in rejecting God's offer of grace. This position on the issue of the freedom of man to accept or reject salvation was and is still termed "Arminian," after its most famous exponent in the period, the Dutch theologian Jacobus Arminius; and once he had adopted it Milton never wavered from it in its basic model, although he perhaps came to modify it in *Paradise Lost*.

As for the Son of God, another of the major characters in *Paradise Lost*, Milton argued that "he who does not exist from himself, who did not beget but was begotten, is not the first cause but an effect; therefore he is not supreme God."[14] Milton's contemporaries would have called him an Arian for this belief—namely that the Son is the first-begotten of all things, and therefore not God.[15] This was perhaps Milton's most dangerous belief; in England, the last two burnings for heresy had taken place not all that long ago, in 1612, in Lichfield and London, for such anti-Trinitarian beliefs. Yet for Milton, philologically speaking, the Trinity was a late and unscriptural notion: he dealt with the problem of the Trinitarian 1 John 5:7–8 ("the Johannine Comma") by dismissing it, correctly, as a textual imposture.[16] His reasoning against the doctrine itself was phrased in logical terms: "since numerical difference flows from essence, those who are numerically two must also be essentially two."[17] Therefore the Father and the Son cannot be one.

This leads us to a fascinating problem in the balance of Milton's thought. An anti-Trinitarian ought logically to be lukewarm about the associated doctrine of the Atonement, or the notion that Christ's sacrifice atones for the sins of mankind, and that it was necessary for such an atonement to have taken place. This was a difficult corner of theology, open to all sorts of objections. At some point around the time of the death of Milton, for instance, the most powerful man in the world, and certainly no Christian, asked a visiting Jesuit "why God had not forgiven his son without making him die; but though he had tried to answer I had not understood him."[18] The traditional argument, following the medieval theologian Anselm's *Cur Deus Homo?*, was that a just God required satisfaction for the fall into sin of all mankind in and through Adam, but that this sin was so great that no single (hu)man could make amends for it. Hence, argued Anselm, infinite

God needed to become finite man so that God-as-Man could punish a Man for a sin that only a God could recoup.[19] But if one does not believe that God-as-father *is* God-as-son, then the spiritual accounts, as it were, fail to balance, and one is forced either into the weaker theory that other, lesser kinds of beings might equally serve the purpose, or that there was in fact no Atonement or Satisfaction at all. What if the whole idea were merely a theologian's fiction, and moreover one rather nastily insistent that God was somehow justice-bound not to show mercy? And if the second Adam was not atoning for the sin of the first Adam, then, so the chain of reasoning relentlessly tightened, perhaps original sin itself was yet another theologian's fiction. This is exactly what the Socinians of Milton's day argued—no Trinity entails no Atonement, which in turn entails no original sin. The arguments they used were those employed by Milton elsewhere: such made-up doctrines were both unscriptural and illogical. Milton himself explained the Arian and Socinian position in a later work, *Of True Religion,* in somewhat ambivalent terms:

> The Arian and Socinian are charg'd to dispute against the
> Trinity: they affirm to believe the Father, Son, and Holy
> Ghost, according to Scripture and the Apostolic Creed; as for
> terms of Trinity, Triniunity, Coessentiality, Tripersonality,
> and the like, they reject them as Scholastic Notions, not to be
> found in Scripture, which by a general Protestant Maxim is
> plain and perspicuous abundantly to explain its own meaning
> in the properest words, belonging to so high a Matter and so
> necessary to be known; a mystery indeed in their Sophistic
> Subtleties, but in Scripture a plain Doctrin. Their other
> Opinions are of less Moment. They dispute the satisfaction of
> Christ, or rather the word *Satisfaction,* as not Scriptural: but
> they acknowledge him both God and their Saviour.

The Socinians, although a real and vibrant church in some countries, existed in Milton's England more as a set of theological possibilities than as an organized sect, but Socinianism was the most intellectually feared theological bugbear of the age, and certain Socinian texts provided even the orthodox with a kind of theological frisson.[20]

Yet Milton proves staunchly orthodox and perforce anti-Socinian in these crucial respects. For all his Arianism, Milton is quite sure about the Atonement as blood sacrifice: Christ redeems us not as a mere moral teacher but by virtue of his execution, redeeming all believers at the price of his own blood. Moreover Christ "must have existed before taking on flesh, whatever more subtle arguments those [i.e., Socinians] who contend that Christ is purely man have thought up to evade this conclusion."[21] Milton was not sure how Jesus could be both a kind of God and a specific man, but he insisted that this was nevertheless so: "There occurs, then, in Christ a mutual hypostatic union of two natures, that is, of two essences, of two substances, and likewise, necessarily, of two persons; yet what prevents properties of each from remaining distinct from each other? And indeed the fact of the matter is self-consistent enough to be so; *how* it is so, is not known, and it is assuredly best that what God wills to be unknown should not be known."[22]

Christ's death, additionally, "fully satisfied divine justice by fulfilling the law and paying the just price on behalf of all men"—not just for the elect. This position Milton implicitly locates as lying between the two extremes of the Socinians and the Trinitarians: "Those who maintain that Christ faced death not in our place for the purpose of redemption but only for our good and by way of an example are vainly trying to evade the evidence of these passages. At the same time I do admit not seeing how those who claim that the son is of the same essence as the Father can adequately explain either his incarnation or his satisfaction."[23]

It is often claimed that in *Paradise Lost* the actual crucifixion and resurrection take place a little too fast in Michael's closing vision, hinging around the almost flippant "so he [Christ] dies, / But soon revives" (12.419–20). But inspection of the theological terminology of the epic shows that it is in line with the Latin theology. In *Paradise Lost*, God too speaks in rigid terms, using the crucial term "satisfaction": "Dye hee or Justice must; unless for him / Som other able, and as willing, pay / The rigid satisfaction, death for death" (3.310–12; compare 12.419, "in this his satisfaction").[24] In *De doctrina*, too, Milton is keen to stress that this kind of morality is not peculiar to the Bible but can be found in the pagan world, citing (slightly ambiguous) examples from the historiography of Thucydides and the poetry of Virgil.[25] So for Milton the Atonement works because the man who died was not a mere man; but nor was he a pure god. He was "a mutual hypostatic union of two natures," and there is no rational way to understand this; "it is best for us to be ignorant of things which God wishes to remain secret." Compare Milton's helpless advice to Adam and Eve in *Paradise Lost:* "know to know no more" (4.637). The peculiar nature of the Son in *Paradise Lost* will be discussed in Chapter 21, where it will be suggested that he is a kind of god-angel hypostatic union when we meet him in the poem, and one who promises to become a god-man hypostasis in order to carry out the work of atonement.

Milton's insistence that God wishes us to be ignorant of some things is a strongly Augustinian moment in a tract named after a famous work by Augustine himself. Augustine too practiced a form a theology that was rationalist unto the skirts of mystery, whereon rationalism was given over for pious contemplation on the limits of human understanding. This moment in Milton's own *De doctrina* is for me the center and the limit of Milton's thought: for at the heart of a rationalist system, there is a piece of mysticism, the theanthropos or god-man. Without it, there is no religion, just the scaffolds of human ratiocination.

Creation takes place in Milton as in most orthodox accounts *through* the Son. Orthodox accounts would also add that the Holy Spirit assisted too, and that this event marked the beginning of time, because there was no time when God was not with his Son and his Spirit.[26] But because Milton insisted that "father" and "son" are relational terms and could have no other status in human languages, God's use of them in scripture can only mean that there was a time when there was a father who had no son. This is a belief that flows from Milton's understanding of accommodation as quoted above: "for he has adjusted his word to our understanding," hence fathers must beget, as opposed to sons who are begotten. Thus the Son, though the second of all created things, is not eternal, and when God created through the Son he must first have created the Son, and so he was creating the universe in time (and seemingly without the assistance of a mysterious third Spirit, who will, however, reappear in *Paradise Lost*).

The most interesting aspect of Milton's creation, however, is his insistence that God did not create out of nothing. As ever, Milton's objections are both logical and scriptural. Logic dictates that nothing cannot act as a cause. As God was the only being in positive existence at the time of the creation, the requisite matter must have come out of God himself, creating through his recently begotten Son. Philological scrutiny of the biblical text produced the same answer. It had long been recognized that the second word of Genesis, past tense of the Hebrew verb "to create," meant in every other occurrence of its use "to create out of something" (such as to make a pot out of clay).[27] This particular site had traditionally been granted immunity from the lexical objection, on the presumption that if God had created out of preexistent matter then God and matter may have existed together from eternity as two opposed principles, the intolerable specter of dualism. In the preface to his own textbook on logic, the *Artis logicæ plenior institutio* ("A Fuller Instruction in the Art of Logic," 1672), Milton derided the kind of evasive theological trick whereby a philosophically palatable conclusion was fixed in advance, and then logic was bent to enforce it; the orthodox position here, in Milton's view, was exactly that.[28] Instead Milton said that it is better to think that body can emanate out of spirit than to affirm an impossibility, that it can emanate out of nothing. So Milton endorsed the orthodox notion that God created a chaos, out of which all substances excepting empyreal or angelic entities were made, but he finds the origin of Chaos in God Himself, not in nothing.

This is not as outlandish as is often claimed. As Gordon Campbell has remarked, the idea that all comes *from* (*ex*, the preposition Milton uses) as opposed to *out of* (*de*) God is a familiar Platonic doctrine, witnessed from Justin Martyr in the second century right up to Henry More in Milton's own time.[29] Justin Martyr, indeed, claimed without any air of controversy that early Christians believed in an initial creation "out of unformed matter," a passage that unsettled early modern commentators.[30] It is also an Aristotelian commonplace that the universe depends on God, but this dependence is not posterior in time: "as we see the *light,* though it *flows* from the *Sun,* yet the *Sun* is never without *light.*"[31] The difference is that while Platonists speak of necessary and eternal emanations, and Aristotelians of an eternal world coeval with its creator, Milton shifts the emphasis onto volition in time: God willed the creation of his Son at a specific moment. This position is also to be distinguished sharply from the pantheism intermittently visible in some interregnum radicals, in which the creation was indeed identified as materially God, such as when Ranters held, or were accused of holding, that God is in the ivy on the wall or in the candlestick on the table. Milton is talking about origins, not about substance as such.

In the orthodox tradition, Creation resulted in two distinct classes of beings. Created things, explained William Ames, are either "immediately" or "mediately perfect." Immediate perfection belongs to those things "having their principles, both materiall and formall, at the first ingenerated in them, and that in a compleat existence." Creatures of "mediate perfection" have a "double existence; first a rude and incompleate, then afterwards a compleat, distinct, and beautified existence." The highest heaven, where God lives, and all the angels belong to the first category, and are subject to no essential change. As beings-perfect-at-once, angels also possess perfection of reason, strength, and speed. Creatures of mediate perfection, on the other hand, suffer change and corruption, and all such things emanate from the primal chaos or "that masse which in the beginning was created, without forme, void, and involved in darknesse, which is called Earth, Waters, the Deepe."[32]

Milton's angels were, however, in another unorthodox move, not created with but before the rest of the universe.[33] As in *Paradise Lost*, so in *De doctrina*, the material universe as we know it was created *as a result* of the angelic fall, and hence Milton's angels are slightly older beings than their more orthodox counterparts. Milton was aware that this was not the standard position, as in the "Arguments" he was asked to supply for each book of *Paradise Lost* he protested "that angels were long before this visible creation, was the opinion of many ancient Fathers," itself a repetition of a similar remark in *De doctrina*.[34] This maneuver also renders their biblical origin mysterious, as many orthodox commentators had—albeit not without misgivings— interpreted the opening verses of Genesis on God creating the heavens and the Earth and then separating the light from the darkness as implicit references to, respectively, the creation and fall of the angels. So in *Paradise Lost* Raphael narrates for Adam, as if performing his own creation epic, the story of the fall of the angels and only then of the cosmic creation itself. This makes good ethical sense within the Miltonic system, as his first commentator, Patrick Hume, rightly remarked: the War in Heaven was "not unrevealed to *Adam*, by so terrible an Example, to fright him from offending his Maker, and to determine him more stedfast and unshaken in his Duty."[35] Milton's angels are also carefully mentally circumscribed: "The good angels do not see into all things in respect of God, as the Papists imagine, but see only, through revelation, those things which God has decided to reveal, and other things through a certain outstanding process of reasoning, but many things they do not know."[36] This again will prove crucial to Milton's narrative design in his epic, for one of the most important moments in *Paradise Lost* is when God tells the angels that he has promoted his Son, and that they will henceforth worship him too. It is this decree that acts as a trigger for Satan's fall, and Satan must therefore have been ignorant of God's plans until that moment.

Most peculiarly of all, Milton's angels are material beings. This is obviously a consequence of Milton's views on creation as from God, as opposed to by God from nothing, but the angels of *Paradise Lost* are not material in any abstract way: notoriously, they eat, defecate, and even have sex (5.401–43, 461–503; 8.615–29). These are not matters Milton discussed in *De doctrina,* another example of how the practice of narrative drew out of Milton new insights about the beings he was modeling, albeit insights to which he might also have been helped by his reading.[37] Milton's epic angels are therefore far more like humans than any other early modern angels, but equipped with an elasticity of body and mind toward which even unfallen man could only strive.

Milton's Adam and Eve in *De doctrina* are less theologically unusual. Following the Western theological tradition, they are created as adults, not as children, as in some Eastern Christian traditions. Adam is mentally agile, as one might expect, but unlike some commentators, Milton does not fill Adam's head with all human knowledge. As for their fall, it is a bleak affair in treatise and epic alike, and Milton endorses a mainstream Reformed judgment of the Fall and its consequences: man is blighted by original sin, albeit capable of accepting or refusing offered grace. This, as discussed above, is the corollary to Milton's views on the atonement. We examine Adam and Eve again in Chapter 19 this time as beings working their way through a narrative rather than just theological concepts.

The final aspect of Milton's system is his view of scripture itself, which has, I believe, an explosive problem at its heart, and the explosion it created was *Paradise Lost*. Views of scripture in systematic texts of this nature tend to stress that even though the Bible appears to have been written by many different people at many different times, they were all assisted by supernatural means to the extent that God "did dictate and suggest all the words in which they should be written," even if He allowed the writers their own historical idiom. Books that look as if they were written "upon some special occasion" are, "in Gods intention," directed to all the faithful through all ages. Each passage of scripture has only one meaning, and this is clear to the faithful. Ames, the source of these quotations, admits that no one ancient version of the Bible has survived utterly intact, but the differences are minor, and nothing important has been lost or maimed. So we can be confident, he says, that the Bible contains all things necessary to salvation, and we need not look beyond it to the traditions and opinions of mere men.[38]

Milton opens his discussion of scripture by affirming its inspired status and its complete clarity on matters pertaining to salvation to those who are not already on the highroad to damnation. Milton then stresses that a good reader of the Bible must possess biblical languages, rhetorical and grammatical sensitivity, and knowledge of sources and context, and of parallel texts.[39] If there is a tension between saying that the Bible possesses complete clarity and yet requires serious scholarship to understand it, then it is a conventional tension—Ames had reasonably solved it by saying that God spoke in the common languages of his original audiences (Hebrew, Greek), and so we need to learn these to understand what was once simple.

Where Milton starts becoming idiosyncratic is in his views on textual integrity and on the "double scripture." Milton accepts that the Bible contains many textual errors, adducing the huge number of extant manuscripts of the Bible, especially of the New Testament.[40] But Milton's real surprise is in his distinction between the external scripture, or the Bible, and the internal scripture, or the Spirit. The latter is the ruler of the former, Milton insists, and can therefore correct it: "on scripture's own witness, all things are in the end to be referred to the spirit and the *un*written word."[41] This is an explosive idea, for in the middle of a treatise consisting mainly of biblical quotation, Milton suggests that biblical text, if found repugnant to the inner conscience, may be safely ignored.

Milton disliked theological labels like "Calvinist" or "Arminian," and tried not to use them. But it is a legitimate question to ask whether Milton's theology in general conforms to any theological school, for no theology is without its own ancestry. In his soteriology Milton is an Arminian, and his view of the Trinity is Arian, as two classic studies affirm.[42] The more outlandish aspects of his theology have often been called Socinian, from his own time to ours. Modern commentary is indecisive.[43] Milton's views that God feels emotions and did not create the world out of nothing find exact Socinian parallels, although Socinians could go much further, on occasion turning God into a kind of enormous sky-alien, himself improvident of the future; and Milton's anti-Trinitarianism perforce overlaps with Socinian arguments.[44] There are many suggestive parallel passages between Socinian and Miltonic texts too: apart from God and his emotions, the much-discussed Exaltation of the Son in *Paradise Lost,* for instance (*PL* 5.600–15), is furnished with an exact anti-Trinitarian gloss by the discussion in *The Racovian Catechism* of the underlying biblical passage.[45] Nevertheless we can now see that Milton was firmly anti-Socinian in the crucial and interconnected areas of the Fall, original sin, and the Satisfaction, three doctrines affirmed by Milton and denied by Socinians: the Miltonic Son, in *De doctrina* as well as in *Paradise Lost,* is still bound to most of the jobs from which the Socinian Son has been freed.

Moving from doctrine to criticism, Milton's views on textual corruption and his strong philological emphasis are legitimately Socinian. More so is his absolute rejection of institutional or patristic authority.[46] But most important is Milton's attitude to logic.[47] Milton often appeals to logic as theologically decisive, even to the emendation of traditional doctrine, because for Milton logic *is* reason (as he explicitly states); and reason, I suspect, is for Milton the manifestation of the internal scripture in almost all its guises.[48] The Socinian tic is to declare a doctrine false because it is simultaneously irrational (implying contradiction) and unscriptural: "for that is repugnant not onely to sound Reason but also to the holy Scriptures," is the common mantra.[49] This is of course Milton's controlling methodology in the *De doctrina* too, and it can be rephrased as the attempted harmonizing of the internal and external scriptures. And when Milton states that equality implied difference, he may be quoting from *The Racovian Catechism:* "For if Christ be equall to God, who is God by Nature, he cannot possibly be the same God."[50] Milton and the Socinians were in turn repeating a logical commonplace, which Milton includes in his own *Ars logica,* set off for emphasis with his famous italic snarl, *evigilent hic theologi:* "Here let the theologians awake."[51]

There is, however, one final pertinent text, structured forcefully as a disputation in logic, for in it there is a chapter on scripture agreeing closely with Milton's own views:

> That the certainty and authority whereof depends upon another, and which is received as Truth, because of its proceeding from another, is not to be accounted the principal ground and origin of all Truth and knowledg.
>
> But the Scriptures authority and certainty depends upon the Spirit, by which they were dictated, and the reason why

they were received, as Truth, is, because they proceeded
from the Spirit:

Therefore they are not the principal ground of Truth.[52]

This is from the third chapter of, once again, Robert Barclay the Quaker's
*Apology,* "Concerning the Scriptures," and it identifies the point where Milton's *De doctrina* advanced toward and indeed right into the Quaker camp.
Elsewhere, Milton's various modifications of orthodox dogma all operated
within the general sphere of Christian agreement that one argued from
scripture as the rule of faith. How devastating, then, that when Milton
turned to that rule of faith, he discovered, like the Quakers, that it was, to
quote Barclay again, "only a Declaration of the Fountain, and not the Fountain it self."[53] But for Milton it also became the charging principle of biblical epic, as Milton had now argued himself into a position in which the
biblical text had become a kind of secondary, literary expression of the indwelling spirit. This was precisely the status Milton would claim for his own
epic writing, and there is a deep, exhilarating sense in which *Paradise Lost*
therefore accompanies the demise of the Bible as a uniquely inspired text.

# 9

## Drafts for Dramas

M ILTON HAD LONG meditated some impressive poem on a biblical or historical subject, and when he first came to plan such a work, he envisaged it not as an epic but as a drama. We know this because sometime after his return from the continent in 1639 he wrote down in his poetic notebook, known today as the "Trinity Manuscript," strings of ideas for such dramas, amounting to sixty-seven possible biblical plays, thirty-three on episodes from preconquest British history, and a further five from early Scottish history—105 possible plays in all. This took place probably between July 1639 and May 1641, and possibly in quite a short window within this period. What prompted this extraordinary bout of planning?

Milton was certainly not thinking about the popular stage, which would soon be shut down by Parliamentary decree, in late 1642. And he himself had a complex relationship with contemporary theater. In his first elegy, written in Latin elegiac couplets and addressed to his friend Diodati, he insinuated that he was currently enjoying the London theaters, but he expressed this in guardedly classical tones and in an initially private poem.[1] Conversely, most of the remarks he made on plays and the theater in published texts treat plays as written texts, and the theater itself as a den of licentiousness. Milton may be posturing a little, but when he confessed in print to play-going, he would admit solely to attendance at *student* plays, at Cambridge, and there, so he says, he hissed and snarled at young priestlings making fools of themselves.

Perhaps in keeping with his suspicion of the contemporary stage, the kinds of plays Milton envisaged in his dramatic drafts were incomprehensible within contemporary English vernacular tastes. The age of the chronicle play had all but closed on the accession of James I, before Milton was even born; and sacred history was almost never represented on the stage, the last, lost example being from 1602. To discover what had inspired Milton we need to look abroad, to the continental dramatic and musical traditions Milton had recently experienced.

For Milton had just visited Italy, and as we have seen, he attended meetings of at least one academy where literary performances included, among the Florentine Svogliati, the recitation of scenes from new tragedies—Nicolo Doni, reading "una scena della sua Tragedia" (a scene of his tragedy). In Rome, Milton also saw some Italian secular opera, notably a revival in February of 1639 at the theater of the Palazzo Barberini of the comic opera *L'Egisto, overo Chi soffre, speri* (*Egisto, or Let He Who Suffers, Hope*) by Virgilio Mazzocchi and Marco Mazzocchi, with a libretto, based on Boccaccio, by Giulio Rospigliosi, the future Pope Clement IX.

Nothing, however, could be further from Milton's own dramatic ideals. But also in Rome the sacred oratorio was enjoying new popularity. A visiting French musician there in 1638–1639 described these oratorios as consisting of "une Histoire du Viel Testament, en forme d'une comédie spirituelle" (a narrative from the Old Testament, in the form of a spiritual comedy), and he mentioned oratorios on Susanna, Judith, Holofernes, and David and Goliath. Milton also surely read some Italian drama—it was said that he bought so many books when abroad that he had to ship them back in chests by boat from Venice.[2] Following a much later remark by Voltaire, it has often been suspected, for instance, that Milton read the *Adamo* (printed in 1613 and again in 1617), a "sacra rappresentatione" of the celebrated actor Giambattista Andreini. Andreini certainly employed allegorical figures (the Seven Deadly Sins, "Mondo," "Carne," "Fame," and so forth) in a manner reminiscent of Milton's first drafts for a drama on the Fall. But he also included God as a speaking character, and there are striking scenes, such as when the newly created Eve wakes up, when she and the serpent debate at length, and when she and Adam argue, Adam torn between his love of Eve and his duty to God. Adam and Eve, fallen, are faced with various personifications of aspects of the sinful world in the manner of Milton's drafts; and the play concludes with Michael's victory over Lucifer, much as in Milton's War in Heaven. Andreini's published text, with prefatory essay and extensive Latin notes in the margins identifying biblical and patristic sources, is adorned with over forty high-quality engravings, one before each scene—this is drama as deluxe, printed artefact.

This bookish form of drama in turn reminds us that writers such as Andreini and indeed Milton had behind them a pan-European tradition of neo-Latin drama. This world beckoned to Milton at every turn. There was the Aeschylean *Parabata Vinctus* (The Transgressor Bound) of Jacque-August de Thou (Paris, 1595, reedited in his *Poemata sacra,* 1599), a drama featuring Satan (the "Parabata") and his fallen angels. In European terms, the late de Thou was the most talked-about historian of his time, and Milton would shortly read his celebrated *Historiæ* right through, a feat that only pales when set within the constellation of similar reading feats performed by Milton in these years. Milton had also met Hugo Grotius in Paris, another giant of European scholarship, and Grotius as a younger man had written two plays, an *Adamus exul* and a *Christus patiens.* Milton proposed versions of both among his drafts, and the latter, indeed, was published in an English translation in 1640 by George Sandys, who honored his text with a long commentary. Then there was the Senecan *Herodes infanticida* by Daniel Heinsius (1607–1608, first published Leiden, 1632), a text which sparked much humanistic debate concerning sacred drama; Heinsius's own *De tragoediae constitutione* (1611) remarked that the biblical story of Joseph furnishes an Aristotelian *peripeteia* and *anagnorisis,* for instance, "in such a way that it excels everything in the tragic poets."[3] Milton too proposed a "Herod massacring," as he called it. If Milton wanted to hark back to specifically British humanistic success in sacred dramatic composition, there was John Foxe the martyrologist's 1556 "comoedia apocalyptica" *Christus Triumphans,* much reprinted, in which Satan's first, eerily Miltonic words are

Hoho quo nunc decidi?
Aut ubi sum, aut quò vertam primum? Nunquam minus
Mei compos in vita prorsus fuerim. Ita

Pugnando, cadendo, bile atque insania
Exagitor: neque quid consilii ineam, scio,
Extorris è cælo eliminor: ubi
Loci nihil est reliquum.[4]

[Ah, whither now have I fallen?
Or where am I, and where first should I turn? Never
In my life have I been so utterly bereft. Thus
In fighting, in falling, by wrath and by folly
Am I harassed: nor do I know what I should do,
Exiled from heaven, I am thrust out of doors, where
There is no place left.]

Finally, and most profoundly, there was the Scottish literary giant George Buchanan, whose neo-Latin dramas had been written for classroom performance in Bordeaux in the early 1540s, but which soon achieved a far wider readership.[5] Buchanan's two plays on biblical themes were an Old Testament drama on Jephtha, and a New Testament drama on John the Baptist. Milton drafted a possible "Baptistes," as he too named it, and it was the narrative from the New Testament that he imagined in the most detail—enough, indeed, for us to be able to work out the general shape of his proposed play. It would have featured a prologue spoken by "the spirit of Philip Herods brother," and it seems quite (strategically?) removed from Buchanan's conception. Likewise in Milton's lists for Old Testament dramas, he simply skipped over the story of Jephtha, perhaps considering the narrative to have been saturated by Buchanan's prior attentions.

Nevertheless Buchanan's somber, politically allusive attitude did influence Milton. His New Testament play pondered the problem of a tyrannical ruler, while his Old Testament drama meditated on the danger of religious boasting while simultaneously exploring the peculiar ethical world of the old law. *Jephthes* dramatized the story of Jephtha, one of the Judges, who rashly promised on the way to battle that "whatsoever cometh forth of the doors of my house to meet me, when I return in peace from the children of Ammon, shall surely be the Lord's, and I will offer it up for a burnt offering" (Judges 11:31). Jephtha won his battle, but the first thing out of his doors was his daughter, whom he was forced therefore by his oath to sacrifice, in anguish, but with her pious acquiescence. This horrid history—the painful righteousness of the Old Testament hero, prone to making unwise oaths, and driven to perform problematic acts as a result of a perceived duty to God—created one of the more widely discussed biblical dramas of the period, and its spirit, its "ethical opacity," haunts Milton's own later play on another Judge with a lack of judgment, *Samson Agonistes*.[6]

Milton, therefore, looked to various continental and learned traditions when he started thinking about plausible plays. But his attitude to sacred drama in particular was likely shaped by some reading in the church fathers he had been doing at this time too. One entry in his commonplace book made at this time concerned patristic hostility to "spectacula," a term that at the time might cover anything from sport and gladiatorial combat to actual theater. Milton chose to interpret certain texts by Tertullian, pseudo-Cyprian, and Lactantius on *spectacula* as specifically concerning drama, and therefore defended, precisely, tragedy, commenting: "For what in all philosophy is more serious or more sacred or more exalted than a tragedy rightly designed; what more useful for seeing at a single view the trials and vicissitudes of human life?"[7] This was probably written just after Milton had returned from his continental tour and was setting up as a teacher, and possibly just before he started putting together his own ideas for dramas.

If Milton's encounter with some of the Fathers was hostile—and he would soon jeer at their "immeasurable, innumerable, and therefore unnecessary and unmerciful volumes"[8]—another piece of his reading in early Christianity at this time would have a more positive influence. We know that Milton read the church historians carefully in Greek just before he left for his European trip, and we have already encountered in Socrates Scholasticus the late fourth-century story of the Apollinares, and how Milton subsequently pressed this anecdote into service in *Areopagitica* (1644).[9] This anecdote gave him a firm and indeed heroic early Christian precedent for recasting sacred texts into secular literary genres, including tragedy and epic. Such precedents from the early church were important for Milton. In the preface to *Samson Agonistes* Milton enlisted the tragedy *Christus Patiens* of the church father Gregory of Nazianzus as a patristic precursor to his own effort—albeit seemingly in ignorance of the fact that by Milton's time scholars had agreed that the work, although ancient, was not Gregory's.[10] Just after his return from the continent, Milton also read in the eighth-century *Ecclesiastical History* of

Bede the account of the earliest recorded Anglo-Saxon poet, Caedmon, who versified stories from the Old and New Testaments.[11]

Perhaps dramatic form inhered in sections of the Bible itself: Milton elsewhere cited Origen's analysis of the Song of Solomon as a "divine pastoral Drama" of two persons and a double chorus, as well as the recent Heidelberg theologian David Paraeus's description of Revelation as, at least from the start of the fourth vision, a tragedy, divided into acts "distinguisht each by a Chorus of Heavenly Harpings and Song between."[12] While he was drawing up the dramatic drafts, Milton was also reading Eusebius's *Preparation for the Gospel,* as he cross-referenced it in his draft for a tragedy on Dinah; this tiny reference is crucial because it shows us Milton seeking to supplement the bare biblical account with extracanonical versions of the same story. In Eusebius Milton will also have encountered fragments of Ezekiel the Tragedian, a Jewish Alexandrian dramatist possibly of the second century BC, who wrote a five-act tragedy on Exodus. These fragments are the most extensive remains of any Hellenistic tragedy.[13]

Milton therefore had a combination of continental, neo-Latin, and patristic traditions in his mind when he first turned to drama, and in general these traditions were more important for Milton's conception of drama than any plays by, say, Shakespeare or Jonson. Most of Milton's ideas for dramas got no further than a proposed subject and a biblical reference, the subject often expressed in a suitably polysyllabic Greek coinage—Gideon Idoloclastes (idol-smasher), Samson Pursophorus (firebrand-bearer), Salomon Gynæcocratumnus (woman-ruled), for instance. That Milton expressed several of these in Greek prompts the suspicion that Milton was not entirely sure whether he intended a Latin or an English text at this stage, an ambivalence, with a final preference for English utterance, documented in Milton's student writing, notably his "At a Vacation Exercise." Nevertheless, Milton evidently opted for English early, as when Edward Phillips later recorded that he had first heard a section of *Paradise Lost* as drama at around this time, in the 1640s, he quoted it—Satan's soliloquy against the Sun (4.32–41)—in English blank verse.

Although most items on Milton's lists evolved no further, some subtleties of construction or theme are intermittently proposed, such as a play on the sons of Eli in which the action was to be "interlac't" with Samuel's vision. A pastoral drama is also mooted twice. A few ideas made it as far as a list of dramatis personae or some rudimentary plotting, notably Old Testament plays on the rape of Dinah, the death of Abias (i.e., Abijah), the story of Abraham and Isaac, and the destruction of Sodom. Milton's little comments and glosses tend to suggest that he was stretching himself to find an extrabiblical angle on his chosen subjects: the play on Abias, for instance, includes a very Greek-looking addition concerning Abias's mother, who "hearing the child shall die as she comes home refuses to return thinking therby to elude the oracle," a plot motif that reminds us of Sophocles's *Oedipus the King* and another futile attempt to evade a prophecy. And the play on Abraham and Isaac, although taking its cue from Genesis 22, thereafter turns its back almost entirely on its source, imagining instead the action as seen entirely from the perspectives of other people, "in the mean while discoursing *as the world would* of such an action divers ways," in Milton's splendidly revealing phrase. The Bible focuses in the main on Abraham and Isaac; Milton's version of the story would have presented a series of other characters wondering and worrying—a steward, a chorus, Abraham's anxious wife Sarah, "some shepheard or companie of merchants passing through," Abraham's concerned personal friends, and then finally an eye-witness messenger, who sets the record straight. Already we can see Milton thinking through the narrative and dramatic implications of otherwise rather sparely reported biblical events, and this is how he would later write *Samson Agonistes.*

This invites the question of whether Milton envisaged his dramas as written to be acted, in the household or otherwise—and surprisingly the evidence here is, at least intermittently, that he did, and that music was to play a part too. In "Baptistes," for instance, "the Gallantry of the town passe by in Processi[on] with musick and song to the temple." In a British tragedy in which William of Normandy slays Harold II in battle, "the first scene may begin with the ghost of Alfred"; later, in Milton's intended Scottish drama on Macbeth, we encounter the ghost of Duncan, a character we do not find in Shakespeare's version.

Yet the biblical story that most caught and held Milton's imagination was that of the Fall of Man. He returned to it four times in his drafts, at greater length and in greater detail than any of his other sketches. What is notable about the earliest drafts is that Milton always thought of this particular play as an acted and not a solely textual affair. Both the two early drafts consist merely of lists of characters, but including several personifications marked as "mutes." Milton soon crossed these out and proceeded to a third, which he called "Paradise Lost," the first appearance of this phrase in Milton's writings. This was divided into five acts:

Act 1: Moses as prologue; a debate on "what should become of man if he fall"; a hymn of creation by an angelic Chorus.

Act 2: The Chorus sings the marriage song of Adam and Eve and describes Paradise.

Act 3: "Lucifer" contrives the Fall; the Chorus relates the angelic rebellion and war.

Act 4: Adam and Eve "fallen."

Act 5: The Expulsion; Adam and Eve shown personifications of the consequences of the Fall, but also Faith, Hope, and Charity; the Chorus "breifly concludes."

Here we can see some of the bones of *Paradise Lost,* as it were, but put together in an order suitable for drama rather than epic. Notable emphases include the Edenic marriage near the beginning, with Eve—so named even before the Fall—taking on a full role; the nesting of the narrative of the War in Heaven in the middle; and the ethical balance of the conclusion, where the ills of a fallen world without are counterpoised with the three theological virtues, a paradise within. We can see elements that will eventually be relocated in *Paradise Lost*—the play, for instance, sets a hymn of creation in the first act, whereas it is turned into a full hexameral narrative and combined with the War in Heaven in the eventual epic, all proceeding from the mouth of Raphael, who has taken over the role of the original "angelic Chorus." Finally, Milton in his first fully narrativized treatment of the Fall omitted the Fall itself. We do not see Adam and Eve in their innocence, a decision which is almost certainly theological rather than simply one of the expedience of imagined staging, as in Milton's (only partially drafted) prologue Moses says that even he, Enoch, and Elijah "cannot se[e] Adam in the state of innocence."

Milton's final attempt at a drama on the subject suggests that as his imagination returned again and again to the matter of Eden, and with the advantage of having tried out many other biblical ideas in the interim, he started to struggle with dramatic structure. Act divisions have now melted away, to be replaced by a continuous narrative, entitled "Adam unparadiz'd." The sketch opens this time introduced not by a human being but an angel, Gabriel. Its action, described by Milton in continuous prose, can be divided into the following events, and I have suggested what seem to me the most logical act breaks:[14]

[Act 1?]

- (a)  Gabriel describes Paradise.
- (b)  The Chorus keeps watch over Paradise after Lucifer's rebellion, and desires to learn more of "this excellent new creature man."
- (c)  Gabriel relates the creation of Adam and Eve, "with thire love, & mariage."

[Act 2?]

- (d)  Lucifer appears, fallen, seeking revenge on man.
- (e)  The Chorus and Lucifer confront one another; Lucifer departs.

[Act 3?]

- (f)  The Chorus sings of the War in Heaven.
- (g)  Lucifer relates "what he had don to the destruction of man" [this is a later insert by Milton].

[Act 4?]

- (h)  Adam and Eve, fallen, appear "confusedly cover'd with leaves," Conscience and Justice accuse "him."
- (i)  The Chorus is told of the manner of the Fall by an angel.
- (j)  Adam and Eve, "but especially Adam," accuse one another; Justice and Reason convince "him," warning of the example of Lucifer's impentitence.

[Act 5?]

(k) An angel is sent to banish Adam and Eve, "but before causes to passe before his eyes in shapes a mask of all the evills of this life & world."

(l) Adam is humbled, relents, despairs, but is comforted by Mercy, who promises the Messiah.

(m) Faith, Hope, and Charity instruct him, and he repents, and gives God the glory.

(n) The Chorus "breifly concludes."

(Note: My act breaks are based on a comparison with the previous draft, borrowing from it the Hymn of Creation as the conclusion of an act, and the Fall and the Expulsion as commencing new acts. This leaves only the break between the second and third acts to be fixed, and I place it after the evident exit of Lucifer following his encounter with the Chorus, exactly in the manner of the end of the fourth book of *Paradise Lost*.)

This final draft displays even more pieces of *Paradise Lost* in embryo, specifically the emphasis on angels and embedded angelic narration (compare *PL*, Books 5–7); a standoff between some unfallen angels and fallen Lucifer in Eden (compare *PL*, Book 4); the boasting of Lucifer about how he effected the Fall (compare *PL*, Book 10); the recriminations of Adam and Eve, especially Adam (compare *PL*, Book 10); and a final vision of the evils of the world, followed by Adam's mixed emotions and eventual repentance (compare *PL*, Books 11–12).

Milton of course never wrote that play, yet we know he got as far as at least Lucifer's soliloquy in Eden about hating the sun, which in my schema belonged to the opening section of Act II. Indeed, Milton must have made a major structural decision by that point, as Phillips says that this soliloquy now opened the tragedy as it was then conceived; this was a play that would now start with defeat. At some point, too, Milton took the momentous decision that the name "Lucifer"—the only name he uses for the Old Enemy in the dramatic drafts—was to be blotted quite out from the epic, which, other than three guarded exceptions (each followed respectively by "so call," "so call him," "so by allusion called," and two deflected into place names),[15] would only be permitted to use Lucifer's fallen name, Satan. But turning the process around also reveals just how different the size and shape of the epic itself is:

*Paradise Lost* (twelve books; 7–8 and 11–12 were the original Books 7 and 10).

1   Hell: Satan and his troops in defeat.
2   Hell: The devils' assembly and Satan's journey.
3   Heaven: Divine theology; the approach of Satan to Eden.
4   Eden: Adam and Eve; Eve recounts her creation; Gabriel challenges Satan.
5   Eden: Eve's dream; the arrival of Raphael; Raphael's narration of the Revolt.
6   Eden: Raphael continues: the War in Heaven.
7   Eden: Raphael continues: the Creation.
8   Eden: Raphael and Adam discuss astronomy; Adam recounts his creation.
9   Eden: Temptation and Fall.
10  Heaven: God sends his Son to Eden; Hell: Satan's return; Eden: recriminations, followed by repentance.
11  Heaven: God's judgments; Eden: the arrival of Michael; the vision of history (up to Flood)
12  Eden: The vision of history (Flood to Second Coming); Expulsion.

Whereas the play, like most previous dramas on the Fall, including Grotius's *Adamus Exul* and Andreini's *L'Adamo,* was set entirely in Eden, using angels either in chorus or as named individuals to narrate events elsewhere, now Milton as epic narrator, in taking central narratorial powers to himself, can range over the whole of the cosmos—"Heaven, Hell, Earth, Chaos, all," as Andrew Marvell described Milton's scope. And although it is indeed the sections in Hell, Chaos, and Heaven that transport the epic far beyond what could have been delivered by the dramatic drafts, we should not neglect the more mundane but equally profound shifts, notably the epic's far greater interest in Eve as an independent character. In the final dramatic draft, Milton still assumes that the theologically important human is Adam: Conscience and Justice accuse "him"; Justice and Reason convince "him." This may well be theologically proper by the standards of the time, and indeed Milton's God too will later use the same reductionist pronouns:

> For man will hark'n to his glozing lyes,
> . . . So will fall,
> Hee and his faithless Progenie: whose fault?
> Whose but his own? ingrate, he had of mee
> All he could have; I made him just and right. (*PL* 3.93, 95–8)

Nevertheless Milton, the narratologist of epic, soon discovered that full interaction between his human protagonists both softened and complicated the hard lines of God's theological stare. There are traces of this in the drafts, especially in Milton's prescient detail that Adam, in the fourth draft, "especially . . . layes the blame to his wife," and is "stubborn in his offence"; here is the germ of the asymmetry in the epic between Adam and Eve's reactions to their sin, the former indeed stubborn in his offence, the latter advising prayer and repentance. For dialogue and debate are proper to dramatic writing, and they are here carried through from their dramatic origins in a manner that enabled Milton to transform the often rather externalized, public exchanges of ancient epic into the internalized ratiocination, even soliloquy, of Milton's more cerebral poem. When, in the prologue to book 9 of *Paradise Lost,* Milton states that "I now must change / Those Notes to Tragic" (9.5–6), it was therefore not so much a change as a return to the earliest and oldest stages of his epic progress.

# 10

## Two Competitors:
## Davenant and Cowley

S O FAR THE emphasis has been exclusively on Milton and his literary and intellectual development, albeit by situating Milton in the context of other contemporary writers and thinkers, and by observing how he reacted to them. This chapter now addresses directly Milton's two main competitors for the epic crown, namely William Davenant (1606–1668) and Abraham Cowley (1618–1667). They were and still are both judged to have failed in their attempts; but these failures can tell us a great deal about the problems that Milton faced too, and the decisions he took.

The prominent poet and playwright William Davenant's first attempt at an epic was in fact a truncated mock epic called the *Jeffreidos,* named for Queen Henrietta Maria's dwarf, the "walking-Thumbe" Jeffrey Hudson; in the *Jeffreidos* Jeffrey is forced by shipwreck to join battle with a half-blind turkey.[1] But Davenant was determined to write a proper epic, indeed a new kind of epic, and he was serious enough about the theory of his experimental epic to publish a *Preface* (Paris, 1650)[2] to his "heroick poem," *Gondibert,* before the actual appearance of the poem itself. This elaborate theoretical discussion was addressed to the philosopher Thomas Hobbes, who had undertaken "daily examination" of Davenant's poem in Paris "as it was writing," and Hobbes in turn composed a response, which Davenant printed with his *Preface*. The next year Davenant finally published in London two and a half of the promised five books of *Gondibert*, prefaced with his and Hobbes's essays, and some admiring poems by the poets Waller and Cowley. *Gondibert*, a poem set in eighth-century Lombardy, told, or at least commenced, the story of its eponymous hero and his love for Birtha. Gondibert however is loved by the princess Rhodalind, the king's daughter; and Rhodalind, in turn, is loved by Oswald. If this was epic, then it was, following in the modern fashion, epic romance.[3] Things did not go well for Davenant, though: despite and because of his elaborate theoretical preparations, his unfinished poem itself was a flop, and one that, because of the fame of its author, gave unwilling birth in to a subgenre of satirical poetry and to a culture, within Royalist circles, of vicious annotation.[4] Nevertheless, there is good reason to think that Milton was aware of this much-discussed poem, which he appears to have imitated in at least one passage in *Paradise Lost*.[5]

Davenant's theory of the epic opened with a critique of available epics. Homer is found wanting because he fabled above nature, treated his muse as a "Familiar" and not as "his rational spirit," and "d[id] often advance his men to the quality of Gods, and depose his Gods to the condition of men." Next, Virgil is criticized for, once again, too much supernaturalism: at the expense of "natural probabilities" we find ourselves too frequently in "Heaven and Hell," with "Gods and Ghosts'; and stylistically, Virgil has too much "gravity"—like a giant, strong but slow. As for Lucan, his poem is simply too historical to be real poetry (Hobbes agreed), and Statius suffered from over similarity to Virgil, again with too much "Heaven and Hell" for a modern sensibility. Among the only two moderns worthy of note, Tasso must be faulted for "his Councell assembled in Heaven, his Witches Expeditions through the Air, and inchanted Woods inhabited with Ghosts"; and Spenser is swiftly dispatched as linguistically obsolete and favoring the "allegoricall" over the "naturall."[6]

Davenant therefore sets out his own theory of the modern epic. It shall be Christian; set in the remote past and in another country, in court and camp; and its characters shall be fashioned "from the distempers of Love and Ambition." As for structure, Davenant's great innovation, prompted surely by his own extensive experience as a dramatist, was to shape epic action by imposing on it a five-act dramatic structure.[7] But instead of blank verse, Davenant chose to adopt a short—perhaps too short—stanza form (ABAB), which he employed with balkanizing rigor, never permitting his sense to be drawn out from one stanza to the next. Davenant's "epic" is in literary-historical terms an astonishingly modernist experiment, even if it was not deemed a successful one: "He is for *unbeaten tracks,* and *new ways of thinking;* but certainly in his *untry'd Seas* he is no great discoverer."[8]

Davenant had only qualified praise for Tasso, and he failed to mention Tasso's own essay on epic theory, the *Discorsi del poema eroico* (1594), itself a meditation on Aristotle's *Poetics*. Nevertheless Tasso's work—recommended, as we saw, by Milton in *Of Education* for teaching "what the laws are of a true epic poem"[9]—shaped most later debates on epic, including Davenant's; and a summary of Tasso's theory will help not only to fix Davenant's own in sharper focus, but also to illuminate what Milton held to be the outstanding theoretical work of its kind.

For Tasso, the epic writer had to achieve the difficult task of combining the verisimilar and the marvelous. The epic setting must be historic, and a religious framework is required. Because, however, the epic poet had to be verisimilar, his religion must be believable, hence the modern epic perforce must overwrite pagan systems of ancient epic with the modern religion of Christianity. The only licit supernatural forces must be those comprehensible within such a religious framework, and for Tasso these are angels, devils, saints, wizards, and fairies. The action itself has to involve noble deeds, including those arising from love and friendship. The question of historicity is complex: an epic in the remote past creates the problem of archaic customs; but one set in the present day creates the even more damaging problem of being too close, impeding poetic invention; and so the past, indeed the remote past, is to be preferred. Epic must also respond to the political order, the best poem functioning under the best political system, which for Tasso is monarchy. Finally, the epic poet is not to meddle in the difficult and dangerous debates of natural philosophy or theology: "He is not to show himself ambitious in natural or theological questions."[10]

We can now see that Davenant responded to Tasso's theory by pressing its modernism still further. Davenant agreed with Tasso that epic had to modernize, but his was a much more thoroughgoing reformation, ejecting all supernaturalism even to the extent, as Hobbes noted, of dispensing with an opening invocation to a muse or a god. This is partly a reaction, and an understandably embittered one, to civil war—Davenant's secularism is a judgment on the religious warfare that had brought about regime change and indeed the very recent execution of the king. He underlined this topicality by placing in the very last lines of his first canto an obvious allusion to current affairs: "Our Reason our Religion does invade, / Till from the schools to Camps it carry warre."[11] In his preface, too, Davenant disavowed the classical idea of inspiration as "a dangerous word; which many have of late successfully us'd." So while Davenant retained several traditional epic conventions—there are versions of a hunt (1.2), a duel (1.4), *fama* personified (2.2), and an *ekphrasis* of divine history (2.6.53–74: Creation, Fall, Flood, Redemption, Resurrection)—these seem somewhat bloodless, missing their traditional mythic underpinning.

Hobbes tactfully upheld most of Davenant's decisions, but he himself displayed an interest in the origins and classifications of genres more akin to the critical approach of the elder Scaliger.[12] He too was a modernizer, however, especially concerning the place of the supernatural in epic: the pagan gods of ancient poetry had been part of their belief systems, but now things are otherwise; moreover, "Beyond the actual works of nature a Poet may now go; but beyond the conceived possibility of nature never."[13] This comment on the "works of nature" also hints that Hobbes, unlike Tasso, might not have objected to the treatment of "natural questions" in epic, and indeed his preface contains several Baconian allusions,[14] concluding on a virtuosic metaphor drawn from contemporary optics: Davenant's poem is like that "curious kinde of perspective [i.e., viewing-tube]" through which multiple figures on a canvas are resolved by the tube into one hidden portrait.[15]

Davenant did not in fact pick over specific natural or theological questions at great length in *Gondibert*, but he made his views on rationality in religion plain, and he also presented at length a description of a scientific institution partly modeled on the fictional House of Salomon in Francis Bacon's *New Atlantis*, and partly on the nonfictional "Office of Address" of the London-based interregnum "intelligencer" Samuel Hartlib. This is the House of Astragon, a scientific college comprehending, anachronistically, all kinds of natural knowledge, from deep sea diving to telescopic astronomy, as well as an Office of Address staffed by "Intelligencers," an anatomy theater, and a library containing all kinds of texts, starting with

Egyptian hieroglyphic rolls, in size "like faln Pillars."[16] Davenant's epic, therefore, showed the marked influence of Baconianism, and Astragon's college
prompted a similar institution in Abraham Cowley's *Davideis*. For the next
epic in the English tradition was indeed Cowley's *Davideis*, first published
in 1656, a more traditional, more influential, yet likewise unfinished work.

Abraham Cowley (1618–1667) was Milton's most irritating competitor.
In the eyes of the world Cowley, the younger man, was the prodigy, the
scholar-poet, the man with epic plans. A precocious sapling of Westminster
School, Cowley had shot into publication in his thirteenth year with his *Poetical Blossomes* (1633), an inoffensive volume containing both narrative and
occasional pieces, and sporting various paratextual blooms, including an engraving of the promising boy, "youngest son of Phoebus." A second edition,
in 1636, included the disheartening information that its two major items
had been written, respectively, at the ages of ten and twelve;[17] it is remarks
such as these which perhaps prompted Milton's own defensive vaunts in
several of the headnotes to his *Poems* of 1645: "don by the Author at fifteen
yeers old" was as early as he could go.[18] Cowley went on to Trinity College,
Cambridge, where he penned several successful comedies, in both Latin and
English, of just the kind Milton was soon to deride in *An Apology* (1642),
with its student actors "writhing and unboning their clergy limbs to all the
antic and dishonest gestures of Trinculos, buffoons, and bawds."[19] Cowley
accompanied the royalist cause to Oxford, and then followed Queen Henrietta Maria to France, working as a cipher clerk and latterly as a spy. He eventually made his peace with the Parliamentary victors, returned to London, and
published more poetry, culminating in his 1656 *Poems*, in which, amid his
protestations of political acquiescence to the ruling regime, his epic ambitions were given full vent. Although Milton was by this point blind, there is
good reason to think that he monitored Cowley and his progress, and he
must have found this politically abhorrent fellow poetically hard to take too.

What we can see today of Cowley's epic development is not quite what
was available to Milton, however. Cowley had first experimented in the
1640s with an epic on the actual civil war that was going on around him
but abandoned it. That he had attempted an epic on contemporary history
was then rendered public knowledge by Cowley himself in his long preface
to his 1656 *Poems*, brought out by Milton's erstwhile publisher Humphrey
Moseley. There Cowley listed all the works of his he was *excluding* from
the present volume, including *"three Books of the Civil War,"* up to the First

Battle of Newbury (September 20, 1643), but abandoned as the royalist cause dwindled. Cowley's artful defense of this nonpublication was that the vanquished ought to accept "a *General Amnesty* as a *favour* from the *Victor*," and not "*rip up old wounds*," a subtle way of announcing both his own allegiance and his peaceableness.[20]

Cowley's *Civil War,* commenced and abandoned probably in the space of at most two or three months, was in fact only found in manuscript after the deaths of both Cowley and Milton, and published in fragmentary form in 1679, the text breaking off mid-verse. In this text, all the rebel names—in the manner of the true names of Milton's fallen angels, "blotted out and ras'd / By thir Rebellion" (*PL* 1.362–63)—were suppressed, replaced by dashes. The full draft, such as it is, was only recovered and published in 1973. It is a fascinating failure: Cowley was in effect trying to construct a kind of politically orthodox version of Lucan's *Civil War,* but was overtaken by events as he wrote. In vain he tried to banish to the realm of myth the conquering forces of history, and in the end he was forced to give up. Before that point, however, he had managed to create some of the traditional epic spaces in his contemporary epic, including a weird, royalist Hell, which has been eloquently described as "a kind of political unconscious of royalist panegyric: all those aspects of political history which do not square with a simply monarchical patriotism are banished to this realm of darkness, from which, however, they then return."[21]

What Cowley did publish in his 1656 folio was a sacred epic, and one in which, with the benefit of hindsight, we can see Cowley recycling passages from his secular epic, which had itself included several tendencies toward the sacred, for instance figuring the opposing armies as if fighting the War in Heaven—"Angels" versus "Fiends."[22] The new, sacred epic was on David, and Cowley defended his transformation of biblical narrative into heroic verse in the strongest terms: "Amongst all holy and consecrated things which the *Devil* ever stole and alienated from the service of the *Deity;* as *Altars, Temples, Sacrifices, Prayers,* and the like; there is none that he so universally, and so long usurpt, as *Poetry.* It is time to recover it out of the *Tyrants* hands, and to restore it to the *Kingdom* of *God,* who is the *Father* of it. . . . All the *Books* of the *Bible* are either already most admirable, and exalted pieces of *Poesie,* or are the best *Materials* in the world for it."[23]

Such an endorsement of divine poetry places Cowley in the tradition of the earlier Cambridge poet, Giles Fletcher, who had prefaced his own di-

vine poems with an essay on the tradition. For Fletcher, the filament of sacred poetry was rooted in the Old Testament, grew through the church
fathers, into the earliest Christian poets, "as sedulous *Prudentius,* so prudent
*Sedulius,*" and culminated in the present age in the Protestant poets Du
Bartas, Spenser, and King James VI and I.[24] Indeed, the tradition of biblical
epic jumped directly from French to English in James VI's *Scottish* court, in
the form of the expatriate musician Thomas Hudson's "Englishing" of Du
Bartas's six-book shorter epic *Histoire de Judit,* first published as *The Historie
of Judith* in Edinburgh 1584 and thereafter in London editions of Du Bartas.
Yet it was not good enough, Cowley himself continued, to versify the odd
biblical story, like Francis Quarles,[25] or to produce a verse treatise on a sacred topic, such as Thomas Heywood with his *The Hierarchy of the Blessed
Angels,* an extremely lengthy creation-and-fall poetic commentary.[26] This is
not to elevate poetry, protested Cowley, but to debase divinity. Cowley in
fact did not reveal what the true divine poet would require, merely looking
forward to the day when his own "weak and imperfect attempt" would be
bettered by some greater man.

Cowley had planned his epic to be in twelve books, and he even explained
how it was to be structured, artfully breaking off after David's elegy on the
deaths of Saul and Jonathan, but before his anointing. This was, Cowley explained, to conform to the practice of Homer and Virgil, who had shown
how epic should only point to its own conclusion rather than narrate it,
much as cardplayers—the comparison is Cowley's—lay down their cards
when it is obvious that they have won.

As it was, Cowley laid down his cards after a mere four books. Yet this
truncated performance was nevertheless, like several of Cowley's other
poems, accompanied by a great deal of self-congratulatory scholarship. Not
only did Cowley bring his preface to a crescendo with his defense of sacred
epic, but he prefaced each book of the *Davideis* with prose arguments,
spotted his margins with biblical references, and appended to each book extensive notes keyed to his poetic text. These notes defend and explain his
poetic practice, often adducing classical parallels or learned sources. Indeed,
Cowley loaded discussions into his notes that he had avoided in the poem
itself. To Cowley the poet's description of Hell as "endless," for instance,
Cowley the auto-annotator commented that this was merely a poeticism,
for Hell has been measured by several commentators. The Jesuit scholar
Leonardus Lessius affirmed Hell to be a Dutch mile in diameter; his fellow

Jesuit Franciscus Ribiera, Cowley continues, proposed 1,600 furlongs or 200 Italian miles; Virgil, in the *Aeneid*, set it twice as deep as the distance between Heaven and Earth . . . and so on, perhaps not entirely seriously, terminating in the scriptural phrase "Utter Darkness."

When Cowley published his volume, he made sure to send a copy, as Milton had done with his own works, to the Bodleian Library, and again like Milton he inserted a manuscript poem into his book, this one in English, and spoken by the book itself, "Humbly presenting it selfe to the Vniversitie Librarie at Oxford." Unlike Milton's poem, long since removed and kept separately, Cowley's remains in its parent volume today.[27] Cowley even tried his hand at a translation (and slight expansion) of the *Davideis* into Latin hexameter, but only the first book was published.[28] And yet his publisher Humphrey Moseley, interestingly, was promising to his buyers the whole four books in Latin in around 1659 or 1660, and so it may be that Cowley saw his scheme further toward completion than has been assumed.[29]

This is a reminder that it was by no means an automatic decision to write an epic, biblical or otherwise, in the vernacular. The most extraordinary English counterexample of learned biblical epics in the mode of Cowley, but here written in Greek hexameter with a facing Latin translation, is the Cambridge classical scholar Joshua Barnes's *Aulikokatoptron sive Estheræ historia* (Courtier-Mirror, or the History of Esther) (1679). Barnes accompanied his own epic on the biblical Esther with scholia—also written in Greek—and even appended a parody in Homeric verse of the original biblical passage. (A lengthy preface reported ongoing work on an epic on Joseph in twelve books too, a work as unforthcoming as Cowley's own.) Barnes's book, in short, was constructed to look bibliographically and intellectually continuous with editions of classical texts, and later in life Barnes would himself produce several such editions, including one of Euripides, itself enriched by Barnes's access to Milton's own annotated copy of that writer.[30]

As Samuel Johnson first spotted,[31] Milton must have had Cowley's (English) *Davideis* read out aloud to him, as he adapted at least one passage from the *Davideis,* and Milton seldom imitated his contemporaries. Cowley says of Goliath:

> His spear, the trunk was of a lofty tree,
> Which Nature meant some tall ship's mast should be.

And here is Milton's Satan:

> His spear, to equal which the tallest pine
> Hewn on Norwegian hills, to be the mast
> Of some great admiral, were but a wand,
> He walk'd with. (1.292–95)

This is an obviously superior but still recognizable imitation, and underlines one of Milton's characteristic imaginative strengths, his geographical reach. Cowley's Heaven and Hell, recycled from his *Civil War*,[32] may also have reaffirmed for Milton the strength of negative comparison, for Cowley introduced both by means of the rhetorical device of *occupatio,* or describing something by negation. This is Cowley's Hell:

> Here no dear glimpse of the *Suns* lovely face,
> Strikes through the *Solid* darkness of the place;
> No dawning *Morn* does her kind reds display;
> One slight weak beam would here be thought the *Day.*
> No gentle *Stars* with their fair *Gems* of *Light*
> Offend the tyr'annous and unquestion'd *Night.* (1.85–90)

And this, in structural parallelism, is his Heaven:

> No pale-fac'ed *Moon* does in stoln beams appeare,
> Or with dim *Taper* scatters *darkness* there.
> On no smooth *Sphear* the restless *seasons* slide,
> No circling *Motion* doth swift *Time* divide. (1.357–60)

As Johnson rather unimaginatively complained, "Cowley's is scarcely description, unless it be possible to describe by negatives; for he tells us only what there is not in heaven."[33] Negative comparison, grammatically common in classical epic, can possess philosophic force, however, for it can insinuate that some things may be strictly indescribable. The closer one gets to sacred things, the more frequently is the poetic tactic of "negative" or "apophatic" theology deployed. It was a device that Milton would press to paradox in *Paradise Lost*: in Hell the lighting conditions are like "darkness visible"; whereas in Heaven the mere skirts of God are "Dark with excessive bright" (1.63; 3.380).

Cowley's poem was politically experimental too. Although Cowley was biographically a Royalist, the fourth book of the *Davideis* reads in many places like a republican experiment, with Cowley in both his verse and his notes sounding a frequently radical note. When the people beg Samuel for a king, for instance, his reply is blunt: "You're sure the first (said he) / Of *freeborn* men that begg'd for *Slaverie*."[34] Cowley's extensive note to this passage even denied that any specifically divine right of kings can be derived from the underlying biblical passage: "It is a vile opinion of those men, and might be punished without *Tyranny,* if they teach it, who hold, that the *right* of *Kings* is set down by *Samuel* in this place. Neither did the people of *Israel* ever allow, or the *Kings* avow the assumption of such a power, as appears by the story of *Ahab* and *Naboth*. Some indeed did exercise it, but that is no more a proof of the *Right,* then their *Practise* was of the *Lawfulness* of *Idolatry*."[35] Cowley presumably came to regret these and similar passages. But they add complexity to his work, and indeed this political—albeit possibly just politic— ambivalence is the most enduring aspect of Cowley's unfinished epic.

Much later, Milton's widow reported that Milton's favorite English poets were Spenser, Shakespeare, and, bizarrely, Cowley.[36] Yet Milton would have found much to deplore or avoid in the *Davideis*. Cowley's style, with its rather restricted set of poetic devices and its jingling overuse of *ploce* (repetition of words, including in grammatical variation) and *zeugma* ("yoking" two or more nouns to one verb), was dating fast. At a deeper level, what has been called Cowley's "epic reticence"[37] extended to his suppression, with one exception, of epic simile; his suspiciously robotic use of hellish and heavenly councils; and his taste for naturalizing explanations in a genre that had formerly thrived on the supernatural. This is an unhappy convergence with the work of his friend Davenant. Nor does Cowley really get behind his hero, David, who is grudgingly awarded his one early moment against Goliath, but who thereafter is a hero in search of a heroic role.

Cowley's rationalizing tendency is additionally fascinating because, especially in his notes, he subjects biblical text to narrative critique. In his second book, for instance, he omits the biblical passage of Jonathan calling for arrows to shoot David, excusing this on the rationalist grounds that it is "a subtilty that I cannot for my life comprehend; for since he went to *David,* and talked to him himself, what needed all that politique trouble of the shooting"; and in Cowley's fourth book, following Hugo Grotius, he revised down a biblical figure of 30,000 chariots to 3,000, as "old *Manuscripts*," including biblical manuscripts, were notoriously erroneous in numbers.[38] These are maneuvers not reassuring to the fundamentalist, and in them we hear again some of the religiopolitical defiance of Davenant, exasperated at what both men perceived as a regime run by religious terrorists. As we saw with his comments on Hell and its dimensions, Cowley's comments on scripture also risk becoming whimsical. This is something he himself implicitly concedes in some of his notes, such as when he decides to award, in Samuel's "college," professorships of astronomy and mathematics to Nathan and Gad respectively, a jocular allusion to the two Savilian chairs at Oxford, established in 1619—"this is a voluntary gift of mine to them, and I suppose the places were very lawfully at my disposing."[39] Cowley had lamely defended his Oxbridge-style biblical college by claiming that this was in fact the origin of the Western universities; but whether he believed this or not, the effect on the epic quality of the poem is dire. Again, Cowley's musings on education in ancient Israel, evidently inspired by Davenant's House of Astragon, have more in common with Cowley's later utopian *Proposition for the Advancement of Experimental Philosophy* (1661), with its model for a "philosophical college," than they do with biblical epic.

Davenant, then, had argued for a new kind of heroic epic poem, modeled on tragedy, philosophically and religiously modernized, and tending, like the more recent Italians, to the romance end of the epic spectrum. Cowley, however, toed a more classical line, preserving epic diction and the heroic couplet, and promoting the notion of the biblical epic. But both displayed rationalizing tendencies, and both introduced a certain Baconian spirit into their epics. Comparing their relative achievements, especially against the Elizabethan attempt of Spenser, soon became a set piece of English criticism.[40] Milton was of course closer to the biblicism of Cowley, but he would have sympathized with Davenant that drama had much to impart to epic. His own practice, however, would decisively resist and reverse many other aspects of these earlier men's projects, most notably Milton's exuberant interest in devils, angels, heavenly and hellish councils, God, and Satan; and he was to show himself, quite against Tasso's strictures, hugely "ambitious in natural or theological questions."

# 11

## Going Blind

A T SOME UNKNOWN date, the well-known London astrologer John Gadbury (1627–1704) drew up John Milton's natal chart or horoscope. It seems unlikely that Milton asked Gadbury to do so, but as Gadbury knew that Milton had been born at 6:30 in the morning, he must have had information from someone close to Milton or access to the family Bible.[1] It is perhaps a test nativity of a notable figure, of a kind often drawn up to see whether nativities and subsequent careers might be correlated. Only the natal chart is preserved, without Gadbury's interpretation of it, but a modern reconstruction has noted one rather ominous aspect: it predicts that Milton would go blind. The prominent astrologer William Lilly, for instance, had included a section in his *Christian Astrology* (1647) on "weaknesses of the eyes," and applying this to Milton's stars, the news was not good: several of Milton's planets were near nebulae at his nativity, and this, it was claimed, portends ill for the eyes.[2]

So it proved. Milton noticed his eyes going from the middle of the 1640s, left one first, then right, and by early 1652 both had failed completely. Physicians have puzzled over Milton's blindness, and the most recent judgment is that it was caused by "intermittent close angle glaucoma."[3] Milton himself was keen to stress that in appearance his eyes remained *sine nube clari ac lucidi,* "cloudless, clear, and shining,"[4] and in *Paradise Lost* he talked about his eyes and what had happened to them: "So thick a drop serene hath quencht thir Orbs, / Or dim suffusion veild" (3.24–26).

Now this is quite medically specific: "drop serene" is a literal translation of the medical term *gutta serena* (also known as *amaurosis*)—but in this poetic context it carries too the (self-rallying?) Latin sense of "serene" as "tranquil," even "joyful." The *gutta serena* was the result of a failure of the optic nerve, and although incurable after a certain point, could be halted if treated early. In contrast, "dim suffusion veild," is a reference to the condition of *suffusio* (*hypochyma* in Greek), the (curable) eye condition caused by humor that had flowed down into the eye. These were opposed by classical and early modern physicians to the incurable condition of *glaucoma,* thought to be caused by the drying out of the lens. Once again, Milton knew all about this from his reading, here probably in the Roman physician Celsus, who had dedicated a long chapter of the sixth book of his *De medicina* to a discussion of types of blindness, and in Aristotle, who opposed *hypochyma* and *glaucoma;* although common medical self-help works of Milton's time contained all the information he would need.[5]

Reading and writing when blind required helpers. In fact, use of such helpers was a practice of many partially or even fully sighted scholars too. Milton's contemporary, the experimental philosopher and chemist Robert Boyle, for instance, whose sight as a young man had been permanently weakened, so he believed, by a bad fall from a horse, used his wealth to employ surrogate readers as well as amanuenses.[6] Milton too employed amanuenses long before he went blind. His nephew Edward Phillips recalled that on Sundays Milton made his nephews learn biblical exposition by dictating to them.[7] When Milton sent his ode to John Rouse of the Bodleian Library in late January 1647, it was likewise in a scribal hand.[8] Blind Milton, however, was confined to such assistance. He struggled on with his state job, but domestic life must have become harrowingly complex when the loss of his eyes was followed by the loss of his wife, in May 1652, leaving him with four young children to raise. He was soon relieved of the burden of one of them, for within two months his only son, also John, had died. Milton must have used his considerable salary as a senior civil servant to employ constant home help.

Milton was horribly mocked for his blindness. To many it was not glaucoma but divine retribution. One reader having seen the blind Milton even wrote on his copy of Milton's *Eikonoklastes:* "the man that wrot this booke is now growne blinde & is led vp & downe," and carefully noted the date: July 11, 1652.[9] The Restoration turned the trickle of abuse into a torrent: "the blind Beetle that durst affront the *Royal Eagle:* That mercenary *Milton* who hath sworn service to prosperous villainy";[10] "the one good eye he [John Hewson, the regicide] hath left, wee'l take it out of his Head, and bestow it upon blind *Milton,* that it may still be worn as an Ornament, in a knaves countenance";[11] "how wonderfully was Mr. *Iohn Milton* . . . strucken blind . . . and could never since, by any art, or skill, either recover his sight, or preserve his Books from being burned by the hand of the common Hang-man";[12] "*Milton* beginning to write an Answer to the late Kings Book against Monarchy, was at the second word, by the power of God stricken blind";[13] "Milton, that writ two Books against the Kings, and *Salmasius* his Defence of Kings, struck totally blind";[14] "Mr Milton . . . a blind adder."[15] He prompted a particularly comic rhyme: "His Justice was as blind as his Friend *Milton,* / Who slandered the *Kings Book* with an ill-tongue."[16] One pamphlet was titled simply—*No Blinde Guides.*[17]

"Do you not sometime reflect on your blindness as a judgment for your writing against King Charles?" one visitor to the famous writer of regicidal prose asked. Milton's riposte hits harder than all the insults above: "I am blind: Salmasius is dead: which is the greater judgment?"[18]

Milton's blindness had been exploited by his opponents as early as the anonymous *Regii sanguinis clamor* (Shout of the Royal Blood) of 1652, an attack that caused Milton a great deal of distress. Already completely blind by the time he received the book, Milton assumed it had all been written on the continent by a slightly shady Franco-Scottish reformed theologian called Alexander More, and thus aimed his counterblasts at this hapless man. The real author, Peter Du Moulin, was a Church of England clergyman; after the Restoration he would argue (unsuccessfully) for the creation of a fortieth article of the English church, to be appended to the standard thirty-nine, stipulating loyalty to the crown.[19] Du Moulin had sent his work to Salmasius and More, who were friends, and the latter had then added a preface and seen the book through the press. It was dispatched sheet by sheet to the intelligencer Samuel Hartlib in London, and copies soon made it independently to Milton, who was handed the book fresh from the press, so he later said, in an actual meeting of the Council of State. Yet another copy then arrived for him from the committee dealing with such matters.[20] When the preface was read out to Milton, he soon heard a famous line of Virgil applied directly to Milton himself: "Monstrum horrendum, informe, ingens, cui lumen ademptum" (A monster, dreadful, shapeless, huge, deprived of sight).[21] Ironically Milton, who has been often criticized for attacking More even after being informed that Du Moulin was the real culprit, was here, at least, absolutely right: the dedicatory preface to the *Regii sanguinis clamor* was indeed More's work. Du Moulin, who in fact did not take advantage of Milton's blindness once in his own text, probably completed the *Regii sanguinis clamor* without knowing of Milton's final descent into the dark. The monster in Virgil alluded to by More was the blinded Cyclops Polyphemus, a sorry figure, tricked by Odysseus, with blood oozing from his one eye socket. Evidently this hurt; Milton spent many pages of the *Defensio secunda* (1654) talking about his blindness.

In response to this one passing Virgilian allusion, Milton defiantly stacked up examples of the righteous blind. From antiquity he named Timoleon of Corinth, the great general and ruler of Syracuse, who in his blindness was visited by foreigners desirous of seeing the great man, as Milton was too, and who was still consulted by the state in his blindness and retirement, as Milton, at least after the Restoration, was not;[22] Appius Claudius Caecus, the early Roman writer and pioneer constructor of civil roads and aqueducts;[23] and Lucius Caecilius Metellus, hero of the First Punic War, who lost his eyes rescuing Rome's sacred Palladium from a fire in the Temple of Vesta and was therefore granted the privilege of riding to the senate in a chariot.[24] These were all heroes from democratic Greece and republican Rome. From more recent history Milton produced the Venetian doge Enrico Dandolo, the Hussite leader John Zizka, and the Italian Protestant theologian Hieronymus Zanchius. For good measure he added Isaac and Jacob from the Old Testament, and recalled from the Gospel of John the miracle of Christ healing the blind man.[25] It is the classic historical sweep of Milton: Greco-Roman republican statesmanship, a crusading doge, two Protestant heroes of the battlefield and of the study, examples enlisted from the Bible itself, and at the end of this righteous tradition, Milton himself.

Milton in his government post was now reliant on total secretarial support, and for his own private literary labors Milton used readers and amanuenses too, some casual, some employed, some perhaps covering both his

official and his private needs. He must have dictated a series of psalm translations, produced as daily mediations in the second week of August,
1653. Later, throughout the composition of *Paradise Lost,* Milton utilized
"whatever hand came next,"[26] and Cyriac Skinner recalled that Milton had
verses composed in his head "against his Amanuensis came"—late amanuenses were greeted with Milton's impatient cry that he "wanted to be
milked." Skinner added that youths sent to Milton from time to time for
instruction often served as amanuenses too, and that "some elderly persons were glad for the benefit of his learned Conversation, to perform the
Office."[27] Aubrey also said that Milton's daughter Deborah "was his Amanuensis," and read to Milton in the learned tongues.[28] Such amanuenses were
not always competent, as Milton at least once complained in Latin about the
insufficient Latinity of the amanuensis—who was of course writing out that
very complaint![29] Milton the narrator would have us believe that his role in
receiving the text of *Paradise Lost* was quite passive:

> If answerable style I can obtaine
> Of my Celestial Patroness, who deignes
> Her nightly visitation unimplor'd,
> And dictates to me slumbring, or inspires
> Easie my unpremeditated Verse (9.20–24)

But Milton the writer's experience was evidently less "Easie," and *Paradise
Lost* the text was the result of hundreds and hundreds of encounters with
many different amanuenses.

Milton's achievement is staggering, and that *Paradise Lost* was of necessity composed as an oral poem only adds to that achievement. Milton is usually held, following Phillips, to have composed most of the epic in the four
or five years around the Restoration, but only in the period each year between the autumnal and vernal equinoxes (late September to late March).[30]
Milton seems to have first dictated the verse in parcels of ten, twenty, or
thirty verses at a time to whatever amanuensis was at hand, and his nephew
recalled that he, Edward, would then have to conform the punctuation and
spelling to Miltonic standards.[31] Given that the average length of a book of
*Paradise Lost* in the first edition is just over one thousand lines, this means
that each book arose out of around fifty bouts of dictation, and these then
all had to be sewn together and revised. Did Milton actually dictate his lines

in near-perfect form? We do not know, but the evidence from the Trinity College Manuscript, Milton's poetic portfolio, shows that he tinkered quite heavily with his earlier poems, especially the masque now known as *Comus,* and there is no reason to doubt that the same was true for *Paradise Lost* too, whatever Milton-as-narrator claimed about his inspiration. Indeed, a slightly later biography of Milton, by Jonathan Richardson, modulated Edward's account, claiming rather that Milton would dictate forty lines in bed in the morning, and then cut them down to half that number. This sounds more plausible, and writing without rhyme may have facilitated such a process, because line endings need not be preserved intact. Nevertheless, Richardson is here obviously borrowing from the biographical tradition of Virgil, who was said to have composed by a similar process of superfluity and reduction.[32]

That *Paradise Lost* was the epic of a blind man soon became an inextricable part of its meaning for readers, as Milton the blind polemicist was transmuted into Milton the blind bard. Andrew Marvell's poem on *Paradise Lost* commences "When I beheld the Poet blind." One of the more curious early compliments paid to Milton is a little Latin manuscript poem by his contemporary the royalist physician and natural philosopher Walter Charleton:

> Maeonides fuerit captus quòd lumine, nullam
> Historiis fateor me tribuisse fidem.
> Id verò ut credam nunc, imò ut credere cogar,
> Efficiunt numeri, docte Poëta tui.
> Nam licet aeternâ tua lumina nocte premantur,
> Tu tamen aeterno lumine digna canis.[33]

> [I thought I put no trust in the tradition that Homer was
> deprived of sight. But your verses, learned poet, show that I
> should believe it now, indeed that I am compelled to believe it.
> For although your eyes are buried in eternal night, you,
> however, sing deeds worthy of eternal light.]

The curiosity is that this is in fact a plagiarism, being an almost word-for-word transcription of an epigram by a sixteenth-century German neo-Latin poet and physician, addressed to a different blind poet, the Italian academician Camillus Falconetus. In both poems, the modern poet's blindness lends credence to the alleged blindness of Homer, rather than the other way around. And it is interesting, too, that Charleton betrays not a hint of political animus here: this learned physician, writing in perhaps the later 1670s, when it would have been so very easy to kick the late Milton whilst down (he died in 1674), hails only the literary achievement. Not everything is politics.

Milton's *Defensio secunda* had approached blindness with defiance. Milton carried this defiance across into *Paradise Lost* itself. He took to himself the lonely symbol of the nightingale, the "solemn" and "wakeful" bird who sings by night three times in Eden (4.602–4, 771; 7.435–36). And the invocation to "holy Light" with which Milton commences Book 3 soon introduces the irony of a blind narrator hailing a light he can no longer physically see:

> but thou
> Revisit'st not these eyes, that rowle in vain
> To find thy piercing ray, and find no dawn. (3.22–24)

Yet just as in the *Defensio secunda* Milton had arranged around him other heroes of blindness, so in *Paradise Lost* he attempts what looks, at first, like exactly the same maneuver, except that his allies here are figures from literature rather than history:

> nor somtimes forget
> Those other two equal'd with me in Fate,
> So were I equal'd with them in renown,
> Blind *Thamyris* and blind *Mæonides*,
> And *Tiresias* and *Phineus* Prophets old. (3.33–36)

Who are these four blind poets? Maeonides (native of Maeonia) is a toponym (occasionally interpreted as a patronym in the period) for Homer, Milton's great epic predecessor. Indeed the very name "Homer," in some of the ancient lives, was etymologically connected with "blind."[34] Thamyris, as Milton says, was also a poet, whose fate was recounted by Homer, in the famous "Catalogue of Ships" section of the *Iliad*:

> the Muses
> encountering Thamyris the Thracian stopped him from
> singing

as he came from Oichalia and Oichalian Eurytos;
for he boasted that he would surpass, if the very Muses,
daughters of Zeus who holds the aegis, were singing against
    him,
and these in their anger struck him maimed, and the voice of
    wonder
they took away, and made him a singer without memory.[35]

In fact the Homeric text says merely that Thamyris was πηρός, or "disabled in a limb," maimed, rather than strictly blinded, but, in an interesting accretion of (blind) Homer and the blind bard Demodocus within *The Odyssey,* Thamyris early became thought of as, like Homer and Demodocus, blind.[36] The name of Thamyris became proverbial. Already by the time of the Greek lexicographer Hezychius (fifth to sixth century), the phrase θάμυρις μαίνεται (Latin: *Thamyris insanit,* English: Thamyris raves) was in use for someone who attempts something beyond his or her ability.[37] As for Thamyris's poetry itself, the first systematic commentator on Milton's *Paradise Lost,* Patrick Hume, has a crucial note on this passage: "*Plutarch* commends his [Thamyris's] Poem, of the *Tytans* Warring against the Gods, in his Book of *Musick*"; and indeed in (pseudo-)Plutarch's essay on music Thamyris is reported as having written such an epic and is, moreover, coupled with Demodocus.[38] Thamyris, like Milton, then, was a poet of heavenly wars. So whereas of these two poets, "equal'd," Milton says, "with [him] in Fate," one embodied success, a figure to comfort Milton and to spur him on, while the other stood for failure—a poet who was blinded because he had dared to aspire above his station. Not only was the maiming of Thamyris an act of revenge, then, it was the punishment of a boaster. In Homer, his was the worst punishment of all, for the Muses made him "a singer without memory." One wonders, too, whether Milton knew of the discussion of the blindness of both Homer and Thamyris in the Greek chorographer Pausanias, who tantalizingly mentioned a lost epic, the *Minyas,* in which it was claimed that Thamyris only paid for his presumption "in Hades," that is, after death. Pausanias, however, confided that he considered both men to have lost their sight through illness rather than divine rebuke, but contrasted Homer, who continued making poetry all his life without despairing, with Thamyris, who gave into his misfortune and gave up his art.[39]

Milton next mentions two other figures, Tiresias and Phineus. The Theban *vates* Tiresias, in the most famous version of his myth, was also blind, but as the result of a complicated chain of events. He had been changed into a woman after striking dead the female of two copulating serpents; striking the male dead seven years later, he was turned back into a man. Because he then revealed that women had more pleasure in sex than men, he was struck blind by Hera, the wife of Zeus, in punishment. Zeus, unable to reverse Hera's act, awarded him prophetic insight in recompense. He is a complex figure for Milton, then: punished by one god, rewarded by another. Of his many appearances in classical literature, perhaps the most pertinent here is in the *nekuia* of the tenth book of the *Odyssey*, an episode then tersely summarized by Lycophron, where Odysseus summons the spirit Tiresias to prophesy for him, and Tiresias tells him his destiny.[40] He was also for Milton a symbol of the burden of having to speak truth when it is going to be unpleasant to do so: in *The Reason of Church-Government* he recalls Tiresias in Sophocles's *Oedipus Rex*, "bemoaning his lot, that he knew more then other men."[41]

Phineus, however, had a unique importance for Milton, who returned to the example of this prophet king several times in his writings. We have just encountered the lost epic the *Minyas*, said to be by Prodicus the Phocaean, featuring the Underworld, and possibly discussing the Argonauts, also known as the "Minyans" after their eponymous founder Minyas. In the surviving *Argonautica* of Apollonius of Rhodes—one of Milton's central texts—Phineus was blinded for being too free with his prophetic powers; nevertheless, he also revealed to the Argonauts the safe path for their journey, just as Milton would later reveal, through his archangel Michael, the future path of mankind. The reference to Tiresias and Phineus in tandem, indeed, by this date meant something personal to Milton, because early on in his blindness, Milton, to return to the *Defensio secunda* once again, had faced his abusers by recalling, in addition to his historic heroes, specifically these two figures:

> Shall I recall those ancient bards and wise men of the most
> distant past, whose misfortune the gods, it is said, recom-
> pensed with far more potent gifts, and whom men treated
> with such respect that they preferred to blame the very gods
> than to impute their blindness to them as a crime? The

tradition about the seer Tiresias is well known. Concerning Phineus, Apollonius sang as follow in the *Argonautica:*

> Nor did he fear Jupiter himself,
> Revealing truly to men the divine purpose.
> Wherefore he gave him a prolonged old age
> But deprived him of the sweet light of his eyes.[42]

Milton repeated the connection in a piece of private correspondence dating from just after the publication of the *Defensio secunda.* On September 28 of that year, Milton wrote a letter to the Athenian scholar and diplomat Leonardos Philaras (1595–1673) in which he explained in detail the medical history of his eyes in the hope that Philaras might obtain for him an opinion from an eminent Parisian physician. After a strictly medical exposition, Milton's literary turn is striking:

> Vapours . . . press and oppress my eyes with a sort of sleepy
> heaviness, especially from mealtime to evening, so that not
> infrequently I think of the Salmydessian seer Phineus in the
> *Argonautica:*
>
>> All round him there then grew
>> A purple thickness; and he thought the earth
>> Whirling beneath his feet; and so he sank,
>> Speechless at length, into a feeble torpor.[43]

Once again, Milton's textual mind turns to the *Argonautica,* and Milton evidently had the entire passage by heart: Jason and the Argonauts encounter wretched Phineus on the coast of the Black Sea; Phineus, to whom Apollo had granted the power of prophecy, "had not the slightest thought even for Zeus himself as he revealed to men the god's holy mind"; so Zeus took away his sight, and forced both longevity and the torment of the Harpies on him. Phineus sinks to his knees in a stupor at the arrival of the Argonauts—the passage quoted by Milton above—and their arrival triggers a bout of prophecy from the old man. The two sons of Boreas weep for Phineus and, as prophesied, resolve to drive off the Harpies, which they then do. But it is openly acknowledged that Phineus has indeed committed a terrible crime against the gods: "It was wretched thoughtlessness which led you to sin against the gods through your knowledge of prophecy."[44] A further bass note sounds when we realize that Milton read this text in an edition with the ancient Greek scholia on Apollonius, and from these he would have learned that blind Phineus appeared in not one but two lost poems attributed to Hesiod, most ancient of poets. The divine blinding of a human seer was therefore a story from the very earliest substrate of Greek myth. And, much more accessibly, Milton would have known from Ovid of a lost Latin epic on the Argonauts by the great Latin scholar poet Varro, in which Phineus must once again have featured.[45]

There is an interesting problem of exegesis here, however, for as we can now appreciate, Milton's recollection of Phineus in the *Defensio secunda* above is intriguingly skewed. Milton states that Phineus is an example of heroic resistance to the gods, where men "preferred to blame the very gods" rather than the human seer himself. But this is at best an optimistic reading of Milton's acknowledged source where, as we have seen, Phineus's guilt is openly acknowledged even by those who reverence and assist him. Milton deflects these details of the Greek poem, substituting them, perhaps, with the parallel passage in the *Argonautica* of Apollonius's Latin imitator, Valerius Flaccus, where there is no criticism of Phineus, who rather calls Jupiter himself unjust (*iniustus*), and claims that he used his powers merely out of pity for the human race.[46] Yet just a suspicion of Phineus's guilt is nonetheless provided by Milton's epithet "Salmydessian" for Phineus, as this comes not from Apollonius but from the play *Antigone* by Sophocles, where Phineus, of the Thracian city Salmydessus, is blinded because he had himself blinded the sons of his first marriage, at the instigation of his wicked second wife.[47] This is related to us by the Chorus, and just after it has sung of this other example of a family falling apart, that other blind seer, Tiresias, enters, bringing the play to its crisis. To this we should add the *Orphic Argonautica*, in reality a much later text but assumed in the early modern period to belong to the oldest stage of Greek poetry. In the *Orphic Argonautica*, again, Phineus is blinded by the two sons of Boreas in revenge for his own blinding of his sons.[48] It is of course hard to be sure which of all these waving tendrils of myth Milton was knotting together when he appealed to Phineus in the *Defensio secunda*, and he had not even started drafting *Paradise Lost* at this point. But the slippage between Phineus the guiltless sage and Phineus the man who said too much is of Milton's making and is a harbinger of his own ambivalence in the epic, as he tries, consciously or otherwise, both to acknowledge and to overcome the difficulties of his own project.

Milton's four predecessors, then, as a group produce a much more complex effect than might at first be assumed—their "Fate," collectively, seems to tilt against their "renown," to use Milton's vocabulary. For at least three of Milton's examples are capable of being read as covert warnings, warnings Milton issues to himself: Is it a mortal's business to handle the things of the immortal?—again, "May I express thee unblam'd?" (*PL* 3.3) The slow reading of this crucial passage in *Paradise Lost* produces an effect that challenges the faster, first encounter; blind Milton sees that he is handling holy things, and he trembles.

# 12

## The Undertaking, Revisited

MILTON PROMISED IN public to write his great work decades before he actually produced it, and he announced this undertaking somewhat incongruously, in two prose works of a political rather than literary nature. It is hard to know what, if anything, Milton's first readers made of these early, and ostensibly eccentric, engagements. Such promises were, however, quite in keeping with the development of Milton's self-conception as a poet. All his life he had obsessed about the career and vocation of the poet, and in order to bring himself into that fold, he studied—and studied to emulate—the lives of earlier poets. When he published his first volume of poems, in 1645, he included in it several older pieces already marked with an awareness of the classical *rota* or "wheel," the idea that the great poet progresses upward through certain fixed genres, mastering each one before progressing to the next level. This image of the wheel "seems to have developed from the use of *rota* as synecdoche for the Classical image of the Muses' chariot."[1]

There were, however, competing models of the *rota*. The most influential, back-formed from Virgil's career, was a tripartite bucolic-didactic-epic trajectory, *Eclogues-Georgics-Aeneid;* or, in the terse formulation of an auto-epitaph foisted on Virgil, "pascua rura duces" (pastures, farms, leaders). There were other ways of spinning the *rota* too: from (erotic) elegiacs to tragedy to epic[2]—or indeed just any progression from genres one could call lighter or comic, to the genres universally accepted as "heavy," tragedy and epic. What mattered was that the author in question was either inter-preted, or labored to present himself, as intentionally constructing (or in some cases no less intentionally resisting) a poetic career based on such a pattern. The example familiar to all Milton's contemporaries was the opening of Spenser's *Faerie Queene,* which had recalled to reject Spenser's earlier pastoral poetry: "For trumpets sterne to chaunge mine Oaten reeds"; as every schoolchild knew, this passage was itself a close imitation of the spurious opening lines of the *Aeneid,* "Ille ego qui quondam gracili modulatus auena / carmen" (I am he who once tuned my song on a slender reed), still printed as genuine in every classroom copy of Virgil in the period.[3]

Needless to say, all such constructions soon collide with biographical re-alities, but this does not render self-presentation irrelevant to the business of interpretation. So as Milton had written elegies and pastorals by the time he started work as a prose controversialist, it actually made sense for Milton to think of himself as having completed the preparatory stages of the po-etic biography, and now qualified to approach the higher level. Milton, in voicing openly this ambition when he did, was to some extent steeling him-self to the work ahead, making a public profession of intent in order to elicit its execution.

A few years later Milton's 1645 *Poems* took further steps to present the poet as engaged on the *rota.* On the Latin side, it contained Milton's elegies, but now with an appendix, also in Latin elegiacs, renouncing these pieces as juvenile and inappropriately erotic. This chilly postscript has often been interpreted as a piece of puritanism, but a hard puritan would simply not have published the elegies at all—rather, Milton the Christian poet is iden-tifying a poetic stage as completed, and then repudiated. Likewise on the English side, "Lycidas," Milton's pastoral elegy for the drowned Edward King, famously concludes by looking forward to "pastures new," a metapo-etical statement that pastoral as a genre had also now been completed, and that preparations could legitimately commence for the final, harder level. The most explicit example of progression, however, comes in the opening lines of "The Passion," which recall Milton's earlier poem of 1629, "On the Morning of Christ's Nativity":

> Ere-while of Musick, and Ethereal mirth,
> Wherwith the stage of Ayr and Earth did ring,
> And joyous news of heav'nly Infants birth,
> My muse with Angels did divide to sing.

This is the poetry of someone who is starting to assume that his poems must be considered not only as a set of texts with horizontal interconnections, but as a vertical record of the development and maturation of the poet himself. "The Passion" is unfinished, indeed abandoned, and it is Milton himself who informs the reader of this: "This Subject the Author finding to be above the yeers he had, when he wrote it, and nothing satisfi'd with what was begun, left it unfinisht." "Nothing satisfi'd"—and yet Milton still preserved and published it, because it was part of his poetic record.

Milton's "On the Morning of Christ's Nativity," the poem with which he chose to open the English section of his 1645 volume (and thereby the volume as a whole, as the English section preceded the Latin), also recalls Virgil's fourth Eclogue, which mysteriously prophesied the birth of a boy savior. This had been interpreted since the time of Constantine and his adviser Lactantius as a pagan prophecy of the coming of Christ—indeed, according to Lactantius, possibly even the Second Coming of the same.[4] The parallelism between these two poems on the coming of the savior, and indeed the resulting destruction of the pagan gods, underscores that Milton, in this section at least, presents himself as Virgilian. But Milton commenced the Latin section of his 1645 volume with his elegies, the genre of Ovid. The first of these, to Charles Diodati, addressed Milton's "exile," a potential period of undergraduate rustication from Cambridge, and Milton underscored the Ovidianism by likening his exile to that of Ovid at Tomis, although he looked forward to the end of this temporary state of affairs.[5] Milton cannot have known that he too, upon the Restoration, fugitive and briefly imprisoned, would fall from political grace and into an internal exile. In the first elegy, Milton quickly passes over his Ovidian moment—Virgil and Homer are swiftly preferred after the comparison to Ovid—but it does show that Milton was open to thinking about his proposed literary career in slightly more flexible ways than his dominant Virgilianism might suggest.

This was fortunate, because not only did the end of Milton's poetic *rota*—the paired *Paradise Regained* and *Samson Agonistes* of 1671[6]—take Milton beyond single epic and into an altogether more complex dialogue between epic and tragedy, but history itself got in Milton's way in the form of the most exciting phase of his adult life: his senior job in the new, kingless commonwealth government, and his sudden and unforeseen rise as the state apologist for the republican political experiment.

Indeed, by the publication of his *Defensio secunda* in 1654, Milton's self-presentation, though still voluble, had shifted in its emphasis. The younger man had declared himself primarily a poet, and if a prose writer at all, then that temporarily, by circumstance. The older civil servant presents a more integrated intellectual biography, however, one that finds Milton more comfortable with his political credentials, which are indeed now dominant: his mission in the 1640s, he writes, was "to promote the cause of true and solid liberty," specifically religious, domestic, and personal liberty. Because, Milton continued, he had already written on the first category (i.e., his tracts against the bishops), and as the Parliament was addressing the final category, Milton in the period of the first civil war turned his attentions to domestic liberty, which he again subdivided into three kinds: marriage (treated by his divorce tracts), education (*Of Education*), and the right of free-thinking ("liberè philosophandi potestas," the *Areopagitica*).[7] This has always struck readers as a little too schematic and self-possessed: in this bracing fantasy, Milton failed to declare, for instance, his own initially disastrous first marriage as surely part of what motivated *The Doctrine and Discipline of Divorce*, nor did he admit external prompts for *Of Education* and *Areopagitica*, which were solicited and elicited by, respectively, the intelligencer Samuel Hartlib and some unwelcome government legislation.

By the *Defensio secunda*, indeed, Milton had gone oddly quiet about his great work. Even his recollection in that tract of his Italian visit, the fullest account we have of this transformational phase, is silent about Milton as a literary figure, let alone as an aspiring writer of epic. In fact this later account, astonishingly, does not mention poetry at all: Milton presents himself as a cosmopolitan, conversing with ambassadors and men of state, and if as a writer, then by implication a political writer. Yet in the 1640s and 1650s Milton had been developing a new kind of vernacular poetry, almost unrecognizable as the work of the same man who had written much of the pastoralizing verse contained in the 1645 *Poems*. The 1645 volume had also included some recently composed sonnets on themes not usually associated with sonneteering: one addressed to the Royalist soldiers advancing on London in the first civil war, asking them to leave the poet and his house alone; and two to women, congratulating them on not their erotic but their moral qualities (Sonnets 8–10). Milton was also soon moved to two sonnets on the reception of his divorce tracts, an unusual manifestation of an author's reaction to a bad review; and his total disillusionment with the Presbyterian party is marked by "On the new forcers of conscience under the Long Parliament." These poems led generically to the political sonnets of the 1650s, written now from a position of power and exemplified by Milton's sonnets to Cromwell and to Sir Henry Vane the Younger, both of 1652, perhaps the earliest examples of the poetry of the completely blind Milton. The former, indeed, was prompted specifically by Milton's alarm at the potential threat to religious freedom of speech represented by a government committee attempting to impose a system of certification on public preachers.[8] Milton had evidently adapted to his new vocation and had even started writing (short) poetry suitable to it, addressed personally to some of the chief men of the state.

None of this is mentioned in the *Defensio secunda,* and its silence may indicate that Milton had not started writing *Paradise Lost* as an epic by this point. This is corroborated by the testimony of Edward Phillips, who located the epic's major phase of composition to the four or five years around the Restoration, probably commencing in earnest in early 1658. Before that point, all Milton had were, in one poetic folder (the surviving Trinity manuscript), his ideas for dramas, including some on the Fall, and in another (now lost) notebook some verse fragments in English, including Satan's address to the Sun, and possibly some pieces of dialogue.

If Milton did finally start assembling *Paradise Lost* in, say, early 1658, then we can be sure that, methodical man as he was, he had settled on a general structure for his poem and had made key decisions about its content. This means that, regardless of what contexts readers may have brought to their political understanding of the poem on its first publication in 1667, Milton in composing the work can have been influenced only at a relatively late stage by the disaster of the Restoration. *Paradise Lost* is in conception and commencement a poem of the Cromwellian period, and Milton's references to the evils of the Restoration, if they are such, are late additions to the text, restricted almost entirely to the invocation before the seventh book.

Not that Milton had much to be happy about in 1658 either. If one of those "Learned Foreigners of Note who could not part out of this City, without giving a visit to a person so Eminent"⁹ were to call in on Milton, say, in early February 1658, he would enter a sorry household. Milton is blind. His second wife dies on the third day of the month. Their infant daughter would very soon follow. It is a sizeable and increasingly fractious family for a sightless man to manage, and Milton is no longer really capable of discharging his official duties. He has not written any major poetry for several years—some psalm translations and a handful of sonnets are not exactly what he had been promising. There are in fact worse times ahead, but for now Milton might be forgiven for writing that he had indeed "fall'n on evil dayes" (7.25), and for complaining that everything had gone completely wrong both in his domestic life and in the political life of his nation. This is the period in which he starts to dictate *Paradise Lost*.

# 13

## Bibliographical Interlude: Publishing *Paradise Lost*

B EFORE MOVING INTO *Paradise Lost* itself, it is right to preface that discussion with an account of the several legal and physical processes that led to its publication. It might now be assumed that a poem of such obviously high quality would make the transition from private project to public book with no difficulty at all. But this is not entirely true. The complexities of the publication of *Paradise Lost* are legitimate parts of its total meaning and cannot be treated as merely of bibliographical interest. This chapter therefore addresses these processes, which shed light not only on Milton's own attitude to his poem, but also on the attitudes of several key players involved in the poem's coming into the light.

Just how *Paradise Lost* was published has long been a matter of obscurity and controversy. The poem itself was ready to go, as it were, by August of 1665 at the latest, when Milton passed the manuscript to his Quaker friend, Thomas Ellwood. And if Thomas Ellwood had been lent a copy in that month, then we may suppose that some of Milton's more established acquaintances had seen or were soon to see the final draft around that time too. That the poem did not appear for another two years had more to do with the twin disasters of early Restoration London: the Great Plague and then the Great Fire. The international scene was also tense. The Second Anglo-Dutch War commenced in March 1666 with a reassuring English victory at Lowestoft, but the tide soon turned in favor of the Dutch. In April and May fears of plague turned into reality; in July the Court abandoned the capital, to return only the following February. In the first week of September, just as the city was getting back on its feet, the Great Fire enkindled. Milton, blind, with his property and assets burning around him, had other things to worry about. It was probably only the following spring, therefore, that he felt that he could resume the push to get *Paradise Lost* published.

We know of only two definite dates here: that of April 27, 1667, when Milton and his chosen printer signed a contract together; and August 20, 1667, when the poem was entered by the printer into the Stationers' Register, the legal guardian of a publisher's rights in the period. As the contract refers to the poem as "lately Licenced to be printed," that must have happened a little before this first date. The following reconstructs the most plausible total narrative, addressing first the licensing of the work, then the printer and his contract, then the surviving manuscript of the first book of the poem, and finally the circumstances of the actual printing and selling of the work.

First, then, comes the license. As we read in the Stationers' Register: "Entred for his copie under the hands of Master Thomas Tomkyns and Master Warden Royston a booke or copie intituled *Paradise lost A Poem in Tenne bookes* by J. M.—vj^d" ["vj^d" is sixpence, the price of the entry].[1] So Milton, who over two decades earlier had published a pamphlet attacking the practice of prepublication licensing, submitted at last to the law he so despised, and in his political defeat, he had no choice. "His copie" did not mean Milton's copy, however, but that of the printer, Samuel Simmons.

Who was the licenser of Milton's poem? Thomas Tomkyns or Tomkins was the son of the organist of St Paul's Cathedral, and the Tomkinses had been a notable musical family since the late Elizabethan period. Both Thomas's uncles were prominent composers and indeed, as his father had been appointed to St Paul's in 1619, Milton, as a schoolboy at St Paul's and living nearby, must have often heard Tomkins Senior play. Later the younger Tomkins became a fellow of All Souls, Oxford, and was a known Arminian.[2] At the time Tomkins was assessing Milton's poem, he had recently left his fellowship to come to London, where he had been appointed rector of St Mary Aldermary and chaplain to Gilbert Sheldon, Archbishop of Canterbury. Tomkins, in the fashion of such henchmen-chaplains, acted as a publicist for Sheldon's political policy, namely the rigid rejection of all varieties of toleration or comprehension for Dissenters. One of Tomkins's tracts, *The Inconveniencies of Toleration*, indeed, was published in the same year as *Paradise Lost*. It is an intelligently argued piece of conservatism: no one believes in total liberty of conscience—"Conscience hath its Rule, may swerve and ought very well to be looked to"—and so the only argument is where the "rule" should be drawn. According to Tomkins, the line should be drawn exactly where it is: in defense of the Anglican settlement, he concludes "Let us then be permitted to continue as we are; seeing it is not agreed in what manner we shall be altered."[3] Tomkins worked hand-in-glove with Sheldon's other chaplain and licenser, Samuel Parker; the Oxford antiquary Anthony Wood recalled with some parochial enthusiasm the privilege of dining with Sheldon, where he watched the two chaplains together at the end of the table, with the great rising prose satirist John Eachard between them, before the three men went off together "to drink and smoake."[4]

Tomkins is named as licenser for some thirty books between the start of his career in mid-August 1666 and early October 1668; *Paradise Lost* is the twentieth of these titles.[5] (Interestingly, in 1670 Tomkins would act again as licenser for Milton's poetry, this time the composite volume of *Paradise Regained* and *Samson Agonistes*.[6]) If we were to ask what else Tomkins licensed around this time, his name can be found at the foot of, to take three examples, the licenses to the prominent Anglican writer and bishop Jeremy Taylor's *The Second Part of the Dissuasive from Popery* (June 29, 1667), to the Duke of Buckingham's chaplain Hugh Davis's *De jure uniformitatis ecclesiasticæ* (On the law of ecclesiastical uniformity) (January 17, 1668), and to the first two parts of the celebrated scholar and divine Meric Casaubon's *Of Credulity and Incredulity* (July 9, 1668). These prose works, in their rather different genres, were all orthodox—against popery, against nonconformity, and against the extremes of believing too much or nothing at all. Indeed, Hugh Davis and Tomkins were friends and allies, and Davis sent his licenser a complimentary copy of his book. *De jure uniformitatis ecclesiasticæ*, a book despite its title written in English, is an impressive theoretical work in the natural law tradition, and Davis occupied a stance diametrically opposed to that of

Milton. His tones toward his antagonists were level, however, and Milton himself, mentioned several times in the book, is criticized merely as "intemperate" against Salmasius.[7] Davis's book was in fact printed by Simmons too, so we would be unwise to see Simmons as politically aligned to Milton because he printed *Paradise Lost*. Indeed, because Simmons evidently had no qualms publishing what was in effect a piece of scholarly propaganda for the Sheldon regime, his dealings with Milton were likely less about ideology and more an example of familial loyalty, as we shall see. It is simplistic to assume direct political transference between a writer and a printer, in either direction.

Tomkins as a licenser was unlikely to find a religious poem problematic. Even quite theologically eccentric poetry, such as the poet Samuel Pordage's bizarre Behmenist creation epic *Mundorum explicatio* (Explanation of the Worlds) (1661), was not entered into the Stationers' Register but appeared to no discernable official dismay.[8] What a licenser was looking for was politically sensitive material—and Tomkins found it. For it was later reported that Milton's simile in the first book of *Paradise Lost*, likening Satan to a solar eclipse, which "disastrous twilight sheds / On half the nations, and with fear of change / Perplexes monarchs" (1.597–99), troubled Tomkins. The report comes from John Toland, the Deist, who wrote a life of Milton a generation after his death. Toland also claimed that Tomkins found "other frivolous Exceptions," but we do not know what these were. (Perhaps the provocative phrase "Athens or free Rome' (9.671)?) Tomkins's eyes had in fact just slid unblinking past an implicit but potentially rather sharp comparison between Charlemagne and Charles II (1.586–87), so evidently it took rather literal prompts to hook the eyes of the censor. "Perplexes monarchs" was an obvious lexical trigger, but in fact the thought is commonplace; eclipses had always been associated with regime change, and although it appears that Restoration churchmen were particularly nervous about astrological doommongers, that Tomkins could isolate this particular exception suggests that he was looking for trouble, as well he might. But Tomkins must have relented, as the passage appears, seemingly unmolested, in the published text. What the anecdote really reveals is that Milton had successfully practiced self-censorship: the published text of *Paradise Lost* is an extraordinary negotiation between Milton's own frequently heterodox beliefs and a manner of expressing them that could also accommodate more orthodox interpretations ("Capable of an Orthodox Construction," in Milton's early biographer

Jonathan Richardson's phrase).[9] This is how a theological epic written by a man whose real beliefs, if more visible, would have been judged heretical in the eyes of most Christian denominations could nevertheless subsequently be adopted by so many of those very denominations as expressive of their own beliefs.

Now that Milton had a license for his poem, he was ready to sign a contract with a printer, and indeed it is implausible to think that an insecure printer would take on work from someone of Milton's reputation without such legal surety. This, however, left the printer to strike a deal with the booksellers, Milton playing no formal part in deciding who would sell, as opposed to who would actually make, his product. This was unusual—authors more commonly did things the other way around, dealing directly with publishers, as Milton had with Humphrey Moseley for his earlier poems, publishers then subcontracting out the work of printing. But Milton went straight for the printer, because he already knew him.[10]

This man was Samuel Simmons, a slightly sorry figure of the Restoration book trade, and very much a step down from the great literary entrepreneur Moseley. Simmons was the son of printers, his father Matthew having been a prominent printer from the mid-1630s until his death two decades later. His business was then taken over by his wife, Mary, who was then joined by their son, Samuel, in around 1662. Matthew had printed several of Milton's prose works in the 1640s, and Milton, disgraced and blind, sought out the son of an old associate for his new work. Compared to his parents, however, Samuel was either a failure or someone who made his money mysteriously, as he cannot have got by on the proceeds of his recorded activities in the book trade. He printed hardly anything, owned the rights to very few copies—*Paradise Lost* was in fact his first copyright possession—took few apprentices, and indeed subsequently sold off all his rights to Milton's poem in 1680, years before his own death.[11] There is a final oddity here—Simmons, a printer by trade, was in effect acting toward Milton as a "publisher," that is, the person who would pay for and register a book. In terms of the book trade, this was a distinct role from that of printer, although many combined them now and then. But Simmons himself was on new territory here, and that is a further reason why both men may have decided to draw up a formal contract.

The contract itself is a remarkable legal survival, if not quite the earliest of its kind.[12] Like all such contracts it was originally one document written out twice, and then cut with scissors into two identical texts following a wavy line: that way, when both halves were fitted back together by their owners, they mutually authenticated each other if the fit were true. The document was witnessed, blind Milton's signature, in the hand of an amanuensis, backed up by that of one Benjamin Green, "servant to Mr Milton." Milton's family seal was then affixed to the document, a spread eagle, which had been the sign above his father's shop in Bread Street. The contract is not a bad deal for Milton, and the fact that it is legally formulated at all is unusual. Milton received £5 upfront, and the contract awarded him with £5 for each subsequent "impression," up to three; he stood to make £20 in all. Such "impressions" were also limited to 1,500 copies, Milton receiving his £5 at the threshold of 1,300 copies sold per impression, which in effect put in place a stable ratio between Milton's and Simmons's profits—the latter could not simply print an impression of several thousand copies and palm Milton off with a payment proportionate to a smaller number. To that end Milton even obtained the right to receive regular reports on how sales were going, and he was entitled to charge the whole £5-per-impression if such reports could not be produced.[13] These reports were to be furnished by Simmons on "Oath," and the seriousness of this is emphasized by an interlinear addition—the oath was to be given "before a Master in Chancery." Milton, in short, was anxious to secure reliable monitoring of sales.[14] And indeed things must have worked reasonably well between the two men, as Milton used Simmons once more, in 1669, to publish his little textbook, *Accedence commenc't grammar.* Was £5—Milton's minimum gain—derisory, excessive, or perfectly reasonable? We lack good evidence from the period, but two anecdotes equally spaced before and after Milton may give us a hint. In 1626, when the great antiquary Sir Henry Spelman offered the royal printer John Bill the manuscript of the first part of his *Archaeologus,* a landmark folio reference glossary of medieval legal and ecclesiastical terminology, he asked for £5 worth of books in exchange. Bill, a major figure in the trade, could without too much difficulty afford such an outlay from his stock. But he turned Spelman down, and Spelman had to pay for the impression himself.[15] And yet when the brilliant young Oxford poet John Philips gave copy to Jacob Tonson of his Miltonic two-book pastiche *Cyder* (1708), a slim quarto of six gatherings, the affluent Tonson, spotting a poem that was sure to sell, paid him £40.[16] So we might say that Milton's bargain, made with a considerably less successful entrepreneur, was most likely a cautious, reasonable, but not overgenerous deal.

Tomkins licensed a manuscript of the poem, not a printed copy. We are extremely fortunate that a portion of this specific manuscript of *Paradise Lost* survives, and this precious document can tell us all sorts of things about how Milton chaperoned his poem from a private, handwritten document, into a commercial object, on sale to people Milton did not and would never know.

While the plague was raging in London, Milton's sometime pupil, the Quaker Thomas Ellwood, had arranged rental for the blind man of a "pretty Box" or cottage in Chalfont St Giles, around twenty-five miles from London, so that Milton could shelter from the metropolis. Quakers were being heavily persecuted in these years, and Ellwood found himself in jail before he could pay a visit to his mentor. On his release, he hurried to do so. After some casual chat, Milton "called for a Manuscript of his," and presented it to Ellwood, inviting him to take it away, read it, and tell Milton what he thought of it. This was a copy of *Paradise Lost,* and this meeting took place in August of 1665. The next year Milton could present a manuscript of its sequel, *Paradise Regained,* to the same man, demonstrating that the two poems were written in close temporal proximity.[17] The copy shown to Ellwood does not survive, or if it does, only in fragmentary form, being the text of the first book alone of the poem, and it is to this manuscript we now turn.

This survival is not, at least initially, because such a manuscript was cherished as a literary relic but simply because the verso of the first folio bore the state licenser's handwritten imprimatur and the signatures of the Warden and Clerk of the Stationers' Company. This meant that the holder of this particular manuscript also held the legal document permitting its publication. As a result it was carefully communicated down the line of owners of the copy of *Paradise Lost*—from Samuel Simmons, the original printer, to Brabazon Aylmer, to Jacob Tonson, who then passed this manuscript, along with a letter explaining its significance, to his nephew, also Jacob Tonson. It survives, too, because of the preposterous edition of Milton by the great classical scholar Richard Bentley—the elder Tonson was so aggrieved by Bentley's wrecking ball of an edition that he sent the manuscript of the first book to his nephew as a refutation of Bentley's claim that Milton's manuscript (which he had assumed to be lost) had been radically revised by some malevolent amanuensis. We reencounter Bentley's Milton at the end of this book.

The original licenser, as we saw, was Thomas Tomkyns. Next to his signature on the surviving manuscript we find those of Richard Royston, warden of the Stationers, and George Tokefield, clerk. Royston was an old grandee of the book trade, "bookseller to three kings," as his epitaph proudly records, and the man behind not only the interregnum publication campaigns of Jeremy Taylor and Henry Hammond, but also the *Eikon Basilike* itself, the best-selling (purported) spiritual autobiography of Charles I, distributed in the immediate aftermath of his beheading. Tokefield was the clerk who had rescued the precious archives of the company in the Great Fire by removing them by cart to his house in Clerkenwell; a few years after this point he would show that the Stationers' clerk had political teeth when he needed them by refusing to enter Milton's friend Andrew Marvell's *Rehearsal Transprosed* (1672) into the register.[18] These signatures, again, guaranteed copyright protection for the legal holder of the manuscript, and this was Simmons, not Milton himself, as copyright in the modern sense of the rights of the author, as opposed to those of the printer or publisher, did not legally exist in England until the Statute of Anne of 1710. (This statute vested the long-term right of copy in the author, while fixing the duration for which another party could hold copyright without renewal.) So with license and copyright in place, Simmons could print this poem by a politically disgraced figure without fear of reprisal or piracy.

That only the first book of the poem was retained in manuscript in turn suggests that it was physically detachable from the rest of the poem, and indeed examination of the structure of the surviving manuscript confirms this.[19] The one-book manuscript is made up of nineteen leaves. Seventeen contain the text and were made by folding nine half-sheets in two and placing them one after the other, the scribe tearing off the last page, as he had finished his work without having to use it. This bundle was then wrapped around with a final sheet, forming the first and last leaves of the integral booklet. That exactly one book is contained in exactly one "fascicule," as such bundles are called, offers us a hint of how Milton organized the physical workbooks for his poem: if he did this for book one, he probably did it for each and every book of the poem. (So ten fascicules for a poem originally of ten books, and when Milton revised the poem into twelve books, he presumably asked his amanuenses to restructure his "project folders" accordingly.) This practice has been well described as one of the "coping strategies" of a blind man, and it was, notably, the very strategy that Milton employed in his overlapping work on the much larger *De doctrina,* the latter divided into fifty-one fascicules, one for each of its fifty chapters, as well as its prefatory epistle.[20]

Yet the surviving manuscript was not itself taken down from dictation but copied from a prior written text. We can tell this because the corrections include some that emend obvious mistakes of the pen and not the ear (the meaningless "sealy" for "scaly," for instance, or "persuers" initially copied, incorrectly, as "perverse" [1.206, 326]), showing that the main scribe of this manuscript was probably not involved with the original, dictated event, as he otherwise would know that these readings were wrong.

The copy we have, indeed, was the manuscript given to the printer, and this is apparent because it bears in its margins the working marks of the compositors who set the poem up in type. Compositors needed to block out in advance how much text of a manuscript they intended to fit on one printed page, so that different compositors could get to work on different sections of the text without fear of overlap or lopsided distribution, and to this end they "cast off," as the process was known, the text before them. Thus in this manuscript the printer has inserted marginal guide numbers every thirty-two lines—and indeed the first edition of the poem settles quickly into thirty-two lines a page.

Nevertheless, the manuscript had a life prior to its role in the print house, for although it was chiefly written by one scribe, it bears all sorts of tinkerings and emendations in a variety of hands—this busy manuscript is the site of perhaps as many as five different scribes working on Milton's text, and it is likely that if the entire manuscript had survived that number would be significantly higher.

The manuscript shows us that Milton, despite his claims in *Paradise Lost* to have been supernaturally donated in his sleep in a series of nightly instalments, revised his text, as we might expect. In his simile of the organ in Book 1, for instance, Milton originally instructed his scribe to write: "To many a hundred pipes the sound-bord breaths" (1.709). Milton then told a later amanuensis, probably here his nephew Edward, to revise the spelling of "hundred" to "hunderd," a Miltonic idiosyncrasy. But he then decided on a last-minute change of phrase: "many a hunderd pipes" became "many a row of pipes," a change that makes his organ a little more three-dimensional in the mind's eye and his line a little less consonantally cluttered. Another, intensifying, revision is to 1.156, where "the Fiend" is changed to "th'Arch-fiend," requiring metrical elision, but elevating Satan to his command role. But vanishingly few of the corrections to the manuscript are actual verbal changes of this kind—the overwhelming majority are tinkerings with spelling and punctuation. These had no effect on the lexis of the poem, but show that the blind Milton was nevertheless preoccupied by orthography: "y" for "i," for instance, struck him as dated, and so "tyme" is typically adjusted to "time." In general, his choices reflect an interest in sound over etymology, and Milton liked to indicate emphasis or metrical quality by tiny shifts in orthography—"heaven" is "heav'n" if monosyllabic; "we" is "wee" if emphatic. (We have seen how these choices may have been influenced by the work of Milton's old teacher, Alexander Gil.)

It is no surprise that Milton's printers struggled. Even the manuscript only partially registers what we can divine of Milton's underlying principles, and his printers in turn were not robots, indeed probably learning, adapting, possibly even resisting as they went. The scholar of this manuscript, Helen Darbishire, nicely noted that Milton liked to draw out the long vowel of "wrath" by spelling it "wrauth," and although the printers failed to implement this in the first book, it thereafter appears in the printed poem (with only three exceptions) as, indeed, "wrauth." It is reasonable to suppose that Milton thus corrected later instances of this word in his complete manuscript, and his printers caught on.

What this signals is Milton's obsessiveness about his text. Most of his contemporaries would have regarded such matters as out of their hands, under the jurisdiction of the compositors, and would not bother taking such trouble over accidentals that might be clean ignored in the print house. Once again, that Milton obsessed so also signals that he was confident his printer would be more obedient to his wishes than was typical. Blind Milton must have received proofs. We can be sure this was so, for "dauntless valour" in the manuscript became "dauntless courage" in the printed text, the kind of change only an author could dictate; and "avoid worse rape" became "prevent worse rape" in publication, before reverting in the second edition to "avoid," additional evidence that Milton not only corrected proofs but continued listening to his poem and revising it even between editions. (We deal with the revision of the poem from ten to twelve books in Chapter 14.)

Milton and his printer did not waste time once they had signed a contract, Simmons probably commencing printing as soon as he could. The evidence concerning the printing of *Paradise Lost* is rather technical, but surviving copies of Milton's poem in its first edition show that it was produced in successive and subtly different "issues." There were four distinct issues, one of 1667 (but with some copies of it dated "1668"), one of 1668, one of "1669" (but probably printed in 1668), and one genuinely of 1669. Interestingly, Milton's printer made minute adjustments to the title page of the poem, and the order in which these changes were made has been reconstructed by the bibliographer of the first edition of *Paradise Lost*, Hugh Amory.[21] The exact form of words in the Stationers' Register matches the third in this reconstructed sequence (the evidence turns on the way in which Milton's name ("John Milton" vs. "J. M.") and the subtitle of his poem are expressed), and this in turn suggests something rather interesting about the printing of the poem. What the tiny changes in the form of the title page of *Paradise Lost* tell is not a story about successive printings as they appeared on the market, but about successive, and it would seem rather nervous, adjustments of the appearance of the poem commencing before Simmons felt comfortable presenting a complete book to the Stationers and then to the paying public. For after Simmons had printed the text of the poem, he then, as printers usually did, used the remaining section of his last sheet to print the title page. At first he identified his poet with confidence— "John Milton." But while the type was still standing, he got nervous and cut this back to the ambiguous "J. M."[22]

Only once the long work of printing was substantially completed did Simmons present the poem to the Stationers' Company, bringing with him both the manuscript (because it bore the legal imprimatur) and one of his fresh copies with its title page in its third state. It was in this form that Simmons carried the completed book to the Stationers, who, despite the anonymity of the book, accepted the license of Tomkins and countersigned it. This was, strictly speaking, all somewhat irregular: the manuscript appears not to have borne the author's name, nor the printed copy; Tomkins's license was not even dated; and therefore when the poem finally appeared, the unsigned and undated *imprimatur*—through gritted teeth it admitted merely that the poem was "Licensed and entred according to order"—was at best incomplete and at worst illegal. But Royston and his clerk were satisfied with Tomkins's signature and accepted Simmons's half-shilling; they had done a good deal of business with the Archbishop's chaplain by this date, and after all this was a biblical poem, not a political treatise or some comment on current affairs.

So the poem was presumably printed by August and was on sale thereafter. We are not quite sure exactly when—on the one hand poetry, with its short lines of predictable length, can be set much faster than prose, and Simmons had a complete copy with a title page in his hand when he went to enter the poem; but on the other hand, this specific state actually bears the date "1668," a common bookseller's trick to keep a book published in late 1667 fresh in the new year, but rather too blatant a fib to tell to customers before, say, October. In favor of a later date is a famous story of the poet Sir John Denham walking into the House of Commons with a sheet of *Paradise Lost,* "wet from the press," and claiming it as "Part of the Noblest Poem that ever was Wrote in Any Language, or Any Age."[23] It is a romantic story, but the incidental detail about Parliament (as opposed to, say, a coffee shop), sounds genuine, and Parliament indeed only reconvened in the second week of October.[24] Whatever the truth of the matter, *Paradise Lost* was a poem that, rather appropriately, appeared as autumn shaded into winter.

In the event, Simmons need not have been so nervous. *Paradise Lost* sold comfortably, although it may just have been overpriced—we are not sure, but *3s* or *3s 6d* seem the most plausible sums, so six or seven times the price of an average playbook or sermon, for instance—and Simmons realized that his fussing over the identity of the author had been oversensitive. So he started selling off further copies with the older title-pages, with "John Milton" standing proud. This is what has caused all the headaches for those who have investigated this issue over the centuries—most of the puzzling variations reflect *pre*-publication indecision.

This narrative also shows us that Milton's manuscript itself had a busy time. Milton initially passed it to Simmons so he could make an informed judgment about whether he was going to print the poem, and with what kind of financial arrangement. Simmons then took it to be licensed. Eventually Tomkins signed it. It was then handed to the printers working under Simmons, who marked it with their printers' symbols, and used it to set the first edition. When the printing was done, it—or at least the fascicule containing the first book—was again picked up and taken over to Royston at Stationers' Hall, along with a printed copy. The manuscript was proffered as it, and only it, bore Tomkins's signed imprimatur, and to this Royston and his clerk now added their signatures. Simmons at that point could pass copies to the booksellers or tell the booksellers that the coast was clear for retail.

For in the event six men sold copies of *Paradise Lost* from their London shops. Perhaps the first issue to appear, with title pages dated 1668 and 1667, was sold by three different booksellers, Peter Parker, Robert Boulter, and Matthias Walker. A second issue, with 1668 on the title page, replaced Parker with Samuel Thompson and Henry Mortlack; the third and fourth issues, dated 1669, were all sold solely from the shop of Thomas Helder.[25] Granted, the recent Fire of London had seriously disrupted the book trade, but this is nevertheless unusual. For an edition to be spread around one or two shops was not uncommon, but six is exceptional. This sense of precariousness is further increased by the recognition that none of these booksellers at this point was a first-rank player in the book trade. Mortlack had a few important authors on his list, notably the extremely productive churchman and scholar Edward Stillingfleet, but the others were recent arrivals, minor players, or nonentities. We might contrast this with the publications of, say, the darling of institutional poets, John Dryden: throughout the 1660s over a dozen literary works by Dryden were all published by one man, the bookseller-publisher Henry Herringman, Humphrey Moseley's Restoration successor as impresario of English belles-lettres.[26] Milton, in contrast, was now outside the literary institution as fabricated by the publishers themselves; that *Paradise Lost* would soon break its way back into that citadel was a crucial step toward the surprise enthronement of *Paradise Lost* as the national epic.

PART TWO

*Paradise Lost*

# 14

## Structure

PARADISE LOST IS designed like a complex clock, where every mechanism influences every other mechanism: changes in the motion in one
part set in motion changes in the others. As Samuel Johnson said with a
sniff—this quotation is the epigraph to this book—it is "a poem which, considered with respect to design, may claim the first place, and with respect
to performance the second, among the productions of the human mind"
(presumably the first in performance is Homer). Nevertheless, although
readers have always felt that there is something exceptionally designed about
the poem, no two will quite agree on how best to discern and rank these
patterns.[1] This analysis of the poem will therefore commence with looking
at ways of talking about the structure of the poem; Chapters 15–21 then
move into its content, namely its cosmology, its experiments with various
epic and nonepic traditions, its persons and poetics, and finally its religious
coherence.

The simplest way of describing the action of *Paradise Lost,* were Milton
to have structured the poem according to chronological order, would be to

split it into its theologically significant episodes, thus (actual distribution, according to the twelve book poem, in square brackets):

1. God's decree concerning the angels (the Exaltation) [Book 5]
2. Temptation and Fall in Heaven (with the War in Heaven, the victory of the Son, and the chasing of the vanquished to Hell) [Books 5–6]
3. Creation of our universe, culminating in the creation of Adam and Eve [Books 7–8]
4. God's decree concerning man (the Prohibition) [Book 8]
5. Temptation and Fall in Eden [Book 9]
6. The curse and expulsion [Books 10, 12]

In fact, Milton famously opened his poem at the end of stage 2 above, in Hell, a disorienting and upsetting strategy (see Chapter 16). Milton was also not content to conclude his epic with the expulsion, and he grafted onto his poem a series of promises and visions to bring the theology of the work full circle, from first fall to final redemption:

7. Sacred (biblical) history from Fall to Flood [Book 11]
8. Sacred (biblical) history from Flood (first destruction of the world) to the Second Adam, with his incarnation, death, resurrection, and ascension [Book 12]
9. Sacred (postbiblical) history to the Second Coming, apocalypse, and judgment (second destruction of the world), after which a renovated world of "New heavens, new Earth" will endure without end. [Book 12]

Investigating the actual ordering of the poem, it is immediately noteworthy that stages 1–4 and 7–9 are in effect discrete poems within *Paradise Lost*, formally narrated by two different angels, namely Raphael and Michael, the former telling of things past, in epic mode, across Books 5 to 8; the latter of things to come, in visionary mode, across Books 11 to 12. Raphael's epic narration is a double poem of martial epic (the War in Heaven) and then scientific epic (Creation), and although the latter easily receives its superstructure from the biblical Work of the Six Days of Genesis 1, the former is of necessity almost entirely unbiblical. This is also why it is the most incongruous section of the poem, because Raphael must reach forward in time and into pagan epic, albeit updated with certain recent technological innovations, to fetch out a fitting poetics of battle.

Michael, conversely, can stick quite closely to biblical text as he works through major Old Testament persons and events in order, and this is partly why his poem is often felt to be less exciting than Raphael's, perhaps more akin to the *Seconde Semaine* of Du Bartas. The *Seconde Semaine* had moved similarly through biblical history, albeit with frequent encyclopedic digressions and only making it as far forward as the biblical Chronicles.

An exact parallel for the whole Miltonic tripartite structure of (1) angelic fall; (2) human fall; and (3) subsequent time to apocalypse is the structure of the second, twelve-book half of Augustine's foundational *City of God,* which had addressed in three balanced subgroups of four books apiece: (1) the origin in the angelic and human falls of the split between the two cities of the righteous and the unrighteous; (2) subsequent biblical time from Cain and Abel to the Apocalypse; and (3) Last Judgment, with eternal punishment and eternal happiness for the appropriate communities. Milton likely knew this, as this way of thinking about Augustine's most important work is not a modern superimposition but Augustine's own structural analysis of his book.[2]

Milton's Michael, however, has little biblical warrant for post-New Testament history, and the shape of the past he adopts for the period between Christ's First and Second Comings is strongly, even radically Protestant.[3] Michael, just like Milton, is sure that spiritual rot will or did set into the church immediately after the apostolic age, and he, like his ventriloquizing poet, laments the early confusion of the sacred and secular powers, recognizing too that most of subsequent sacred history will be taken up with the persecution of a righteous minority by the "far greater part" of the unrighteous (12.508, 517, 533). Milton as narrator also displays little optimism about the clergy, commenting of Satan's first entry into Eden, "So clomb this first grand Thief into Gods Fould: / So since into his Church lewd Hirelings climbe" (4.192–93), a poetic echo of the title of his 1659 prose tract, *Considerations touching the likeliest means to remove hirelings out of the church.* This is a version of Protestant history first heard from Milton in the anticlerical passages of "Lycidas," but fully radicalized only in Milton's first prose pamphlet, *Of Reformation* (1641).[4]

Two and a half decades later Milton still held to it. Following this version of history, Milton downgraded the entire patristic period to one of "grievous wolves" (12.508) and took a strongly negative view of Constantinian Christianity, when the powers of church and state had coalesced following the adoption of Christianity as the official state religion by the emperor Constantine after the Battle of the Milvian Bridge in 312. It is important to recognize that Milton's dim view of Constantine—a view he almost certainly derived directly from his reading of Dante, the first major exponent of this radical revisionism, itself then reinforced by Petrarch and Ariosto—was rare even within Protestantism.[5] Milton's archangel in *Paradise Lost* was stating as visionary truth an interpretation of church history that no orthodox Restoration churchman could accept.

As for the end of time itself, Milton's God first predicts Apocalypse in discussion with his Son (3.323–41), informing him that in the end the Son will come to judge the quick and the dead, sending all "Bad men and angels" to Hell, which shall thereafter "be forever shut." "Meanwhile," God continues, "The world shall burn," and the saved will live on it after it has been purified by fire. It is slightly ambiguous what Milton thinks will happen next. The Father does predict of his Son that "Then thou thy regal Scepter shalt lay by, / For regal Scepter then no more shall need, / God shall be All in All" (339–41). But is this for the saved or will this include the dissolution of Hell, previously "forever shut," too? Michael repeats these basic outlines at the end of the epic, predicting an apocalypse culminating in "New heavens, new Earth," and "eternal bliss," after which the elect will live in heaven or indeed on a renovated planet, burnt pure of its corruptions (12.463–65, 549, 551). When this will happen is left prudently open by the poem, which however separates Christ's Ascension and the Last Judgment in one place by a single semicolon (12.458, and compare 12.539). Milton is not being explicitly apocalyptic here, in the sense of predicting an imminent Second Coming, but he does leave the possibility hanging over the poem. This is perhaps audible too in his famous complaint that he is living in "evil dayes" (7.25, 26). This is usually read as one of the few exclusively contemporary, Restoration references in the poem, an antiestablishment rattle. But the phrase has suggestive sacred overtones too. Paul in Ephesians, for instance, tells the Children of Light to walk wisely "because the days are evil" (5:16, ὅτι αἱ ἡμέραι πονηραί εἰσιν). This kind of language became intensified among early Christians, for instance in the distinctly apocalyptic Epistle of Barnabas, one of the oldest Christian texts, where "evil days" (the language is the same as in Ephesians: Ἡμερῶν . . . πονηρῶν) reappears, now explicitly as a sign of living "in these final days" (ἐν ταῖς ἐσχάταις ἡμέραις)—the righteous must stick together as the world ends around them.[6] So in *Paradise Lost,* too—we do not know when the end of days will come, but it may be tomorrow.

In terms of the scheme presented above, it might seem that Milton only narrates in his own voice that section of sacred history that concerns, strictly, Paradise Lost. But this is in fact not true, for Milton spends his two first books dealing with the aftermath of the angelic fall, first from the perspective of Hell (Books 1–2), and then from Heaven (Book 3), and finally from Eden (Book 4 and the first half of Book 5). This underlines just how innovative Milton's narrative disruption is. The temporal start of the poem comes in the middle of Book 5, when God, in Raphael's inset epic, utters his decree. This triggers the rest of the theological stages listed above, which are recounted in order from Books 5 to 10, followed by the final two proleptic, visionary books. In contrast, the first four and a half books stand a little outside the bare theological frame of Creation-Fall-Redemption. The books of Hell (1–2) are strongly paganized, this unsettling effect itself part of Milton's moral project; the book of Heaven (3) is largely theological in a manner almost uncomfortably extrabiblical, as Father and Son theologize to one another like Protestant scholastics; and the books of unfallen Eden (4, first half of 5) present innocence seen through difficult grids of pagan fables, extrapolating an entire georgic economy from the slightest of biblical prompts. Milton, of course, believed in the basic narrative truth of his entire structure, but he front-loaded his poem, as it were, with episodes narrated in his own voice yet of the most extreme difficulty for both writer and readers—three realms unknowable in themselves to fallen man: Hell, Heaven, and the now inaccessible world of prelapsarian Eden.

In a performance quite surpassing the ambitions of pagan epic, Milton's poem therefore describes almost the totality of imaginable time, from the time in Heaven immediately before the angelic revolt to the Second Coming. It is not quite the totality of time, however, for what happened in Heaven before God's "imperial summons" of the heavenly host to hear his decree concerning his Son (5.584, 602) is not narrated. This was not part of theological time as available to human comprehension, and, notwithstanding a few hints, Milton piously left it alone.

The internal structure of Milton's epic relies primarily (but not entirely) on its formal division into books. Here, however, we face a critical conundrum, for Milton first published *Paradise Lost* in ten books in 1667, and then re-vised it into twelve for the second edition of 1674, the latter being the ver-sion universally followed thereafter. Milton did this by dividing the two longest books (the seventh and tenth in the first edition) in half, and slightly rewriting the breaks to smooth their edges.[7] Why did he effect such a rad-ical change? The conundrum is that any convincing argument for revision needs both to identify what led Milton to cast the poem in ten books in the first place and to identify what advantages the revision offered that did not result in internal confusion. The critic, in short, needs to find good reasons for both arrangements.[8]

The most obvious external control is the precedent of tradition. None of the ancient epics available to Milton had an odd number of books, with the exception of Silius Italicus's *Punica,* regarded anyway as imperfect; the other oddity was Quintus Smyrnaeus's *Posthomerica* in fourteen. Only Lucan, the poet of civil war, had left an epic in ten books. But the main tradition seems always to have exploited the series $1 \times 2 \times 3 \times 4$ and multiples gener-ated within it. Milton's revised twelve books therefore chimed with Homer (twenty-four),[9] Virgil (twelve), and Lucretius (six), as well as Claudian (three, albeit unfinished), Apollonius (four), his Latin imitator Valerius Flaccus (eight, perhaps meant to be extended to twelve), and Statius (twelve again). The lost epic by Apollinaris the Elder on the biblical books of Kings was again, according to Socrates Scholasticus, in twenty-four books, and Nonnus, who wrote heroic verse in both pagan and Christian modes,[10] employed twenty-four books for his pagan epic. Among the moderns, Vida wrote six books; Spenser also left fully complete only six books, although he intended twelve or perhaps twenty-four; and Cowley completed four of a projected twelve. (Italianate stanzaic epics, as less obviously tied to classical precedent, were more variable in this respect.)[11]

Milton's initial ten-book structure is therefore unusual. Because the only major precedent is Lucan, this has encouraged some readers to detect sus-tained, if usually implied, republican engagement with the problem of civil war.[12] Lucan's *Pharsalia,* written in the first century, brooded over the civil war between Julius Caesar and Pompey the Great, which had culminated in the Battle of Pharsalus in 48 BC. For the *Pharsalia* (also known as *De bello civili* or "The Civil War") presented the victories of Caesar not as divinely ordained but as the secular acts of a tyrant. War is atrocious and civil war the worst atrocity of all. When the Caesarians are victorious at Pharsalus in Book 7, Lucan explicitly laments the loss of liberty, "That liberty nere to returne againe."[13]

Now Lucan certainly could put tinder into dangerous hands: Milton studied the English antiquary and historian William Camden's *Annals* carefully, and in it he will have read the account of the rebellion of the Earl of Essex against the elderly Queen Elizabeth, egged on by his secretary, Henry Cuffe. Cuffe, in this version, persuaded Essex to arms by quoting Caesar's rallying cry in Lucan: "Arma tenenti omnia dat, qui justa negat" (He who denies what is just, gives up everything to the enemy in arms).[14] The Lucanic translations of Milton's contemporary Thomas May have also recently received shrewd reappraisal. David Norbrook, for instance, notes that the dedications to individual noblemen placed before each book of May's complete version of Lucan, published in 1627, were politically sensitive, and it may be no accident that they were hastily excised from most copies.[15] As Norbrook extensively demonstrates, the Jacobean and Caroline "English Lucans" generated a politically charged poetry that was, however, capable of manipulation in more than one direction, as the example of Royalist Cowley's *Civil War* attests.[16]

*Paradise Lost* is inevitably marked by Lucan, who was not just the poet of civil war but the poet of the ambiguous villain: his victorious, eloquent Caesar is a tyrannical and manipulative leader. Thus Satan's insincere republicanism in his various addresses to his faction in *Paradise Lost* cannot help but evoke Caesar's similarly spurious rhetoric to his troops in the *Pharsalia*. The Lucanic narrator, with his frequent interjections, has also reminded some commentators of Milton himself, intruding into his poem to admonish and complain. Additionally, Lucan provided several potential undertexts for Miltonic passages. To take only three examples, Satan's uncertain voyage across Chaos may imitate Lucan's Caesar crossing the Adriatic; the reduction of the devils into various serpents in Milton's tenth book recalls a virtuosically sibilant snake catalogue in the Latin epic; and the bridge Sin and Death build across Chaos somewhat surreally evokes Caesar's bridge of boats across the harbor at Brindisi.[17]

Nevertheless there are difficulties with seeing *Paradise Lost* as politically, let alone structurally, Lucanic.[18] As the passages above indicate, Lucan supplied specifically and perhaps solely Satanic undertexts, and this renders any "republicanism" derived from this source extremely problematic, even if we grant that these problems were already present in Lucan's portrayal of

Caesar. As Norbrook says, Satan's speeches must have left Milton's first republican readers "endlessly perplexed."[19] At a more general level, Lucan (as
Cowley, abortively, in Milton's time) was interpreting recent history, indeed
civil war, in heroic verse, and this removed him from the mainstream of epic
tradition, as many critics from Servius to Hobbes concluded.[20] Lucan's
pagan, disappointing, rather reckless universe must be contrasted with Milton's precise moral laboratory, where divine providence and human freedom
seek balance, without either overwhelming the other. And in terms of the
ten-book symbolism, Lucan's poem was obviously unfinished—indeed
Thomas May completed it for him in both Latin and English—and it is im-
probable that Milton would assert numerological kinship for his grand design with an imperfect and incomplete structure. So without denying the
rather complex influence of Lucan, we must seek the key to the poem's
structure elsewhere.

A clever model has been suggested by David Quint, who has proposed a
structure for the poem based on circularity—or, to describe it differently,
symmetry around an axis placed at the center of the poem:

| | | | | |
|---|---|---|---|---|
| 1 | Construction of Pandaemonium<br>Idolatry<br>Catalogues of devils and shrines | | 10 | Expulsion from Eden<br>Cessation of Oracles<br>Catalogue of seats of empire |
| 2 | Demonic lack of mortality<br>Satan acclaimed | | 9 | Adam and Eve's mortality<br>Satan hissed |
| 3 | Son's offer of Atonement | | 8 | Adam and Eve's Fall |
| 4 | Eden<br>Eve's account of her creation | | 7 | Creation<br>Adam's of his creation |
| 5 | War in Heaven<br>Abdiel's heroism | | 6 | War in Heaven<br>The Son's heroism[21] |

This is a rich way of parsing the epic. We start in Hell and we end leaving
Eden. The demonic parliament acclaims Satan in Book 2, an acclaim that is
turned into hissing in Book 9. The Son offers to redeem in Book 3 the sin
Man will commit in the parallel Book 8. Eve explains her first moments in
Book 4; Adam his own in Book 7. Books 5 and 6 cover the War in Heaven,
with the heroism of Abdiel in the war's opening phase facing the corre-

sponding heroism of the Son in its closing phase. Quint also detects some subtler but no less important patterns, notably the parallelism of the catalogues of devils and of places; and the plights of the immortal devils in Hell, unable to choose any meaningful destiny, balanced against the fortunes of Adam and Eve, who after the Fall must now choose one of the two ways, of spiritual life or spiritual death.[22]

Quint perhaps regrets that Milton chose to break this pattern, but it can be observed that some of this proposed structure depends, as all such do, on omission. One of the most obvious structural parallelisms of the poem, for instance, is of the hellish and heavenly councils, in Books 2 and 3 respectively—in the first, no one will answer Satan's invitation to undertake the mission to undo man, and so Satan himself volunteers; in Heaven, God's question of who will undertake the mission to restore man is answered by his Son. And there are some asymmetries here too: in the first edition, the invocations come before Books 1, 3, 7, and 8, which is not nearly as satisfactory as the geometrical distribution in the second edition, before the first and third books of each half respectively (thus 1, 3; 7, 9). My own view is that the ten-book structure was satisfying as a working model for the epic because it placed the War in Heaven at the center of the poem, wrapped it around with the Edenic books, placed episodes in both Heaven and Hell on either side, and supplied a suitable overall trajectory by commencing in physically unredeemable Hell, and concluding in spiritually redeemable Eden. Nevertheless, Milton perhaps came to think that the final, prophetic book of this first edition was just too long, at 1,541 lines, and threatened to overwhelm his structure. It was over twice as long as his shortest book, Book 4. Splitting it required the splitting of another book, so that an even number of books would be retained. Milton's decision was a good one: not only did it rebalance the books of his poem successfully, but it also brought it into a more satisfying relation with the dominant ancient tradition, and better organized the invocations. For "Lucanic" critics this will make the poem disappointingly "Virgilian," but if republican Lucan's ten books did not after all influence the ten books of Milton's first edition, then departing from that arrangement need not imply a corresponding political change of heart. Indeed, Milton's more openly political statements persist unchanged between first and second editions.

The new twelve-book structure also suggests some equally plausible subdivisions. We might, for instance, divide the work into three sets of four books: the first a "Sataniad" following Satan from Hell to Eden; the second, paralleling the Homeric "Apologoi," a retrospective core, containing Raphael and Adam's recollected narratives; and the third concentrating on the Fall itself and its aftermath, including Michael's visionary account of the future. Satan is the focus of the first; the Son of the second; and Adam and Eve of the third. It also shifts the center of the poem away from the principled angel Abdiel, who in the first version connected the two halves; now, more impersonally, but more grandly, War in Heaven faces Creation across the central divide of the poem. This also harmonizes with the new division between the final books: antediluvial Book 11 ends with the Flood, the world destroyed; postdiluvial Book 12 opens with the world restored.[23] But, as John Hale has commented, the risk with this kind of process is that twelve factorizes so well: arguments can be made for a $4 \times 3$ arrangement, as well as a $2 \times 6$, and these can be defended too, especially the latter. Yet the placing of the invocations now at the starts of Books 1, 3, 7, and 9 indeed suggests a poem divided into two halves (n.b. "Half yet remaines unsung," 7.21), but with these halves then subdivided in 1:2 ratios (in the deliberately underdetermined scheme below, into a satisfying 2:1 1:2 / 2:1 1:2 mirror):

| | | | |
|---|---|---|---|
| 1 | Hell | 7 | Eden [Creation] |
| 2 | Hell | 8 | Eden [Creation] |
| 3 | Heaven | 9 | Eden [Fall] |
| 4 | Eden | 10 | Eden [Fall] |
| 5 | Eden [War in Heaven] | 11 | Eden [Vision of the future] |
| 6 | Eden [War in Heaven] | 12 | Eden [Vision of the future] |

This arrangement also allows the poem to contrast the opening of its first half, in Hell, in despair, with the opening of the second half, where Creation itself gestures to a final optimism beyond the Fall—and we need it, given how conflicted and depressing most of Michael's vision of the future is.[24] The first half is also now a narrative circuit—it opens after the end of the battle with which it concludes. The second half is circular in its way too, but reaching into the future—it opens with the Creation of Genesis, and it closes on Conflagration, with a Second Creation to come out of the ashes of this same world. We can overlay this structure with the myriad individual doublings and contrasts set up throughout the epic, but without breaking the basic clarity of a series of internal joists and planks, all hewed in proportions answering to the factors of the number twelve. Beyond this we venture at our own pleasure and risk. Thus the ten-book *Paradise Lost* had its undoubted strengths of symmetrical parallelism around a central axis; but the twelve-book *Paradise Lost,* binding itself further to the epic tradition, retains symmetry, while surpassing its earlier configuration in balance and harmony.

# 15

## Creating a Universe

THE TOTAL COSMOS in which the action of *Paradise Lost* takes place
embraces Heaven, Hell, Chaos, and the created universe. The first
three of these spaces are vast, perhaps unfixably so (Chaos, for instance, is
"illimitable" [2.892]); the last is so tiny and indeed fragile in comparison that
Milton can only express it by simile: "This pendent world, in bigness as a
star / Of smallest magnitude close by the moon" (2.1052–53). Nevertheless,
Milton's cosmos is mappable, as it were, chiefly because of Satan's piloting
through most of its realms, paired with Milton's precise, or at least proportionate, statements about distances.[1]

At first, there was God, like the mathematician's infinite set: "Boundless
the Deep, because I am who fill / Infinitude, nor vacuous the space" (7.168–
69). Next there was Heaven. We do not know what happened there in the
beginning, but it is later explained that God created at least the angels
through his Son. We do not know if Heaven itself was created out of Chaos,
but Chaos is ontologically weird, where "time and place are lost" (2.894).
Chaos is that part of absolute infinite space on which God has not (yet)

imposed organization. In the Aristotelian physics of Milton's education, it is matter without form. Heaven and Hell have castle-like defensive boundaries, but Chaos is something altogether different, of indefinite extension, a being, zone, and condition all at once. Chaos the being, when we encounter him in Book 2, is accompanied by six other abstractions, and it is a sign of the difficulty of this section that in Milton's first edition, the compositors failed to set the names of these six things in their proper italics, as if they could not tell whether these were abstract concepts or personifications (2.962–67).

Milton's whole description of Chaos is an acceleration of Hesiod on Tartarus in the *Theogony*.[2] God's notorious "dark materials" for the making of new worlds are a transformation of the obscure "springs and ends" (πηγαὶ καὶ πείρατα, 738) of earth, hell, sea, and heaven found in Hesiod's Hell; Satan's actual journey mirrors and intensifies Hesiod's lines on the conjectural traveler in his pagan Tartarus, buffeted about, in strikingly kinetic verse, "this way and that" (ἔνθα καὶ ἔνθα) by "blast upon blast" (πρὸ θύελλα θυέλλῃ):

χάσμα μέγ᾿, οὐδέ κε πάντα τελεσφόρον εἰς ἐνιαυτὸν
οὖδας ἴκοιτ᾿, εἰ πρῶτα πυλέων ἔντοσθε γένοιτο.
Ἀλλά κεν ἔνθα καὶ ἔνθα φέροι πρὸ θύελλα θυέλλῃ
ἀργαλέη· (740–43)

[It is a great gulf; and if a man were once within the gates, he would not reach the floor until a whole year had reached its end, but cruel blast upon blast would carry him this way and that.]

As ever, Milton goes further. Hesiod's whole year is stretched into an eternal present: had not a random upsurge borne him aloft, Satan, "Fluttring his pennons vain," "to this hour / Down had been falling" (2.933, 934–35). Chaos as a zone seems to be infinite in one direction at least.

Milton's discussion of the materials of Chaos appears to combine the language of a traditional four-element physics with the voguish lore of "atoms." Indeed, it is in Book 2 that Milton gives his most vigorous statements on the warring physics of Chaos, matter not worked on by the organizing forces of Creation wielded by the Son in Milton's seventh book:

> For hot, cold, moist, and dry, four Champions fierce
> Strive here for Maistrie, and to Battel bring
> Thir embryon Atoms; they around the flag
> Of each his Faction, in thir several Clanns,
> Light-arm'd or heavy, sharp, smooth, swift or slow (2.898–902)

This is in fact a typical Milton compression and acceleration of a passage in Du Bartas, very near the start of the latter's poem, likewise on Chaos, in terms themselves recalling the atomism of Lucretius as well as, more conventionally, the opening of Ovid's *Metamorphoses*. As Du Bartas writes:

> Where th'Elements lay iumbled all together,
> Where hot and colde were iarring each with either;
> The blunt with sharp, the dank against the drie,
> The hard with soft, the base against the high;
> Bitter with sweet . . .
> This was not then the World: 'twas but the Matter,
> The Nurcery whence it should issue after;
> Or rather, th'*Embryon*[3]

Hot and cold and moist and dry are conventional, but "blunt" and "sharp," and especially "Bitter" and "sweet," come from Lucretius's second book, where he discusses the shapes and forms of his atoms, proposing that bitter and sweet tastes in the mouth arise from the impact of sharp and blunt atoms, respectively.[4] Milton, however, overlays the account too with a military conceit: the four elements are "Champions" accompanied by infantry-like "Atoms," who gather round their "flag" in unmistakably Scottish "Clanns," just a hint of civil-war-inspired Celtophobia in Chaos.[5] This will later play into Milton's views on dubiously heroic militarism.

Milton's Chaos is so strange, indeed, that it can look like a zone of the poem in which metaphysical dualism applies, the principle that the positive and negative forces of the universe have existed coeternally. (We might recall one of the most striking and problematic lines of the physician Samuel Barrow's poem on Milton set before the second edition of *Paradise Lost*: "Et sine fine Chaos, & sine fine Deus"—"Both Chaos without end, and without end God.")[6] Chaos is where Night, not Light, is explicitly called "eldest of things" (2.962), Light otherwise being the first created thing elsewhere in the poem (3.1). John Leonard in a brilliant essay has therefore insisted that the poem here presents Chaos itself as eternal, notwithstanding what we feel the poem at large, theologically, ought to be presenting.[7]

Milton, I suggest, is also here parodying, first, Hesiod's lines on Chaos and his offspring,[8] but then, more subtly, the various elaborate divine genealogies of the Gnostic heretics. These heretics of chiefly the second century AD constructed divine genealogies by pairing personified qualities or "hypostases," usually to make up larger sets. In Milton's Chaos, Chaos as a hypostasis is at first paired with Chance (2.907, 910), but this is then revised to Chaos paired with his "consort" Night, with Orcus and Ades paired below them, then Demogorgon on his own, then a further pairing of Rumour and Chance, then Tumult and Confusion, and finally Discord, in a 2:2:1:2:2:1 symmetrical pattern (2.959–66).

Compare the best-known Gnostic genealogy, that of Valentinus of Alexandria, as described by the church father Irenaeus in his *Adversus haereses,* the cornerstone text of Christian heresiography. Valentinus taught his followers that before the material creation, among invisible and ineffable things, there was first of all Abyss, with his consort Silence. They generated Intellect and Truth. These four "aeons" formed the first divine "tetrad." Next came Word and Life, then Man and Church, the whole eight forming the first "ogdoad." These were followed by further subdivisions, grouped into a further five (the first "decade") and six ("dodecade") pairs, the whole thirty aeons forming the "pleroma," the complete first family of premundane beings.[9] The created universe is, in effect, a chaotic abortion of the most junior aeon. This is merely the opening phase of this Gnostic theogony, but it is enough for our present purposes—Milton transplants Gnostic thought patterns into his Chaos, but for ultimately satirical effect.[10] No more did Milton believe that there were real beings called Tumult and Confusion, than he believed in the "vain genealogies" of Abyss and Silence and their fellows. Gnosticism, superficially orderly, is really chaotic, and Chaos itself takes on a tinge of absurdity by the reverse comparison to the "science falsely so called" (1 Tim. 6:20).

Nevertheless Chaos certainly preceded Hell, as the personified Chaos fears recent developments on his borders, "Weakening the sceptre of old Night" (as if his consort were really the primal power?). On one side there had been the creation of Hell; and, after that, on the other, the new "heaven and Earth":

> another world
> Hung o'er my realm, linked in a golden chain
> To that side heaven from whence your legions fell (2.1002,
>     1004–1006)

Hell was therefore created in expectation of the angelic fall, and Milton in a curious passage imagines Hell as a living being trying to get up and run away from the falling angels heading for it, but in vain, as a carefully impersonal "Fate" (rather than, explicitly, "God") holds Hell, terrified, in place:

> Hell heard th'unsufferable noise, Hell saw
> Heav'n ruining from Heav'n and would have fled
> Affrighted; but strict Fate had cast too deep
> Her dark foundations, and too fast had bound. (6.867–70)[11]

Chaos regrets the arrival of Hell insofar as it encroaches on his territory. Then, in a momentarily unsettling phrase, he complains about a further innovation: "Now lately Heaven and Earth, another World" (2.1004). At first that "Heaven" is worrying—Chaos cannot mean Heaven itself, the realm of God. But when he continues with "another World" we decide that "Heaven and Earth" is here a phrase for the visible universe, our universe of stars and planets. Chaos then confusingly uses "Heaven" again in its empyreal sense: the new universe is connected "To that side Heav'n from whence your Legions fell" (2.1006). The reader is being deliberately disoriented. Then, as Chaos concludes,

> If that way be your walk, you have not farr;
> So much the neerer danger; go and speed;
> Havock and spoil and ruin are my gain. (2.1007–1009)

Regardless of Milton's cautions in *De doctrina* that the *substance* of chaos is morally neutral,[12] these are not the words of a morally neutral *being* Chaos—the imperative "speed" means "succeed," and success in Chaos's opinion is if Satan can cause more "Havock and spoil and ruin." When in fact such "ruin" results in the construction of a bridge over Chaos by Sin and Night, Chaos complains about that too (10.415–18). Chaos may be a "womb," in a famous transposition of a line of Lucretius's *De rerum natura* into Milton's epic;[13] but if so this is a womb where things are merely "abortive," "embryon" (2.441, 900). If there is a parallel here to Lucretius, it is to that poet on the early blunders of the world-wombs of creation, where monsters were brought forth instead of viable organisms.[14] As is explored in Chapter 18 this is also a parody of genuine Creation, in Book 7, where God, in another section debating the merits of the Lucretian creation, commands the animals to spring out of the Earth, perfect and fully formed.

Elsewhere, we are told in considerable detail about the new world linked to Heaven: Satan approaches the "firm opacous globe" (3.418) of the created realm from the side of Chaos, and finds wandering on its surface monsters, giants, suicides, pilgrims, and monks—a rare moment of pure, sour, satire in the epic (3.455–97). It is also only at this point that we hear of the seemingly solid, concentric spheres of our universe:

> They pass the Planets seven, and pass the fixt,
> And that Crystalline Sphear whose balance weighs
> The Trepidation talkt, and that first mov'd. (3.481–83)

These lines have traditionally been held to be serious, detailing the seven planetary spheres, the sphere of the fixed stars, and the crystalline sphere of conventional celestial physics. But Leonard, picking up on a warning first issued by the Richardsons in their 1734 commentary on *Paradise Lost*, rightly suspects these lines of being satirical—"They" who "pass" are after all the deluded friars and monks, and we cannot therefore trust this passage as describing what Milton himself believes.[15] Certainly, his angels fly about on light rays without bumping into spheres. And Milton had already been satirical about crystalline spheres and walking on the moon in his student "De Idea Platonica"—the (fabulous) ideal Platonic Form is mockingly to be sought among "ordines decemplicis" (tenfold ranks, i.e., spheres), or on the globe of the moon.[16]

Corroboration for the view that the passage in *Paradise Lost* is ironic can also be found in its simultaneous allusion to hostile accounts available to Milton of Persian or Mithraic religion, specifically the fabled ascent through the seven spheres, a trope also rife in Gnostic systems. The church father Origen, for instance, in his polemic against the pagan physician Celsus, sneered at religions that promised a sevenfold ascent, whereas "in no part of the genuine and divinely accredited Scriptures are seven heavens mentioned."[17]

We should not make this passage do too much work, however: revising the tone of these three lines to heed their mockery will not render Milton a convinced or consistent Copernican. His created universe is nevertheless still enclosed in at least one sphere, a hard external shell. This has excited much comment, as this is a clear reference to the Epicurean model of our *mundus* or universe as one among many, separated from the void around it by the *moenia mundi* or "walls of the world." But whereas the Lucretian walls separate our universe from its neighboring universes, like bubbles in a bath, Milton's walls separate us from the surrounding Chaos, and the present existence of other universes is unconfirmed.[18] The external surface of the globe of the world is illuminated only on the side facing Heaven, and the link between the two realms is a version of the biblical vision of Jacob's Ladder (see Genesis 28:10–22). This linking chain connects the globe to a gem-studded gate "underneath" (around?—we also need to flip our perspective vertically at this point) the entrance to Heaven, which stretches into a crystal sea. The connecting ladders can be let down and drawn up, and that they (always) lead directly down to the top of Paradise means the Earth has to be geostatic in this universe (3.501–39). The structure is biblical, but also Homeric, Zeus claiming he could draw up all the other gods as well as creation on a chain.[19]

It is pagan heroic poetry that also supplies prompts for the relative distances of Hell, Heaven, and the World. Milton's Hell is "As far removed from God and light of heaven / As from the centre thrice to the utmost pole" (1.73–74). The "centre" to the "pole" is the distance from the center of the Earth to the boundary with Heaven (so including the length of the Heaven-Earth chain / ladder); and thus Hell is twice as far from Earth as Earth is from Heaven, as the poem encourages us to think of these zones as in a line, a conceit going back to Hesiod, where the distance is expressed in terms of a falling anvil—there it is nine days' fall from Heaven to Earth; and a further nine days' fall from Earth to Tartarus.[20] Virgil, whom Milton follows, then doubled the demonic distance: in the *Aeneid*, Tartarus is twice as far down as Olympus is up.[21] There is some initial conceptual difficulty in Milton's reckoning, because we have been elsewhere assured that distances across Chaos are unimaginably large, and that the created world is vanishingly small—as small, we have seen, as the smallest star next to the Moon (2.1053). But as the Moon in that simile stood for Heaven itself, we must rather accept that Heaven is the really vast zone, with the infinitesimal created world hard by it, and Hell, separated by Chaos, two Earth-Heaven spans further away.

Milton's created universe does not exactly resemble its lapsarian successor. In Book 10, after the Son has judged the fallen pair of humans, God sends angels out to alter the structure of the heavens. Before the Fall, as Alastair Fowler has so meticulously demonstrated, the equatorial (or equinoctial) and ecliptic planes were the same thing. That is to say, the imaginary great circle traced by the points of intersection of the terrestrial equator and the enclosing celestial sphere is the same circle as the one in which the Sun takes its annual path. In our lapsarian world these circles are at slight angles to one another, the Sun tracing its path through the zodiac, not the equator, and so they intersect at only two, opposite, points, and these we call the equinoxes. This is because the Earth and the Sun do not in our world have parallel axes: one tilts with respect to the other. Before the Fall, there was no tilt, so these circles were the same, and therefore of course intersected at every point. Thus there was permanent equinox—that is why nights and days are the same duration in Eden, and, at least astronomically speaking, there are no seasons. The prelapsarian world simply remains in the season in which it was created, "eternal spring" (4.268). Milton had found a cosmic mechanism whereby the old fables of the golden age could be given a precise astronomical cause. Eve's meal table features "All *Autumn* pil'd, though *Spring* and *Autumn* here / Danc'd hand in hand" (5.395–95), an allusion to the equivalence of the vernal and autumnal equinoxes, and their static persistence in unfallen Eden. So when Milton in his second invocation laments in his blindness, "Thus with the year / Seasons return, but not to me" (3.40–41), he is lamenting the loss of something that only fully came to be in the fallen world.

Placing the prelapsarian poles directly overhead also has the effect of fixing the longitudes of the constellations: they may perform one revolution in twenty-four hours, but stars no longer rise and set as they appear to do with a tilted pole; there are no seasonal variations, no winter constellations, for instance; no ascending or descending signs; and the signs and constellations were one and the same. ("Precession," a postlapsarian

phenomenon, subsequently "backs" the signs westward against the constellations.) Satan first sees this pristine order from the circumference of the
globe of the created world, on which he is standing: looking down, he can
see Libra on one side and, diametrically opposite, Aries ("the fleecy star,"
because of the ram's coat) with Andromeda above (3.558–60). God actually
creates one of these constellations to stop an impending fight between Gabriel, hanging his scales in the heavens as a symbol to desist (4.997–98, Libra,
between "Astraea" [Virgo] and Scorpio). This is Milton's transformation of
the classical "catasterism," whereby a thing or person is turned into a constellation, "yet seen": thus in Aratus, slightly ironically for this passage,
Virgo as Justice lived on Earth among men in the Golden and Silver Age,
but removed herself to the heavens with the coming of the Bronze Age.[22]
(Is there an inconsistency here, however, Satan having already "seen" Libra
in Book 3?)[23]

After the Fall, therefore, God instructs the angels to tilt the Earth from
its upright position with respect to the Sun, or to tilt the Sun with respect
to the Earth, "twice ten degrees and more"—the Miltonic narrator is typically coy, leaving either possibility open (10.668–78). The observed effect is
the same, for the Sun now appears to move through the signs of the zodiac,
alternately ascending and descending, from Aries, in which it was created,

> To Taurus with the seven
> Atlantic Sisters, and the Spartan Twins
> Up to the tropic Crab; thence down again
> By Leo and the Virgin and the Scales,
> As deep as Capricorn, to bring in change
> Of seasons to each clime (10.673–78)

Over time such changes cause corresponding malign astrological influences
("sidereal blast," 10.693) and the arrival of the various winds, four northern
(Boreas, Caecias, Argestes, and Thrascias), two south (Notus and Afer), then
the "levant" and "ponent" (i.e., eastern and western) winds Eurus, Zephir,
Sirocco, and Libecchio (10.699–706). (Milton is here once again gesturing
to his prized Aratus, as to follow star signs with weather signs follows the
order of Aratus's *Phaenomena / Diosemeia*.) These are all classical winds carried through into contemporary anemological charts, but there is a deliberate instability, even ambiguity here—Milton names only ten or perhaps

eleven winds (for "levant" might be "Levant," the east wind itself), rather than the twelve[24] or twenty-four[25] winds of classical tradition, let alone the sixteen of actual maritime wind roses.[26] This is because Milton's intention in this whole section is to emphasize that all the symmetrical and orderly charts of the astronomers and meteorologists, with their neat zodiacal band of twelve signs and their equally neatly distributed twelve winds, obscure the fundamental fact that all these phenomena are the results of disorder, an unnecessary and blighted structure. Our "regularity" is simply damage.

We do not know exactly when in terms of elapsed human time Milton believed his narrative had taken place, but we may be sure that he considered it a firmly historical event, and to have occurred specifically, give or take twenty years or so, around 4000 BC. This is roughly when the Hebrew Bible placed creation, and the many hypotheses circulating in Milton's time all gathered around this date. There is no indication that Milton entertained the alternative chronology offered by the Greek (Septuagint) text of the Old Testament, a version of the biblical text that had been obsessing scholars other than Milton particularly since the arrival in England of the celebrated Codex Alexandrinus, initially presented to the monarch in 1624. And none more so than the Codex Alexandrinus's keeper, Patrick Young, the royal librarian, and Milton's acquaintance. The case for the stretched chronology of the Septuagint, courtesy of its longer-living Patriarchs, was bolstered for some by the dissemination by Jesuits missionaries in the 1650s of the recently translated Chinese king lists, which, when reckoned against the standard Hebrew text of the Old Testament, appeared to stretch back before the Flood—a problem which could be solved by adopting by the Septuagint reckoning.

Did Milton know about this controversy? He did, for his correspondent Henry Oldenburg, one of the first secretaries to the Royal Society of London, informed Milton by letter in 1656 about the forthcoming work of Martino Martini, the China Jesuit whose *Atlas Sinensis* (1655) and forthcoming *Sinicæ historiæ decas prima* (1658) first promulgated in the West the huge spans of Chinese imperial history, stating explicitly that the way to integrate this into Western reckonings of time was to favor the Septuagint over the Hebrew or "Vulgate" chronology.[27] But was Milton persuaded? Not at all. He merely told Oldenburg that "the ancient Chinese calendar, from the Flood on, which you say is promised by the Jesuit Martini, is doubtless eagerly anticipated because of its novelty; but I do not see what authority or support it could add to the Mosaic books."[28]

Moving from absolute time to time as it is measured in Paradise, because it is perpetual spring before the Fall, timekeeping in Eden is somewhat simplified. As the Sun *always* reaches its height at midday, it functions as the hour hand of a huge celestial twenty-four-hour clock, as does the conic shadow it casts at night. The Sun therefore rises at 6 a.m. and sets at 6 p.m., and when Milton says that the shadow of night is "Half way up hill this vast sublunar vault" (4.777), he means the point halfway between sunset and midnight, that is to say, 9 p.m. So time is easily and regularly measured in quarter- and in eighth-circles of a twenty-four-hour dial as traversed by the Sun, and Milton typically expresses time in Paradise by means of this solar clock. Next, in a brilliant adaptation of Hesiod's *Theogony* ("where Night and Day draw near and greet one another as they pass the great threshold of bronze: and while the one is about to go down into the house, the other comes out at the door"),[29] Milton institutes an exactly analogous system for Heaven, except that the necessary fluctuations in brightness are created by a revolving light-show housed centrally underneath God's throne, and not a circumferential journey of two different principles (6.4–12).[30] Thus Milton connects the mundane and supramundane zones of the poem into the same timeline.

So with time itself rendered measurable, Milton can now schedule his entire poem. The actual chronology of the poem is complex but consistent, and Milton is so careful to specify precise durations that we are invited to be likewise careful in monitoring them. We can track definite statements about time throughout the poem, as long as we bear in mind that Milton often reckons a day, in the Jewish manner, from evening to morning. The poem opens with Satan and his crew having wallowed, vanquished, in Hell for nine days (1.50); Pandaemonium is then built in one hour (1.697). The same day Satan departs on his mission, and arrives in Eden at noon the next day (4.564–65); it is just after 9 p.m. that night when Satan whispers at Eve's ear in bed (4.776–77). The next morning in Eden (5.1) Eve recounts her troubled dream to Adam, and Raphael is sent by God to talk to Adam, being given until sunset to do so (5.229). Raphael's inset narration then provides us retrospectively with the earlier chronology for the poem.

Following Raphael's reckoning, God's Decree elevating his Son is the first event in time as it can be measured (5.600). At midnight, Satan, as Raphael recounts, suggests rebellion to Beelzebub (5.667); before dawn the third part of the angels has set up camp in the north and held debate. The faithful Abdiel resists, and is back in front of God's throne by dawn (6.2). God declares battle, which is waged for three days, Messiah triumphing on the third day

(6.406, 524–25, 669). These are the first four days of the poem. The vanquished angels then fall through the void for nine days before being shut in (newly created) Hell (6.871). At that point, God then commences the creation of our universe through his Son, lasting for six days (7.216–550), followed by a seventh day of rest, the Sabbath (7.581–82). Raphael now concludes his narration and continues to discuss astronomy and obedience with Adam until sunset (8.630–32).

Meanwhile, Satan has been circling the Earth for seven nights, and reenters Eden on the eighth (9.58–67). On the same day he effects the Fall, and all the remaining action of the poem takes place on that day and the next (11.184); Fall and Expulsion are separated by one night.

Resolving this back into a coherent chronology from God's Decree to the Expulsion is not simple, as there are several concurrent strands, and we must also count with inclusive reckoning. But the best interpretation, following Fowler, is this:

| Day: | Event: |
| --- | --- |
| 1 | God's Decree concerning his Son, followed that night by rebellion |
| 2 | War in Heaven: the first day |
| 3 | War in Heaven: the second day |
| 4 | War in Heaven: the third day, and Messiah's victory |
| 5–13 | Nine days' fall from Heaven to Hell |
| 13–22 | Nine days lying vanquished in Hell |
| 14–20 | Hexameron and Sabbath |
| 22 | Revival of Satan, erection of Pandaemonium, and Satan's departure for the new world |
| 23 | Satan arrives in Eden at noon and whispers to Eve at night |
| 24 | Raphael's visit |
| 24–31 | Satan's week of circling the Earth |
| 32 | Fall and Judgment |
| 33 | Expulsion |

Thus Milton managed to work several symbolic quantities and durations into his epic schedule: the War in Heaven, involving the host Heaven split into three equal parts, takes three days, also the number of beings involved in godhead; and the week of Hexameron and Sabbath is balanced by Satan's own week of circling the Earth. There is no biblical warrant for the twin demonic periods of nine days—reminiscent, however, of the nine days of plague visited on the Greeks at the beginning of the *Iliad?*

Milton's construction of a coherent cosmos and chronology for his poem is meticulous, and it must have required very careful cross-checking as the composition evolved. And although Milton is describing a world that existed, and then soon afterward ceased to exist in quite the same way, thousands of years before his own time, readers have always noticed that Milton re-acts to more recent developments too. The subject of the poem might be ancient, but the poem itself discusses contemporary discoveries. Milton is sparing in his explicit modernism, however. In all of *Paradise Lost,* he mentions only two modern historical figures by name: Columbus (9.1116) and Galileo (5.262), the one standing for geographical, the other for astronomical, exploration.

As for Columbus, the modern voyages of discovery had become the subject of modern epic from the famous *Os Lusíadas* (*The Lusiads,* 1572) of Luís Vaz de Camões, on Vasco da Gama and his travels.[31] Earlier, however, Ariosto's *Orlando Furioso* had already linked ancient heroism and modern exploration. Andronica, asked by Astolfo whether the Eastern nations ever set sail for the West, or the Western nations for the East, says that, at present, they do not. She continues:

> Ma volgendosi gli anni, io veggio uscire
> da l'estreme contrade di ponente
> nuovi Argonauti e nuovi Tifi, e aprire
> la strada ignota infin al dì presente:
> altri volteggiar l'Africa, e seguire
> tanto la costa de la negra gente,
> che passino quel segno onde ritorno
> fa il sole a noi, lasciando il Capricorno.

> [But with the passage of time I see new Argonauts, new
> Tiphyses hailing from the lands which lie furthest to the West,

who shall open routes unknown to this day. Some of them
shall round Africa, following the shores of the black peoples
right on past the limits whence the Sun returns to us after
leaving Capricorn.]

Ultimately,

altri lasciar le destre e le mancine
rive che due per opra Erculea fersi;
e del sole imitando il camin tondo,
ritrovar nuove terre e nuovo mondo.[32]

[Others shall leave to their right and left the Pillars established
by Hercules, and, following the circuit of the sun, discover
new lands, a new world.]

Ariosto's conception of modern epic as a kind of evolution of the story of
Jason and the Argonaunts, the subject of Apollonius of Rhodes's *Argonautica,* was likewise an idea that would appeal to Milton.

Milton too alludes to the recent voyages, but, significantly, it is only in
the aftermath of the Fall that we first hear of the East and West Indies in
close succession. The fig leaves with which Adam and Eve clothe themselves
are identified as Malabaric or Deccan *banyan,* the Indian fig (9.1101–1104);
and Milton supplements "such of late / Columbus found the American so
girt / With feathered cincture" (9.1115–17). That Milton sequences this so—
the fig leaves of shame encountered by the modern explorer—associates
the Fall with new (here geographical) knowledge; and it also fleetingly
associates Adam and Eve with the Taino of Hispaniola, and therefore, by
implication, Columbus with Satan. This is one of Milton's many parallels
between the Edenic and the colonial situation, an association that provoked
ambiguous feelings in Milton, as J. Martin Evans explored in a fine book.[33]

The Columbus passage also glances at the problem of recently discovered cultures apparently operating outside the economy of not only Christian
knowledge but maybe also Christian anthropology itself. Are the semi-naked
Americans perhaps not even of the seed of Adam? Milton raises this possibility only to close it off. A recent and widely decried hypothesis, that of the
"Preadamites" (Men before Adam), had proposed that original sin was not a

universal affliction, as the whole world had been populated long before Adam and Eve enacted their comparatively late, special drama. This hypothesis was known to Milton, but he had no patience at all for such outrageous (and, as he would have snorted, French) *libertinage;* the fact that the Americans are here only semi-naked (the "feathered cincture") affirms that they too know shame.[34] So they are also the children, if the somewhat forgetful children, of Adam.

Milton's purpose in such an association is to recognize that technology and the achievements it permits, such as navigation—or telescopes—are ineluctably postlapsarian developments. Before the Fall, Adam and Eve had no fire, and so, Milton is careful to explain, no smelted gardening tools other than the ones given to them by the visiting angels, in lines that eerily evoke the complementary pagan myth of Prometheus (9.391–92).[35] Milton has nothing positive to say about the luxurious cultures of the Far East and the primitives in the far west, but knowledge of them in itself is no bad thing, and Milton revels in his own global reach.

To a certain extent this is also true of Milton's use of Galileo and his extensive allusions to the new astronomy.[36] Milton, like any reasonably well-informed contemporary, was fascinated by the theories of Copernicus and Galileo, and the latter, as a victim of the (Roman Catholic) Church, had already become an important symbol for Milton of intellectual freedom, the *libertas philosophandi.* Milton, as we saw, had met Galileo in Italy, and it is highly likely that he managed to bring back a copy of Galileo's controversial and banned *Dialogi* with him, as in *Areopagitica* Milton snorted that he had seen an Italian book with *five* imprimaturs, and this is the only publication licensed thus to have been traced.[37] English academics were proud of the fact that, unlike many of their continental counterparts, they were technically free to debate heterodox or novel ideas in philosophy, including natural philosophy, no opinion being officially proscribed. Many continental centers of learning could not boast such freedom. But English scholars were careful not to appear dogmatic about such ideas, lest they fall into unsupple certainties about things that were, after all, matters about which reasonable people might disagree. Even after the Restoration, what we tend to regard as the major discoveries of the period might still be viewed with studied equanimity by figures at the heart of Britain's nascent scientific institutions.[38]

It is in this spirit that we should read the famous astronomical debate between Adam and Raphael in the eighth book of *Paradise Lost*—Raphael is more than happy to entertain Adam's cautiously proposed Copernicanism, but this has to be debated as an interesting paradox within the context of biblical geocentrism. "Not that I so affirm" (8.117), Raphael coyly warns, before rehearsing the Copernican cosmos in extensive and speculative detail. We might compare the terminology of the imprimatur granted to John Wilkins's classic 1638 speculative study, *A Discovery of a World in the Moone*, arguing that the moon might be a planet like ours: *perlegi haec paradoxa* (I have read through these paradoxes), wrote the censor. Indeed, Milton's whole discussion is related to the rhetorical device of *occupatio* or *praeteritio* ("And let me not mention," followed by extensive mention), but here given moral application: "Solicit not thy thoughts with matters hid" (8.167), Raphael concludes.

Milton's reticence in such matters indeed may go further than the balanced tones of an academic's *libertas philosophandi*. It is another test not only for Adam and Eve, but for the reader and for Milton himself, for if unfallen Adam and Eve are to be told to keep their curiosity in check, then their narrator and readers must do so too. This is likewise true of Milton's interest in that quintessentially English branch of early modern experimentalism: magnetism, or the "magnetical philosophy," which took the Colchester physician William Gilbert's *De magnete* (On the Magnet, 1600) as its manifesto.[39] Gilbert's final book had proposed that the sun itself was a huge magnet, and that heavenly bodies, including the Earth, spun magnetically on their axes. Raphael alludes to magnetism when he talks of the sun's potential "attractive virtue"; and we have already heard, explicitly, of the sun's "magnetic beam" earlier in the poem (8.124; 3.583).[40] But Raphael is posing a question, "What if?," and the earlier mention is part of a typical Miltonic either / or construction: the stars "Turn swift their various motions, or are turned / By his [the sun's] magnetic beam," both possibilities being left open. As ever, engagement is not assent, although it is worth pondering, as Kepler did when he read Gilbert, that magnetism can perform what was once delegated to the spheres of traditional physics. Magnetism, albeit here tentatively proposed, allows space to become permeable.[41]

Perhaps most strikingly, Milton exploits Satan's voyage from the shell to the center of the new universe to introduce speculation about alien life. This was a question that had vexed medieval and early modern theologians, but which had recently received new and troubling energy. Galileo's *Nuncius Sidereus* (Venice, 1610) had carefully avoided open support of the hypothesis of lunar civilization, but Kepler's excited response to Galileo, his *Dissertatio cum Nuncio sidereo* (Prague, 1610), indeed imagined cities on the moon. This soon spawned a new lunar literature, culminating, in England, in the first piece of English science fiction, Francis Godwin's *The Man in the Moone* (London, 1638).[42] The Galilean influence on Milton was spotted early: as Milton's first commentator, Patrick Hume, remarked on Milton's phrase "Space may produce new Worlds" (1.650): "to the continuing of these Conceits, the Spectacles of *Galileus* have not a little contributed."[43] But Milton once again proffers with one hand what he withdraws with the other:

> Stars distant, but nigh hand seemd other Worlds,
> Or other Worlds they seemd, or happy Iles,
> Like those *Hesperian* Gardens fam'd of old,
> Fortunate Fields, and Groves and flourie Vales,
> Thrice happy Iles, but who dwelt happy there
> He stayd not to enquire (3.566–71)

Note Milton's repeated "seemd" (compare the identical repetition at 5.617, the one-line origin of sin); and "but . . . stayd not" is faintly but undeniably sardonic. Indeed, although Milton returns several times to the notion of alien life in *Paradise Lost,* his allusions are never unequivocal. Milton accepts that beings might exist "Betwixt the angelical and human kind" (3.462), and he does suspect, I grant, that they, along perhaps with "Translated saints" (Enoch, Elijah), may perhaps live on the moon. But this is an attempt to accommodate types of beings widely accepted in Christian and indeed pagan tradition,[44] and it is embedded in a passage otherwise tinted with satire. Raphael also introduces at length the argument from analogy that the moon may well be inhabited, and that this analogy might be applied to other suns (8.144–52). Again, this is in the context of his conjectural discussion with Adam, a discussion curtailed by Raphael's own injunctions not to think about it too much: "Dream not of other Worlds" (8.175). Satan assumes that in theory all the "shining orbs" might be inhabited (3.670), and with him agree the unfallen angels. Yet crucially they insinuate that such habitation is "destined" (7.622), and so set aside for the future—these are solar systems waiting to be colonized by the expanding populations of the unfallen, should they remain unfallen, not planets inhabited with peculiar and nonhuman realms of life. Milton is worlds away from Kepler, for instance, whose posthumous *Somnium* (1634) imagined screaming reptiles on the moon, living and dying in a day, like short-lived versions of the dinosaurs of which he could not have known.[45] As for Milton's Galileo, when he descries lands on the moon, they are "imagined lands" (5.263); although Galileo's observations are not in themselves called into question, his interpretation of them is. The moon he sees is a "spotty globe," a sign that sin has taken hold in the heavens: new technology confirms rather than challenges the lapsarian universe (1.291). Thus Milton's own obvious fascination with these ubiquitous questions of seventeenth-century thought is constantly held in check; but although his interest in the new science is self-admonished, it is not effaced.

Milton, perhaps surprisingly, also does not contest the basic truth of astrology: heavenly bodies exert an influence over earthly bodies. Once again, however, this is presented as dismal lapsarianism, at least in its malign consequences: God directs his angels to manipulate the formerly benign heavens so that

> To the blank moon
> Her office they prescribed, to the other five
> Their planetary motions and aspects
> In sextile, square, and trine, and opposite,
> Of noxious efficacy, and when to join
> In synod unbenign, and taught the fixed
> Their influence malignant when to shower (10.656–62)

This is mainstream astrology, rooted in the second-century Alexandrian mathematician Ptolemy's *Tetrabiblos,* and practiced unchanged in its elements in Milton's day. Milton is once again providing an etiology for received opinion, rather than challenging that opinion itself. And with his usual twist, he suggests that astrological influence is yet another aspect of divine punishment. There were "progressive" voices in Milton's time, for those who must think of the historiography of science in those terms—but Milton was not one of them.

# 16

## Epic Disruption

P*ARADISE LOST*'S DEEPEST organizational debt is, inevitably, to its epic predecessors. Like the *Odyssey* and the *Aeneid, Paradise Lost* is designed so that it does not follow the order of time, but starts at a significant point in the middle of the action, *in medias res* (into the middle things), returning only later to certain chronologically prior episodes. Thus it features inset, retrospective narration in the manner of the "Apologoi" of the *Odyssey* (the fourth to twelfth books, in which Odysseus narrates his wanderings for his Phaeacian hosts), and likewise the books of the *Aeneid* (two and three) in which Aeneas recounts the aftermath of the Battle of Troy before the court of Dido in Carthage.[1]

Yet Milton's most interesting engagements with prior epic structures are usually disruptive. Chapters 17 and 18 explore in detail some of the more precise and interesting operations Milton performed on the available traditions of the martial and cosmogonic epic, exemplified in the root poems of Homer's *Iliad* and Hesiod's *Theogony*, respectively, as well as some of the nonepic traditions Milton comprehends, notably georgic and tragedy. But to begin we need only recognize the typical epic ingredients adapted by Milton for sacred use and appreciate the creative violence done to these traditions. Epics require gods and heroes, battles, the supernatural, voyages, conflicts of loyalty or love; at the narrative level they feature debates between superhuman beings, adventures against monsters, a descent to the underworld or an ascent to the heavens; at the technical level, epic diction tends to favor repeated epithet, repeated passages, lists—especially of names and places—and lengthy descriptions of armor and clothing.

All of these elements are of course present in *Paradise Lost* but, as it were, at right angles to the tradition, for epic imitation in Milton carries with it a subtle incrimination of what it imitates. Milton's gods are God; his heroes, innocent of clothing and armor alike, garden rather than duel; his battles, conducted by angels, are surreal morphs of classical warfare, fought by deathless shape-shifters; the supernatural is firmly limited by God's providential eye; the uncouth voyage is undertaken by the moral foe of the epic; and the conflicts of loyalty and love are uniquely domestic in focus: "domestick" Adam (9.318) and his economic Eve provide the major, indeed sole, human focus of the poem. At the narrative level the debates take place first, acceptably enough, between various devils, something familiar from Marco Vida's *Christiad* (1535) and Torquato Tasso's *Gerusalemme Liberata* (1581), as well as several English neo-Latin "gunpowder plot" poems[2]—but then, outrageously, between God himself and his Son, usually considered to be two-thirds of the same being, seldom encountered debating; the monsters, notably Sin, Death, Chaos, and Ancient Night, hover problematically between beings and allegories; and descents and ascents multiply and interconnect, undertaken by devils, angels, Adam and Eve, the Son, even Milton's muse and the epic narrator himself.

Technically, however, Milton furnishes as close to an English version of epic diction as he can manage: he eschews stanzaic verse and, vehemently, rhyme, so that his blank verse recalls the unrhymed hexameter of the ancients; he is careful to repeat epithets and on occasion whole sections of verse; and he delights in lists, whether of the pagan names of the fallen angels, the competing intricacies of pagan fable itself, or the ringing proper names of world geography. Yet always here too Milton is pressing boundaries: his blank verse was a deliberate affront to the conventions of English versification; his repetitions carry unique theological current; and his lists boast a historical and geographical range that by implication renders classical epic parochial.

Such a technique of disruption is manifest right from the start, as *Paradise Lost* opens like the negative print of recognizable epic. Achilles was the obvious precedent for the martial hero; Odysseus, the man of *metis* or "cunning," with his twin talents for disguise and deceit, was condemned to wander after a defeat; Aeneas, fleeing Troy, combined these roles and was also destined to found a new nation. There were other questing voyagers in the epic tradition, notably Jason, who sought a forbidden object. The divine wars of the *Theogony* featured as their central action a successful rebellion: Zeus indeed dethroned Cronus. The opening book of *Paradise Lost* combines all of these components—we are at once presented with a martial, exiled, cunning, wandering hero, bent on establishing his new kingdom. But this hyper-hero is Satan himself, his strength spurious, his exile from Heaven, his cunning mere fraudulence, his quest one of revenge following a failed coup, and his "new kingdom" is to be our fallen world. This is why Satan so troubled early readers, because in all available epic senses he was the "hero" of the poem, and yet from every theological or ethical stance he was the ultimate villain, the Old Enemy. Milton was colliding the two unavoidably dominant ways of making sense of his poem, or indeed any literary text—reading in terms of its genre and the expectations of that genre, and reading in terms of its subject and its inherent moral qualities. Milton's first intention here was to commence from the outset his critique of classical epic and the model of heroism it promoted; his second intention, by commencing so aggressively, was to challenge, even to shock, the reader into a particularly alert form of reading.

If Milton disrupts epic tradition, then what kind of epic is his own? This is a question the first edition of the poem perhaps invites by omission, for Milton published it as a poem, as it says on its title page—not, as we might expect, as a heroic poem, or an epic. The poem obviously has some kind of relation to epic, but we are in effect invited to work out for ourselves what this is.

C. S. Lewis once influentially distinguished what he called primary from secondary epic: the former records heroic deeds so that they are not forgotten; the latter is literary, an artistic interpretation of the traditions, themselves often literary, of such heroic legends. The former may glamorize or amplify what are at heart historical events; the latter can treat its mythic material as a pretext for more philosophical or theoretical departures.[3] Milton on this understanding is more Virgil than Homer, more secondary than primary—the robed and garlanded *aiodos* has been replaced by a man at a desk in a library. Perhaps we might even call Milton tertiary, Alastair Fowler has suggested: a Virgilian secondariness has itself been subjected to antiheroic treatment, and reduced to subsidiary function within a new, Christian framework.[4]

Perhaps the most astonishing act of epic disruption performed by Milton, however, is a consequence of his blindness. Milton's age believed that the origins of poetry were oral, and some scholars were even debating the possibility that the Homeric text represented not what Homer himself had performed, but what later editors had constructed. This disintegrationist theory could be traced back at least as far as the first-century AD Jewish historian Josephus, who claimed in a famous passage that Homer did not write his poems down, but that his scattered songs were transmitted by memory and only later stitched together into the longer epics. This problem, therefore, was pondered by early modern editors of Homer, and the so-called Homeric question is older than we might assume. For instance, the German philologist Obertus Gifanius prefaced his 1572 edition with a discussion of the textual history of Homer, repeating Josephus's remarks and adding that the isolated sections (*partes*) of Homer had been assembled in a manner that nevertheless betrays the odd internal discrepancy. Moreover, wrote Gifanius, the first true edition of Homer, that commissioned by the sixth-century BC Athenian ruler Peisistratus, contains the latter's own verses interpolated here and there.[5] Milton, in his blindness, was therefore returning to a manner of oral dictation coeval with the lost original stages of epic composition, even as it was a culmination of all surviving (because written down) epic. Milton, in short, was a bard because he was blind. This also allowed Milton to present his poem as a series of, as it were, translations: first dictated to Milton in his sleep, *Paradise Lost* was then dictated by him when awake, and only at that point did it materialize as a textual record, a transcript, in a process that perhaps even protects the reader from exposure to the process of divine inspiration.[6]

Although it is true that Milton's technique might be described as that of Lewis's secondary or, better, Fowler's tertiary epic poet, it is clear that Milton was in a special way a writer of primary epic too. He believed in the historical truth of what he was writing; he was memorializing events too serious to be regarded as merely literary; and above all he conceived of himself as returning to, and returning literature to, its primal origins, in the biblical narratives of struggle, loss, and expulsion. Moreover, although Milton had a library and his poetry was correspondingly bookish, by the time he was writing *Paradise Lost* in earnest, he could no longer see to read—reading for Milton of necessity had been replaced by memory and recitation. Without retiring Lewis's distinction, therefore, we may define Milton's epic identity in a different manner. In Chapter 5 we noted that Milton's curriculum was, for want of a more contemporary term, not just humanist but Hellenistic. Indeed, in one important sense Milton, at least as a teacher, was closer to a Hellenistic scholar than a humanist, because he had a particular passion for technical and lexicographical works and projects, and displayed a surprising but comprehensible suspicion of mainstream historical texts. He was attracted to systematic work too, and was busy compiling a systematic theology in a period in which most people had given up doing so.

Milton as an epic poet is Hellenistic too. This may be argued even though the term was not available to Milton, it being our version of the nineteenth-century German "Hellenismus," created to describe the historical period falling between the death of Alexander in 323 BC and the emergence of the Roman Empire. By extension it came to describe the literature of this period, which for Milton signified Greek literature, especially as developed by a core group of writers associated with Alexandria and the Museum founded there, so early modern scholars said, by Ptolemy II Philadelphus. The Museum included the famous library of Alexandria and was the site of the translation of the Torah into Greek, the original Septuagint, following the order of Ptolemy II.[7] The scholarly emphases of these writers under the Ptolemies were three: philology, poetics, and science. The names most obviously associated with these enterprises are Callimachus, Theocritus, Apollonius, Aratus, Lycophron, Eratosthenes, and Archimedes. The library was famous for work in criticism, notably the efforts of Zenodotus in standardizing the text of Homer, and for systematic descriptions of rhetoric and grammar.

Milton was steeped in, and identified with, this tradition. When Milton recommended "Phalereus" on rhetoric in *Of Education,* he meant Demetrius of Phalerum, who worked at the library.[8] As for grammar, the first systematic description of Greek was composed by Dionysius Thrax, the pupil of Aristarchus, and provided the model for all Western grammars up to and including Milton's own published Latin grammar. Callimachus compiled the first bibliography of all Greek writers, and apart from his surviving poetry, he was known to have written a lost work "on the origin and causes of sacred matters, which was entitled *Aitia* [Causes]," which later provided the pattern for Ovid's *Fasti*.[9] Theocritus invented bucolic; Apollonius revived epic; and Aratus (not actually an Alexandrian, but claimed by them as one of theirs) versified the constellations, thereby positioning technical or didactic intent as part of the remit of poetry too. This would later license the poems of, say, Nicander and Oppian, both again authors Milton taught. Lycophron, we saw, was owned and carefully annotated by Milton, and it is hard to understate the influence on Milton's poetics of the trio of Theocritus, Apollonius, and Aratus. Indeed, the original poetic Pleiades in literary history was the Alexandrian Pleiad, numbering among it, depending on which account is followed, Callimachus, Theocritus, Apollonius, Aratus, Nicander, and Lycophron.[10] Milton's strongly technical interests in literature likewise have a Hellenistic feel to them; Milton, as well as being a writer himself, was a student of language: a collator of texts, a grammarian, and a lexicographer.

If we are to seek four signal qualities of the kind of poetry associated with the poets of the Alexandrian Museum, they are, first, a penchant for technical matters, particularly lists (geographical, astronomical, zoological); second, an antiquarian interest in etiology and comparative mythology, often displaying virtuosic scholarship; next, a lexicographical and rhetorical passion for etymology and verbal experimentation; and finally, a resultant self-conscious poetic voice, a narrator aware of himself as such and correspondingly manipulative of his reader. Now it is evident that these are also signal aspects of Miltonic epic style—at once technical, antiquarian, etymological, and all deployed by a narratorial voice insinuating a particularly complex relation to the reader.

This can be illustrated by discussing Milton's relationship with Apollonius of Rhodes, the poet of Jason and the Argonauts, a writer who particularly influenced Milton, something frequently noted by Milton's earlier editors. As a teacher, Milton drilled his students in the four books of the *Argonautica,* and his own quotations from the work show how deeply this Hellenistic epic had taken hold of Milton too, from as early as his academic *prolusiones,* and especially in his blindness, as we saw.[11] Apollonius narrated the voyage of "the well-benched Argo through the mouth of the Pontos and between the Dark Rocks, to gain the golden fleece," as the epic commenced.[12] It was a poem of expulsion, wandering, trials, and a homecoming; it featured, for instance, encounters with a blind seer, a serpent wrapped around an apple tree, the first combat with a robot in Western literature, and a particularly difficult romance between Jason—an epic hero nevertheless capable of weakness, sexual passion, and even depression—and the conflicted Colchian princess and witch Medea.

Apollonius is an antiquarian poet too, his epic replete with etiological myths both astronomical and geographical. He also crafted a narratorial voice of considerable complexity and self-awareness: myths are juxtaposed and debated, and ironies grow up in the gaps between allusion and the readers' encircling knowledge. At the structural level, the *Argonautica* features songs within the song, notably a cosmogony sung by the bard Orpheus, which we examine here and in Chapter 18. The artistry of the whole narrative relies on structural parallelism between the two halves of the poem, turning the *Argonautica* into a kind of narrative circuit, as befits a circular voyage, ending where it began. These are all aspects of Milton's epic and its design too. Of course, much of this is also Virgilian, but the structural role of Apollonius in what was visible of the epic tradition was coming to be appreciated in Milton's time. As Jeremias Hoelzlinus, editor of the major seventeenth-century edition of Apollonius, stated in his preface, "Virgil's *Aeneid* could not have been as it is, had there not been Apollonius," and he followed this with a list of borrowings of incident, theme, and device. Milton may have been Virgilian; but Virgil was Apollonian.[13]

Milton absorbed Apollonius's epic into *Paradise Lost,* and pieces occasionally break the surface, as in the description of Satan's own voyage as more dangerous "then when *Argo* pass'd / Through *Bosporus* betwixt the justling Rocks" (2.1017–18). Satan, indeed, is a kind of Argonaut himself,[14] and a triangulating simile may be found toward the end of the *Argonautica,* when the Argo, trying to find a way out of the river Triton, is likened to a snake turning this way and that.[15] Apollonius's depiction of the blind seer Phineus was also particularly important to Milton, who returned at least three times in his writings to Phineus.

Milton's most virtuosic use of Apollonius, however, seizes on a passage near the beginning of the *Argonautica,* where the bard Orpheus sings of how Ophion and Eurynome first ruled Olympus but were deposed by Cronus and Rhea.[16] Milton transposes and adapts this passage into Book 10 of his epic, discussing how knowledge of the actual Fall was dispersed by the devils into heathen traditions, where it was

> fabl'd how the Serpent, whom they calld
> *Ophion* with *Eurynome,* the wide

Encroaching *Eve* perhaps, had first the rule
Of high *Olympus* thence by *Saturn* [the Latin equivalent of
    Cronus] driv'n
And *Ops* [the Latin equivalent of Rhea] (10.580–84)

Here Milton's equation of Ophion with Satan / the Serpent and Eve with Eurynome brings both of his own falls, angelic and human, into alignment: for "Ophion" (etymologically "serpent") can stand for the serpent of the terrestrial fall, while the mythic allusion is to a pagan report of a primal battle in heaven, a theomachy, and hence by extension to the angelic fall led by the "Old Serpent" of Revelation 12:9. Particularly Hellenistic, too, is the prosodically and etymologically innovative "wide / Encroaching *Eve*," for here the etymology of Eurynome (from εὐρύς, "wide," and νόμος, "law") is transferred to Eve, as a suggestion of how Eve (who is "wide-encroaching" in the sense of, first, one who has transgressed boundaries; and second, of one who has encroached on her posterity by involving them in her sin) could turn into Eurynome. It is a virtuosic piece of transferred epithet, of etymological antiquarianism.

This is in fact one of Milton's most antiquarian references. The earliest surviving references to Ophion and Eurynome in literature available to Milton are in the fragments of Pherecydes of Syros, a sixth-century BC Presocratic philosopher, reported by the Byzantine encyclopedia known as the *Suda* to have written a prose theogony in ten books, based on "the secret books of the Phoenicians"—and he was also reported by the church fathers to have recalled an original cosmic battle between "Ophioneus" and "Kronos."[17] This deep cultural memory of some battle involving a primal serpent was homed in on by mythographers of the Fall. For instance, the Spanish humanist Joannes Ludovicus Vives in his standard commentary on Augustine's *City of God*—printed in most of the better editions of Augustine, in both Latin and English—glossed Augustine's comment that Satan had chosen the serpent as "fit for his work" with *"Pherecides* the Syrian saith the diuells were cast from heaven, and that their chiefe was *Ophioneus,* that is, *Serpentine."*[18] The conflict of Saturn with some atavistic opponent was alluded to in other works probably read by Milton: in the church father Tertullian's *On the Crown,* for instance, Tertullian mentioned how Pherecydes had written of "Saturn" as "crowned" (i.e., with the crown of military victory) before all others, an allusion to his primal victory over an (here unnamed) enemy.[19] The fragments of the earliest Greek philosophy, in other words, themselves bore witness to, at least as far as Milton was concerned, an even earlier drama.

Finally, Milton also seems to have pondered the next surviving epic iteration of the Argonauts, namely the first-century AD *Argonautica* in eight books (probably unfinished) of Valerius Flaccus. This Latin hexameter poem is an imitation of the Greek original, but refocused in turn through a strongly Virgilian lens.[20] Miltonic pieces of Argonautic material are inevitably hard to attribute to a specific version—Homer recalled the Argonauts, as did Theocritus in two odes, and Catullus in parts of the longest of his poems[21]—but two rather striking possibilities have been suggested for indebtedness, specifically, to Valerius.[22] First, Milton's famous simile of Vulcan / Mulciber falling from heaven seems, despite its ultimately Homeric origin, very close indeed to Valerius's version:

> vertice caeli
> devolvit; ruit ille e polo noctemque diemque
> turbinis in morem, Lemni cum litore tandem
> insonuit. (2.88–91)

> [Down from the top of heaven / he [Jove] cast him [Vulcan];
> from the pole he fell, by night and by day, / like a whirlwind,
> when at last he resounded upon the Lemnian shore.]

Milton's account is a slow-motion rewrite of Valerius's already retarding verse, extending "night" and "day" to "Morn . . . Noon . . . Eve . . . A Summers day," and trailing an allusion to Lucifer, a falling star:

> thrown by angry *Jove*
> Sheer o're the Chrystal Battlements; from Morn
> To Noon he fell, from Noon to dewy Eve,
> A Summers day; and with the setting Sun
> Dropt from the Zenith like a falling Star,
> On *Lemnos* th'*Ægæan* Ile: (1.741–76)

The second proposed Miltonic imitation of Valerius concerns the exordium of Milton's epic itself. Epic exordia fall into a number of distinct patterns, to do with the sequencing of how the subject is laid out and how the singer relates himself to the song. Homer, for instance, immediately addressed his muse and stated his subject in his opening lines: "The wrath sing, goddess, of Peleus' son"; "Tell me, O Muse, of that many-sided hero." Virgil opened with his subject and a verb of narration in the first person: "Of arms and the man I sing." This approach—to state the subject, and then to invoke the song, either one's own or that of the muse—can be stretched to a double invocation, such as to a muse and to a patron. Thus Milton in *Paradise Lost* states his subject and follows this by a double invocation:

> Of Mans First Disobedience, and the Fruit
> Of that Forbidden Tree . . .
> Sing Heav'nly Muse, that on the secret top
>     . . .
> And chiefly Thou O Spirit . . .
> Instruct me, for Thou know'st; Thou from the first
> Wast present,
>     . . . What in me is dark
> Illumin, what is low raise and support;
> That to the highth of this great Argument
> I may assert Eternal Providence,
> And justifie the wayes of God to men.

This is much in the manner of Valerius Flaccus. As he opens his epic:

> Prima deum magnis canimus freta pervia natis
> fatidicamque ratem . . .
> Phoebe, mone . . .
>         . . . tuque o, pelagi cui maior aperti
> fama, Caledonius postquam tua carbasa vexit
> oceanus . . .
> eripe me populis et habenti nubila terrae,
> sancte pater, veterumque fave veneranda canenti
> facta virum.
>             . . . nunc nostra serenus
> orsa iuves, haec ut Latias vox impleat urbes.

[The first straits navigated by the mighty sons of gods I sing,
and of the prophetic ship . . .
Phoebus, be thou my guide . . .
. . . and thou too, that didst win still greater glory for opening
up the sea, after the Caledonian ocean had borne thy sails . . .
do thou, holy sire, raise me above the nations and the cloud-
wrapped earth, and be favourable unto me as I hymn the
wondrous deeds of old time heroes. . . .
Look kindly now on me and aid my essay, that the sound of
my voice may fill the cities of Latium.]

Note how Valerius, as Milton, states his subject immediately, but as a double subject ("straights" / "prophetic ship"; "disobedience" / "fruit"). Note too how both poets emphasize the foundational nature of their narratives by placing "first" in the first line—indeed in Valerius "first" is the first word of his poem. (This in turn imitates Apollonius's first words, "ἀρχόμενος σέο" [first thou].) Valerius calls on Phoebus and then the emperor Vespasian ("tuque o," itself an allusion to the Virgilian exordium to the first Georgic [1.12]); Milton on the (perhaps identical) "Heav'nly Muse" and "Thou O Spirit." These might be regarded as coincidental echoes, but Valerius's "raise me above the nations and the cloud-wrapped earth" finds a surer Miltonic parallel in "what is low raise and support . . . to the highth of this great-Argument," and both conclude by promising the achievement that will flow from such assistance: "that the sound of my voice may fill the cities of Latium," "That . . . / I may assert Eternal Providence, / And justifie the wayes of God to men."

There are differences between the two epic exordia, of course, and these further fix Milton's precise project. Pagan Valerius will sing himself (*canimus*), the verb used by Virgil (*cano*), Lucan (*canimus*), and Statius (*canam*). Milton, in the manner of Homer, Hesiod, and the more recent Christian bard, calls for someone else to sing, to educate him ("Sing Heav'nly Muse," "Instruct me"). Although Milton and Valerius both emphasize the "first" things, Milton, digging under and against his source, knows who was really there in the beginning—"*Thou* from the first."

# 17

## Military Epic

THE CENTRAL BOOKS of *Paradise Lost* are a nested epic, indeed two epics, Books 5 and 6 being a poem of angelic rebellion and war, followed in Books 7 and 8 by a poem of creation, all narrated by the angel Raphael. These epics within an epic are delivered to Adam and Eve after an Edenic meal prepared by Eve, fruitarian and nonalcoholic:

> fruit of all kindes, in coate,
> Rough, or smooth rin'd, or bearded husk, or shell
> She gathers, Tribute large, and on the board
> Heaps with unsparing hand; for drink the Grape
> She crushes, inoffensive moust, and meathes
> From many a berrie, and from sweet kernels prest
> She tempers dulcet creams (5.341–47)

Milton's calm repast in Eden shuns the luxury of epic feasting:

> Rais'd of grassie terf
> Thir Table was, and mossie seats had round,

And on her ample Square from side to side
All *Autumn* pil'd, though *Spring* and *Autumn* here
Danc'd hand in hand. A while discourse they hold;
No fear lest Dinner coole (5.391–96)

The meal is significant, for in placing Raphael's narration after eating, Milton signals that he is imitating one of the oldest epic narrative strategies, that of the poem delivered after a dinner.[1] This is one of the richest implied genealogies in Milton's epic and merits full digestion. Indeed, Milton prompts us to pause, for the passage immediately before the one just quoted runs

Whatever Earth all-bearing Mother yields
In *India* East or West, or middle shoare
In *Pontus* or the *Punic* Coast, or where
*Alcinous* reign'd (5.338–41)

"Pontus" is another allusion to Apollonius of Rhodes's *Argonautica*, where the Argo navigates that distant coast and receives the hospitality of the Colchians far in the northeast; "Punic" is a reference to Carthage, of Punic (Phoenician) origin, where Aeneas and his men tarry; and "Alcinous" is the ruler of Phaeacia (Scheria), who entertains Odysseus in Homer's *Odyssey*. These were places where meals were had—opulent, carnivorous, and boozy—and after which epic songs were sung.

The second of Milton's nested epics, his scientific poem of Creation in Books 7 and 8, is examined in Chapter 18; here we concentrate on the first part of the subnarration, Milton's military epic of War in Heaven, a somewhat incongruous story for naked and unarmed Adam and Eve, before this point quite ignorant even of the concept of battle. And whereas for his scientific section Milton had as his guide a long tradition of hexameral epic rooted in the opening chapter of the Bible, for the War in Heaven he had almost no biblical sources at all and therefore relied on the machinery of the pagan epics of war. The War in Heaven rested almost entirely on just three verses of the Bible, Revelation 12:7–9:

And there was war in heaven: Michael and his angels fought
against the dragon; and the dragon fought and his angels,

And prevailed not; neither was their place found any more in
    heaven.
And the great dragon was cast out, that old serpent, called the
    Devil, and Satan, which deceiveth the whole world: he was
    cast out into the earth, and his angels were cast out with
    him.

On this slight foundation Milton raised much of his war effort, as had many
Christian poets before him, and he found his infrastructure in a tradition
rooted in the epics recounting divine (Hesiod, Claudian, Nonnus) as well as
human (Homer, Virgil, Lucan) battling, culminating in various early modern
poems, chiefly in Latin and Italian.[2] And although Milton's decision to
include the War in Heaven has strong precedent, at least one other contemporary English hexameral poet considered the angelic rebellion to be
something on which, as the scriptures were almost silent, we should be silent
too: "But circumstances that we cannot know / Of their rebellion and their
overthrow / We will not dare t'invent."[3]

Raphael narrates the War in Heaven to Adam because God tells him
to do so. As Milton states in the prose "Argument" set before the fifth
book,

God to render Man inexcusable sends Raphael to admonish
him of his obedience, of his free estate, of his enemy near at
hand; who he is, and why his enemy, and whatever else may
avail Adam to know.

"*Why* his enemy"—God wants Adam and Eve to be in full possession of the
historical facts, so that when they do fall, they cannot plead ignorance of
the causes and consequences. Raphael acknowledges the difficulty and
danger of his task, promises that he will use simile where "human sense"
would otherwise be baffled, but also suggests that Heaven and Earth might
not be so totally different:

how last unfould
The secrets of another world, perhaps
Not lawful to reveal? yet for thy good
This is dispenc't, and what surmounts the reach

Of human sense, I shall delineate so,
By lik'ning spiritual to corporal forms,
As may express them best, though what if Earth
Be but the shaddow of Heav'n, and things therein
Each to other like, more then on earth is thought? (5.568–76)

Raphael does not answer his rhetorical question, but Milton's materialism would indeed entail that heavenly reality is at least not incomprehensible to man—angels are after all made out of matter just as people are, albeit more rarefied.

Nevertheless, there are two audiences for Raphael's martial epic, and the kinds of reactions they can have slightly differ. The first audience is of course Adam, and this poem is performed for him in order to explain who Satan is, and how he and his crew fell through their own wickedness and were justly crushed. This is therefore the structural counterpart to the spurious epics sung by the demons in Hell, who "complain that Fate / Free Vertue should enthrall to Force or Chance" (1.550–51). The second audience is the fallen reader, who unlike Adam has a full knowledge of warfare, the history of warfare, and the literary history of that warfare. This reader cannot but help find the whole conflict rather surreal, differing from real warfare in several crucial respects; and this reader may also suspect, as many have, that Milton is therefore passing judgment on the literary traditions of battle poetry and on the ethics of such traditions.

The War in Heaven is narrated across Books 5 and 6, and is the direct outcome of God's Exaltation of his Son. After the Exaltation, there is dancing, and after dancing the hungry angels dine, in circles. Then Heaven sleeps, with the exception of God, the angels who sing in turns around God's throne—and the discontented angel who will after his fall be known as Satan. Satan, disliking what he calls God's "new Laws," thereon inspires rebellion, and draws with him a third of the heavenly host, setting up camp in the northern parts of Heaven. God and his Son laugh to themselves at Satan's plans, and Satan himself faces the challenge of the constant seraphim Abdiel, who, when he realizes Satan's actual intentions, rebukes him and returns south to the faithful. This act of free angelic decision making and loyalty concludes the fifth book, underlining that the angels, like Adam and Eve, are responsible for their own actions.

Abdiel arrives back to find that preparations for war are already underway, and God, after praising Abdiel's faithfulness, instructs Michael and Gabriel to lead the godly troops. Battle is joined, with Abdiel and Satan exchanging just words, and then Michael and Satan exchanging words and blows, much to the latter's disadvantage. The first day's fighting concludes with victory to the virtuous; but the fallen angels, in temporary withdrawal, make the technological leap forward of inventing ordnance, which in the second day's fighting looks, initially, as if it might give them the edge. Here the fighting, having leapt forward technologically, now becomes intermingled with the literary topoi of *gigantomachia*, accounts of primordial warfare between gods and giants, as mountains are uprooted by the righteous angels and thrown back at the wicked. This sets the stage for the final intervention. Up until this point, the fallen third of heaven has faced a numerically equal, unfallen third; but now God, who has reserved the final unfallen third for this intervention, sends his Son in his chariot to conquer, and the Son indeed vanquishes Satan, driving him and his party into Hell, and returning in triumph to Heaven. (Earlier, in Book 2, Chaos had recalled this endgame, seen, however, from below, as it were.)

The fighting itself is a confection of classical combat maneuvers, translated and amplified by Milton with extraordinary dexterity. *Acies,* for instance, means in Latin both the edge of a blade and an army in battle array, ready to charge, as in Virgil's "Haud aliter Trojanæ Acies, Aciesque Latinæ / Concurrunt" (Not otherwise did the Trojan edge and the Latin edge rush together). Milton finds both meanings at once with his "On the rough edge of battle" (5.108).[4] Again, his "Clashing bray'd, horrible discord" is a virtuosic combination of "clashing" from *klazein* and "bray'd" from *brachein,* two noisy battle verbs from Homer. The swordplay between Michael and Satan is Miltonic technique at its most kinetic:

> it [Michael's sword] met
> The sword of *Satan* with steep force to smite
> Descending, and in half cut sheere, nor staid,
> But with swift wheele reverse, deep entring shar'd
> All his right side; then *Satan* first knew pain,
> And writh'd him to and fro convolv'd; so sore

The griding sword with discontinuous wound
Pass'd through him (6.323–30)

There is even a touch of Spenserian diction here—"griding" for "cutting"
appears in *The Faerie Queene,* as in "To her weapon run in mind to gride / The
loathed leacher."[5] Such diction implicates the poem in chivalric action, which
is important because Milton will later disown such models of heroism.

This passage, however, also illustrates the weirdness of the fighting. The
unfallen angels do not feel pain, and angelic bodies are anyway all slightly
permeable, something just audible in "shar'd" above, which means primarily "sheared," as of a solid, but still carries the more ordinary "shared" as
the sword enters Satan's body like a knife into jelly. Homer's warriors die of
their wounds, but his immortal gods when punctured bleed not blood but
ichor, and can be healed by balms that coagulate to seal up wounds.[6] Milton's
Satan, with only a small leak, similarly self-heals:

but th'Ethereal substance clos'd
Not long divisible, and from the gash
A stream of Nectarous humor issuing flow'd
Sanguin, such as Celestial Spirits may bleed. (6.330–33)

The demonic invention of cannon again builds on a passage in Spenser,
who in a simile had pointed to the "divelish" origins of the "yron Engin," a
combination that would soon become inevitable in English poetry following
the Gunpowder Plot of 1605.

As when that divelish yron Engin wrought
In deepest Hell, and framd by Furies skill,
With windy Nitre and quick Sulphur fraught,
And ramd with bullet round, ordaind to kill,
Conceiveth fire, the heavens it doth fill
With thundring noyse[7]

So in Milton's war, Satan, questioned by the battle-shattered Nisroc, tells
how the earth will yield "materials dark and crude, / Of spiritous and fierie
spume,"

> Which into hollow Engins long and round
> Thick-rammd, at th'other bore with touch of fire
> Dilated and infuriate shall send forth
> From far with thundring noise among our foes
> Such implements of mischief as shall dash
> To pieces (6.478–79, 484–89)

Milton breaks and resets elements of Spenser's stanza, repositioning "Engins," "rammd," "fire," and "thundering noise," as Satan explains his new invention to his delighted troops. The Satanic cannon is initially effective: the triple-barreled weapons are concealed within the ranks of the fallen angels, marching "in hollow Cube," and then revealed as the front lines part to either side. The effect only seems devastating: "down they fell / By thousands, Angel on Arch-Angel rowl'd" (593–94). But Raphael adds that this was really just because the good angels were wearing their encumbering armor—otherwise they might easily have dodged, or miniaturized themselves (595–97). So after this initial setback, the angels remove their armor, and, paradoxically restored to full strength by disarming, they find a way to put a stop to the bombardment:

> They pluckt the seated Hills with all thir load,
> Rocks, Waters, Woods, and by the shaggie tops
> Up lifting bore them in thir hands (644–46)

These they drop on their enemy, crushing devils and cannon together. The devils too are hurt by their armor, and as their bodies become more densely material through their sin, they find it harder, but not impossible, to shapeshift out of their plight. As the war moves into this new phase of mountain throwing, God and his Son intervene for victory on the third day, the Son swooping in at the head of a vast army on his extraordinary chariot, a vehicle "instinct with Spirit" (752), but also borne by four four-faced cherubs.

Much of this may sound surreal and even burlesque, but Milton was drawing on biblical texts and current exegesis of such texts, especially Revelation, for the details of his battle. The division of the citizens of heaven into thirds rests on Revelation 12:4; the removing to the north on Isaiah 14:13; the throwing of mountains Luke 23:30 and Revelation 6:16; and the

Son on his throne-chariot is closely modeled on the visions of Ezekiel 1:4–27. Even the miniature gunpowder epyllion had received biblical sanction, namely the exegesis of Revelation 9:17–18 on the lion-headed horses: "and out of their mouths issued fire and smoke and brimstone." Joseph Mede in his celebrated *Clavis* or "Key" to Revelation had interpreted these verses as predictive of ordnance, specifically the cannon used by the Turks in their 1453 capture of Constantinople: "that new kinde of instruments of war . . . I meane gunnes sending forth fire, smoak and brimstone." Milton was simply applying this reading retrospectively, helped along his way by precedents in Ariosto as well as Spenser, as well as the gunpowder poem tradition, in which he too of course had written poems.[8] In the early eighteenth century Joseph Addison anticipated the objections of many modern critics who have found the battle too close to burlesque by comparing it with the Latin poet Claudian's fragmentary epic, the *Gigantomachia*. Claudian's thrown pieces of land could easily appear burlesque: the whole river Enipeus, for instance, is scooped out and tossed like a grenade, wetting the giant bearing it; and the isle of Lemnos is torn up with Vulcan's smithy still burning inside it. Addison rightly remarked that Milton toned down this kind of thing.[9]

Milton's treatment, however, also intersects with the tradition that the Fall is connected with technological innovation, of science in its darker ethical form. This is a Promethean motif, that story itself often interpreted as a paganization of older Jewish myths about the angels who corrupted men by teaching them the arts and sciences.[10] There is a hint of this in Eden too, where prelapsarian food is fresh and uncut, and the technology of cooking by fire will have to be discovered by fallen Adam. Fallen Adam also receives in his visions from Michael accounts of the discoveries of his descendants, who develop metalwork by observing the properties of forest fires, or ores washed out by rivers (11.566–70).

Nevertheless, the War in Heaven continues to disturb. There may be precedents for it, biblical and literary. But Milton's astonishing battle poetry is unnerving to the fallen reader because we can see, as Adam cannot, that several different kinds of warfare, literary and real, are taking place all at once. The language is initially of classical and medieval warfare—swords are the chief weapons, but arrows are also mentioned twice (6.546, 845). The angels fight hand-to-hand, again as in classical epic. But the invention of cannon then suddenly modernizes the conflict, bringing it into the age of gunpowder. We cannot forget that Milton had just lived through the Bishops' Wars

(1639–1640), the Scottish Civil War (1644–1651), the Irish Confederate Wars (1641–1653), the three English Civil Wars (1642–1651), and then war with the Dutch, twice (1652–1654, 1665–1667), by the publication of *Paradise Lost*. The Wars of the Three Kingdoms, the name often given to the totality of the civil conflicts between 1639 and 1651, saw the first serious use of cannon on English soil. Yet when the English fired their cannons at one another, they were, unlike the angels, ripped to shreds: at the royalist storming of Leicester in May 1645, for instance, Colonel St George and his company "in a bravery" approached right up to the cannon's mouth—and were "by it shotter'd into small parcels." The same battle also saw the use of handguns and "hand-granadoes," which "terribly burnt our men."[11] The wounds inflicted by cannon in particular were horrific: the larger pieces fired balls, but the smaller ones were often loaded with bags of shrapnel and nails. Milton has Raphael look specifically into the future of this kind of warfare when he breaks his narration to address Adam directly:

> yet haply of thy Race
> In future dayes, if Malice should abound,
> Some one intent on mischief, or inspir'd
> With dev'lish machination might devise
> Like instrument to plague the Sons of men
> For sin, on warr and mutual slaughter bent. (501–6)

"Mutual slaughter"—this is a reference not to some Ottoman assault on the walls of Constantinople but to intestine, civil war.

Yet all this technology is then in turn erased by mythic *gigantomachia,* a sacred reworking of Claudian's poem, which commences with the Earth herself telling her giants to rip her apart and throw her parts at their common enemy, the gods: "sunt freta, sunt montes: nostris ne parcite membris" (Here are seas, here are mountains: spare not the limbs of my body).[12] Finally, the Son on his chariot is a vision from the Old Testament, and he sweeps away not just Satan and his crew, but war itself. Swords, cannons, and even mountains now seem puny, even preferable fates to this, as the vanquished angels lament (6.839–43, an echo of Revelation 6:16: "And [they] said to the mountains and rocks, Fall on us, and hide us from the face of him that sitteth on the throne, and from the wrath of the Lamb"). Milton's War in Heaven, then, collapses in on itself, a bizarre synchronism of all wars past and present, imagined or real. Raphael's epic of war is itself then superseded by his epic of Creation; and, finally, the Miltonic narrator turns his back on battle poetry itself in the invocation to Book 9:

> Not sedulous by Nature to indite
> Warrs, hitherto the onely Argument
> Heroic deem'd, chief maistrie to dissect
> With long and tedious havoc fabl'd Knights
> In Battels feign'd (9.27–31)

This is on the surface of it a rejection of the chivalric tradition of Boiardo, Ariosto, Tasso, and indeed Spenser, all poets hitherto dear to Milton. Now he forces his narrator to reject them, and with that rejection too comes, inevitably, an ethical judgment on his own enforced war music.[13]

Before concluding this chapter, let us digress briefly on what we first hear about the War in Heaven at the beginning of the poem, for we are prepared for the battle by witnessing its aftermath. This is our first experience in the poem as readers, for the fallen angels of the opening two books are singed with defeat, and their language and activity is marked by the war just fought and lost. One of the more subtle indications of this is musical: the fallen angels "move / In perfect phalanx to the Dorian mood / Of flutes and soft recorders" (1.549–50), whereas before the fall the loyal angels are inspired, we later learn, by "instrumental harmony" (6.65) as they prepare for conflict. The devils, therefore, are described as listening to ancient music, modal ("mood") and monomelodic, while the angels in contrast are listening to harmonic or contrapuntal music, that is music written in several different parts, all interweaving. This is music as Milton heard and played it—we might imagine Milton Senior's own five- and six-part fantasias in the contrapuntal style, the Italianate and rather retrospective *prima practica*.[14] For a moment the devils therefore sound as if they have slipped back a little in time, musically devolved in falling.

Nevertheless we later learn that the devils do retain musical knowledge of harmony even after their fall:

> Thir Song was partial, but the harmony
> (What could it less when Spirits immortal sing?)
> Suspended Hell (2.552–54)

So when he has his demons marching to soft recorders Milton is gesturing to something other than just modal music. The allusion, in fact, is not just to "Dorian" as the mode suitable, as Plato had said, for "the utterances and the accents of a brave man who is engaged in warfare or in any enforced business," but to a famous passage on the Spartans in Thucydides, and to Aulus Gellius's discussion of this passage in the *Noctes Atticæ*.[15] Gellius's subject is war music, and he observes that it was part of the awesome discipline of the Spartans that, rather than the blare of trumpets and horns, the Spartans heard softer flutes or pipes (*tibiæ*) as they marched into battle. This was to calm the warriors down, so that "by this quiet, pleasant, and even solemn prelude the fierce impetuosity of the soldiers was checked."

Some of the devils do need to calm down. In Hell, some form inconclusive philosophical discussion groups, while others compose epic poems on their own defeat:

> Others more milde,
> Retreated in a silent valley, sing
> With notes Angelical to many a Harp
> Thir own Heroic deeds and hapless fall
> By doom of Battel (1.546–50)

But the wilder sort stage Olympic games, both on the ground and in the air (1.528–32, 546–51, 557–61), while still others

> with vast *Typhoean* rage more fell
> Rend up both Rocks and Hills, and ride the Air
> In whirlwind; Hell scarce holds the wilde uproar. (2.539–41)

Typhon or Typhoeus was the many-handed, many-headed monster who warred, unsuccessfully, against Zeus,[16] and the rending of rocks and hills is an early hint of *gigantomachia*. The devils here, as if stuck in the rut of their own defeat, reenact the battle they have just lost.

One of the earliest reactions to Milton's War in Heaven was the Latin poem by Samuel Barrow, one of the two poems—the other was Andrew Marvell's English effort—placed before the second edition of *Paradise Lost* (1674). Barrow spent most of his poem thundering forth on Milton's battle in tones that show that, for him at least, this was the fulcrum of Milton's achievement. But just over a century after *Paradise Lost* had first been published, Samuel Johnson snorted at the War in Heaven in his deeply ambivalent treatment of Milton in the *Lives of the Poets* (1769–1771). Earlier readers, however, had also spotted problems. One thought the whole thing quite impious, a collision of the "gravity and seriousness" of the subject with "the adventrous flight of Poets," resulting only in "romantick Battels in the Plains of Heaven, a scene of licentious fancy."[17] Conversely, what worried another reader was that the imaginative success of the War in Heaven ran the risk of misleading us into believing it as doctrine.[18] This success depended partly on its technological modernism, prompting the ironic remark of this reader (the inventor Sir Samuel Morland, writing in 1695) that "one of these Armies dug up the Terrain of Heaven, and with the Materials they there found, made Powder, Bullets and great Guns (it is a pity that Bombs were not in use when he wrote that Treatise)."[19] For Morland, Milton was "a late very learned Author" who was nonetheless in such descriptions "Lude[ns] cum Sacris" (playing with sacred things) in the manner of "Poets and Painters." Note the fascinating slippage here. For Milton was of course a poet, yet Morland presents him as a "learned Author" writing a "Treatise," a sign that Milton's theological seriousness was causing at least this reader to become confused about what kind of activity Milton was performing. This was precisely the worry of our first reader above, the Nonjuror Charles Leslie, who equally feared the conflation of the divine with the poetic. The Jacobean-Caroline poet and playwright Thomas Heywood, in this respect, had been careful in his lengthy poem *The Hierarchie of the Blessed Angels* to stress the allegorical nature of the war in heaven—no actual "Lances, Swords, nor Bombards."[20] Finally, Morland's intensely visual reaction to the War in Heaven is rendered all the more fascinating by the fact that he was himself blind when he wrote this reaction—he, like Milton, may well therefore have only heard *Paradise Lost* read aloud.

# 18

## Scientific Epic

T HE FALL OF the angels leaves Heaven perhaps feeling a little empty, as God jests, but he immediately rejects the idea that there is any necessity for him to repopulate his territory. Nevertheless, eventual repopulation is God's plan, as he soon explains, moving from a grammar of possibility ("can") to one of intent ("will"):

> I can repaire
> That detriment, if such it be to lose
> Self-lost, and in a moment will create
> Another World, out of one man a Race
> Of men innumerable, there to dwell,
> Not here, till by degrees of merit rais'd
> They open to themselves at length the way
> Up hither (7.152–59)

God thus tasks his Son with the creation of Heaven and Earth, and this is the cosmogony of the seventh book of *Paradise Lost*, the hexameron at the center of the poem, a song of creation after a song of war. In a typical Miltonic temporal inversion, this hexameron, narrated by Raphael, is of course based on, but temporally precedes, the exposition of Moses himself in the first chapter of Genesis. Milton, in a prolepsis for Raphael's later narration, had in fact encoded in miniature Moses's cosmological poem in the exordium to the entire epic:

> That Shepherd, who first taught the chosen Seed,
> In the Beginning how the Heav'ns and Earth
> Rose out of *Chaos*    (1.8–10)

At the beginning of Chapter 17, it was shown how the sequencing of Raphael's narration after a meal is significant: after the feast comes the epic poem. Raphael tells first of war and then of creation, but in fact the two traditions, martial and scientific, had long been intertwined in epic and in epic commentary. This intertwining is of such fundamental structural importance to both the epic tradition and to Milton's manipulations of it that the bulk of this chapter is given over to an analysis of why and how war and creation traditionally interacted. It also returns us to the fundamental fact of Milton's self-presentation as a poet, namely his inspired blindness.

In the eighth book of the *Odyssey*, the bard Demodocus sings three songs at an extended feast. The first and last recount stories from the Trojan War, visibly upsetting Odysseus; the middle one, after an athletic contest in the middle of the feast, relates the affair of Ares and Aphrodite, caught and trapped in his net by Aphrodite's husband, the lame forge-god Hephaestus. Demodocus, as was discussed in an earlier chapter, was commonly thought of as blind, robbed of his sight by the Muses. He is thus Milton's archetype inside the epic tradition.

The performance of Demodocus was then imitated in the *Argonautica* of Apollonius, which early on features a quarrel at a feast, soothed by a poem, this time not of human or divine strife, but of cosmogony and astronomy. After dinner, to mollify an argument between Idas the Argonaut, who stands for force and bluster, and Idmon the seer, a man of introspection and intelligence, the bard Orpheus takes up his lyre and defuses the situation with music:

> ἤειδεν δ᾽ ὡς γαῖα καὶ οὐρανὸς ἠδὲ θάλασσα,
> τὸ πρὶν ἐπ᾽ ἀλλήλοισι μιῇ συναρηρότα μορφῇ,

νείκεος ἐξ ὀλοοῖο διέκριθεν ἀμφὶς ἕκαστα·
ἠδ᾽ ὡς ἔμπεδον αἰὲν ἐν αἰθέρι τέκμαρ ἔχουσιν
ἄστρα σεληναίη τε καὶ ἠελίοιο κέλευθοι·
οὔρεά θ᾽ ὡς ἀνέτειλε, καὶ ὡς ποταμοὶ κελάδοντες
αὐτῇσιν νύμφῃσι καὶ ἑρπετὰ πάντ᾽ ἐγένοντο.[1]

[He sang of how the earth, the heavens, and the sea—
Once upon a time united with each other in a single form—
Were sundered apart by deadly strife:
And how a position fixed for eternity in the sky is held
By the stars and the paths of the moon and the sun:
How the mountains rose up, and the origin of sounding rivers
With their own nymphs, and all creatures on the ground.]

The whole passage, "a kind of cosmic overture to the poem,"[2] is a close imitation of its Homeric antecedent, and in turn it is the source of Virgil's transformation of Homer's heroic wandering bard Demodocus into the more mysterious figure, as we shall see, of Punic Iopas. Furthermore the cosmological song of Orpheus resonates on into Milton's epic with a surprising, retrospective harmonic, for in the Christian tradition Creation was indeed "sundered apart by deadly strife," namely the angelic rebellion.[3]

Milton's nearest inspiration, however, is from the *Aeneid,* where all these traditions, and more, converge. At the end of the first book, once again after a meal,

> cithara crinitus Iopas
> personat aurata, docuit quem maximus Atlas.
> hic canit errantem lunam solisque labores,
> unde hominum genus et pecudes, unde imber et ignes,
> Arcturum pluuiasque Hyadas geminosque Triones,
> quid tantum Oceano properent se tingere soles
> hiberni, uel quae tardis mora noctibus obstet.

> [long-haired Iopas
> Sounds the golden lyre, he whom great Atlas taught.
> He sings of the wandering moon, and of the sun's labors,
> Whence the races of men and beasts, whence rain and fire,
> Of Arcturus, the rainy Hyades, and the Two Bears,

Why in winter suns so hurry to dip themselves
In Ocean; and what delay retards the slow nights.]

Iopas is described as "crinitus" (long-haired), the attribute of Apollo, but his song is seemingly even more scientific than that of Apollonius's Orpheus, underscored by the reference to Atlas, here the legendary inventor of astrology and astronomy.[4] Through this description Virgil was also here alluding to the evergreen Aratus as the poet of constellations and weather signs, and perhaps also—especially through the line "unde hominum genus et pecudes, unde imber et ignes" (whence the races of men and beasts, whence rain and fire)—to the more recent scientific poem of Lucretius, Virgil's elder contemporary.[5]

Additionally, the passage refers to Virgil himself, much as blind Demodocus was often interpreted as a Homeric self-reference. For Virgil had earlier manipulated the idea of nested poems in his pastoral *Eclogues*. The sixth eclogue, for instance, opens with talk of martial poetry—"reges et proelia" (kings and battles)—but when Silenus actually commences his song within an eclogue, he starts once again with cosmogony, reminding us of the oldest Greek cosmogony, Hesiod's poem of that name:

Namque canebat uti magnum per inane coacta
semina terrarumque animaeque marisque fuissent
et liquidi simul ignis; ut his exordia primis
omnia, et ipse tener mundi concreuerit orbis[6]

[For he sang how, through the great void, seeds
Of earth, and soul, and sea, and liquid fire
Were gathered together; how from these elements
All things arose, and the young globe of the world itself grew]

Virgil then seals the Hesiodic origin of this eclogue by Silenus's reference to "the old Ascraean," Hesiod himself, Ascra being his birthplace.[7]

Virgil in the Iopas passage is also, however, directly quoting verses from his own *Georgics*, specifically from the second, where they can be found embedded in a self-referential passage:

Me uero primum dulces ante omnia Musae,
quarum sacra fero ingenti percussus amore,

accipiant caelique uias et sidera monstrent,
defectus solis uarios lunaeque labores;
unde tremor terris, qua ui maria alta tumescant
obicibus ruptis rursusque in se ipsa residant,
quid tantum Oceano properent se tingere soles
hiberni, uel quae tardis mora noctibus obstet.[8]

[Let the Muses, sweet to me before all things,
Whose secrets I bear, struck with a huge love,
Receive me, and show the ways of the heavens and the stars,
The defects of the sun, and the varying labors of the moon;
Whence earthquakes, by what force the high seas swell
Over protruding rocks, and again retreat upon themselves,
Why in winter suns so hurry to dip themselves
In Ocean, and what delay retards the slow nights.]

It might seem, therefore, that the trajectory of the nested narration in epic moves from the heroic to something closer to the cosmogonic / scientific.[9] And this is exactly what happens in *Paradise Lost,* as Raphael moves from the War in Heaven to the Creation.

The interesting complication is that quite early on in Homeric criticism there developed an allegorical method of reading Homer's myths, whereby seemingly heroic actions in fact stood for cosmic principles. For instance, the second song of Demodocus in the *Odyssey,* the one narrating the story of Ares and Aphrodite, was interpreted as an allegory for how the forces of Love and Strife led to the Creation. Part of the original motivation here was to exonerate Homer from the charge of impiety, and Virgil himself was fully aware of this tradition of pious allegorism. The seeming contrast between the heroic and the scientific, in other words, was in this tradition merely that, *seeming;* behind the former lay the latter, and "the ideal Homeric bard thus stands revealed as a cosmologer."[10] This approach was revived in the early modern period, and editions of ancient exponents of this allegorical school of criticism proliferated, for instance the *Homeric Problems* of the fourth-century BC philosopher Heraclides of Pontus, which Milton studied too.

A final complexity of the Virgilian reworking is the ethnic location of this particular banquet and bard. Iopas appears at a Carthaginian banquet, and Carthage was a Punic colony. The substitution of more obviously entertaining tales of heroism with an austere kind of scientific poetry has in its sights a Roman sense that Carthaginian civilization, destroyed by the Romans at the conclusion of the Third Punic War, had developed in a different direction, and that their literature had tended to the technical or scientific. Virgil himself probably picked this idea up from the elder Pliny, who recalled that the libraries of Carthage had been handed over by the victorious Romans as a gift to the petty kings of Africa, with the one condition that the twenty-eight books of "Mago" on agriculture be translated from Punic into Latin. Pliny makes frequent reference to this Mago, as do the Roman *authores de re rustica*.[11]

Milton's own knowledge of all these texts and traditions was total. To start with Demodocus himself, Milton recalled exactly this poet and his effect in one of his college poems, "At a Vacation Exercise," itself spoken amid a feast:

> Such as the wise *Demodocus* once told
> In solemn Songs at King *Alcinous* feast,
> While sad *Ulisses* soul and all the rest
> Are held with his melodious harmonie
> In willing chains and sweet captivitie.[12]

Even in this student poem, Milton's cosmological ordering is apparent. Envisaging a true epic subject, he imagines his muse starting with the gods and passing to the deeds of men via a kind of scientific poetry closer to Hesiod than to Homer. There is even a sense of primeval strife:

> tell[ing] at length how green-ey'd *Neptune* raves,
> In Heav'ns defiance mustering all his waves;
> Then sing of secret things that came to pass
> When Beldam Nature in her cradle was (43–47)

The whole passage, moreover, is instinct with the Virgilian passage from the *Georgics* cited above—note the correspondence between Virgil's "sacra" and Milton's "secret things."

As for the influence of the cosmogonic poetry of Hesiod—whose poetry, as we have seen, furnished Milton with not only his cosmology but also models for several episodes, including that of Sin and Death[13]—it is crucial to recognize that Milton's age tended to suspect that Hesiod, with his tales

of creation and cultivation, represented an earlier stage of human development than Homer. Julius Caesar Scaliger, for instance, declared Hesiod Homer's senior, albeit assuming that they were roughly contemporary. The debate
concerning the respective antiquity of Hesiod and Homer was then given
a fillip in Milton's time by the English scholar John Selden, hailed by Milton
as "the chief of learned men reputed in this Land."[14] In 1628 Selden published his *Marmora Arundeliana,* an edition of a collection of inscribed stones
recently acquired from overseas by the Earl of Arundel. The most famous
of these stones, still on display today in Oxford's Ashmolean Museum, and
which Selden boasted he had deciphered by means of that new invention
the microscope, was and is still known as the Parian Marble, from the island where this distinctive kind of white marble was quarried. On this stone
are recorded memorable events stretching, seemingly, from the sixteenth
century BC to the period of the marble's own carving, in the fourth century
BC. The Parian Marble, the oldest Greek record of its kind, placed both
Hesiod and Homer as early as the tenth century, yet it awarded Hesiod
priority in time over Homer by about a generation.[15]

Modern scholars accept neither this dating nor this sequencing, but in
artistic terms the early modern acceptance of the priority of Hesiod over
Homer suggested once again that the most primal kinds of poetry were,
therefore, cosmogonic (Hesiod's *Theogony*) and georgic (Hesiod's *Works and
Days*). A striking dramatization of this decision occurs in the Neo-Greek
biblical epic on Esther, the *Aulikokatoptron* ("Courtier-Mirror," 1679), by Milton's younger contemporary the Cambridge scholar and poet Joshua Barnes.
In Barnes's epic, a Persian court bard called Terpsimbrotus sings, again at a
feast, of the wars in heaven, and of the creation of the world from Chaos,
and of how the elements arose one from another—a performance influenced by both Genesis and Hesiod, as well as the performances of Orpheus
and Iopas in Apollonius and Virgil, respectively.[16] This assumption that the
earliest datable poetry dealt with the earliest known times was only strengthened by early modern encounters with other ancient Near Eastern myths
of creation.

Milton was deeply engaged with both Apollonius and Aratus; we have
encountered his manipulations of the former, and in his own copy of the latter
he cross references it with Lucretius at the crucial line 5 of Aratus, the one
quoted by the Apostle Paul to the Athenians ("For in him we live, and
move, and have our being; as certain also of your own poets have said, For

we are also his offspring," Acts 17:28).[17] We also know that Milton studied the major surviving exponent of the allegorical approach to Homer, Heraclides of Pontus, for in 1637 he purchased the *Allegoriæ in Homeri fabulas de diis* ("Allegories in Homer's Stories about the Gods," usually known today as the *Homeric Problems*) in the Basel, 1544 edition; this copy of Milton's again survives. In this text, many of the classic epic episodes received philosophical explanation—the fall of Vulcan / Mulciber from heaven, for instance, is interpreted as allegorizing the distinction between the pure element of fire and fire as encountered on earth.[18] Even though the Phaeacians were slaves to pleasure, Heraclides argued, there is philosophy in their song, and he reports too the interpretation mentioned above, that Ares in Demodocus's song is truly the principle of *Neikos* (Strife), and Aphrodite the force of *Philia* (Love), an attempt to read the passage as a cipher for a specifically Empedoclean physics of creation. Heraclides even wondered if the passage were not also a technological allegory for working at the forge.

Despite the suggestive evidence provided by Pliny and the agricultural writers, it is hard to know what Virgil made of the putative Punic tradition. That Milton, however, might have divined some cosmogonical lore in the deep cultural past of Iopas's song is rendered likely by the existence of an intermediary text, later than Virgil, but reporting earlier material, and which we know Milton also read with care. This was the church historian Eusebius of Caesarea's *Preparation for the Gospel*. Eusebius was a third- to fourth-century Christian scholar of Greek descent, whose *Ecclesiastical History* was the cornerstone of Christian historiography, just as his *Chronicle* was the founding text of Christian chronology. Milton was wary of Eusebius's politics, particularly his adulation of the first Christian emperor, Constantine, a ruler whom Milton distrusted—a sign, we saw, of notable radicalism—for brokering too close an alliance between church and state. But the *Preparation for the Gospel* provided Milton with a thesaurus of fragments of otherwise lost ancient texts.

The *Preparation for the Gospel* has a simple, even simplistic argument. Eusebius "prepared" pagans for the gospel by arguing that although pagan cultures may have preserved fragments of the truth, these are ultimately confused memories of Hebraic writings and traditions. It is a kindly doctrine: rather than rejecting pagan learning outright, as a few of the more zealous Fathers wished, the Christian (and indeed the pagan) has merely to accept that the origins of such wisdom lie in a Jewish past, and its destiny in

the Christian present. Polytheism and idolatry are later errors of interpretation, and can be stripped away as such. In order to demonstrate this thesis
to his satisfaction, Eusebius redacted extensive passages of ancient writers
often surviving now only through these redactions, and for this reason
his book was pored over by Renaissance scholars not in need of conversion
but eager to recover scraps of lost literature. It also bequeathed a basic
framing method of comparatism to early modern historians of myth and
ancient history: if we suppose a common source, we can now associate geographically and textually disparate traditions; and likewise such different
traditions can be assumed to point to a common source. This methodology, for instance, deeply influenced Sir Walter Ralegh's extremely popular
*History of the World* (1614, several subsequent editions), read and owned by
Milton too; as one early reader wrote in the margins of his copy to Ralegh's
chapter on this assumption: "note that Homer Plato, & Pithagoras had
read Moses 5 bookes & thence stolne their divine sayinges of one god."[19]
Nevertheless, although such Eusebianism made for good poetry, it should
be recognized that as a model for the actual history of religion it was falling
under increasing suspicion in Milton's age. "Modern Eusebianism," as it
has been termed, was undergoing some modifications and challenges, and
G. J. Vossius's highly influential *De theologia gentili* of 1641 explored in encyclopedic detail the philosophical idea that all versions of pagan idolatry
were not simply pieces of ancient plagiarism, but mistaken, if ultimately
monotheistic, nature-worship.[20] Indeed, it may not be a coincidence that
one of the only scholarly enterprises in Restoration England committed to
upholding the strong thesis that all pagan philosophy was merely a distortion of Jewish wisdom was the vast *Court of the Gentiles* (4 vols., 1669–1677)
of the nonconformist divine Theophilus Gale, working deliberately outside the scholarly mainstream and suffering from the consequences of such
isolation.[21]

Regardless of how aware blind Milton was of contemporary academic
developments in the historiography of religion, we know Milton earlier read
Eusebius's book with minute attention, for in his drafts for biblical dramas he
referred to an account of the rape of Dinah found not in the biblical account
but in the ancient Hellenistic Jewish poet Theodotus, specifically and solely
as preserved in Eusebius. In Eusebius, therefore, Milton would also have
found further suggestive literary precedents, namely fragments of the Jewish
dramatist Ezekiel, the earliest surviving writer of biblical tragedy, and even

some mysterious hexameters from an otherwise lost biblical epic *On Jerusalem,* by one Philo.[22]

As for Punic wisdom, Eusebius in *The Preparation for the Gospel* also repeated the story that the very inventor of writing, the mythical Cadmus, had been a Phoenician. But for the early moderns by far the most important fragment of supposed Punic literature preserved in Eusebius was the primeval creation narrative of the Phoenician hierophant Sanchuniathon, as reported by his Greek translator Philo of Byblos, to whom we also owe much of our knowledge of Pherecydes. Sanchuniathon, a priest of the Phoenicians said to have flourished before the Trojan War, provided an account of the origin of the universe in which the forces of a controlling providence were puzzlingly absent.[23] This reported text was, in the eyes of the scholars of Milton's time, one of the oldest nonbiblical writings still in existence,[24] much older than other ancient Near Eastern accounts of origins available in, for instance, the fragments, or legends, of the Babylonian Berosus and the Egyptian Manetho, both also reported in Eusebius's book.[25] Milton was well aware of such oriental traditions and had already in his student poem "De Idea Platonica" made good satirical currency of the antiquity of the "Assyrian priest" knowledgeable of "ancient Ninus" and "primal Bel," probably a reference to Hierombalus, priest of Ieuo, Sanchuniathon's declared source in Eusebius.[26] Nevertheless, such traditions were seen as already corrupting the purer tradition of Moses, himself conventionally dated to the middle of the second millennium BC.[27] As Eusebius said, "the polytheistic error of all the nations . . . [took] its beginning from the Phoenicians and Egyptians."[28]

Sanchuniathon's creation arose out of mist and chaos, eventually generating something called *mot* (utterly puzzling to contemporary commentators: perhaps, via Hebrew, for "decay" or "death"? A personification of Pluto? The Egyptian for "mother"?—no one was sure),[29] from which in time came intelligent life, initially in the form of egg-shaped beings called *Zophasemin.* Eusebius complained of the account's *atheotes,* "its lack of any divine agency in the process of origin."[30] Modern scholars regard the embedded "Sanchuniathon" fragment as based on genuine ancient accounts but in comparatively modern forms—perhaps two different city-state traditions, combined with a verse cosmogony—and subsequently somewhat contaminated by later Hellenistic motifs, mostly of Philo's own imposition.[31] But its origin in divine scripture was accepted even by the most critical of early modern commentators, Joseph Justus Scaliger, son of the aforementioned Julius Caesar Scaliger of the *Poetics*. Philo had proposed that the first Phoenician god, Taautes, was the same as the Egyptian deity-scribe Thoth; Scaliger the younger, however, cut vertically down to the Hebrew word for Chaos, *tohu,* as encountered at the start of Genesis: *tohu* and *bohu,* chaos and void. The text therefore contained traces of the Genesis cosmogony.[32] Closer to the time of Milton's epic, Edward Stillingfleet, in his *Origines Sacrae,* accepted Sanchuniathon as at least relatively ancient, and speculated that the heretical theogonies of the Gnostics were derived from it, quite a close hit. Once again he saw the text as unwitting testimony for the earlier accounts of Moses: in his phrase, "we may in this *dungeon* find out many *excellent remainders* of the *ancient tradition.*"[33] Milton himself expressed the same sentiment in *The History of Britain*: "oft-times relations heertofore accounted fabulous have bin after found to contain in them many footsteps, and reliques of somthing true, as what we read in Poets of the Flood, and Giants little beleev'd, till undoubted witnesses taught us, that all was not fain'd."[34] Indeed, just as Milton was finally going blind, there appeared the first printed edition of the *Chronographia* of Georgius Syncellus, which preserved the Babylonian creation myth of Oannes, the fish-prophet who arose from the Red Sea, human feet poking out below its tail, and who, like a kind of eastern Prometheus, taught ancient man "the knowledge of the disciplines and of letters, the procedures of the crafts, how to build cities and erect temples, how to establish laws, how to understand geometry, to collect seeds and fruits, and how to become civilized." Despite his failing sight, Milton almost certainly purchased this expensive book, and had probably already studied the account provided by John Selden in the latter's *De diis Syris* ("On the Syrian Gods").[35] There, Selden equates Oannes with biblical Dagon, whence Milton's *"Dagon his Name, Sea Monster, upward Man / And downward Fish"* (1.462–63); the temple in which the denouement of *Samson Agonistes* takes place is also notably that of *"Dagon* thir Sea-Idol" (13). The Byzantine chronicler George Syncellus, from whom the quotation on Oannes above is taken, then went on to record the attack on "Thalatth" by "Belos," beings we can recognize from modern Assyriology as the Babylonian Tiâmat, primordial chaos-goddess, sundered by Bel (Marduk) to form the heavens and the earth, yet another creation myth based on a primal act of violence.[36]

Milton's Creation may not look as if it depends on some primal sundering, but it does take its prompt from the expulsion of the fallen angels, and

Milton's—as we have seen slightly unusual—sequencing of the Creation after the angelic Fall therefore brings his narrative closer to all these pagan accounts of primal strife. Once again, martial and scientific modes prove to be closely related, and Milton presumably thought that the presence of primal strife in the various pagan cosmogonies was indeed the Chinese-whisper legacy of the first, angelic disobedience as he narrated it. He had available to him this literary tradition of pagan cosmogony in an impressive series: he knew that bards encountered in epics had sung of strife and creation, both literally and allegorically, from Homer and Hesiod, through Apollonius, and into Virgil. Such traditions were not just literary for Milton, but inhered in ancient Near Eastern accounts already under debate by patristic authorities and subsequently by their early modern readers. This, for the scholar-poet Milton, was a scholarly as well as a literary tradition, and it stretched back far earlier than the Greeks.

The Miltonic Creation is, following Augustinian tradition, instantaneous, but providentially narrated as a series of six "days" of work. Creation is effected by the Son, as Word, and with him he takes an immense army of "winged Spirits, and Chariots wing'd," the latter drawn "From the Armoury of God, where stand of old / Myriads between two brazen Mountains lodg'd / Against a solemn day" (7.199–202), that solemn day being an interesting prolepsis of the Son at the other end of time, when he will come not to make but to judge the world.[37] The Son and his enormous retinue then peer down into the waves and wilds of Chaos, and the Son commands these to be still. He next uses his "golden compasses" to "circumscribe" the visible universe (7.255, 256), and it is within this radius, extrapolated into a sphere, that the phases of Creation will take place. The Son, now referred to as "God" in the manner of the original hexameron of Genesis, then speaks Creation into being in successive stages—including, in another ominous prolepsis, the rivers "With Serpent errour wandring" (7.302). As Milton puts in place the furniture of Creation—light, earth, water, heaven, plants, planets, stars, fish, fowl, and animals—he expands on the terse verses of Genesis, even managing to encode ethical and political comment into Creation. The "Parsimonious Emmet" or ant, for instance, is heralded as "Pattern of just equalitie perhaps / Hereafter, join'd in her popular Tribes / Of Commonaltie" (7.487–89), that triplet "equalitie . . . popular . . . Commonaltie" carrying an unmistakably republican charge.

Finally, God creates man. In the biblical account, the plural "Let us make man in our image" (Gen. 1:26) was traditionally interpreted as a proof text the Trinity; in Milton, it is quite literally a conversation between Father and Son: "the Omnipotent / Eternal Father . . . thus to his Son audibly spake" (516–18). Man is made by God; woman is made from man, "Female for Race" (530); and dominion is granted to them over the rest of creation, but "of the Tree / Which tasted works knowledge of Good and Evil, / Thou mai'st not; in the day thou eat'st, thou di'st" (542–44). Creation is crowned by the return to Heaven of the Creator, and here the reader learns the true origin of Psalm 24, as the angels, long before David, sing:

> Open, ye everlasting Gates, they sung,
> Open, ye Heav'ns, your living dores; let in
> The great Creator from his work returnd
> Magnificent, his Six days work, a World. (565–68)

Psalm 24 was traditionally held to be the one David sang as soon as the place of the Temple in Sion had been revealed to him; typologically it referred to Christ and his Church; and prophetically it celebrated the dominion of God over the whole universe.[38] Here it looks back to the conclusion of Creation itself, as the gates of Heaven literally open to receive back the all-creating Word, accompanied by his angelic retinue.

Milton's biblical hexameron of course differs from the various pagan models open to him, but it nevertheless draws on them. Broadly speaking, as Milton's architecture for Hell and Chaos borrowed from Hesiod, so his account of the Creation of the smaller, internal universe in which we live is in dialogue with the classical Epicureanism of Lucretius, specifically the passages from *De rerum natura* on how life arose.[39] The Epicurean Creation was encountered in the fifth book of *De rerum natura*, where is explained the manner of the creation of plants, animals, and people. As Thomas Creech, the seventeenth-century Oxonian translator of Lucretius, rendered one of the crucial sections of the poem:

> And therefore *Parent-Earth* doth justly bear
> The name of *Mother*, since *all* rose from Her.
> She now bears Animals, when softning *Dew*
> Descends, when *Sun* sends heat she bears a thousand new.[40]

Or, as Thomas Stanley explained in the instalment of his influential *History of Philosophy* dedicated to Epicureanism and published in 1660, "concerning Animals themselves, it is likely that the earth, retaining this new genitall seed, brought out of itself some little bubbles, in the likenesse of little wombs, and these when they grew mature, (nature so compelling) broke, and put forth young little Creatures.[41]

Milton, probably following the French scholar and Epicurean revivalist Pierre Gassendi, or his English adaptor the physician Walter Charleton, likewise proposed through Raphael the spontaneous generation of at least the lower fauna from Lucretian "wombs" in the primal earth. But his creatures, unlike the uncertain first creatures of Lucretius, spring forth already mature, perfectly formed:

> The Earth obey'd, and strait
> Op'ning her fertil Woomb teem'd at a Birth
> Innumerous living Creatures, perfet formes,
> Limb'd and full grown (453–56)

Milton's adult lion pawing its way out of the ground is especially memorable:

> The Tawnie Lion, pawing to get free
> His hinder parts, then springs as broke from Bonds,
> And Rampant shakes his Brinded main (464–66)

Nothing could be further from Lucretius's first creation, with its monsters and byproducts:

> Besides, the *Earth* produc'd a *numerous* train
> Of *Monsters,* Those her labour wrought in vain;
> Some without *hands,* or *Feet,* or *mouth,* or *eyes,*
> Some *shapeless* lumps, *Nature's* Absurdities;
> Dull, *moveless things*

These, however, soon died out; only creatures well-adapted to their environment and endued with "Craft, strength, and swiftness" survived, a theory of competition of species that was, however, not linked in Milton's time with a theory of variation of species.[42] Milton's view of the creation of the fauna, therefore, is willing to meet Epicurean models halfway—but only halfway. His Creation is still subservient to the voice of God. The Earth itself did not and could not act spontaneously, but "obey'd" the divine command; and it produced no *"Monsters,"* and suffered no extinctions, twin affronts to divine providence.

The major difference, however, between the Lucretian view of creation and Milton's (as well as Gassendi's and Charleton's) modification of it, was that the former account assumed that man, indeed *all* the first people, sprang up in the same manner as the lesser creatures, independently, dotted throughout the world from the very first. As Thomas Stanley in his *History of Philosophy* continued, "some little bubbles and wombs, sticking to the roots of the earth, and warmed by the Sun, first grew bigger, and, by the assistance of nature afforded to infants, sprung from it a connaturall moisture called milk, and that those thus brought up, and ripened to perfection, propagated Mankind." Or as Creech translated Lucretius, "Thus for a certain time *Mankind* she [Earth] bore / And *Beasts.*"[43] This was to carry Epicurean notions to a destination to which almost no early modern thinker was willing to go, despite the seductive solution it offered to explaining at one stroke how people can be found all over the Earth, even in seemingly unbiblical continents such as the Americas. The spontaneous generation of people from out of the ground in all parts of the world (known as "autochthony") was also part of the Preadamite hypothesis, as known to, and disapproved of by, Milton. For Milton, God may well have infused the Earth with vital seeds at the beginning, enabling the spontaneous generation of animals (indeed, he uses the chymical term "Fermented" (281)).[44] Nevertheless the Bible is explicit that God himself made Adam out of the Earth, and then Eve from his rib. They, rather than the Earth, will beget their subsequent children. A barrier between the animal and the human kingdom was thus erected, and this was crucial to maintaining the theological distinction that humans, made by and in the image of God, have souls, and can be saved—whereas animals do not, and cannot.

# 19

## Pastoral Tragedy

CHAPTER 9 EXPLORED the origins of *Paradise Lost* in drama. And although Milton later turned to epic, he did not turn away from drama; his epic contains within it a kind of pastoral drama, which when plotted through the four core Edenic books (4, 5; 9, 10) is tragic in genre, as Milton confirms in the invocation to Book 9 (9.5–6). In Chapter 9 it was noted that Milton in his dramatic drafts twice mentioned a possible pastoral among his dramas, in addition to the Edenic sketches he prepared. This chapter investigates how such ideas of drama persisted into Milton's epic, and how they became modified by their new epic responsibilities.

Pastoral poetry was for J. C. Scaliger the most ancient kind of poetry; he did not suspect that poetry about leisure in the countryside is more likely to be written by sophisticated urbanites. Milton's understanding of the genre was likewise rooted in two texts of his classroom, the *Idylls* of the third-century BC Greek poet Theocritus, and behind him the *Works and Days* of the primal Hesiod. Theocritus's *Idylls* contain several different types of poem, notably bucolics, such as the famous seventh idyll, on a harvest, inside which the goatherd Lycidas sings his own poem.[1] *The Works and Days,* in contrast, is a rugged, didactic work, delivered by Hesiod to his immoral brother Perses. Hesiod commences with the story of Pandora. Because Prometheus had stolen fire from Zeus, the father of the gods ordered Hephaistus to make an artificial woman out of earth and water, who when sent to man opened the jar of human miseries.[2] Hesiod then narrated the five ages of the world: golden, silver, bronze, the age of heroes, and lastly the age of iron. The rest of his poem is taken up with gnomic moralisms and an almanac for the farmer's year of hard labor, with advice on religious observances. Here in sum was a kind of fall epic in itself: the origin of suffering in a tempting woman, the succession of ages of labor, and how man must till the earth in the sweat of his brow and respect the gods. Milton, with characteristic contaminating irony, explicitly links his Eve to this original narrative of Hesiod in his fourth book, where Eve is

> in naked beauty more adorn'd,
> More lovely then *Pandora,* whom the Gods
> Endowd with all thir gifts, and O too like
> In sad event, when to the unwiser Son
> Of *Japhet* brought by *Hermes,* she ensnar'd
> Mankind with her faire looks, to be aveng'd
> On him who had stole *Joves* authentic fire. (4.713–19)[3]

Bucolic poetry in the Latin tradition fell into eclogue and georgic, the former, with its fondness for shepherding and love, looking to Theocritus, the latter, with its sterner commitment to agriculture and virtue, to Hesiod. It helped that Virgil had progressed from the former to the latter, as it implied a moral trajectory the future artist might traverse too.[4]

Milton's Eden adapts bucolic and tempers it with georgic. Adam and Eve, for instance, are musical like the shepherds of bucolic poetry, but their instruments are their voices alone, and theirs is devotional verse, for the practical purpose of praise. The prose argument to the fifth book of *Paradise Lost* identifies "Thir Morning Hymn at the Door of thir Bower," and this hymn, a prelapsarian fusion of the set and the freely inspired, is "More tuneable then needed Lute or Harp" (5.151; the hymn is 5.153–208). Even when Adam and Eve seem most relaxed, they are tending, in the manner recommended by the *authores de re rustica,* to their *oeconomia,* their household. Sometimes one is working and the other resting, as when Raphael finds

Adam sitting in the door of his little house sunbathing, while Eve potters around inside making supper and fruit juice (5.299–300; compare Adam's words at 9.232–33: "for nothing lovelier can be found / In Woman, then to studie houshold good"). But Adam, although he may enjoy a moment to lean on one elbow in the morning and gaze on his slumbering wife (5.11–12), is clear that there is always georgical work to be done:

> we must be ris'n,
> And at our pleasant labour, to reform
> Yon flourie Arbors, yonder Allies green,
> Our walk at noon, with branches overgrown,
> That mock our scant manuring, and require
> More hands then ours to lop thir wanton growth:
> Those Blossoms also, and those dropping Gumms,
> That lie bestrowne unsightly and unsmooth,
> Ask riddance, if we mean to tread with ease. (4.624–32)

There are no true seasons as yet, but Milton embeds a principle of fecundity into his paradise that requires equal and opposite labor to keep it in check. It is a "delightful task," however, because shared: "Which were it toilsom, yet with thee were sweet," says Adam to his wife (4.437, 439). This is essential to the design of the argument of the tragic books, because not only does Adam assume the necessity of childbearing for the purposes of better gardening ("More hands then ours"), but he gives Eve an at least somewhat plausible argument for her later desire to garden apart—that way, more work will get done.

Adam's comment on more hands also points to one of the more surprising aspects of Milton's Adam and Eve, namely that, although the narrator piously tries to avoid describing too directly the act itself, Adam and Eve have sex (4.738–49), as indeed do the angels (8.622–29). This is unusual but again logical: Milton accepts that Adam and Eve were created without sin and as sexually mature adults, and that therefore the actions of sexually mature adults are not in themselves sinful and may, indeed must, take place in Eden, even just for pleasure. Both Adam and Eve, however, envisage raising children in Eden (compare Eve at 9.622–24). Again this is essential to the design of the tragedy: when Adam confides in Raphael just how much he admires Eve, lapsing into some dangerous talk on her erotic sway, Raphael rebukes him "with contracted brow" (8.560). These are the two internal dramatic motors of the human fall: the necessity for more gardening and an overactive love of woman.

One of Milton's earliest editors, the poet Elijah Fenton, claimed in his 1725 edition that he could detect many fragments of the original play, even as they lay partially submerged in their new epic ocean.[5] This became something of an editorial vogue: Francis Peck then took up Fenton's earlier hint in 1740, producing a five-act schema and even a reconstruction of the original Act 4, scene 2.[6] And indeed it seems reasonable to suppose that some of the verse of the earlier drafts went into the final product, although extracting these elements from the final compound is in practice well-nigh impossible. Some guesses, however, are quite plausible: in addition to the solid testimony of Phillips that Satan's soliloquy to the Sun was a part, indeed the opening lines, of one of the dramatic drafts, C. S. Lewis thought he had found two more. The first is one of Satan's speeches in book nine where Satan rather stagily describes himself as "thus wrapt in mist" (9.158), despite the fact that the narrator has just done so too ("involv'd in rising Mist," 9.75), a suggestive dittography. A little later, Satan is glad to catch sight of Eve without Adam, "for I view far round" (9.482), a performative waggle again redolent of a dramatic character explaining his motions in the way a narrated character need not.[7]

It does not matter that we cannot be sure whether these examples are pieces of some *ur*-tragedy or not. The important thing is that the genre of tragedy survived into the epic, and its legacy lies in the characterization and plotting of the pastoral-tragic books. For Milton characterizes in a far more philosophically complex fashion than the epic genre had hitherto required for its protagonists, and his dialogue owes more to dramatic than to epic precedents. Indeed, it perhaps owes something to contemporary English drama, for Milton's prized Greek tragedians staged dialogue somewhat differently: the classical dynamic of long solo utterances juxtaposed with faster dialogue is modulated in *Paradise Lost* into a broader range of conversational forms.

In Milton's drama-in-an-epic there are three important characters, namely Satan, Adam, and Eve. At some point after Milton stopped tinkering with the pages of the Trinity College manuscript, he replotted his play so that Satan was now the first person to appear in the action. We can see at once that Satan had become no wooden tempter but a conflicted intellectual being. The speech Phillips reported having heard from this early point in the work's development, a speech initially of Satan's defiance, continues in the epic:

> Ah wherefore! he deservd no such return
> From me, whom he created what I was
> In that bright eminence (4.42–44)

This soliloquizing Satan is a dramatic character, who vacillates and regrets, who even interrogates himself: "Hadst thou the same free Will and Power to stand? / Thou hadst" (4.66–67). Indeed the more popularly celebrated Satan of *Paradise Lost*'s first two books, Satan in Hell, "Vaunting aloud, but rackt with deep despare" (1.126), was developed by Milton out of this earlier Satan in Eden. Satan's dramatic origins also provide one explanation for the enduring ethical problem of the readerly experience the poem: Satan appeals to us as a character not (just) because we are wicked and respond to wickedness, but because he is, quite literally, something out of a play.

As for Adam and Eve, they are placed in Eden immediately as adults, but their experiences from their points of creation, and indeed their memories of their creations, are unequal. Milton is here perhaps responding to the biblical necessity of getting Eve away from Adam for the temptation by rendering their experiences before that point carefully asymmetrical. Eve's dreams are interfered with by Satan; Adam's are not, and indeed we learn nothing of his dreams. Adam learns directly from Raphael about the angelic fall; Eve learns indirectly, by overhearing (7.50–51; 9.275–76), and it is assumed that she, not invited to participate in the main dialogue and absent for the debate on astronomy, will receive additional tuition at second hand by Adam, who will kiss her when she asks difficult questions, and

> intermix
> Grateful digressions, and solve high dispute
> With conjugal Caresses, from his Lip
> Not Words alone pleas'd her. (54–57)

Chapter 20 looks at how their memories of their creation differ, and Adam and Eve were never intended to be equal:

Not equal, as thir sex not equal seemd
For contemplation hee and valour formd,
For softness shee and sweet attractive Grace,
Hee for God only, shee for God in him (4.296–99)

Both accept, or learn to accept, this Pauline hierarchy as the natural state
of things. Eve even tells Adam that she is happier than he, because unlike
her husband she gets to enjoy two superiors (4.445–48).

Eden, even unfallen Eden, is an emotional place, and Adam and Eve can
get worried, if not quite upset. Adam, on hearing of Eve's dream, says that
it "Affects me equally; nor can I like / This uncouth dream" (4.97–98); these
are not untroubled robots of perfection. Eve's reaction to Adam's reassuring
words on her dream is to shed two tears, and "wip[e] them with her haire"
(5.131); Adam kisses two more from her eyes—and thus, as Dennis Danielson
has remarked, there are tears even in unfallen Eden.[8] As Adam, yet unfallen, awaits fallen Eve's return in Book 9, holding his soon-to-be-discarded
crown of flowers, he frets, his heartbeat stumbling: "Yet oft his heart, divine of
somthing ill, / Misgave him; hee the faultring measure felt" (9.845–46).

Differences between Adam and Eve are also expressed—especially as they
have no clothes to be described—in terms of their hair. Milton, acquiescing
with the Apostle Paul on hairstyles, presents us with a sensual Eve who

as a vail down to the slender waste
Her unadorned golden tresses wore
Dissheveld, but in wanton ringlets wav'd
As the Vine curles her tendrils, which impli'd
Subjection (4.304–8)

Whereas for sensible Adam

Hyacinthin Locks
Round from his parted forelock manly hung
Clustring, but not beneath his shoulders broad (4.301–3).

Notwithstanding that faintly priggish last remark, Milton was evidently
much taken with hair, which grows on everything in *Paradise Lost* from angels to trees.[9] His description of Eve's "tresses . . . Dissheveld . . . in wanton

ringlets" reminds, even rebukes, the fallen reader that there is no way of describing prelapsarian beauty, let alone sexuality, without a postlapsarian pang of desire. This in particular wracks Satan, who seems to know that "Eden" in Hebrew means, etymologically, "pleasure" or "delight," and fully understands that for Adam and Eve this means sex:

> Sight hateful, sight tormenting! thus these two
> Imparadis't in one anothers arms
> The happier *Eden,* shall enjoy thir fill
> Of bliss on bliss, while I to Hell am thrust (4.506–9)

Although the inequality between Adam and Eve is neither presented nor experienced as unfair, it is nevertheless another necessary motor of the fall. Satan in the serpent is keen to locate both Adam and Eve, but especially Eve, apart and alone, as he fears Adam's "higher intellectual" (9.421–22, 483). But, crucially, the stages by which Eve removes herself from Adam are her own doing. This is the narrative counterpart to the difficult discovery of Augustine that Eve (and subsequently Adam) must have resolved to sin, secretly, internally, before any successful temptation or public act of disobedience could take place. The tempter can only tempt the temptable.[10]

We can use the "Adam Unparadiz'd" dramatic draft discussed above as a control on the shape of Milton's final performance. A five-act distribution of the material, compressed, would look something like this:

Act 1:
   Gabriel describes Paradise, the angelic rebellion, and the
   creation and marriage of Adam and Eve.

Act 2:
   Lucifer appears, fallen, seeking revenge on man, is confronted
   by the Chorus, and flees.

Act 3:
   Chorus sings of the Rebellion; Lucifer, after the event,
   recounts how he has just perverted man.

Act 4:

Adam and Eve, fallen, accuse one another.

Act 5:

Adam and Eve are banished, despair, and finally repent.

(Readers will note that this is also structurally equivalent to Milton's third draft, the one he first called "Paradise Lost.") Comparing this to how Milton arranged his material in the final epic, we can see that the material covered by our putative acts one and two became Milton's fourth book; half the third act was absorbed into Raphael's narration; the other half became Milton's ninth book, and the final two acts his tenth. What is immediately obvious is that Lucifer's recounted temptation is replaced by a lengthy narration and depiction of the Fall itself—an entire book, indeed, and the human heart of the epic itself. In particular, there is no elaboration in the drafts of Eve's necessary role in the process, being her three interactions, first with Adam (separation), then with Satan (temptation, her own fall), then with Adam again (his fall). We can assume that Lucifer in the drafts explained how he found and tempted Eve, but there is no hint in these earlier sketches of the other stages of this process—of how Eve, without any prompt from Satan himself, debated with Adam the respective merits of gardening together versus apart; and of how she returned, fallen, and convinced him to fall too. This is therefore revealed as Milton's crucial strategic realization, relatively late in his thinking about this narrative: Eve had to resolve to go off alone, and in order to preserve the intellectual character of Adam and Eve's partnership, this resolution must arise out of debate, and Adam must freely suffer Eve to garden alone. Likewise after Eve's return, Adam's own fall had to be an extensively meditated action. So Milton had to create three sequential discussions. The first takes place between Adam and Eve, and concludes with Eve's upheld resolution to garden apart (9.205–384). The second, between Eve and Satan, results in her fall (532–833). The third, between Eve and Adam, ends in his (856–989).

We know something is wrong at once between Adam and Eve, because Eve speaks first; hitherto in the epic she had not initiated discussion. Her request to garden alone, however, addresses a need in Eden that the narrator too has just conceded: "for much thir work outgrew / The hands dispatch of two Gardning so wide (9.202–3). Adam's response is that their future off-spring will assist them, an indication, as we saw, that Milton's Adam is a family man, and that Milton understood the curse of Genesis 3:16 not to be childrearing itself but only the pain now associated with it. Adam is in principle content for Eve to garden alone, but in practice he knows that they have a foe, lurking "somewhere nigh at hand." Eve protests her "firmness"; Adam tries to reassure her that he is merely seeking to prevent the dishonor of an attack, not doubting the resilience of their defense. But he is admonitory too, reminding Eve that their hidden enemy had after all managed to ruin angels. Eve's response is seemingly the classic Miltonic theory of virtue: to be tried and found worthy is better than not to be tried at all. But is this the right response in context? Her arguments stray into overconfidence and self-sufficiency, and Adam's response is exact: "Firm we subsist, yet possible to swerve." Nevertheless he decides that his wife's freedom must be respected: "Go; for thy stay, not free, absents thee more."

At this point Eve has not sinned and will remain "yet sinless" (9.659) for some time to come. But she has been overconfident in her own powers of resistance, a departure from the ideal of marital cooperation Adam advises. (Adam's magnificent argument, so unlike the prose of the theologians, is that he and Eve will want to behave well, and to look good, in each other's company.) This is the first step toward the Fall, and over this first dialogue hang the words of Paul: "Let the woman learn in silence with all subjection. But I suffer not a woman to teach, nor to usurp authority over the man, but to be in silence. For Adam was first formed, then Eve" (1 Tim: 2:11–13).

The second step is Satan's dialogue with Eve. In an immediate parallelism to the first dialogue, Satan addresses Eve as superior, as "sovran," asserting as well that *she* was the one made in her maker's image, rather than Adam (9.538). This inversion of hierarchy is in contrast to Eve's actual intellectual performance against the Serpent, which, in the context of what we know Eve knows, is poor. She marvels at the speaking snake, without once suspecting what it really is, despite Adam's parting warnings. The Serpent claims that his voice and "capacious mind" were effected by the fruits of a certain tree, and that his new-found intelligence has directed him to worship Eve, "Sovran of Creatures, universal Dame" (9.612)—again that bogus claim of female sovereignty. Eve asks which tree it is, and the Serpent leads her there. Despite Eve's identification of the tree as the Forbidden Tree, she still at no point divines Satan in the Serpent. As long as she does not realize this, she has no defense against his next (fallacious) argument—that he, a snake, has (individually) eaten and has not died, and so the prohibition must be (universally) false. This is what any student versed in his Aristotle on logical fallacies, as Milton was, should immediately identify as the fallacy of *converse accident:* because X is (individually) true of A does not make it (universally) true of all other examples. (Milton detailed this exact fallacy in his own *Ars logicæ.*)[11] Eve does not catch this, and the tree, Satan can thus insist, is indeed "Mother of Science," a perversion of one of the standard ways in which Eve herself is greeted in the epic, as "Mother of Mankind," "Mother of human Race" (1.36, 5.388, 11.159–60; 4.475).

Eve is persuaded; but her acquiescence, importantly, is voiced internally to herself in soliloquy before she performs the external act. Her act of taking is itself a recollection of an earlier moment, in a dream: "she pluck'd, she eat [*sic*, for ate]" (9.781) reaches back to "He pluckt, he tasted" (5.65), the moment in Eve's dream when the dream-Satan broke the prohibition that Eve now breaks here. This raises the difficult problem of the extent of the influence of Eve's dream on her future actions: she is after all not just doing what Satan wants, but reperforming his actions as experienced in her dream, at his prompting. Eve completes the pattern of inverted sovereignty by applying the word to the Forbidden Tree itself: "O Sovran, vertuous, precious of all Trees / In Paradise" (9.795–96). Like some Celt, Eve now worships a tree, the symbol of her final, pagan debasement.[12]

The third step is Eve's persuasion of Adam. This is a quite different encounter, another inversion, for this time it is the tempter who is deceived, whereas the person being tempted is not. Eve's opening address to Adam— once more she initiates dialogue—on how the forbidden tree "is not as we are told" (9.863), is greeted by him with horror: "while horror chill / Ran through his veins, and all his joynts relax'd" (9.890–91). This again reaches back to Eve's dream, where *she* had felt exactly the same on Satan's bite of the apple: "mee damp horror chil'd" (5.65). Adam's chill, however, is because he, without having to debate the matter extensively, knows, or at least thinks he knows, that this means that he must now fall too, freely. Eve had spoken to herself, internally, just before her fall; Adam now does so too, but this time in agonized, imagined dialogue with his wife, to whom he is not actually talking. His acceptance of what must now happen comes within a dozen lines of realizing what has just happened to Eve: "And mee with thee hath ruind" (906), he ruefully resolves.

Adam's ensuing dialogue with Eve is a peculiar exercise in Adam reconciling himself to the sin about to take place, while Eve, still not quite grasping the facts, champions his "exceeding Love" (960). Marriage, the institution that should have kept them together in innocence, but did not, will now keep them together in their fall. Eve still does not see that this has been Satan's doing; and Adam, indeed, only half-faces the problem with his vague talk of "som cursed fraud" (904; compare 1068–69, where it is again ambiguous whether he has really worked out what has happened). Adam's completion of the Fall is nevertheless "Against his better knowledge, not deceav'd, / But fondly overcome with Femal charm" (998–99), just as Raphael had feared. This is the final step in this phase of the drama, and hanging once again over it, in continuation, are the words of Paul, directly following on from the previous quotation: "And Adam was not deceived, but the woman being deceived was in the transgression" (1 Tim. 2:14). This core drama of the three dialogues, of course, is transformed in its epic setting by the circumventing narratorial voice, commenting on the action and then placing it by simile inside the echo chambers of comparative pagan mythography and history; this is the subject of Chapter 20.

Milton's original drafts for a drama on the Fall all placed an emphasis on the aftermath of the Fall equal to if not greater than that placed on the Fall itself. In the drafts this was because Milton originally did not plan to dramatize the process of the Fall at all; it was easier and safer to depict Adam and Eve already fallen. In the epic, this has all changed. Now that the Fall has been reconstructed with a dialogic intensity hitherto unseen in literature, the aftermath moves into structural parallelism, as Milton balances the story of how we got into this mess with the story of how we at least began to get out of it. This action occupies the end of the ninth and the tenth books.

Satan's temptation of Eve hinged on what seemed true to Eve: that the Serpent as mere snake could now talk and reason. The snake tells her that before the forbidden fruit had turned him into a philosopher, he had lived a life solely of food and sex: "nor aught but food discern'd / Or Sex" (9.573–74, perhaps the earliest use of "sex" thus). After both Eve and Adam have eaten the fruit, Milton inverts this exactly: before, they had truly been philosophers; now, they think first of food ("nor known till now / True relish" [1023–24]), and then of sex ("There they thir fill of Love and Loves disport / Took largely, of thir mutual guilt the Seale" [1042–43]). This is followed by the inversion of their prelapsarian dialogue, as mutual appre-

ciation turns into mutual recrimination. Nakedness, which was their shame-
less covering, is now itself covered by shame: "hee cover'd, but his Robe
/ Uncover'd more" (1058–59; reversed by the Son at 10.216–23). At this point
too, Milton inserts a simile to Samson shorn, a reference that looks forward
to his own *Samson Agonistes*:

> so rose the *Danite* strong
> *Herculean Samson* from the Harlot-lap
> Of Philistean Dalilah, and wak'd
> Shorn of his strength (1059–62)

The couple now argue, and the book of the Fall concludes:

> Thus they in mutual accusation spent
> The fruitless hours, but neither self-condemning,
> And of thir vain contest appeer'd no end. (1187–89)

This is the thirty-second time in this book alone that Milton has introduced
the saturating word "fruit" or its antonym "fruitless," and it completes the
pun first recklessly set in motion by Eve herself standing before the Forbidden Tree: "Fruitless to mee, though Fruit be here to excess" (648).[13]

Milton's tenth book is an extraordinary mixture of biblical reprises and
reprisals, with lengthy imagined additions, exploring the mental experience
of the aftermath of the Fall. Adam is slow to accept responsibility, and Milton
underlines this by making Adam struggle to admit to the Son what has happened, delaying his syntax line after line:

> This Woman whom thou mad'st to be my help,
> And gav'st me as thy perfet gift, so good,
> So fit, so acceptable, so Divine,
> That from her hand I could suspect no ill,
> And what she did, whatever in it self,
> Her doing seem'd to justifie the deed;
> Shee gave me of the Tree, and I did eate. (10.137–43)

The opening and closing verses are biblical. Indeed, in the King James Bible,
we also have two exact lines of blank verse: "The woman whom thou gavest

to be with me, [ / ] she gave me of the tree, and I did eat" (Gen. 3:12). Milton takes these over almost unchanged, but Adam defers and defers, throwing up subclause after subclause in an attempt to delay the main verb, to excuse in advance the inexcusable.

Compare Eve: she says, merely, "The Serpent me beguil'd and I did eate" (162); the King James Bible has: "The serpent beguiled me, and I did eat" (Gen. 3:13). Two words have swapped places for metrical reasons, but otherwise Eve sticks exactly to her text. She declines to imitate the "loquacious" (10.161) excuses of her husband. That precise word is interesting, for "loquacious" was long thought to have been a Miltonic coinage. Now that many more early modern texts are electronically searchable, we can see that this is false: the earliest use traced so far is from Francis Meres back in 1598: "so more admirable is constancie and silence in women, because their sex is mutable and loquacious."[14] What this underlines is that Milton reverses the sexist commonplace: Adam is the babbler here, not Eve.

In the medieval tradition of the pseudepigraphical *Life of Adam and Eve*, the fallen couple when expelled from Eden first "spent seven days mourning and lamenting in great grief" before setting off on their adventures.[15] Milton, however, places the stage of lamentation between judgment and expulsion, so that, as God had hoped (11.113), by the time Adam and Eve are finally ejected from Paradise, they have come to a stable spiritual understanding of their predicament and their destiny; they may move on to tackle the world without much further weeping: "Som natural tears they drop'd, but wip'd them soon" (12.645). This again is a major but logical ethical innovation: Milton wishes to trace the origin of proper (fallen) prayer and spiritual regeneration to actions first performed in Eden. Before such regeneration, however, Adam and Eve progress through a series of discussions that must have been especially uncomfortable for readers who believed that these beings literally were their first parents. Adam imagines his readers rebuking him, as we ourselves complain: "Ill fare our Ancestor impure, / For this we may thank *Adam*" (735–36). His subsequent lament first criticizes God for making him at all, before retracting this impiety. But Adam then hopes for sudden death, and reasons that "All of me then shall die" (792), a sentiment that implies that the soul will die with the body. This hope is then succeeded by the fear that punishment after death might, on the contrary, be eternal, and this eventually drives Adam into almost Satanic misery:

> To *Satan* only like both crime and doom.
> O Conscience, into what Abyss of fears
> And horrors hast thou driv'n me; out of which
> I find no way, from deep to deeper plung'd! (10.841–44)

This is a reprise of Satan's famous description of his internal life when he first alights in Eden in Book 4:

> Which way I flie is Hell; my self am Hell;
> And in the lowest deep a lower deep
> Still threatning to devour me opens wide (4.75–77)

Adam's lament, like Satan's, is now to himself; and when Eve approaches him he greets her with a litany of insults. Eve's response is striking: she offers to take the sin entirely on herself (935–36), a course of action Adam had just debated with himself but had rejected as too heavy a burden for him to bear, even if shared with Eve (834–37). Adam regards Eve's offer as unrealistic, but it does soften his anger, and he recommends—the first sign of a return to the practice of working together as a married couple—that they "strive / In offices of Love, how we may light'n / Each others burden in our share of woe" (959–61).

But if Adam has had his episode of wild and whirling words, Eve, in another parallelism, now has hers. She recommends that they abstain entirely from sex, so that there is no possibility of procreation; and, if abstinence should be too hard, then they should commit suicide, at once (986–1006). This is again strong stuff for a reader who is listening to his or her primal mother. Adam has now regained moral control of the relationship, however, and meditating the terms of the triple Curse just pronounced by the Son— work, childbirth, the enmity of the Serpent—he realizes that there is a future destined for them out of Eden, and that they will reach it through a combination of prayer and technological ingenuity.

Milton thus manages to bring mankind from Creation, through Fall, to Repentance, all inside Eden; and it is only once Adam and Eve, again of their own free, if now damaged, will, have reasoned themselves into a position of repentance that God can now command Michael to expel them. Thus concludes the drama of the Fall.

# 20

## Contamination and Doubles

IN CHAPTER 18, we touched on the pertinence to Milton's intellectual
project of Eusebius of Caesarea and his collections of ancient classical
fragments, *The Preparation for the Gospel*. Eusebius preserved such fragments
in order to suggest that in their recognizable but imperfect recollection of
the true historical past, they simultaneously confirmed that past and condemned themselves as perverted accounts of it. *Paradise Lost* displays a kind
of literary Eusebianism too, and the first half of this chapter further explores
and then complicates this Eusebianism, suggesting ultimately that Milton's
poetry is less assured about its power to impose on the reader such a firm
line between the authentic and the merely antique.

In *The Preparation for the Gospel*, Eusebius reports from an otherwise lost
portion of the first-century BC Greek historian Diodorus Siculus the story
of Euhemerus, the man who found the islands where the real "gods" had
lived. This gave rise to the term "Euhemerism," the notion that pagan fables are based on actual historical happenings, corrupted into myth over
time.[1] A Euhemerizing text of the classical period popular in Milton's age
was the *On Incredible Things* of the rationalizing paradoxographer Pa-

laephatus, where natural explanations of seemingly supernatural events are given.[2] This was one way of dealing with myth—to treat it as history in disguise. Euhemerism was adopted by some of the earlier church fathers, for instance Lactantius, who argued that the pagan gods were merely memories of powerful men, deified after their deaths. A more exciting and indeed agonistic view was, however, decisively asserted by Augustine, who taught that the pagan deities were fallen angels in disguise.[3] This is not Euhemerism because it is not a rationalizing or even secularizing theory, but rather the annexation of one system of religious belief by another. This Augustinian view is Milton's too, evident for instance in his multilayered account of how the architect-devil responsible for building Pandaemonium in Hell was later "fabl'd" into the pagan deity Mulciber:

> Men call'd him *Mulciber;* and how he fell
> From Heav'n, they fabl'd, thrown by angry *Jove*
> Sheer o're the Chrystal Battlements; from Morn
> To Noon he fell, from Noon to dewy Eve,
> A Summers day; and with the setting Sun
> Dropt from the Zenith like a falling Star,
> On *Lemnos* th'*Ægæan* Ile: thus they relate,
> Erring; for he with this rebellious rout
> Fell long before (1.740–48)

The structure of Milton's account is in several ways not dissimilar to that of, for instance, Palaephatus. Palaephatus typically related a myth (parallel to "Men call'd him *Mulciber*" above), stated in a phrase that this is an error (e.g., "τὸ δ'ἀληθὲς ἔχει ὧδε" "but the matter is truly in this wise"; compare "thus they relate, / Erring"), and then gave his own explanation (in the pattern of "he . . . / Fell long before"). The difference is that Milton, following the Augustinian tradition, corrects one belief with another: these are indeed all supernatural occurrences, but only one religious framework offers the right explanatory system.

The actual poetry Milton generates, however, is not as simple, not as clean, as this theory might suggest. What renders Milton's verse particularly intellectually rich and melancholy is a property I shall call "contamination." In classical poetics, *contaminatio* describes the process of blending source texts to create a new text, usually with reference to drama, and takes its rise from Terence's comments in the prologue to the *Andria* on mixing together plays.[4] A famous example in English from a generation or two before Milton is Shakespeare's *Comedy of Errors*, a virtuosic fusion of two plays by Plautus, resulting in an entirely fresh drama. Miltonic contamination, as I shall define it, is a little different. This is really a class of *imitatio*, the transformative / combative imitation of a source text or texts,[5] here carried out in a manner that simultaneously subjects its source to a (usually ethical) critique, but which also finds itself contaminated by that very association. It is hard, in other words, to shake off the imitated text. Contamination, to be precise, is what happens when classical *imitatio* is Christianized. Without compromising faith, contamination recognizes the "fallenness" of both text and reader. Because this renders Milton's moral project somewhat ambiguous in its actual performance, "contamination" is the fitting term.[6]

That this really is contamination and not simply a dirty reading of a cleaner situation is, I admit, partly an aesthetic judgment. Some of the most powerful passages of *Paradise Lost* depend on the reader reacting to these passages with an intense mixture of pleasure and melancholy, and this in turn relies on an invincible affection for the pagan classics. True, to an unbeliever, this sense of contamination is in these more secular times more an intellectual appreciation of a historical problem, lacking the glow of piety, but the remaining current is quite strong enough—it is not hard to sympathize with loss.

On this understanding, *Paradise Lost*, notwithstanding its obvious debt to the Bible, especially to the King James version, therefore contains many components assembled from materials the epic simultaneously tries to reject as impurities, with mixed success. The theoretical difficulty of pagan referents in a Christian narrative was a critical commonplace, and had been perceived, for instance, by Milton's hexameral predecessor, Du Bartas. To those who would wish "that these words of *Flora, Amphitrite, Mars, Venus, Vulcan, Iupiter*, and *Pluto*, &c. were banished out of my booke," Du Bartas replied in his preface to *La Sepmaine* that he had "sowne them slenderly; and when I vse them, it is by a Metonymy . . . making some allusions to their Fables, which hath been practiced till this time by those who haue written Christian Poems. Poesie hath been so long times seasoned and seized of these fabulous termes, that it is impossible to dispossesse her but by little and little thereof." Du Bartas then retreats even further from this rather timid defense, insisting that he had at least made a start on the necessary depaganization of poetry, and he looks forward to one after him "who will wholly purge her."⁷ The problem with this position is that its logical terminus would be a Christian poetry that owed nothing to the pagan classics at all; and Milton, following a more aggressive tradition of assimilation rooted in the Latin poetry of Englishmen,⁸ could see that this was an absurd and self-defeating ambition for a writer attempting a genre that could only be recognized as such by engagement with its pagan antecedents.

Milton's engagement nevertheless produces a slightly sticky effect, where some of the terms of Milton's pagan referents transfer up to Milton's own text and do not evaporate. In two examples, both from famous sections of Milton's fourth book, the fallen reader, exhausted after three books of Hell, Heaven, and Chaos, is finally given some time in the green world of Eden. In the first example, Eve recounts to Adam the story of her creation, but in an episode that is so obviously extrabiblical that the reader is encouraged to ponder what kind of comparison is being proffered here. Eve's account also bears some relation to Platonizing allegory, but for now its importance lies in its more obvious, primary reliance on Ovid's story of Narcissus:

> That day I oft remember, when from sleep
> I first awak't, and found my self repos'd
> Under a shade of flours, much wondring where
> And what I was, whence thither brought, and how.
> Not distant far from thence a murmuring sound
> Of waters issu'd from a Cave and spread
> Into a liquid Plain, then stood unmovd
> Pure as th'expanse of Heav'n; I thither went
> With unexperienc't thought, and laid me downe
> On the green bank, to look into the cleer
> Smooth Lake, that to me seemd another Skie.
> As I bent down to look, just opposite,
> A Shape within the watry gleam appeerd
> Bending to look on me, I started back,
> It started back, but pleas'd I soon returnd,
> Pleas'd it returnd as soon with answering looks
> Of sympathie and love; there I had fixt
> Mine eyes till now, and pin'd with vain desire,
> Had not a voice thus warnd me, What thou seest,
> What there thou seest fair Creature is thy self (4.449–68)

The resemblance to Ovid's tale of Narcissus and Echo has been dutifully noted by commentators since Hume: "*Milton* has improved the Fable of *Ovid*, by representing *Eve* like a She *Narcissus* admiring her self."[9] The improvement, for Hume, lies in its greater plausibility: Narcissus should have known better, but Eve, newly created, has that excuse. On Hume's reading this is at least partially a disjunctive comparison: the reader is encouraged to distinguish between the predicaments of Eve and Narcissus.

Comparison against the text of Ovid assists this side of the reading.[10] In Ovid, Narcissus is an ambiguous youth, "poteratque puer iuvenisque videri" (able to be seen as either a boy or a young man *or* both as a boy and a young man). Narcissus is also a fool, vain and deceived, unlike the adult and intellectually sophisticated Eve. He plunges his arms into his stream but cannot grasp his image. He is also a victim of divine vengeance for scorning the nymph Echo, who pines away into just her echoing voice. Narcissus's death was predicted in Ovid by Tiresias—another subtle incorporation of that figure into *Paradise Lost*—and Narcissus in his death turns into the flower. Even his name is slightly dulling, for the flower named after him deadened the senses (compare our word *narcotics,* from Greek *narkein,* "to numb"). Eve stands in comparison to all this. She is female, is not vain, and has as yet no one to deceive her. Narcissus breaks the skin of his pool with his hands; Eve just looks with her eyes. Nor is she a victim of divine vengeance at this juncture; quite the opposite, as she is led away from her reflection and toward Adam, her truer image. Powerless Echo in Ovid is in Milton the voice of the all-powerful. The comparison, we might initially decide, is wholly negative.

Nevertheless, there is a more problematic, associative side to the comparison. There are indeed certain properties of Narcissus that cannot transfer to Eve, notably his gender. But what are we to do with all the persistent points of contact? Eve, for instance, is throughout *Paradise Lost* likened to flowers, and she gives them their names. Contact can also be morally troubling: Narcissus is culpable, and Eve worryingly confesses that "there [upon her pool] I had fixt / Mine eyes till now, and pined with vain desire, / *Had not* a voice thus warned me." Half of the force of the comparison pulls Eve away from Narcissus; the other half draws her back; and they both join in the word "vain," with its double senses of vanity and fruitless. Like Narcissus, Eve too is both a *iuvenis,* young but at least sexually mature, and something, in terms of experience, much younger. The reader is not easily able to define precisely where the line within Miltonic allusion is to be drawn between conjunctive and disjunctive simile, between positive and negative comparison.

It might be objected that Milton's narrator is quite clear in other cases about how the reader is supposed to react to morally problematic episodes. When Satan vaunts in book one, for instance, the narrator is quick to qualify and condemn: "Vaunting aloud, but rackt with deep despare" (1.126); and as for pagans and their myths of Mulciber, "thus they relate, / Erring" (1.746–47). But only an inert reader would accept that things are always, or even in those cases, this simple. Even when Milton's grammar itself tries to persuade us that a comparison is negative, its cognitive effect is residually positive too, and indeed in our second example it seems fairly obvious that Milton intends this doubleness, as he piles up several comparisons in series. Milton is presenting unfallen Eden to his fallen reader:

> Not that faire field
> Of *Enna,* where *Proserpin* gathering flours
> Her self a fairer Floure by gloomie *Dis*
> Was gatherd, which cost *Ceres* all that pain
> To seek her through the world; nor that sweet Grove
> Of *Daphne* by *Orontes,* and th' inspir'd
> *Castalian* Spring, might with this Paradise
> Of *Eden* strive; nor that *Nyseian* Ile
> Girt with the River *Triton,* where old *Cham,*
> Whom Gentiles *Ammon* call and *Lybian Jove,*
> Hid *Amalthea* and her Florid Son
> Young *Bacchus* from his Stepdame *Rhea's* eye;
> Nor where *Abassin* Kings thir issue Guard,
> Mount *Amara,* though this by som suppos'd
> True Paradise under the *Ethiop* Line
> By *Nilus* head, enclosd with shining Rock,
> A whole days journy high, but wide remote
> From this *Assyrian* Garden, where the Fiend
> Saw undelighted all delight. (4.268–86)

This is signally Miltonic: the reader is presented with a number, four in all, of precomparisons to the zone Eden, some with their own internal ramifications. These four zones are (1) Enna, in central Sicily, scene of the rape of

Proserpina; (2) the grove of Daphne by the river Orontes, near Antioch, where there was an oracle of Apollo and a sacred spring named for Castalius; (3) the Arabian island of Nysa near the river Triton, where the baby Bacchus was hidden from Rhea, Ammon's wife, by his parents Ammon and Amalthea; (4) Mount Amara, the high mountain just under the equator where the kings of Abyssinia quarantine their sons from external interference. As one realizes when taking this passage apart, each of the precomparisons has its own darker internal narrative. Thus (1) the myth of Ceres and Proserpina is a crop allegory for the seasons—which will of course be initiated by the Fall-to-come in Milton's poem. The rape of Proserpina (= Eve) by Dis / Hades (= Satan) is also the subject of Claudian's *De raptu Proserpinæ*, a poem constantly alluded to by Milton and already a popular candidate for allegorical exegesis, as for instance in Leonard Digges's 1617 translation, prefaced by a threefold "Historicall," "Naturall," and "Allegoricall" exegesis of the poem.[11] (2) Daphne and the Castalian spring carry a typical negative / positive balance: the latter is a symbol for inspiration, but the former is named for Daphne, who early on in Ovid's *Metamorphoses* is chased by Apollo and escapes rape by turning into a laurel. (This transformation is grotesquely reimagined by Milton's friend Marvell in "The Garden" as indicative of Apollo's sexual desire for *plants:* "Apollo hunted Daphne so / Only that she might Laurel grow.") Then, (3) the birth of Bacchus from adultery is employed by Milton as a means of coordinating both classical and Christian types of syncretism: Ammon, this Libyan king, was identified in pagan tradition with Jupiter on the one hand and biblical Ham (Cham) on the other. This tale of adultery subtly underlines that for Milton classical myth was not simply fiction but garbled history, often biblical history, distorted by later pagan retellings. (I suspect Milton gleaned this passage from his reading of Walter Ralegh's *History of the World* (1614).)[12]

Indeed, this sense of growing historicity is amplified by the fourth comparison, to Mount Amara, a comparison drawn this time not from ancient mythographies but from modern travel accounts, almost certainly the one printed by Samuel Purchas in his *Purchas his Pilgrimage* (1626). Purchas, relating the account of Luis de Urreta, a Spanish Dominican, provides us with several striking details:

> This Hill is situate as the Nauill of that Ethiopian Body, and
> Centre of their Empire, vnder the Equinoctiall Line, where the

Sunne may take his best view thereof, as not encountring in all
his long iourney with the like Theatre, wherein the Graces and
Muses are Actors, no place more graced with Natures store, or
furnished with such a store-house of bookes. . . . But greater
Iewels then those are kept in Amara, the Princes of the Blood
Royall, which are sent to this hill at eight yeeres old, and neuer
returne thence, except they be chosen Emperours.[13]

The comparison with a "Theatre" reminds us that Milton's Eden is also "a
woodie Theatre" (4.141), and indeed Purchas's extended account of the situation of Amara provides an obvious model for the geography of Milton's
own high garden:

It is situate in a great Plaine largely extending it selfe euery
way, without other hill in the same for the space of 30.
leagues, the forme thereof round and circular, the height
such, that it is a daies worke to ascend from the foot to the
top; round about, the rock is cut so smooth and euen, without
any vnequall swellings, that it seemeth to him that stands
beneath, like a high wall, wheron the Heauen is as it were
propped: and at the top it is ouer-hanged with rocks, jutting
forth of the sides the space of a mile, bearing out like mush-
romes, so that it is impossible to ascend it, or by ramming
with earth, battering with Canon, scaling or otherwise to win
it. It is aboue 20. leagues in circuit compassed with a wall on
the top, well wrought, that neither man nor beast in chase
may fall downe. The top is a plaine field, onely toward the
South is a rising Hil, beautifying this Plaine, as it were with a
watch-tower, not seruing alone to the eye, but yeelding also a
pleasant spring which passeth through all that Plaine, paying
his tributes to euery Garden that will exact it, and making a
Lake, whence issueth a Riuer.[14]

This is Milton's account of Satan approaching Eden:

So on he fares, and to the border comes,
Of *Eden,* where delicious Paradise,

Now nearer, Crowns with her enclosure green,
As with a rural mound the champain head
Of a steep wilderness, whose hairie sides
With thicket overgrown, gottesque and wilde,
Access deni'd; and over head up grew
Insuperable highth of loftiest shade,
Cedar, and Pine, and Firr, and branching Palm,
A Silvan Scene, and as the ranks ascend
Shade above shade, a woodie Theatre
Of stateliest view. Yet higher then thir tops
The verdurous wall of paradise up sprung:
Which to our general Sire gave prospect large
Into his neather Empire neighbouring round.
And higher then that Wall a circling row
Of goodliest Trees loaden with fairest Fruit,
Blossoms and Fruits at once of golden hue (4.131–48)

Milton's Eden, in short, is modeled on what was at least claimed to be a real place. There is even a kind of metaphorical congruity between the fabulous library of Amara, assumed genuine by some English scholars, and said to contain all books ("their number is in a manner innumerable, their price inestimable"), and *Paradise Lost* itself, encompassing all literature, ancient and modern.[15]

This list, then, moves from the mythic origin of the seasons through to contemporary travel accounts, and concludes by granting Eden geographical specificity: "this *Assyrian* Garden." It also suggests a variety of interconnections between biblical, pagan, and even modern narratives. And yet for all that the reader has nevertheless been confronted for almost twenty verses with a list of what exactly Eden is *not,* and these gardens rehearse a series of narratives of rape, actual and attempted, of adultery, and of imprisonment. The grammar may insist that these are not Eden; and yet the content refuses to disperse. Who can unthink that Proserpina was dragged off by Dis (Pluto), that Daphne was chased by Apollo, that the Nyseian Isle hid the offspring of adultery, and so forth, in this tiered set of comparisons, a technique repeated throughout the epic.[16] Milton's fallen gardens all allude to the coming fate of Eden, and they contaminate our encounter with Eden as a yet unfallen space. If there is any didacticism here, it is that we cannot easily shun the pagan inheritance of humanist education. Du Bartas had looked forward to one "who will wholly purge" poetry of such an inheritance; Milton, however, confronted this problem by absorbing and displaying it, and a reading of *Paradise Lost* that can detect only hostility to the pagan masters of the epic genre has mistaken the admonitory pronouncements of Milton's epic narrator for the deeper complexity of Milton himself.

The counterpart to this sort of vertical contamination is what I term horizontal contamination, the allied structural technique of twinning. Almost every significant event in *Paradise Lost* has its twin (and sometimes twins become triplets or interact with other twins). Horizontal contamination is the poetic product of an ethical philosophy, once again, that regards evil as disarmingly close in appearance to the good; virtue therefore must struggle to separate the good from the evil.

Sometime just after he returned from Italy, Milton wrote down in his commonplace book under the heading "Malum morale" (moral evil) a quotation to this exact effect from the early African Father Tertullian:

> in malo morali potest multum esse admistum boni idque arte singulari, nemo venenum temperat felle, et hellaboro, sed conditis pulmentis et bene saporatis ita diabolus letale quod conficit, rebus dei gratissimis imbuit &c.[17]

> [In moral evil much good may be mixed, and that with singular craft; "no one mingles venom with gall or hellebore, but with seasoned, fine-tasting dishes; thus whatever deadly dish the devil cooks up, he steeps it with things most pleasing to God," etc.]

The idea that bad speech can be likened to cooking is as old as Plato's *Gorgias,* where Plato cautions that the relation of sophistry to actual justice is analogous to that of cookery to medicine. Milton himself had tapped into this traditional association in his student feasting poem "At a Vacation Exercise," where he heralds his switch into English verse with the faintly luxurious promise: "The daintiest dishes shall be serv'd up last" (14). What the Christian tradition adds is the demonic ingredient: the devil, and indeed all devils, will entice us with fair words.

Milton had already dramatized this in his rather unmasquelike *Maske . . . Presented at Ludlow-Castle,* with its continuous rather than episodic presentation, focusing, often at great length, on the moral problem of appraising the words of strangers. Although the actual staging of this masque will have been collaborative, it was nevertheless probably Milton's idea to present the first *peripeteia* of the drama, Comus's imprisonment of the Lady, as in "a stately Palace, set out with all manner of deliciousness: soft Musick, tables spred with all Dainties."[18] Yet the audience of this masque *are* sitting in a stately palace set out with all manner of deliciousness, music, and dainties while they watch a drama presenting a stately palace set out, again, with all manner of deliciousness, music, and dainties. Somewhat austerely for a festive occasion, the first audience is asked to ponder the similarities between the licentious and the virtuous inflections of the same scene, and to make sure that they stay firmly on their own (virtuous) side of the action. It is notable, too, that the surviving performance text of the masque is shorter than the printed version, especially in this scene. For Milton revised his text, and more than once, in order to transform it from what had been acceptable as an acting script for mainly very young actors—the Lady was fifteen, and she was the oldest of the child actors—into a readerly text, where the moral questions of how to distinguish seeming from genuine virtue are amplified.[19]

In some senses it is surprising that Milton, a few years after he had written *A Maske,* bothered writing down the Tertullian extract into his reading log at all, as it was such a patristic commonplace. Milton, for instance, was also reading Ignatius of Antioch around this time, and in his Epistle to the Trallians Ignatius had commented of heretics that they mixed true doctrine "with their own poison, speaking things which are unworthy of credit, like those who administer a deadly drug in sweet wine."[20] That Milton saw fit to front his commonplace book with this sentiment—for although it was not the first thing Milton entered in the order of time, it was what he chose to place as the first visible entry in his notebook—underlines its symbolic importance. A commonplace book in moral philosophy should start with such an affirmation.

Indeed, Milton placed only one further comment on this opening page, and the two comments may be read in tandem as the twin terminals of Milton's ethical circuitry. His second comment, confected from two works of the church father Lactantius, "the Christian Cicero," also addresses the problem of evil, but this time from the divine rather than the demonic end of the system. Note, however, Milton's slightly worried annotation to this piece of patristic reading:

> Cur permittit deus malum? ut ratio virtuti constare possit. virtus enim malo arguitur, illustratur, exercetur quemadmodum disserit Lactantius l. 5. c. 7. ut haberet ratio et prudentia in quo se exerceret, eligendo bona, fugiendo mala. lactan. de ira dei. c. 13. quamvis et hæc non satisfaciunt.

> [Why does God permit evil? "So that reason may correspond to virtue." For virtue is made known, is illustrated, and is exercised by evil, as Lactantius argues [in *Divine Institutes,*] book 5, chapter 7, that reason and prudence might have something by which they may discipline themselves in choosing good things and fleeing evil things. Lactantius, *On the Anger of God,* chapter 13—however much these arguments fail to satisfy.]

Milton, in short, knew that evil came disguised as good, and this would in time underpin his literary presentation of devilry in *Paradise Lost* and *Paradise Regained,* where Satan and his crew are almost always encountered in some shape-shifted form or disguise. But although he broadly accepted these twin propositions, from very early on Milton nevertheless worried about the ultimate coherence of this system as a theodicy, or an answer to the question of why God permits evil at all. One of the poles of his system was incontrovertible—"And no marvel; for Satan himself is transformed into an angel of light" (2 Cor. 11:14)—but the other, that God permits this to exercise us, perturbed Milton: "haec non satisfaciunt" (these things fail to satisfy). *Paradise Lost,* formally identified as a theodicy by its narrator (1.25–26), would attempt an answer to this exact question, this time not by merely affirming the moral healthiness of struggle, but by investigating the original story of how this situation came to be. In a striking piece of Miltonic continuity, the later epic rises to the implicit challenge set almost three decades earlier on the first page of the commonplace book.

The use of literary doubling to explore the nature and origin of evil was not invented but inherited by Milton. The idea of the demonic simulacrum was, as we saw, biblical and patristic, but the specific literary debt—perhaps Milton's major "device" debt to any single author—was to the Elizabethan poet Edmund Spenser and his unfinished epic *The Faerie Queene* (1590, 1596).[21] Spenser was one of the very few English poets Milton ever mentioned, and it is no accident that he praises Spenser, "whom I dare be known to think a better teacher then *Scotus* or *Aquinas*," in the course of one of his more famous passages on virtue as only elicited by combat with vice: "That vertue therefore which is but a youngling in the contemplation of evill, and knows not the utmost that vice promises to her followers, and rejects it, is but a blank vertue, not a pure."[22] Spenser, for Milton, was not a good poet merely because he was a didactic poet (there was no available articulated literary theory that taught otherwise), but because his didacticism relied on the use of doubles and copies, and on the challenge to the reader to distinguish these correctly. In Spenser as in Milton this had a confessional edge: the popish Catholic is apt to produce and to be deceived by images and idols, worshipping the copy for the real thing; the Protestant is confirmed as such by resisting such eye worship, probing the reality behind the image.

Obvious transplantations of this Spenserian dynamic into Milton's productions include the central problem of *A Maske*, where the Lady in the forest is captured not by force but by guile: Comus is in appearance to her a "Gentle villager" or "good Shepherd" (304, 307), and the irony of her subsequent moralizing on how such "courtesie" is "sooner found in lowly sheds / With smoaky rafters, then in tapstry Halls / And Courts of Princes" (322–25) is that this otherwise slightly hostile sentiment in an indeed tapestried hall is, in this specific encounter, an error. Milton's inheritance from Spenser could be very complex in this regard, for instance in his "Captain or Colonel" sonnet, where the vocabulary again shows a surprising, sunken affinity with Spenserian lexis and narrative. Milton's poem imagines a knight in arms before the entrance to a bower: this is, on the surface of it, poeticism for a soldier before poet Milton's house ("the Muses Bowre"), and Milton is asking him to leave him alone. But one level lower, it is also a complex inversion of Acrasia's Bowre of Blisse, destroyed by the knight Guyon in some famous stanzas of *The Faerie Queene*.[23]

Miltonic doublings in *Paradise Lost* take place at the simplest level in repeated words, and especially repeated doublets of opposed words. Perhaps the most important such doublet is "descent" / "ascent," and cognates. These words appear dozens of times throughout *Paradise Lost*, and help to create the impression that the universe of the poem is one in which all sorts of things can go up and down, both spatially and morally. The central symbol of this is the ladder connecting Heaven and the visible universe, seen by Satan from surrounding Chaos, a corridor able to be extended or retracted: "The Stairs were such as whereon *Jacob* saw / Angels ascending and descending" (3.510–11). For Satan, descent is humiliation: at his change from angel to snake in the book of the Fall, he cries "O foul descent!" (9.163); this is soon followed with "But what will not Ambition and Revenge / Descend to?" (168–69), an uneasy formulation, as "Ambition" usually rises, and "Descend," here intended to mean "resort," retains its air of decay and humiliation. Such passages display a demonic confusion of spatial and moral categories, already evident in Satan's first speech in Pandaemonium to his fallen comrades: "From this descent / Celestial vertues rising will appear / More glorious and more dread then from no fall" (2.14–16), and a little further on in the same speech he repeats the doublet: "That in our proper motion we ascend / Up to our native seat: descent and fall / To us is adverse" (2.14–15, 75–77). The word continues to be used by the wicked in negative or aggressive senses: Satan applies it twice to Sin and Death, for instance, as an instruction of how to use their new causeway to "descend" on Eden to "kill" mankind (10.94, 98).

Yet spatial descent is not of itself a bad thing, and indeed Milton relies on one particular descent, when he calls on his muse: "Descend from Heav'n *Urania*" (7.1). In Heaven the moral and physical categories are carefully separated out by God when he discusses the Incarnation with his Son: "Nor shalt thou by descending to assume / Mans Nature, less'n or degrade thine owne" (3.303–4). The angel Raphael comes "descending" to Eden; and in Eden "All perfect good" from God "descends" to man (5.363, 399, the latter again at 7.513). Adam then thanks the "condescention" (8.9; he repeats the term at 8.649) of Raphael as divine historian, deigning to relate heavenly matters to earthly beings; and Adam, after hearing Raphael's narration, later says "from this high pitch let us descend" (8.198), as he recompenses Raphael's story of Creation with that of his own earthly creation. God, inside Adam's narration, in response to Adam's request for a suitable mate, teases him, pointing to his own divine singularity and the "infinite descents" between him and his creatures (8.410). In Raphael's narration of the War in Heaven, the pivotal moment is when the Son "Ascended" (6.762) in his chariot; earlier in the battle, Michael's sword falls "descending" (6.325) on

Satan's, a usage picking up on the angels' "descending" to tread on their fallen counterparts, recalled by the latter right at the opening of the epic (1.327). After the Fall the Son will "descend [ . . . ] strait" to judge Adam and Eve (10.90, repeated at 337, from Adam's point of view), and fallen man will require "Prevenient grace descending" (11.3). At the end of the epic, "descend" is used four times in forty lines as Raphael and Adam come down from the hill of speculation, in preparation for the expulsion and the journey ahead (12.588, 606, 607, 628).

Milton leans on this doublet at least superficially because it alludes to one of the most famous of all Virgilian spatial moralisms: "facilis descensus Averno / . . . / sed revocare gradum superasque evadere ad auras, / hoc opus, hic labor est" (the descent to Hell is easy . . . but to climb back up, and to escape to the upper air, that is the difficulty, that the labor).[24] Milton builds this allusion into his narrator's voice at the opening of the third book, as the epic narrator, tracking the path of Satan himself, flies out of Hell and up through Chaos, alongside the created world, to Heaven:

> Taught by the heav'nly Muse to venture down
> The dark descent, and up to reascend,
> Though hard and rare: (3.19–21)

The polarity of the Virgilian allusion is reversed, however, in the description in Book 10 of the bridge built from Hell to Eden by Sin and Death as "from hence a passage broad, / Smooth, easie, inoffensive down to Hell" (10.304–5). The narrator may "reascend," but most of us will slide the "Smooth" way "down."

The ascent / descent doublet has a deeper importance, as it is also the means by which Milton negotiates his relationship with Platonism. Platonism, in this context, means a philosophy of intellectual and spiritual ascent and descent, where God is at the top of the scale, and created beings slide up and down below him. The strongest piece of such Platonism in *Paradise Lost* is Raphael's ontological lesson for Adam:

> O *Adam,* one Almightie is, from whom
> All things proceed, and up to him return,
> If not deprav'd from good, created all

Such to perfection, one first matter all,
Indu'd with various forms, various degrees
Of substance (5.169–74)

This has rightly been seen as a passage exemplifying what modern commentators have called Milton's theological "monism": "*one* first matter all."[25] It also might suggest on a first reading a kind of free elasticity—"proceed," "return," as if creation were a kind of respiratory movement, God breathing out and at length breathing back in his creation. But there is a qualification: man is only in such a condition as long as he is "not deprav'd from good." As man was in the event indeed depraved from good, this ontology no longer applies.

This situation might be compared with the strongest statement of ontological Platonism formulated in the renaissance, namely Pico della Mirandola's heady *Oration on the Dignity of Man* of 1486, in which Pico also imagined God talking to Adam in Eden. But Pico's God hands over to Adam radical freedom:

Igitur hominem accepit indiscretae opus imaginis, atque in
mundi positum meditullio, sic est alloquutus. Nec certam
sedem, nec propriam faciem: nec munus ullum peculiare tibi
dedimus o, Adam, ut quam sedem quam faciem, quae munera
tute optaueris, ea pro voto, pro tua sententia habeas &
possideas. Definita caeteris natura intra praescriptas a nobis
leges cohercetur. Tu nullis angustiis cohercitus pro tuo
arbitrio, in cuius manu te posui tibi illam praefinies.[26]

[Therefore He made man, a work of indeterminate form, and
placed him in the middle region of the world, saying: "We
have given to you, O Adam, no certain seat, no fixed aspect,
no gift specific to you alone, so that you may upon your own
judgment have and hold the seat, the aspect, the gift that you
desire for yourself. A fixed nature for all other creatures is
limited within laws prescribed by us. But, coerced by no such
straightnesses, you, following your own judgment, will
prescribe your own end, which I have placed in your hands."]

This is Pico's defense of free will, as the side note in the 1506 edition of Pico's works points out, and Milton's God would support at least that goal. But Pico's God concludes by telling Adam that he is neither mortal nor immortal, neither a beast nor a god, but capable of making himself either. Milton's God could never come out with such dangerous stuff. Yet at this divine offer exclaims Pico: "O summam Dei patris liberalitatem, summam et admirandam hominis foelicitatem!" (O highest generosity of God the Father, O highest and most admirable good fortune for man!). Pico's Adam is a limitless being, but Milton's Adam, very much the more orthodox of the two, is a being who is told to keep his curiosity in check, not to pry too far into God's ways, and above all to honor the prohibition of the Forbidden Tree as a pledge of his obedience.

*Paradise Lost* contains, however, an embedded Piconian narrative as a doublet to the actual Fall, in the form of Eve's aspiring dream, her own (in Fowler's phrase) "narcotic epic" (5.28–93). Adam and Eve do not know, as the reader does, that this dream was demonically inspired by Satan, squat at Eve's ear in the likeness of a toad (4.800–803). Eve therefore recounts to Adam an experience the origins of which neither of them can really explain. She recalls how, in her dream, she was awoken in moonlight and led by a "voice" (she thought it Adam's) to the Forbidden Tree, where she encountered one like an angel, who, wondering "is Knowledge so despis'd?," ate of the tree and made her do likewise. Eating empowers flight, and Eve and her tempter soar upwards: but "suddenly / My Guide was gon, and I, me thought, sunk down." This sudden flight failure snaps Eve out of her dream.

This whole passage is supercharged with groups of keywords that feature throughout the epic, notably fall words ("fruit," "taste," "sweet," "pluck"), and aspiring words ("merit," "ascend," "exaltation"). The undertone of forbidden knowledge is reinforced by the immediate classical referent, the story of Daedalus and Icarus in Ovid, underlined by Eve's "My Guide was gon," which reworks Ovid's "deseruitque ducem" (he [Icarus] deserted his guide [Daedalus]).[27] Note the careful difference, however: in Ovid, it is Icarus who in his "audacious flight" (*audaci . . . volatu*)[28] deserts his leader, whereas in *Paradise Lost* it is the leader who disappears, a moment that presumably corresponds to the moment earlier narrated when the angel Ithuriel pokes the toad with his spear, at which Satan explodes into his own form, "the grieslie King" (4.810–11, 821). Eve in her dream is ambiguously culpable, as the shady angel by the tree literally presses the fruit onto Eve's lips, such "that I, methought, / Could not but taste" (5.85–86). The episode also simultaneously looks backward within the epic to Eve's narration of her own creation in Book 4, where again a voice led her from one place to another (4.467), and forward to the Fall itself in Book 9, where Satan will capitalize on the arguments first rehearsed here. Nevertheless his are Piconian arguments, and when the dream-Satan complains that the fruit is "Forbidd'n here, it seems, as onely fit / For God's, yet able to make Gods of Men" (5.69–70), he sounds like Pico's God, and Milton will approve neither of them. "Knowledge" here is also *gnosis* in the sense in which the word was used by the Gnostic heretics, and just as Milton subtly parodied Gnostic cosmogony in Chaos, so here in this Satanic dream is the knowledge of the Gnostics' "science falsely so called" (1 Tim. 6:20). There is no real aviation to be had from eating fruit.[29]

Doublings and doublets, then, function both at the level of specific words and also at the level of episodes. Perhaps the most obvious doubling in the epic is the close parallelism of Hellish and Heavenly zones and activities: the devils continue to imitate many of their former practices, but now abortively or in confusion. For instance, when Satan asks the assembled devils in Pandaemonium who will undertake the difficult voyage to undo mankind, all are "mute," until Satan himself volunteers, precisely so that when God in Heaven asks the assembled angels who will undertake the difficult voyage to restore mankind, all are again "mute," until the Son volunteers himself (2.417–29; 3.217–26).[30] We have looked at the major Edenic example of this structural technique, but there are many others too, notably Satan's address to the Sun, in which he curses the Sun (4.32–41), cantilevered in the epic's structure against Adam's address to the sun, where he, conversely, asks the Sun to instruct him how to praise the Creator (8.273–82).

These are oppositions, but they are not, and there are seldom ever, simple oppositions in *Paradise Lost*. The heavenly assembly is, initially, as mute as its hellish counterpart, and although Satan starts off cursing the sun, as his speech develops he vacillates between defiance toward God, and, as we have seen, an astonishing capacity for regret. Satan's blasphemies offended some early readers of Milton, but conventional devilry on its own has little power to shock—demons, after all, are supposed to behave like that. Milton's Satan is shocking because his wickedness is accompanied by such disturbingly complex feelings of remorse. This Satan works his way into his readers not because he blasphemes but because he cries.

We now conclude with two examples of complex "horizontal" twinning, both drawn from accounts of origins, the first from Sin's account of her origin, and the second from the contrasting accounts from Eve and Adam of, once again, Eve's creation. When Satan encounters his daughter Sin, at first he does not recognize her or their offspring Death. She has to remind him of her origin:

> All of a sudden miserable pain
> Surprised thee, dim thine eyes, and dizzy swum
> In darkness, while thy head flames thick and fast
> Threw forth, till on the left side opening wide,
> Likest to thee in shape and countenance bright,
> Then shining heavenly fair, a goddess armed
> Out of thy head I sprung (2.752–58)

This is, almost, the origin of evil. But it takes place, so Sin explains, "at the assembly, and in sight / Of all the seraphim with thee combined / In bold conspiracy" (2.749–51), suggesting that conspiracy, which must also be the product of evil intent, was then already underway. The full narrative context is only granted to the reader later in the epic, when Raphael—who after all was not there and is relying on divine prompt—narrates the consequences of God's decree: chronologically, the earliest evil in the poem comes in the line "All seemed well pleased, all seemed, but were not all" (5.617). Evil is then given a story with the account of the sleepless Satan, moved by both "envy" and "pride" (662, 665), a twinning of the two traditionally debated motives for his fall, whispering rebellion to his initially unnamed "associate" (696), and gathering after them "the third part of heaven's host" (710). Raphael says nothing of the peculiar birth of Sin; but conversely Satan and Sin do not mention the Exaltation—they are, as it were, "dizzy," even amnesiac, about their own falls.[31]

Sin and Raphael therefore differ in their perspectives. Sin thinks allegorically, as she is an allegory herself; whereas Raphael thinks in literal, narrative terms. It is useful for Milton to present Sin to us first, because the narrative origin of evil was perhaps the hardest philosophical problem facing Christian exegetes of the Genesis narrative: Adam and Eve fell because Satan tempted them; but who then tempted Satan? As the only allowable answer was "no one," the question had to become rather how did sin arise, without external prompting, within Satan's mind? This was the question that obsessed the most philosophical of the Latin Fathers, Augustine, in his *City of God,* a foundation text in the Western tradition and one carefully meditated by Milton at a number of different times in his life. After long debate, Augustine's astonishing conclusion was that humans not only must not, but cannot, seek the origin of the first evil will: it was something that had no cause, and was therefore beyond rational apprehension.[32] Milton in effect provides the poetic counterpart to this crux by presenting the origin of sin first as the origin of Sin, an allegorical character. To a philosophical imponderable Milton provides a local habitation and a name.

It also allowed Milton to manipulate more horizontal twinnings. The vertical twin of the origin of Sin is of course the birth of Athena from the head of Zeus, most immediately from the account in Hesiod.[33] The horizontal connections are, on the one hand, to the divine gestation of the Son from the Father, in Milton's implicitly Arian theology; and, on the other hand, to Eve, in her creation, and also once again at her "watery gleam" (4.461), contemplating her own image. That the Son was not unbegotten but generated from the Father was of course Milton's belief, as we know at great length from his *De doctrina Christiana.* In *Paradise Lost* he is perhaps necessarily subtle on this point, but here he presents a devilish parody of such generation, even to the production of the third member of this satanic trinity, Death:

> Thyself in me thy perfect image viewing
> Becam'st enamoured, and such joy thou tookst
> With me in secret, that my womb conceived
> A growing burden (2.764–67)

But there is also a horizontal connection to Eve, for the birth of Sin out of the left side of Satan's head parodies Eve's creation from the left side of Adam (8.465), another extrabiblical, although traditional, detail. The contrast also emphasizes that Eve was created out of Adam's side by God, whereas Satan's own thought (inside his head) is responsible for Sin. The deeper connection, however, is to Eve's watery image:

> there had I fixed
> Mine eyes till now, and pined with vain desire,
> Had not a voice thus warned me (4.465–67)

The Son is created by God's (sexless) contemplation of his own image; Sin is created by Satan's (erotic) contemplation and indeed violation of his own image, which is simultaneously him and yet female. Eve, contemplating her own image, is drawn away, instructed that happiness will, for her, be found in a complementary being, not in a mere copy of herself. As we saw, Narcissus broke the skin of the water, plunging his arms into his image, and Satan too completes his diabolic trinity by creating his own travesty of the Holy Spirit through his "secret" sex with his daughter. Eve, however, does not violate her image; she merely looks. So she can be led away from this path, in safety, at least for a time.

Eve's flirtation with a narcissistic version of herself is reported by her in her speech recounting her own creation, a virtuosic combination of not only Ovid, as we have seen, but also Homer as interpreted by Neoplatonic writers such as the third-century scholar Porphyry. For in his influential allegorizing essay *On the Cave of the Nymphs* Porphyry argued that Homer's cave from the Ithaca episode of *The Odyssey*, along with many other similar caves of especially Zoroastrian and other ancient mystery traditions, was a symbol of the material realm, and the water flowing through it of the soul's descent into matter and generation.[34] It is notable that Milton suffuses Eve's creation with this specifically Neoplatonic light, perhaps even with a tinge of the pagan mystery traditions, something he entirely withholds from his account of Adam's first moments.

After Eve has been drawn away by the voice, she is led to Adam. There is an interesting potential narrative lacuna here. In Eve's account she came to consciousness under flowers and followed the sound of waters issuing from a cave. In Adam's account he awoke to find Eve "not far off" (8.481) rather than right next to him, and Eve potentially therefore managed a short, unremembered stumble between being fashioned by God and waking under flowers, perhaps an analogue for the soul's forgotten descent into matter. This fleeting narrative tremor, however, turns into a fissure when we compare the recollections of Adam and Eve of their first meeting. Eve is quite explicit that she at first considered her own image to be more attractive than Adam, and she initially fled him; she remembers a different order of things, however short-lived that was.[35] Adam for his part accepts that Eve turned away from him at the point of their first encounter, but he interprets this moment—in a passage that might almost be suspected of displaying embarrassment were it on the other side of the Fall—as modesty, and an initial rejection soon overturned by his "pleaded reason." Again, Eve's account provides a counterpoint to this interpretation. According to Adam, on the creation of Eve he uttered a prayer of thanks directly to God, containing the marriage formula "Bone of my bone, flesh of my flesh" (8.491–99). But Eve reports this speech as directed at her, not God: "Return fair Eve, / Whom fly'st thou? Whom thou fly'st, of him thou art, / His flesh, his bone" (4.481–83). This is a famous crux, for although Eve reports her version of events from the position of having now accepted Adam's natural superiority (4.489–91), she recalls a time before this acquiescence; and Adam's account, with its subtle incompatibilities, only serves to underline that Eve in her very first state was already acting with independence.

Further scrutiny deepens the fissure. Eve's creation, as we noted, is tinged with the idea of the Neoplatonic descent from mentality into matter, and it is fitting then that she materializes, as it were, looking down, mute. In contrast, Adam, in an account that is all ascent, looks up, springs up, and talks: "Straight toward heaven my wondering eyes I turned, / . . . By quick instinctive motion up I sprung / . . . My tongue obeyed and readily could name / Whate'er I saw" (8.257, 259, 272–73). Adam's quick brain then deduces that because he can perceive created things there must be a Creator, and such a Creator is due worship.

The two accounts of the origin of evil discussed above offer different perspectives, allegorical and then literal, on the same event, an event perhaps unknowable in itself. An argument can be made that the differing perspectives of Adam and Eve on their creations perform a similar function. Eve's creation feels more influenced by allegory, as pure, self-dependent mentality contemplating itself is drawn down into materiality and dependency. The creation of Adam on the other hand is more literal, and indeed more biblical. But it is hard to deny that notwithstanding this consideration, the contrast between Eve and Adam here is troubling, and portends what is to come.

# 21

## Justifying the Ways of God to Men

I T  I S  O F T E N  claimed that *Paradise Lost* stands or falls as a poem as it suc-
ceeds or fails to carry out its opening intention: to "justifie the wayes of
God to men" (1.26). It is presumably true that Milton meant what he said
in this line; and if it were to be demonstrated that, within the principles of
his own religious system, Milton had indeed stumbled in his performance,
then he would have to concede some kind of failure. Milton, unlike some
of his modern readers, was not at liberty to sport with the terms of his own
Christian beliefs.[1]

Nevertheless, a poem may display many different kinds of value, or perform some tasks better than others, and most readers have been happy to
find meanings in the poem independent of its theological success or otherwise. Some have gone further, and declared that the (perceived) failure of
the theology is either irrelevant to the success of the poem or alternatively
in some way contributory to that very success. A few readers over the centuries have pushed this last permutation into a statement of intention: Milton
meant this (perceived) failure.

Attractive though that last proposition has been to a few critics and writers, no convincing form of interpretation can view *Paradise Lost* as an elaborate trick played on its pious narrator by its impious creator. But it is still legitimate to ask whether Milton succeeded in his stated aim; and it is also reasonable to think that the overall artistic achievement of any poem is linked to its intellectual coherence. This is also a question of taste: readers of the last century or so have relished the artistic effects of tension or ambiguity, "energies" running counter to the stated purposes of the text or inferred intentions of the author; many, indeed, locate their version of literary value in such "energies." But there is no point either in claiming that Milton intended such instabilities to destabilize his poem beyond repair or in exonerating him if any such instabilities indeed overwhelm his structure.

The question of Milton's achievement in this regard is complicated because Milton to a measurable extent inherited, rather than created, the system he explores. Adam and Eve in the Garden of Eden, perhaps the most elaborated world myth west of the Zhou and north of the Berbers, had received such precise and profound attention by Milton's time that his own interpretation inevitably runs in deep grooves carved ever deeper by theologians, writers, and everyday believers before him. God created Adam and Eve, set them a test which they failed, and then held them and their posterity responsible for that failure. Almost nobody in Christendom professed otherwise. There is no victory to be won in holding Milton entirely responsible for such a mythology.

From the point of view of literary interpretation, it is best to search for what Milton brought to this tradition—what is Miltonic about Milton—without necessarily forgetting that he was at least responsible for ensuring that the entire circuitry of the array could still bear appropriate current. But if we wish to attack (or indeed praise) Milton's God for being God, we must be careful to distinguish between what is an attribute or a process that, so to speak, God imposes on Milton, compared to attributes and processes that Milton imposes on God.

Recall Milton's theological Arminianism: he believed that God had given man freedom to accept or reject salvation. Arminianism can in fact more precisely be defined as the adoption of specific stances on five theological debates, all parts of soteriology, the study of who shall be saved. These were the central questions debated at the Synod of Dort in 1618–1619, a major international symposium of Protestant theologians, having been crystalized into five topics in a 1610 "Remonstrance," drawn up by the followers of Jacobus Arminius: predestination, corruption, conversion, redemption, and perseverance. A Calvinist would argue that only a limited number of people are the elect and have been predestined to be so; that we are rendered totally depraved by the Fall, incapable of winning grace for ourselves; that grace, once given, cannot be resisted; that Christ only atones for the elect; and that the elect persevere in their state of grace and cannot fall from it. The Arminians countered each of these points, claiming in their Remonstrance that salvation is offered to all and not to a predestined minority; that humans were not entirely depraved by the Fall and might, albeit with some divine assistance, win grace; that grace has to be accepted and therefore can be resisted; that Christ therefore died for everyone who freely accepts him; and that one can indeed fall from a state of grace. The Synod of Dort anathematized these views, and the "Canons of Dort" were immediately translated and published in England, supplying the framework and terms for most subsequent debate.[2] "Calvinist" and "Arminian" by this point had already become complex words, capable of bearing political and ecclesiastical as well as theological meaning, and more than capable of polemical distortion.[3] Here we are chiefly concerned with their theological meanings.

The God of *Paradise Lost* is theologically Arminian, vociferously so, albeit with some interesting complications. To take each of the five points again: even though some will reject it, salvation is offered to all: "offerd grace / Invites" (3.187–88). God promises that after the Fall "once more I will renew / His [man's] lapsed powers (3.175–76; compare 11.1–4). The Son's sacrifice atones for every fallen human who accepts it: "His [Adam's] crime makes guiltie all his Sons, thy [the Son's] merit / Imputed shall absolve them who renounce / Thir own both righteous and unrighteous deeds" (3.290–92). As for resisting grace and persevering in it, God is clear that "if they will hear, / Light after light well us'd they shall attain, / And to the end persisting, safe arrive" (3.195–97)—and so safe arrival is only a consequence of human persistence and relies on a free choice to hear or not to hear: "*if* they will hear." The reason why God is an Arminian is that for Milton to argue otherwise would be to deprive man (and angel) of moral agency:

Freely they stood who stood, and fell who fell.
Not free, what proof could they have givn sincere
Of true allegiance, constant Faith or Love,
Where onely what they needs must do, appeard,
Not what they would? (3.102–6)

From his first full statement of this position in *Areopagitica* in 1644, there under the strong influence of his readings in the church father Lactantius,[4] Milton never wavered significantly from this basic ethical philosophy. That he conceptualized it as the most important distinction between Calvinist and Arminian positions is confirmed by his last prose work, *Of True Religion* (1673), in which he deprecated the use of "sect" words (Lutheran, Calvinist, Arian, Socinian, Anabaptist, Arminian), while nevertheless offering thumbnail sketches of what was at stake in such differences. His Calvinist "is taxt with Predestination, and to make God the Author of sin; not with any dishonorable thought of God, but it may be overzealously asserting his absolute power, not without plea of Scripture." Whereas his Arminian "is condemn'd for setting up free will against free grace; but that Imputation he disclaims in all his writings, and grounds himself largly upon Scripture only."[5] Even were Milton's *De doctrina* never to have been recovered in the nineteenth century, it would be still be obvious where the later Milton's sympathies lie.

It is, however, also important to recognize some fundamental shared ground between Calvinists and Arminians. Neither party contested the basic premise that original sin itself existed, and that all Adam and Eve's posterity suffer from it by direct biological inheritance, and that this is not just a universal ethical sickness but a matter of universal culpability. As Milton's God says, man has committed "Treason," and "He with his whole posteritie must dye, / Dye hee or Justice must"; and, as we have seen, "His [Adam's] crime makes guiltie all his Sons" (207, 209–10, 290). Milton therefore in no sense believed in man's radical freedom. Before the Fall, freedom depended on obedience. After the Fall, freedom relies, once again, on making the right choices. The difference between before and after the Fall is in this respect a matter of degree, not kind, and man's postlapsarian weakness is itself an admonishment of his dependence on God. As Milton's God declares,

Upheld by me, yet once more he shall stand
On even ground against his mortal foe,
By me upheld, that he may know how frail
His fall'n condition is (3.178–81)

These lines summarize Milton's whole general ethical theory: we are all "frail" and "fall'n," we may yet "stand," but only "Upheld by me." This is a version of the free will defense, but one with a strong lapsarian flavor: we may still be free to choose, but our power of choice is impaired. This was not so for Adam or indeed the angels, however, who need not have fallen in the first place: "Sufficient to have stood, though free to fall" (3.99).

There is a complication within Milton's Arminianism, however, as a fine book by Stephen Fallon has explored.[6] God announces within his general theory a special subset, a class of people to whom are granted unusual powers:

Some I have chosen of peculiar grace
Elect above the rest; so is my will. (3.183–84).

These people "of peculiar grace" are distinguished from "The rest" (185), who are those who must strive under normal ethical conditions. These rest are the ones encountered above who, "if they will hear," and persevere, shall "safe arrive." This is a problematic modification of Arminianism because within it Milton is creating a specially elected group, and, as Fallon discusses, this is not something easy either to square with Milton's general ethical theory or to extract from Milton's formal theology, the *De doctrina*. Is this, Fallon wondered, perhaps a late (i.e., post-Restoration) addition to Milton's design? There is in fact at least a hint of this in the *De doctrina*, but the problem remains: Milton usually insists that we are all free to fail, but here it seems that a few of us are fated to succeed.[7] It is also quite the reverse of appeasing the state censor by ambiguous conformity, for an ivory tower for the elect situated in the corner of otherwise Arminian territory does rather stick out amid all the surrounding language of free choice. Milton, in Fallon's judgment, was in effect creating a theological category for himself and a few hardy forbears, and steeling himself facing forward into an increasingly hostile environment. More than this: he was in fact courting a version of what is termed "single predestination," which has some difficult consequences, namely that for all his talk of free will, Milton may well have decided that he personally was "Elect above the rest." Milton's own freedom, that is to say, was nevertheless constrained within the limits of his election; although fallen, he was still too good to sin *quite* like the rest of us.

The soteriology of Milton's epic, then, is Arminian with modifications. But is his system of falls, angelic and human, itself persuasive as a justification of God's ways to men? Justifying this performance requires us to treat the two different kinds of falls separately.

## THE ANGELIC FALL

The angelic fall is the genuinely mysterious fall, one that had cast a long mythological shadow, but, as far as the literalist Christian exegete was concerned, with disturbingly little developed biblical substance to flesh out even basic details of what had happened.[8] Unlike the human fall it had—at least according to God—no tempter, which is how God distinguishes it from the later fall in Eden:

> The first sort by thir own suggestion fell,
> Self-tempted, self-deprav'd: Man falls deceiv'd
> By the other first (3.129–31)

There are difficulties with God's interpretation of the narrative here—only Eve is truly "deceiv'd"; Adam, explicitly, is "not deceav'd" (9.998)—but theologically the problem is obvious: what caused the first fall? What does "by thir own suggestion" actually mean?

This was a problem that had been debated most influentially by Augustine in *The City of God,* who came to the remarkable conclusion that the causation of the first *mala voluntas* or "evil will" in the entirety of creation could not be spoken of by humans with any philosophical success or religious safety. Now it is significant that Augustine placed this discussion in the context of his debate concerning the angelic, rather than the human, fall: it is the first fall of all that is the hardest to contemplate. Milton, now moving beyond where Augustine dared to tread, dramatizes this problem at the moment in the fifth book of the Exaltation of the Son in Heaven, perhaps the most anxiously debated episode of the entire poem. God declares to the assembled heavenly host that "This day I have begot whom I declare / My onely Son" (5.603–4). The angels are ordered to "confess him Lord" (608) or suffer expulsion from Heaven. No reason is given. God here conspicuously does *not* use one of his keywords so frequently elsewhere applied to the Son, namely "merit," as in the earlier line "By Merit more then Birthright Son of God" (3.309). Instead God pares back angelic stability to an act of mere obedience or disobedience in the face of pure assertion. This is certainly "arbitrary" in the sense of an action arising from God's considered will or pleasure; but is it "arbitrary" in the other seventeenth-century sense of the word, that is, merely at whim, tyrannical? This latter sense is often applied to God by Satan (his "arbitrary punishment / Inflicted," for instance [2.334–35; compare 2.359, and 2.909 on "Chance"]); whereas Raphael uses it in its former sense to Adam when he admonishes him that "to stand or fall" lies "in thine own Arbitrement" (8.640–41).

To decide whether God's promotion of his Son in the manner reported by Milton through Raphael to Adam is arbitrary in its considered or tyrannical senses requires discussion of the Son himself. Milton is somewhat coy in *Paradise Lost* about the earlier history of the Son—who he was and what he was doing before his Exaltation. In the invocation to the third book, the narrator hails a being called "holy Light," who is "ofspring of Heav'n first-born," and who played a decisive role in the creation of this visible universe, "Won from the void and formless infinite" (3.1, 12). This being is slightly more likely to be the Son than the Holy Spirit, but it is nevertheless similar to the being addressed in the first invocation, where a "Spirit" is addressed who was also engaged in the work of creation, again, of this visible universe and not the larger realm in which our universe is placed (1.17, 19–22). Later in the poem, when God is instructing his Son—whom he calls, as elsewhere, his "Word"—to create the visible universe, he sends him out to do so with his "overshadowing Spirit" (7.163–66; he does, however, add "and might" to "overshadowing Spirit," subtly destabilizing the identity of the Spirit as a being rather than an attribute). This makes sense of the opening invocations: Son and Spirit were both there at the creation of our universe.

The question is what the Son was doing before this, and indeed what he was doing, if anything, before the creation of the "higher" universe in which our created universe sits. He does seem to be eternal in some sense in the poem. He is addressed in the invocation to Book 3 as the "Coeternal beam" "of the Eternal," "Bright effluence of bright essence increate," statements that suggest his coeternity with his Father, albeit qualified by the narrator's uncertainty whether the Son may rightly be so called: "May I express thee unblam'd?" (3.1–6). (In *De doctrina*, Milton makes the distinction clearer: God is "aeternus" or eternal, without beginning or end; whereas the Son is merely perpetual, without end.)[9] The hymning angels of Book 3, at any rate, confirm that they consider the Son to have created them and their surrounds:

> Hee [God] Heav'n of Heavens and all the Powers therein
> By thee [the Son] created, and by thee threw down
> Th'aspiring Dominations (3.390–92)

So we can be sure on internal evidence that Milton held the standard view that God created the heavens through his Son, and he created all the living things in the heavens (i.e., the angels) by that means too. The poem does not, however, say that the Son created Chaos. Later on, the Son "threw down" the rebelling angels; and later still he performed a second creation, on behalf of his father and with some help from a "Spirit," of the visible universe. Later still, he became incarnate as a human.

In effect the Son has three different phases of existence. In the helpful phrase of Albert Labriola he is "thrice begotten literally."[10] First, he is begotten by his Father. At this point in his existence he is the Word, and created the Heavens and the angels. God then exalts him, and expresses this as, literally, a second begetting: "This day I have begot whom I declare / My onely Son" (5.603–4). This is in one sense a political begetting, as its direct quotation of Psalm 2 suggests: "I will declare the decree: the LORD hath said unto me, Thou *art* my Son; this day have I begotten thee" (Psalm 2:7). The context of this psalm is the political power of the Lord's anointed on the earth: God laughs at the heathen, saying: "Yet have I set my king upon my holy hill of Zion" (2:6). In Psalms, therefore, "begotten" does not mean gave birth to or generated, but simply appointed. Now, God's begetting in Milton's Heaven is also a political appointment: his Son is now king (God uses the slightly less inflammatory word "Head") in Heaven, "Vicegerent" to the mysterious being who rules all planes of all realities, and must be treated as so. "All knees" must "bow" to him (606–8). But this is not solely a political begetting, in which the word merely means appointing. This is the Son entering the second phase of his existence, begotten as an angel. God is not presenting to the angels a being with whom they are readily acquainted; this is something new in Heaven:

> *This day* I have begot whom I declare
> My onely Son, and on this holy Hill
> Him have anointed, whom ye *now* behold
> At my right hand (5.603–606, my italics)

The Son's third begetting will be as a human, born of woman. So the Son is indeed begotten three times: as Word, as "Head" angel in Heaven, and as Man.

Readers will feel at once that to describe the Son as God and Man does not feel peculiar. To describe him as an angel, however, is more unusual. Nevertheless, there is strong logic to the position. God asks the angels which of them will volunteer to stand in as a blood sacrifice for man. It is imperative that they have the freedom to be able to say yes or no to this request. It is also imperative that this is not an empty request from God—the angels, we are invited to believe, possessed, individually, the capacity to offer some kind of atonement for man's sin. All these angels, additionally, are good angels. And yet

> He ask'd, but all the Heav'nly Quire stood mute,
> And silence was in Heav'n: on mans behalf
> Patron or Intercessor none appeerd,
> Much less that durst upon his own head draw
> The deadly forfeiture, and ransom set. (3.217–21)

The Son, of course, steps in, but only after Milton has allowed the tension to build. Now the Son has to possess some parity of being with the other angels or God's request would simply be ironic, something Milton's own words as narrator do not suggest: "And now without redemption all mankind / Must have bin lost" (222–23). It is necessary for the angels to be offered and to decline—it is not a test of their goodness or obedience, merely their courage—so that when God applauds the Son's offer by calling him "By Merit more then Birthright Son of God" (309), it means something significant to the angels. As Labriola argues, materially the Son also has to be an angel because he lives, moves, and battles in the angelic material space; the "Vice-gerent" has to be accessible to the realm over which he reigns. God, conversely, does not move at all, and is acknowledged by different beings to be "inaccessible" (2.104, 3.337, 7.141). This is not to argue that the Son is *only* an angel in this period (let alone *only* a man when incarnated); rather, his second and third begettings laminate his divine origin onto successive realms: the Word becomes Word-in-Heaven, and then Word-on-Earth. That he is the Word-in-Heaven as a God-angel is precisely what Abdiel confirms in his angry words to Satan:

> Thy self though great and glorious dost thou count,
> Or all Angelic Nature joind in one,
> Equal to him begotten Son, by whom
> As by his Word the mighty Father made
> All things, ev'n thee, and all the Spirits of Heav'n
> By him created . . .
>
>    nor by his Reign obscur'd,
> But more illustrious made, since he the Head
> *One of our number thus reduc't becomes* (5.833–38, 841–43, my
>   italics)

Nevertheless, the angelic rebellion takes place before the Son has made his offer to take on flesh—indeed, he makes that offer at the point where God reveals that he foresees that the angelic rebellion will ultimately result in Adam and Eve falling as well—and it has to be said that there is no "merit" in him visible at the point of his Exaltation. This may suggest that when God simply orders his angels to treat the Son as their "Head" he is indeed acting arbitrarily in Satan's sense of the word. But there is an ethical logic to this position too. God sets a test to Adam and Eve in Eden, one that in and of itself is harmless—a harmless apple, forbidden. Milton himself insists on this in his *De doctrina:* it is no test of obedience to be told to abstain from something that is obviously harmful anyway.[11] What is required of an obedience test is an element of arbitrariness in a middle sense, neither a considered command nor an improper imposition, but a preference not based on the nature of the thing preferred. For the three senses compare: (1) "we went to arbitration," (2) "I resist arbitrary impositions," and (3) "it was left arbitrary" (these correspond to the *Oxford English Dictionary's* "arbitrary," A2, A4, and A1, respectively). Sense 1 is akin to saying that God's judgment will control the proceedings, just as sense 2 rejects such a judgment as an imposition. Sense 3 respects the indifference of the thing commanded. As John Rumrich has argued, just as there has to be a test in Eden, so too must there be a test in Heaven, a positive command that can be obeyed or disobeyed.[12] From the *De doctrina* we learn Milton's judgment that "the good angels do not see into all God's thoughts. . . . They know by revelation only those things which God sees fit to show them." So the crucial question for the poem is: when God orders the angels to bow to his Son do they know exactly who this being is? The hymning angels of Book 3, albeit at a later chronological point, seem to know that they were created by the Son. Abdiel certainly does when he resists Satan. Do the angels who fall? Later they deny this: in a fantasy of complete autochthony, they "Know none before us, self-begot, self-rais'd" (5.860). It is a hard question to answer, as God does not make the choice easy either by reminding his audience who they are dealing with or by declaring that the Son is being promoted for merit rather than birthright. Is this provocative of him? The poem is slightly open here. On one reading it is not provocative in any negative sense, because God has the right to command such obedience from the angels, and it is also imperative in Milton's ethical universe that the command must be, in the middle sense delineated above, arbitrary. One reading, indeed, is that the angels at this point do not and should not know that the Son is their Creator. If they did, it would not be a test. Abdiel and the good angels gradually realize that it is so, as they grasp that a mystery has taken place whereby God has become Angel, but they do not automatically, already know this; they have to think it through and to assent.

Satan rejects this mystery, and his fall is immediately consequent on God's decree: "All seemed well pleased, all seemed, but were not all" (5.617). We have discussed the complexities in Chapter 20 of how Milton presents us with Sin's subjective account of her origin, and then only later with Raphael's more objective narration of Satan's rebellion. What is even more obscure is how Satan manages to draw so many after him. God later says that Satan, at least in his creation, was identical in rank to Michael (6.690), and he evidently commands a significant proportion of the angelic host. In his rebellion, he speaks first to his lieutenant—we do not hear the prelapsarian name of this angel, but he is the one who later will be named Beelzebub—and infuses "Bad influence" into his "unwarie brest" (695). But the removal of the majority of Satan's party to "The Quarters of the North" (689) is by a trick: Satan tells Beelzebub to pretend that they are all going there merely to prepare "Fit entertainment to receive our King / The great *Messiah*" (690–91). Once there, Satan wins them all over in a single speech (772–802), with the prominent exception of Abdiel—"but his zeale / None seconded" (849–50). Milton had little narrative choice here. He had inherited the statistic that, but no information on the means whereby, one third of the heavenly host went over to Satan. So this process happens unnervingly swiftly in *Paradise Lost,* almost as if the more important outcome for Milton was the chance to invent the very Miltonic Abdiel,

> Among the faithless, faithful only hee;
> Among innumerable false, unmov'd,
> Unshak'n, unseduc'd, unterrifi'd (5.897–99)

What are the strengths of Milton's angelic fall as a model? First, Milton carries the principle of free obedience and so also free disobedience into heaven; he closes the ethical and philosophical gap between angel and man. This allows the angelic fall to be understood much better by us humans; for the same reasons it also works better as a warning to Adam and Eve.

What are the weaknesses? Milton cannot easily explain why this fall affects some and not others, why Satan and not Michael—and that is why it is important that God states that Satan and Michael were equal in their creation. For Milton, it is enough that angels, like men, were created "Sufficient to have stood, though free to fall" (3.99). I suspect that Milton also thought with Augustine that the origin of the evil will that causes some and not others to act on this freedom is not something that can be discussed in itself. This is a model that therefore rests very heavily on the free will defense that it is better to have free will than to be prevented, absolutely, from sinning. And this is what Milton's God explicitly says (3.100–11). Nevertheless, God's description of the fallen angels as "Self-tempted" remains problematic, because it is only true if we interpret "self-" here as referring to "beings of the same kind," because only Satan is truly self-tempted in the more obvious sense of the prefix, of being tempted by one's own self. (Satan, presumably, would claim that in fact God tempted him.)

## THE HUMAN FALL

In theological terms, the human fall differs only slightly from the angelic one; but in narrative terms it differs in two crucial respects: there is a Tempter from outside the human realm, and Adam and Eve fall for different reasons.

We have examined the drama of Adam and Eve and their falls in Chapter 19; what remains to be discussed here is how this second fall fits into the theodicy of the poem as a whole.

Eve and Adam have different falls. This is perhaps the profound ethical discovery of the poem, taking its prompt from Paul in 1 Tim. 2:14: Eve is deceived, but Adam is not. They both could have chosen to do otherwise, but their paths to sin are different. Here is the Fall dramatized, and drama has brought to the theology it explores a greater complexity and naturalism, centered on the life of a couple in love. Nor does Milton abandon his protagonists at the Fall. In fact, across Books 9 and 10 Milton expends slightly more verse on Adam and Eve fallen than unfallen, as they work their way from recrimination to repentance.

From the point of view of theodicy what is the strength of this model of the human fall? Eve is sympathetically portrayed as loyal but intelligent, capable of holding her own in an argument, capable of getting her way without any sinful intent. Adam is no household tyrant but respects her liberty, specifically her liberty to work alone. This all goes wrong, but it is terribly plausible: Eve departs from Adam against his advice, but not out of malice, and when Adam decides to fall with her, he falls for love. God theorizes on a plane above such subtleties: he speaks as a theologian, repeating theological keywords, mainly to do with how "Man" as a category behaves; Milton, however, details the human workings behind the theological concepts, investigating just what kind of personal processes could lead to the known result.

What are the weaknesses? God is insistent, as we saw, that "Man falls deceiv'd / By the other first." This, he continues, is why man will find mercy and the fallen angels none. This is not what happens in Book 9, however, for Eve, rather than "Man," is "deceiv'd," and Adam is not. What makes Adam and Eve psychologically so plausible is that they are not copies of one another; but this difference also troubles the absolutes of the theologian. Milton presents us with two different misuses of free will in Eden, and in light of the undeceived fall of Adam, we might rather wonder why the possibility of redemption is not offered to the fallen angels too. Conversely, is there not a case to be made that Satan tricked some of the angels too, speaking "with calumnious Art / Of counterfeted truth" (5.770–71)? Perhaps the humans, both deceived and undeceived, are not so different from the angels. Again, the differing conducts of Adam and Eve map rather closely onto their differing creations, the one moment in their instantly adult lives for which they are not morally responsible. The Fall in Eden is therefore considerably messier than that in Heaven—a Satanic dream is eventually followed up by a successful temptation, and Eve at the point of her fall, deceived, believes Satan's claims; but then Adam on the cusp of his own fall does not believe Eve's claims, regardless of what he drunkenly says afterward. The free-will defense has to work very hard here. Milton, we again must suppose, is forced to say that *even though* Eve looks as if she is worryingly less capable than Adam to have resisted, *nevertheless* it was within her power to have done so. This is not by any means an intolerable position, but it does place some strain on how convincing we may choose to find it.

That, however, is the theological judgment. From the point of view of Milton the narrative poet, he again had limited choice in the matter. He had to get his characters moving, and move them through a plot with a biblically authorized *peripeteia* ("Now the serpent . . . said unto the woman, Yea, hath God said, Ye shall not eat of every tree of the garden?," Gen: 3:1), and *anagnorisis* ("And the eyes of them both were opened," Gen. 3:7). How else was he to effect his narrative? Seen from this perspective, it is a remarkable balancing act, a narratological success of moving his protagonists from one end of their story to the other, and a theological success, so we may tentatively grant, of insisting that the freedom of the agents concerned was adequate to cope with the problems they encounter.

Within the parameters of his belief system, therefore, Milton, I propose, did an extraordinarily fine job of juggling narrative and theological responsibilities. Those who wish to push the case for the prosecution of Milton a little further, however, will swiftly move away from the actual falls and turn their attention to the rest of the poem. Adam and Eve and the angels, after all, are culpable and are punished for it. But are there not other culpable, and unpunished, even unpunishable, beings in this poem? And, if so, would this not render the whole thing rather unfair?

Such an investigation, again, ought to exclude episodes that are merely inherited by Milton. As for Miltonic novelties, the lynchpin example in the poem is the Exaltation of the Son in Heaven, a motif more traditionally found in the form of the devil refusing to worship Adam (as even in the Quran) rather than the exalted Son. We have rehearsed a defense of that episode as replicating in Heaven the challenge of free obedience set to Adam and Eve in Eden. Commentators, however, point to many other moments in the poem where the design of the universe seems tipped toward the possibility of a fall. In Eden, we have seen that Raphael delivers his warning to Adam alone, despite the fact that it is Eve who will be first tempted and first to fall; it is to place a great deal of responsibility on both Adam and Eve to assume adequate transmission of this warning. There are problematic pieces of conduct at the angelic level too, for instance the capture *and then release* of Satan at the end of Book 4, when God intervenes to stop the impending fight between Gabriel and Satan by setting Libra in the heavens, but this time an articulated Libra, with one weighted pan signifying "parting" and the other "fight" (4.1003). Fowler has argued that God freights his scales with a meaning larger than that perceived by both Gabriel and Satan: they think it is just a judgment on Satan (for this, Milton's prompt is Daniel 5:27, the writing on the wall at Belshazzar's feast: "TEKEL; Thou art weighed in the balances, and art found wanting"); whereas God, pondering all of time, sees through to the ultimate consequences of "parting" (temptation, fall, incarnation, redemption) and "fight" (mankind safe but untested). In this case we can argue that God is making sure that the conditions for the Fall remain in place, because he can have it both ways: either mankind will exercise free will properly, or mankind will not, in which case God has an ultimate solution for that too. Whether it is fair for him to have it both ways is a harder question.

Indeed, as we push back into the chronologically earlier parts of the poem, we encounter other instances of God intervening so that the Fall might take place. As Satan approaches the created universe, the retractable stairs connecting Heaven and the created world are at that very moment "let down, whether to dare / The Fiend by easie ascent, or aggravate / His sad exclusion from the dores of Bliss" (3.523–25)—that dare sounds on the one hand like mocking distraction and on the other like goading. At the beginning of their discussion in Book 3, God informs his Son that Satan is coming back,

> whom no bounds
> Prescrib'd, no barrs of Hell, nor all the chains
> Heapt on him there, nor yet the main Abyss
> Wide interrupt can hold; so bent he seems
> On desparate reveng (3.81–85)

God terminates in a typical shift of agency—"so bent" does the work of "because he is so bent"—but we have seen even earlier that the "barrs of

Hell" were only released for Satan because his offspring Sin has the key, a key given to her by God: "which time this powerful key, / Into my hand was giv'n" (2.774–75). Milton shields the passage with a passive ("was giv'n"), but there is no real doubt about the giver. We are told right at the start of the poem that God will permit Satan to be "Left . . . at large to his own dark designs" (1.213), but God does more: he hands Sin the key to Hell so that she can open the gates for Satan, and God then stops Gabriel from fighting Satan off from Eden.

These and other examples have recently been collected together under the heading of "contributory negligence."[13] Everyone in the poem, it seems, is negligent in some way. This is obviously so for the fallen angels and the humans, but God and the angels, in this reading, have their own failings too: at points where they could have acted, they did not. The problem with this line of argument is that Milton has so obviously *introduced* rather than *suppressed* such elements, that he must have a reason for doing so which is not to implode, perversely, his own poem. Once again it is a matter of exacerbating the central test of the poem: God is determined that the temptation will happen; he is equally determined that it is within the moral ability of Adam and Eve to withstand this temptation, even though he knows they will not. What these examples of negligence really show is God's commitment not to "praise a fugitive and closter'd vertue, unexercis'd & unbreath'd."[14] Milton is, at least, being consistent, and also extremely bold. He need not have made God quite so keen to ensure that the Temptation would take place, but he considered the principle of free virtue under trial important enough that God acts, repeatedly, to preserve it. Milton's writing in this respect is polemical: this is an aggressively Arminian epic, bent on emphasizing that God himself created and will respect, at all costs, free will.

We may find faults in Milton's theodicy if we wish. Here, the case for its internal consistency has been made as far as possible. There are of course some difficult moments. Milton's category of "peculiar grace" is one of them: given that he himself endorses its existence, could it not have been vouchsafed to Adam and Eve, thereby preventing a great deal of misery? Or is such grace, paradoxically, only available to the fallen? More worrying is the difference in capacity between Adam and Eve, their qualitatively differing creations, and their differing motivations for falling. These defy simple theological appraisal, and Milton presumably recognized this as he was writing. This is perhaps why he placed so much emphasis not simply on the Fall, but on how Adam and Eve gradually pick themselves up after it. Man and Woman too—with some "Prevenient Grace"—contribute to the theodicy of the poem:

> Thus they in lowliest plight repentant stood
> Praying, for from the Mercie-seat above
> Prevenient Grace descending had remov'd
> The stonie from thir hearts (11.1–4)

# 22

## Becoming a Classic

WHEN THE ANTIQUARY John Aubrey came to assemble materials for a life of Milton after the poet's death in 1674, his rough notes show that he tracked down several people who had known Milton in person. He interviewed Milton's widow Elizabeth; his brother Christopher; a former pupil "Mr Packer"; Abraham Hill, treasurer to the Royal Society; Andrew Allam, an Oxford don interested in Milton's biography; possibly even Milton's "apothecary" on his last illness; and Edward Phillips, the most important of Aubrey's witnesses when it comes to Milton as a writer.[1]

At first Aubrey did not know of the elder Phillips boy, Edward (his brother John, also Milton's sometime pupil, having been a year younger). Aubrey had evidently called in on Milton's widow, probably in 1681, to ask what had become of Milton's papers. She told him that she had kept her husband's letters—"a great many . . . from learned men his acquaintance, both of England & beyond sea," now sadly lost—but had given the rest of his papers to his nephew, one Phillips, who might be found near the Maypole in the Strand. Aubrey's interview notes have a blank for Phillips's first name. But Aubrey soon tracked Edward down, and interviewed him quite extensively.

Aubrey and Phillips seem to have hit it off—Phillips gave him plenty of information and not just on his uncle; presented him with a copy of his own work on grammar, the *Tractatulus*, fresh off the press (1682); and even mentioned to Aubrey that he had in his possession unpublished poetry by Milton, too hot to handle. (These were Milton's panegyrics on Cromwell and Fairfax, which Aubrey tried to coax from Phillips, without success.)

Edward wrote down notes for Aubrey—the almost complete bibliography of Milton's writings in chronological order among Aubrey's papers is in Edward's distinctive hand, as is an important revision of Aubrey's own prior, disordered list. So is a firsthand account of Milton as a teacher. On a separate piece of paper, Elizabeth scrawled in an unpracticed hand the date and time of Milton's birth, an entry copied from the family Bible. On this piece of paper Aubrey then set down Phillips's famous account of the dictation of *Paradise Lost*: "His invention was much more free and easie in the Equinoxes, than at the solstices; as he more particularly found in writing his Paradise Lost." This passage is then crossed out, Aubrey supplying, still from Phillips, an improved version: "All the time of writing his <u>Paradise lost,</u> his <u>veine</u> began at the Autumnall Equinoctiall and ceased at the Vernall or thereabouts (I belieue about May) and this was 4 or 5 yeares of his doeing it. He began about 2 yeares before the K. came in, and finished about 3 yeares after the Ks Restauracion." Against *Paradise Lost* and *Regained* in Aubrey's own list of Milton's works, finally, Edward has written: "Edw. Philips his Amanuensis." He then paused, and added "cheif" before "Amanuensis." "Cheif" may be a vague term when pressed, but there is no reason to doubt that Edward played the dominant role in assisting Milton to write. His hand is visible in some important corrections to the manuscript of the first book of *Paradise Lost*, which survives, and it is unlikely that Edward would have deceived Aubrey about his involvement in *Paradise Regained* too.

Not only was Edward the dominant scribe of *Paradise Lost*, but he was one of its most important early publicists.[2] He thought the poem was perfection itself, and soon found occasion to say so in print, albeit in Latin and tucked at the back of a schoolroom reference work that he had been employed to revise. This was the *Phrasium poeticarum thesaurus* of the German educationalist Joannes Buchlerus, to which Edward appended his own essay on classical drama and a survey of the best modern poets, both male and female, of Europe. This is a fascinating document because Phillips also used the occasion to evaluate Milton's major contemporaries, notably William

Davenant and Abraham Cowley, whose own attempts at epic we have encountered. His praise for these mere pretenders to epic is muted: Davenant
certainly "bragged" (*gloriatus est*) of *Gondibert*, "a poem which calls itself heroic, and indeed it was a grand beginning; but he who would attempt such
things must observe the economy and decorum of the great poets" (i.e.,
Davenant had failed to do so). As for Cowley and his *Davideis:* "a poem
dubbed heroic, and that not wrongly so—if only he had consistently observed proper invention and decorum."[3] Can we hear his uncle's judgments
in these comments? In any case, happily there has recently been published
a work, Phillips declares, in which at last the true qualities of a heroic poem
are displayed, to perfection:

> Poema quod sive sublimitatem Argumenti, sive Leporem
> simul & Majestatem Styli, sive sublimitatem Inventionis, sive
> similitudines & descriptiones quam maximè Naturales
> respiciamus, verè Heroicum, ni fallor, audiet, Plurium enim
> suffragiis qui non nesciunt judicare censetur perfectionem
> hujus generis poematis assecutum esse.[4]

> [a poem, which if we should consider it either for its sublimity
> of argument, or for its at once charming and majestic style, or
> for its sublimity of invention, or for its similes and most
> especially its descriptive passages, it will be granted, if I am
> not mistaken, truly heroic; for it will be estimated by the
> approbation of those who know how to judge to have attained
> perfection in this kind of poem.]

Phillips then repeated this praise in a work written this time in English, and
which included a revised version of his survey of modern poets, now in al-
phabetic order. This is his *Theatrum Poetarum* and Milton gets his own entry,
but Edward declined to comment at length, protesting—or so it would
seem—that "it will better become a person less related than my self, to deliver his judgment."[5] Actually Edward proceeded to say exactly what he
thought of his uncle, but he tucked this into his entry for his own brother,
John, a poet of modest reputation who had written, among other poems, a
travesty of Virgil. John Phillips is described as the nephew and disciple of
"an Author of most deserved Fame late deceas't, being the exactest of

Heroic Poets, (if the truth were well examin'd, and it is the opinion of many both Learned and Judicious persons) either of the Ancients or Moderns, either of our own or what ever Nation else."[6]

This kind of praise had in fact greeted the poem very shortly after its publication. One of the earliest private responses we have to *Paradise Lost* is that of an old parliamentarian Presbyterian, Sir John Hobart (1628–1683). Writing to a cousin in January 1668, Hobart sent a copy of the book, with his highest recommendations: "I must confess I haue been strangely pleas'd in a deleborate & repeated reading of him . . . truly I never read any thing more august, & w^thall more gratefull to my (too much limited) understanding." The language of the poem, indeed, was archaic, reminiscent of "Spencers way," and the author, like Homer, blind. Hobart also maintained— as would Phillips—that "in y^e opinion of y^e impartiall learned," the poem was "not only aboue all moderne attempts in verse, but equall to any of y^e Antient Poets." A subsequent letter, in which Hobart's praise for the poem only intensified, identified the poet, and yet the contrast in Hobart's judgment could not be starker: "a criminall & obsolete person, & many of his words being ye last [i.e., obsolete] some moderne creticks will condemne him for being guilty (in this booke as well as others) of ye first [i.e., criminality] too." This reader, a staunch Presbyterian and therefore hostile to the Independent and regicidal politics of "Mr Milton," as he finally named him, was forced to draw a firm line between the excellence of the poem and the criminality of the poet, who, along with his other publications, was evidently a known quantity to both Hobart and his cousin.[7]

For a work of literature from this period to achieve classic status, however, it tended to require four things: republication in deluxe folio format, commentary, translation, and imitation. As we saw in Chapter 10, Abraham Cowley attempted to accelerate this process for himself by publishing directly in folio, writing his own commentaries, and even providing his own Latin translations—without lasting success. Conversely, Milton left us almost no statements on *Paradise Lost,* in contrast to his former loquacity about his own planned artistic development. Nevertheless, the poem made it into folio—and not just that, but illustrated folio—in 1688, published by that great broker of literary reputations Jacob Tonson; and a commentary tradition grew up around *Paradise Lost* with extraordinary rapidity.[8] This was inaugurated by Patrick Hume, an otherwise obscure schoolmaster, who prepared a line-by-line commentary on *Paradise Lost* suitable to be printed with Tonson's sixth edition of the poem in 1695; it must have been a Tonson commission.[9] It is 321 folio pages in length—longer than the poem itself, a sign of things to come—and almost every subsequent work on the poem, including this one, owes some debt of detail to Hume's work. Hume, whose commentary responded equally to the biblical and classical foundations of the epic, was convinced that Milton had indeed overcome Homer and Virgil, and amid his huge mass of philological comment and source hunting, Hume has moments where he is simply spell-stopped. Commenting on Milton's "Night invests the Sea" (1.208), for instance, Hume dutifully notes the origin of the verb in French and two parallels in Virgil, but then suddenly pauses in mere appreciation: "All exact Night-Pieces, yet is this one word [*Invests*] strangely significant." (Presumably this strangeness results from "invests" being a synonym for "besieges," suggesting Night as a military force, and Book 1 is all about the fallen forces of darkness; compare the haunting conclusion of Book 4, as the fiend "fled / Murm'ring, and with him fled the shades of Night.")

Perhaps the most peculiar commentary, however, was that of the great classical scholar Richard Bentley, whose 1732 edition of *Paradise Lost* has presented readers with a puzzle and a challenge ever since Bentley declared that blind Milton had been deceived by his amanuensis, an unscrupulous "Editor" who rewrote the text of the dictated poem before sending it to the printer. This hypothesis assumed explicitly the nonexistence of any authorial manuscripts and implicitly that the proofreading process had either failed or had been faked. This was proposed by Bentley in order to explain what he interpreted as the published poem's huge failings in grammar, rhetoric, logic, and prosody.[10] Although Bentley did not openly state this, he also found fault with Milton's theology. Bentley indicated all of this by printing the Tonson text, unadulterated, as his vulgate, but italicizing what he believed to be the Editor's sinister interpolations, placing the "restored" readings in the margins. Copious footnotes justified the ways of Bentley to Milton. The result is a work of extraordinary violence. Was this conspiracy theory, or a vicious joke of some sort?

Few have been able to accept that Bentley believed his own theory, but opinions about Bentley's influences, motives, and performance differ. Critics such as Joseph Levine have noted that in practice Bentley's own footnotes soon forgot that the erring soul behind the text's imperfections was supposed to be the editor and not Milton himself; after a while, they become one and the same offender. As Bentley's most recent scholar, Kristine Haugen, points out, Bentley was, in this closing phase of his career, editing the Latin astrological poet Manilius on exactly the same supposition—that an alleged interpolator had insinuated himself between the author and the reader, and Bentley was going to remove him. Indeed, the editorial strategy of positing interpolation in order to remove it went back at least to Scaliger; what was audacious here was that Bentley was performing his restoration on a very recent English artifact, not a text in one of the classical languages of remote antiquity. As Haugen says, "the putative interpolator justified Bentley's interventions rather than determining them."[11] If the method itself was not unknown to textual criticism, its use here was nevertheless outrageous, as the leading classical scholar of his age exercised an almost territorial sense of authority over this vernacular *parvenu*.

Even before it was published, Bentley's edition was attracting negative comment. He was also lying about the manuscript evidence, as we know Bentley borrowed the manuscript of the first book of *Paradise Lost*, from which he took notes. Indeed, Bentley was the despised Master of Trinity College, Cambridge, and it seems significant that our first recorded sightings of Milton's "Trinity College Manuscript"—if not a text of *Paradise Lost* then at least collateral evidence for Milton's techniques of composition—date from immediately after the appearance of Bentley's edition. I wonder whether the "discovery" by the fellows of Trinity of Milton's poetic papers lying neglected in their library was not prompted by the edition of their hated master.[12] And yet the Bentley edition, for all its notoriety, performed the positive service of insisting that the text comes first, and that the critic, regardless of the stature of the author in question, must make sense of that, and that includes the courage to make value judgments. Bentley was presenting the critic as an independent being, one whose powers extended beyond mere praise or exegesis; what better way to demonstrate this exalted conception of the critic than to take on the largest, most impressive, and indeed most problematic work to have appeared in the vernacular in Bentley's lifetime? And although Bentley lost the war, he won some battles. Consult a scholarly edition of *Paradise Lost* at the lines 7.321 ("The swelling Gourd," emended from "The smelling Gourd") and 7.451 ("Let th'Earth bring forth Soul" for "Let th'Earth bring forth Foul"), and you will find that Bentley's interventions in these places have indeed been accepted into the textual tradition.

As for attention from languages other than English, *Paradise Lost* became a translated text with astonishing rapidity when compared with other English vernacular texts.[13] This was itself partly owing to its epic genre, which was easier to assimilate to continental literary traditions than some more exclusively insular developments, especially theatrical traditions. English was also not, or only just becoming, an important language in the international world at this date: when we look at nonliterary genres of English scholarly writing, many now classic texts remained inaccessible to continental readers other than through summaries in reviewing journals, published usually in French or Latin. It is significant, therefore, that the first major attempt to put *Paradise Lost* into another language came from the pen of a German speaker who was bilingual in English and who had worked in England for the government as a translator at the same time as Milton himself. Theodore Haak of Neuhausen in the Palatinate, who had known Milton personally since at least 1648, worked on his manuscript translation of the epic, of which three books still survive in manuscript. This happened over some period between the initial publication of the poem, and around 1678–1680, when Haak's acquaintance Ernst Gottlieb von Berge visited England and was presented by Haak with a copy of his unfinished translation. Rather too shortly afterward, in 1682, Von Berge published a complete version of *Das Verlustigte Paradeis* under his own name, with only slight acknowledgment of Haak. A comparison with the surviving portion of Haak's manuscript has demonstrated that *Das Verlustigte Paradeis* relied heavily on Haak's work, and the first published German version should therefore be thought of as a collaboration, if one not sought by Haak, between two German speakers, one of whom had known and worked with the English poet himself.[14]

The next vernacular into which *Paradise Lost* was translated, if somewhat abortively, was Italian. Again this arose because the continental translator had become personally involved for a time in English intellectual circles. This was the Italian virtuoso and man of letters, Lorenzo Magalotti (1637–1712), who visited England in 1668, and in his rich account of this visit, the *Relazione d'Inghilterra,* he included lists of famous writers, books, instrument makers, musicians, beauties, and so forth. Milton does not appear in Magalotti's list of "English Poets'; but under his index of "Some Exceptional Books" we find, amid an otherwise largely inoffensive list of the notable books of the time, Milton's *Tenure of Kings and Magistrates* (1649), a striking indication that even in the Restoration the work was recognized, if not endorsed, for its rhetorical force.[15] While he was in London Magalotti also attended a couple of meetings of the Royal Society, of which Haak was a fellow, and to which Milton's sometime colleague and correspondent Henry Oldenburg served as secretary.[16] Magalotti was a literary Anglophile, and in old age he translated not only some of *Paradise Lost* but also the Miltonic *Cyder* of John Philips (no relation to Milton's own nephew John Phillips). Magalotti commenced his translation work on Milton sometime before 1709, because in a Latin elegy of that year by the English envoy-extraordinary to Genoa and Tuscany, Sir Henry Newton, we hear of his work:

> Sed cùm Cœlestem referat mirantibus Orbem,
>     Miltonique comes, nobile surgit opus;
> Tum Superum redeunt acies, atque acta Deorum;
>     Resque simul Superum, Verba, Modosque legunt.[17]

[But when he [Magalotti], the companion of Milton, draws
down for our astonishment the heavenly sphere, a noble work
arises, and then return the battle-array of the immortals, and
the acts of the gods; and at once they survey the deeds, words,
and ways of the celestial beings.]

This suggests either the devils or the angels and their wars, and in fact only part of Book 1 survives in Magalotti's version, perhaps all he completed. Magalotti translated blank verse into blank verse, with a surprisingly jerky effect for readers overfamiliar with the original and no longer sensible of its own hyperbaton. With his frequent elision, verb delay, and double negatives, Magalotti delivers back some of Milton's own complexity:

> La temeraria, & a tutti noi fatale
> Prima dell'uom disobbedienza il Pomo
> Della vietata pianta, onde si amaro
> Ne fu il sapore, & si funesto il Seme
> E'il chiuso Paradiso, in fin che un Grande
> Ma pur Uomo egli ancora, il grave immenso
> Danno non ne rifece, & il primo onore
> Non ne rende della beata Sede:
> Canta O musa Celeste[18]

[Very literally: "The rash and fatal to us all / First disobedience of man, and the apple / Of the forbidden tree, whence so bitter / Was the taste, and so deadly the seed / And paradise closed, until a great / Yet nonetheless grave and immense man / The damage repair and the original honour / Restore of the blessed seat / Sing heavenly muse"]

However, the main language into which *Paradise Lost* passed was not a modern vernacular, but Latin. There had been some attempts to put notable English vernacular poems into Latin before this date, but these were isolated examples.[19] But in Milton's case, indeed, this language dominates the translation history of the epic for its first century, and unsurprisingly so. Such translations, at first partial, started appearing from 1686, when one J. C. published the first book in Latin as *Paradisus amissa,* identified as a collaboration by several hands *eadem Natione* (of the same nation), a suggestion that the publication was looking to a continental readership. J. C. promised a translation, already completed, of the other "nine" books of the poem too, if this pilot Latin publication were successful. Oddly enough, as this makes clear, the team was evidently working from the ten-book edition, an indication that not everyone had registered Milton's revision to twelve books. Another fragment appeared in 1694, the section of the fifth book where Eve relates her dream to Adam, this time translated by Charles Blake of St John's College, Oxford; this man also assembled (but did not manage to bring to publication) an edition of Alexander Gil the younger's unpublished Latin verse. Thomas Power of Trinity College, Cambridge, then published in that town a Latin translation of the first book alone in 1691, leaving the rest in manuscript in his college, where it still is. The previous year the Scotsman William Hogg had managed to Latinize not only all of *Paradise Lost,* but *Paradise Regained* and *Samson Agonistes* too, and would make his way to *A Maske (Comus)* in 1698. Impecunious and prolific, Hogg had earlier paid the same compliment to the biblical books of Job and Ecclesiastes, and would pay it once again in 1699 to Richard Blackmore's *Prince Arthur* (the English original dating from 1695), an Arthurian vernacular epic of the kind Milton himself had meditated over half a century earlier, only to shun. Hogg's main Milton volume was dedicated to, because funded by, the wealthy physician and colonial adventurer Daniel Coxe; Hogg, who wrote, as he said, out of fear of hunger, died homeless on the streets of London.

Latin versions of Milton thereafter abound, and they could become quite luxurious. The winner of this category is William Dobson's sumptuous version in two volumes, the first published at Oxford in 1750 and the second at London in 1753. This included Dobson's translation with the original text in English below it on each page, so that the reader could compare versions and enjoy Dobson's artistry. Dobson, a young lawyer of New College, Oxford, was said to have been promised £1,000 by the rich politician and critic William Benson on the completion of the work, and Dobson's nose was kept to the desk by receipt of the interest on that sum during his progress.[20]

Some of the earlier Latinizers of Milton at least tried to claim that their desire was to communicate the poem to a continental audience. This was never really plausible, but by Dobson's effort, there was no attempt to deny that translating *Paradise Lost* into Latin was, paradoxically, a thoroughly English thing to do, made by and for Englishmen. It reassured the English, particularly those involved in education, that they lived in harmony with the classics, and that a classical curriculum was thoroughly English in spirit. They could prove this to themselves by reversing Milton's travel from the classics into the vernacular by turning him back into his source languages, a latter-day mutation of the old humanist practice of "double translation." There were even some efforts in Greek, albeit rarely published; an exception is Thomas Stratford's 1770 attempt at the first book, which was actually presented in parallel with Dobson's Latin.

This mentality has left a very long tail. Rhetoric could be and was long taught in English-speaking schools by using Miltonic examples where classical ones might once have served. ("Zeugma—'flown with insolence and wine.'") For centuries, the punishment of "Georgics" at one of the older English schools involved the copying out of chunks of Latin hexameter; in living memory this could be replaced with passages of Milton.

The third way in which a poem became a classic was if it prompted imitation. This is a colossal category, as Milton came to dominate, oppress, some might say crush, the developing literary canon.[21] The Tonson dynasty of publishers must share some responsibility here too, for Milton could not become a classic without also becoming a publishing phenomenon. Indeed, when Tonson the elder had his portrait done by Sir Godfrey Kneller, he had himself depicted proudly holding his illustrated folio edition of *Paradise Lost*. But even before Tonson acquired the copyright of the poem, it had begun its slow march to dominance. This could produce some odd side effects, notably the attempt to put unruly Milton back into rhyme. The most famous example is Dryden's rhymed opera (never performed) *The State of Innocence*—very popular indeed, with ten editions to 1703—but there are other examples, such as John Hopkins's 1699 version of the fourth, sixth, and ninth books ("The primitive loves"; "The battel of the angels"; "The fall of man"), choice books of religious action. Hopkins's motive is an insult in several different directions at once to Milton's conception of the ideal reader, but it shows that Milton was not thundering at straw men (and perhaps straw women) in his note on his own verse. As Hopkins whined, "His work like the Tree of Knowledge is Forbidden to the Ladies, to those I mean who would Tast the Apples, but care not for Climbing to the Bough, and I have heard some say, *Mr. Milton* in Rhyme would be a Fine thing."[22]

These were minority voices, however, and Milton's rhymelessness begat a dominant eighteenth-century tradition, that of blank-verse georgic. The most prominent examples, across the century, are the aforementioned John Philips's *Cyder* (1708), James Thomson's *The Seasons* (1726–1730), William Somervile's *The Chace* (1735), and William Cowper's *The Task* (1785). In no sense, however, was this a linear progression from awe to frustration at the Miltonic yoke; no serious imitation is at peace with its predecessor, and eighteenth-century Miltonic poetry phases in and out of mock-Miltonic even within individual texts. Cowper, for instance, commences with outrageous bathos: "I sing the Sofa."

John Philips's *Cyder* is particularly complex.[23] This fine poem drew on serious prose discussions of cider manufacture—just as Somervile in *The Chace* would later provide practical advice on kenneling—and opens by promising "*Miltonian* Verse" on its theme, a compositional strategy Philips had first adopted for his brief, experimental, mock-heroic "The Splendid Shilling, in Imitation of Milton" (1701, corrected text 1705). In the interim had appeared *Cerealia, An Imitation of Milton* (1706), once attributed to Philips but now known to be by Elijah Fenton, who would go on to edit Milton and write his biography. *Cerealia,* however, a mere beer-is-better-than-wine romp, topples into pure burlesque (e.g., "Full of thy Pow'r infus'd by Nappy ALE, / Darkling He watch'd the Planetary Orbs"),[24] whereas Philips's *Cyder,* in contrast, was serious georgic, albeit in turn soon attacked by the anonymous *Milton's Sublimity Asserted* (1709) for not being sublime enough.

Both Philips and Fenton, moreover, emanated from conservative High-Church Tory Oxford, an early sign that the Miltonic style would be tugged at by Whig and Tory in turn.[25] The Whig Thomson, for instance, treated Tory Philips as the link connecting him to Milton in lineal succession; but Philips had sounded a more complex note of political regret as he turned, partially, to face his stylistic master with sorrow and rebuke:

> And had that Other Bard,
> Oh, had but He that first ennobled Song
> With holy Raptures, like his *Abdiel* been,
> 'Mong many faithless, strictly faithful found;
> Unpity'd, he should not have wail'd his Orbs,
> That roll'd in vain to find the piercing Ray,
> And found no Dawn, by dim suffusion veil'd!
> But He—However, let the Muse abstain[26]

Such regret was necessitated by political circumstances; but perhaps the most profound difference between Milton and his georgical imitators is that Milton had written of paradise *lost*, whereas his eighteenth-century followers adapted his depiction of unfallen Eden to present it as a vision of what England could be—a taming, if not quite a disavowal, of the strong lapsarianism at the heart of Protestant Milton's epic. English Georgic is still at heart Virgilian Georgic: how to improve the land.

Miltonic pastiche had in fact commenced early, perhaps with Dryden's *State of Innocence* and after him with the Earl of Roscommon's "Essay on Blanc Verse," a verse paragraph inserted just before the conclusion to the second edition (London, 1685; first edition 1684) of his verse *Essay on Translated Verse*.[27] At this point, Roscommon switched from rhymed to blank verse, and into italics, to signify pastiche, noting his source as the sixth book of *Paradise Lost*, the War in Heaven. Roscommon's *hommage* stands at the spring of the second tradition of Miltonic imitation, the strand that looked not to the georgic but to the martial books of *Paradise Lost*. An almost forgotten example of this tradition is the interesting *Præ-Existence* of 1714, an anonymous poem that exploited the unnarrated space of the nine days' fall of the fallen angels to argue in Miltonic verse for the heterodox doctrine of the preexistence of human souls; we humans were in fact present at the angelic rebellion in a former life as angels, and not sufficiently loyal angels.[28] Nevertheless it is a sign that the baroque elements of Milton's War in Heaven were already dating that this section declined in popularity quite quickly, reaching a nadir with Samuel Johnson's *Life* of Milton. The ultimate assault-by-imitation was, however, launched by Alexander Pope, whose *Rape of the Lock* (1712, rev. 1714, 1717) trivialized Milton's epic structures by domesticating them. His Cave of Spleen is Milton's Hell; and his sylphs and gnomes Milton's warring angels and demons, now mere powerless "machines" of generic contrivance. When one of Pope's tiny sylphs is cut in two by a pair of scissors, the wound soon closes (in parentheses), in (derisive) imitation of Milton's self-healing angels: "Fate urged the shears, and cut the Sylph in twain, / (But airy substance soon unites again)."[29] Milton's own angels, by implication, are converted into conventions, robbed of independent existence, and the glittering, dead eyes of Alexander Pope stare back on *Paradise Lost* with no friendly intent.

Imitation dissipates, or expands, into influence, and the subsequent dispersal of *Paradise Lost* into literature and culture is a story for elsewhere. But attitudes to Milton were for some centuries barometric of literary taste in general, as some anecdotes will show. Milton was rediscovered as an oral poet, for instance, by William Blake and then by the Wordsworths: Alexander Gilchrist's *Life of William Blake* (1863) recalls how Blake and his wife would sit naked in their garden house reciting parts of *Paradise Lost* ("'Come in!' cried Blake; 'It's only Adam and Eve, you know!'").[30] More austerely, Dorothy Wordsworth recorded in the Grasmere Journals how in February 1802, "after tea," she read aloud from *Paradise Lost* to her brother (whose sole confessed drinking bout, incidentally, had earlier taken place in Milton's student room in Christ's). Whereon "we were much impressed & also melted into tears"; extraordinary, given that she was reading to William specifically from the eleventh book, perhaps the least glamorous of the twelve.[31]

Beginning in the late eighteenth century, Milton's physical remains became fetishized as well, starting with his bones, some of which were dug up and sold in 1790 by a sexton. A lock of hair became a victim of poems by John Keats and James Henry Leigh Hunt, the latter seeing at once the transference between the modern poet beholding Milton's hair and blind, trichophiliac Milton imagining inwardly the hair of "Adam and his bride / With their rich locks." While Milton was increasingly adopted as the political darling of various causes perhaps more revolutionary than even Milton had been called to espouse, his very personal effects (mostly fakes) became commodities. The culmination of this tendency—we recall Milton's bitter satire on the relic-waving monks of the "Paradise of Fools" (2.489–96)—was a plan, hatched in the 1880s, to disassemble Milton's surviving house in Chalfont St Giles and relocate it to America, a kind of bizarre Protestant version of the flying Shrine at Loretto. This prompted a patriotic countermovement to purchase the house by local public subscription, and the first subscriber was Queen Victoria, who gave £20.[32]

The institutionalizing of criticism in university departments in the twentieth century led to several stunts of Miltonic "dislodgment," starting with T. S. Eliot's fatuous comments, commencing in his essay on Marlowe published in *The Sacred Wood* (1921) and terminating in his 1947 lecture on Milton before the British Academy, although among them is the occasional fine phrase, such as his comment on blank verse after "the erection of the Chinese Wall of Milton."[33] Meanwhile, and more interestingly, the influence of Milton's lapsarian narrative had leaked into utopian / dystopian literature, especially as that form modulated into science fiction, as in Yevgeny Zamyatin's brilliant dystopian work, *We* (1921 in Russian, but banned and unpublished; the first edition was therefore in English, 1924), or C. S. Lewis's pious *Perelandra / Voyage to Venus* (1943), which, with its Venusian Paradise Retained, works as a kind of fictional counterpart to Lewis's influential *Preface to Paradise Lost,* published the previous year. *Paradise Lost* was by this time a staple of the school curricula of the English-speaking world, and although serious study of the epic has now gradually moved from secondary to tertiary educational institutions, the books of Hell or of the Fall are still often studied in secondary schools.

Nevertheless, despite the continued spectral presence in contemporary culture of *Paradise Lost,* even if at one or several removes, the underlying supposition about the function of the poem has changed radically. Although he perceived the dangers in divulging divine secrets, Milton persisted because he thought they were divine, and his early readers at least felt they could agree on that. Milton and these readers, that is to say, shared a basic belief in the truth of his subject. Moreover, because Milton's epic diction borrowed from and was in turn nourished by the language of the King James version of the Bible, *Paradise Lost* insensibly became part of the English language in its devotional mode. Indeed, for centuries *Paradise Lost* functioned in English-speaking territories as deuterocanonical scripture. In 1763, for instance, John Wesley, who had spent his adult life working *Paradise Lost* into his educational and pastoral ideas, published *An Extract from Milton's Paradise Lost with Notes* in pocket format, evidently so it could function as a pocket Testament.[34]

That view has quietly disappeared. When Milton's epic is defended from a theological point of view today—as, to some extent, I have defended it—what is being defended is now usually taken at best as an allegory for truths no longer held to have literally taken place in the manner biblically reported; or simply no longer held to be truths at all. For the vast majority of readers, both those who defend and those who attack Milton's project, they are addressing, with pleasure and admiration, even with frustration and awe, what is for them merely the greatest technical masterpiece in the English language. This is our view today, and Milton would not like it.

# Appendix

## MILTON'S CLASSROOM AUTHORS

| Phillips (1694) | Phillips to Aubrey (1682) | Milton (1644) |
|---|---|---|
| **INITIAL LANGUAGE TRAINING** | | |
| | | Cebes, Plutarch, Plato Quintilian |
| **LATIN** | | |
| Cato | Cato | Cato |
| Varro | Varro | Varro |
| Columella | Columella | Columella |
| Palladius | | |
| Celsus | | Celsus |
| Pliny the Elder | | Pliny the Elder |
| Vitruvius | | Vitruvius |
| Frontinus | | |

## MILTON'S CLASSROOM AUTHORS

| Phillips (1694) | Phillips to Aubrey (1682) | Milton (1644) |
|---|---|---|
| **LATIN** (*continued*) | | |
| Lucretius | Lucretius | Lucretius |
| Manilius | Manilius | Manilius |
| | | Virgil, *Georgics* |
| | | Seneca, *Natural Questtions* |
| | | Pomponius Mela |
| | | Solinus |
| | | Cicero |
| | | Comedy |
| | | Political authors |
| | | Law, including Justinian |
| | | Logic |
| | | Rhetoric, including Demetrius of Phalerum, and Longinus |
| | | Poetics, including Horace |
| **GREEK** | | |
| | | Plato |
| | | Aristotle |
| | | Theophrastus |
| | | Orpheus |
| | | Theocritus |
| Hesiod ( / Homer) | Hesiod | Hesiod |
| Aratus | Aratus | Aratus |
| Dionysius Periegetes | Dionysius Periegetes | Dionysius Periegetes |

## MILTON'S CLASSROOM AUTHORS

| Phillips (1694) | Phillips to Aubrey (1682) | Milton (1644) |
|---|---|---|
| **GREEK** *(continued)* | | |
| Oppian | Oppian | Oppian |
| | | Nicander |
| Quintus Smyrnaeus | Quintus Smyrnaeus | |
| Apollonius of Rhodes | Apollonius of Rhodes | |
| pseudo-Plutarch, the *Placita*, and on education | | Plutarch |
| Geminus | | |
| Xenophon, *Cyropedia* and *Anabasis* | | Xenophon |
| Aelian | | |
| Polyænus | | |
| | | Diogenes Laertius |
| | | Timaeus of Locri |
| | | Demosthenes |
| | | Hermogenes of Tarsus |
| | | Sophocles and Euripides |
| | | Comedy |
| | | "Grecian lawgivers" |
| **GEOMETRY, ARITHMETIC, AND ASTRONOMY** | | |
| Urstitius | | |
| Ryff | | |
| Pitiscus | | |
| Sacrobosco | | |
| | "some rudiments"; | |

## MILTON'S CLASSROOM AUTHORS

| Phillips (1694) | Phillips to Aubrey (1682) | Milton (1644) |
|---|---|---|
| **GEOMETRY, ARITHMETIC, AND ASTRONOMY** (*continued*) | | |
| | "the use of the globes" | |
| | | "the rules of arithmetic, and soon after the elements of geometry"; "the use of the globes and all the maps"; "any compendious method of natural philosophy" |
| **MODERN LANGUAGES** | | |
| Villani in Italian | | "the Italian tongue": |
| D'Avity in French | | comedies in Italian |
| | | Castelvetro on the *Poetics* |
| | | Tasso on epic poetry |
| | | Mazzoni on Dante |
| **BIBLICAL LANGUAGES** | | |
| New Testament in Greek | | |
| Pentateuch in Hebrew | | Hebrew |
| Targum in Aramaic | | "Chaldee" (i.e. Aramaic) |
| Matthew in Syriac | | "Syrian dialect" (i.e. Syriac) |
| | | Church history "ancient and modern" |
| [English] | | "the Saxon and common laws of England, and the statutes" |

# Notes

NOTE: in the following endnotes, publishers are usually supplied only for modern imprints, and are suppressed for early modern imprints unless otherwise pertinent. References to classical and patristic texts follow received textual divisions, and no edition is specified unless that specific edition is under discussion. Titles to classical and patristic texts are given in English or Latin, depending on the form most commonly encountered by modern readers.

## NOTES TO CHAPTER ONE

1. John Milton, *Defensio secunda* (London, 1654), in the translation in Milton, *Areopagitica and Other Writings* (London: Penguin, 2014), 308–9.

2. *The Reason of Church Government Urg'd against Prelaty* (London, 1641), 37. It was actually published at the end of January 1642.

3. *Of Reformation* (London, 1641), 89.

4. *A Modest Confutation* (London, 1642), sig. A3r–v. The work was probably by Bishop Joseph Hall, or his son, or both, as its involved defenses of Hall's own literary satires suggest. To "bezel" (or "bezzle") is to fritter away or to guzzle.

5. *An Apology* (London, 1642), 11–17.

6. All citations from *Paradise Lost* unless otherwise identified are to the 1674 twelve-book edition and incorporated into the text, under the abbreviation PL for *Paradise Lost*, followed by book number and line number(s), so that PL 1.16, for instance, means Book 1, line 16.

7. "*Salust* to thee and *Siluester* thy frend, / Comes my high Poem peaceable and chaste" (3); Drayton's preface signals Marcus Hieronymus Vida's *Christias*, George Buchanan's *Jephthes*, and Du Bartas as his inspirations. Milton himself saluted Vida's poem in "The Passion," line 26.

8. Josuah Sylvester, "Urania," in *Du Bartas His Devine Weekes and Workes Translated* (London, 1611), 658.

9. As first noted by Benjamin Stillingfleet, in Henry John Todd, ed., *Poetical Works of John Milton* (London, 1801), 6:426. See more generally George Coffin Taylor, *Milton's Use of Du Bartas* (Cambridge, MA: Harvard University Press, 1934). There is an excellent modern edition of Sylvester's translation in two volumes, *The Divine Weeks and Works of Guillaume de Saluste, Sieur du Bartas,* ed. Susan Snyder (Oxford: Clarendon Press, 1979); see esp. 1:72–95, on the translation's influence in England.

10. Du Bartas, *Devine Weekes and Workes Translated,* 2 = PL 3.373; Taylor, *Milton's Use,* 71.

11. Snyder, in *Divine Weeks and Works,* 1:85, brilliantly adduces the Shakespearean precedent: "Unhous'led, disappointed, unanel'd," from *Hamlet.*

12. In Milton's grumpily defiant defense of his blank verse, he commented that "not without cause therefore some both Italian and Spanish Poets of prime note have rejected Rime both in longer and shorter Works." The reference to the Italians is probably to Torquato Tasso and his religious epic *Il Mondo Creato.* But there is no appropriate Spanish poem, we are told, and it seems likely that Milton was recalling a passage in the Elizabethan royal tutor Roger Ascham's *Scholemaster* (1570), in which he talks of translations from Homer into Spanish blank verse by Gonzalo Pérez (1550). See Carl W. Cobb, "Milton and Blank Verse in Spain," *Philological Quarterly* 42, no. 1 (1963): 264–67, and Gordon Campbell, "Milton's Spanish," *Milton Quarterly* 30, no. 3 (1996): 127–32. If this interpretation is correct, it is an interesting elision of epic and the translation of epic. Cobb additionally comments that Juan de Jáuregui translated Tasso's *Aminta* into blank verse (Rome, 1607), defending such unrhymed verse in his preface.

13. Du Bartas, *Devine Weekes and Workes Translated,* 245 ("The Imposture").

14. Interestingly, however, lineation (in multiples of five) was employed for the Latin version of the (prose) *Eikon Basilike* (London, 1649), as translated by John Earle.

### NOTES TO CHAPTER TWO

1. The former is lost, but the latter, in the 1640 London edition, is in the library of Jesus College, Cambridge. See also Edward Jones on Young in the *Oxford Dictionary of National Biography* (Oxford: OUP, 2004) [hereafter *ODNB*], and especially Jeffrey Alan Miller, "Milton and the Conformable Puritanism of Richard Stock and Thomas Young," in Edward Jones, ed., *Young Milton: The Emerging Author, 1620–1642* (Oxford: Oxford University Press, 2012), 72–103; the Jesus College inscription is reproduced on page 87.

2. *Areopagitica* (London, 1644), 31.

3. "Elegia quarta," lines 29–38, 87–94.

4. The major discussions of the Gils are Michael McDonnell, *A History of St Paul's School* (London: Chapman and Hall, 1909), 156–97; McDonnell, *The Annals of St Paul's School* (London: governors, 1959), 172–73, 174, 180, 183–220; McDonnell, *Registers of St Paul's School* (London: governors, 1977), 113–15, 117–22; Donald

Lemen Clark, *John Milton at St Paul's School: A Study of Ancient Rhetoric in English Renaissance Education* (New York: Columbia University Press, 1948), chap. 4; Bror Danielsson and Arvid Gabrielson, eds., *Alexander Gill's Logonomia Anglica (1619)* (Stockholm: Almqvist and Wiksell, 1972), esp. pt. 2, 9–53.

5. Trinity College, Cambridge, MS O. 10. 22, discussed in McDonnell, *History of St Paul's School*, 265–66, and T. W. Baldwin, *William Shakspere's Small Latine & Lesse Greeke* (Urbana: University of Illinois Press, 1944), 1:118–22.

6. *Of Education* (London, 1644), 2.

7. Milton advertised his two psalm paraphrases as written when he was fifteen, the earliest such date he attached to a poem. The undated verses in elegiacs and lesser asclepiads found with Milton's commonplace book in 1874, along with a prose theme on early rising, are not in Milton's hand and can at best be only circumstantially attributed to him; they may just as easily be pupil exercises from the 1640s. Milton's Greek theme "Philosophus ad regem" (published in the 1645 *Poems*), however, smacks of St Paul's, as does the Latin "Apologus de rustico et hero" (only acknowledged in the 1673 *Poems*), being an imitation of Mantuan; perhaps Milton did not set his age to these precisely because that would identify them as mere schoolwork. When Milton sent his only postschool Greek poem to Gil the younger, he stated that it was the first Greek composition of his "since I left your school" (*The Complete Prose Works of John Milton* [hereafter *CPW*], ed. Don M. Wolfe et al., 8 vols. (New Haven, CT: Yale University Press, 1958–1982), 1:321–32.

8. Milton to Henri de Brass, July 15, 1657: "ut dicam quod sentio, Sallustium cuivis Latino historico me quidem anteferre" (*Epistolae familiares* (London, 1674), 53–55, translation in *CPW*, 7:500–501).

9. McDonnell *Annals*, 187–89; and *Registers*, 95, 114, 118.

10. McDonnell, *Annals*, 177–78, 184; and *Registers*, 114, his authority being the Mercers' Company Acts of Court for March 10, 1609, printed in original spelling as Document XXII in Danielsson and Gabrielson, *Alexander Gill's Logonomia*.

11. The National Archives, PRO, PROB 11 / 169, fols. 211v–212v. We should not make a Talmudist of Mrs. Gil, who may have been left the learned bibles merely as an asset, but among the other books bequeathed to her it is intriguing to find the works of Henry Ainsworth and Richard Greenham, preachers distinctly toward the puritan end of the spectrum.

12. Alexander Gill, *Logonomia Anglica* (London, 1619), sig. B2v.

13. Alexander Gill, *Logonomia Anglica*, 2nd ed. (London, 1621), 20; Helen Darbishire, ed., *The Manuscript of Milton's "Paradise Lost," Book I* (Oxford: Clarendon Press, 1931), xxxiii–xxxv; see the corrections there to *PL* 1.2, 662. Mechanical repeaters of the belief that Darbishire's conclusions were successfully overturned several generations ago might like to consult Alan Ward, "Milton's Spellings Again," in *Five Hundred Years of Words and Sounds: A Festschrift for Eric Dobson*, ed. E. G. Stanley and Douglas Gray (Cambridge: D.S. Brewer, 1983), 157–64.

14. The fullest studies of this underappreciated work's character remain those of Arthur Barker, "Milton's Schoolmasters," *Modern Language Review* 32 (1937): 527–36, and Ruth Marie Baldwin, "Alexander Gill, the Elder, High Master of St Paul's

School: An Approach to Milton's Intellectual Development" (PhD diss., University of Illinois, 1955), 137–86.

15. Alexander Gil, *The Sacred Philosophie of the Holy Scripture* (London, 1635), 2nd pag., 36.

16. Gil, *Sacred Philosophie*, 2nd pag., 53–54. "Chymical" because Gil cites the "Novum lumen Chemicum," i.e., the Polish alchemist and physician Michael Sendivogius's work of that title.

17. Gil, *Sacred Philosophie*, sigs. (*2)v, (*)1v. Compare also Gil's long comment on 66–67.

18. Francis Cheynell, *Chillingworthi novissima* (London, 1644), sig. E3r.

19. Gil, *Sacred Philosophie*, sig. [(*3)]r.

20. *Areopagitica* (London, 1644), 10 (note the spelling "suttlest"). Milton in fact transposed the whole passage from an entry in his commonplace book (William Poole, "Milton and the Beard-Hater: Encounters with Julian the Apostate," *Seventeenth Century* 31, no. 2 (2016): 166).

21. Socrates Scholasticus, 3.16.

22. "On the Morning of Christ's Nativity," lines 186–88.

23. Virgil, *Eclogues*, 9.33–34.

24. Virgil, *Eclogues*, 2.58–59.

25. Milton, *Epistolae familiares*, 11: "rerum Poeticarum judicem acerrimum, & mearum candidissimum." On Gil and Milton see Leo Miller, "On Some of the Verses by Alexander Gil which John Milton Read," *Milton Quarterly* 24, no. 1 (1990): 22–25; and Gordon Campbell in *ODNB*. For the necessary redating of the letters to Gil, see Eugenia Chifos, "Milton's Letter to Gill, May 20, 1628," *Modern Language Notes* [hereafter *MLN*] 47 (1962): 37–39, and Gordon Campbell, *A Milton Chronology* (Basingstoke, UK: Houndmills, 1997), 35, 38, 40.

26. See McDonnell, *Annals*, 203–10, and David Cressy, *Dangerous Talk: Scandalous, Seditious, and Treasonable Speech in Pre-modern England* (Oxford: Oxford University Press, 2010), 143–46.

27. Anthony Wood, *Athenæ Oxonienses*, ed. Philip Bliss (London: Rivington et al., 1813), vol. 3, col. 43, citing two letters from Joseph Mede to Sir Martin Stuteville of Dalham, dated 15 and 22 November 1628 (these are, respectively, British Library, MS Harley 390, fols. 454r–55v, and 457r–58v). One wonders at Mede's source ("my author").

28. *Original Papers Illustrative of the Life of John Milton*, ed. William Douglas Hamilton (London, 1859), 69.

29. This was not the last time in the coming years prominent London headmasters would become victims of the state. In 1639 Laud took as another victim Lambert Osbaldeston, headmaster of Westminster, who was fined even larger sums than Gil, and condemned likewise to have his ears tacked to the pillory in the presence of his students. He fled. A little later, the headmaster of Merchant Taylors was sacked, this time by the Parliamentary powers, and replaced with the scholar-printer William Dugard. Dugard himself was destined for a colorful

career—imprisoned for printing material offensive to Parliament, before being released and "turned" to print Milton's own works in defense of the regicide. For both see *ODNB.*

30. When he was released has been misunderstood. He received a royal pardon only in late 1630, but in one of his groveling letters to Laud, dated November 23, 1629, he explicitly claims to have been released by that date ("Tandem (propitio Deo) post quindecim [*sic*] mensium ærumnas optimum Regem tetigit hominis omnibus fortunis exuti miseratio; vitâ Ille me priùs donaverat, nunc etiam carcere solutum luci reddidit," East Sussex Record Office, FRE 690, 62). So he was in fact at liberty for about a year before his formal pardon.

31. British Library, MS Egerton 2725, fol. 72r.

32. *Epistolae familiares,* 9–10.

33. Trinity College, Cambridge, MS O. 3. 53, fols. 64r–68r, which may have come to that college, like Milton's poetical working manuscripts, through the abandoned papers of Daniel Skinner.

34. *Epistolae familiares,* 14.

35. Alexander Gil, *Parerga* (London, 1632), sig. A5v: "Et si in evolvendâ hac farragine incideris in alia tenuiora; verum ubi ad *Sylvam-Ducis,* aut *Gustavi* Magni gesta perveneris, ea re malim imitari, quam cætera reprehendere"; sig. [E6]r. "Arma priùs cecini, cùm panderet inclyta portas / Sylva Ducis Batavis." Unlike the former, the latter poem achieved an English translation, by William Hawkins, published in 1632.

36. *Epistolae familiares,* 9.

37. Some similarities of detail suggest that a front-runner is Henry Hexham, *A Historicall Relation of the Famous Siege of the Busse, and the Surprising of Wesell* (Delft, 1630).

38. Milton, "Elegia Tertia," lines 11–12; Gil, *Parerga,* 37. Compare the sixth prolusion's reference to Buckingham's 1627 expedition to the Île de Ré (*Epistolae familiares,* 133 = *CPW,* 1:285). "Elegia quarta," to Thomas Young in Hamburg, is also marked by worrying rumors of impending attack.

39. *Epistolae familiares,* 10: "Nescio sane an Henrico Nassovio plus gratuler de urbe capta, an de tuis Carminibus"; for the siege, see Maarten Roy Prak, *The Dutch Republic in the Seventeenth Century: The Golden Age* (Cambridge: Cambridge University Press, 2005), 66–69.

40. Gil, *Parerga,* 37.

41. Gil, *Parerga,* 38. The final line is indeed a Virgilian half-line.

42. Collected now in Elizabeth R. Wright, Sarah Spence, and Andrew Lemons, eds. *The Battle of Lepanto* (Cambridge, MA: Harvard University Press, 2014).

43. Thomas Heywood, *The Hierarchie of the Blessed Angels* (London, 1635), 144; compare 341 on the (lack of real) angelic weapons.

44. Both were included in the collection now at East Sussex Record Office, FRE 690; there are two manuscript copies of the latter in the Bodleian (MS Tanner 306, fols. 78r–79r; MS Rawl. D 398, fol. 180r–v).

45. For these poems see chiefly Estelle Haan in her edition of Fletcher's *Locustæ*, Supplementa Humanistica Lovanensia IX (Leuven, Belgium: Leuven University Press, 1996), xxv–xxix. Haan considers Milton's epigrams to allude to James VI and I's own "Premonition" prefaced to the second edition of his *Apologie for the Oath of Allegiance* (London, 1609).

46. Dana Sutton, "Milton's *in Quintum Novembris, anno aetatis 17* (1626): Choices and Intentions," in *Qui Miscuit Utile Dulci: Festschrift Essays for Paul Lachlan MacKendrick*, ed. Gareth L. Schmeling and Jon D. Mikalson (Wauconda, IL: Bolchazy-Carducci, 1998), 373. Sources and analogues are presented by Estelle Haan, "Milton's 'In Quintum Novembris' and the Anglo-Latin Gunpowder Epic," *Humanistica Lovaniensia* 41 (1992): 221–95; and 42 (1993): 368–401, as well as in her edition of Fletcher's *Locustæ*.

47. "In Quintum Novembris," line 23.

48. Pliny, *Natural History*, 2.53; mentioned again at 29.14.

49. Augustine, *City of God*, 4.23.

50. Ovid, *Fasti*, 6.731.

### NOTES TO CHAPTER THREE

1. For Cambridge and Christ's College, see David Masson, *The Life of John Milton*, 7 vols. (London: Macmillan, 1881–1896), 1:111–320, still the most detailed account; John Peile, *Christ's College* (London: Robinson, 1900); Peile, *Biographical Register of Christ's College, 1505–1905*, 2 vols. (Cambridge: Cambridge University Press, 1910, 1913); Harris Francis Fletcher, *The Intellectual Development of John Milton*, 2 vols. (Urbana: University of Illinois Press, 1956), 2:2–54; Victor Morgan, *A History of the University of Cambridge*, vol. 2, *1546–1750* (Cambridge: University of Cambridge Press, 2004); Quentin Skinner, "The Generation of John Milton," in *Christ's: A Cambridge College over Five Centuries*, ed. David Reynolds (London: Macmillan, 2005), 41–72; and David Hoyle, *Reformation and Religious Identity in Cambridge, 1590–1644* (Woodbridge, UK: Boydell, 2007).

2. A particularly macho list can be found in John Bickerton Williams, *Letters on Puritanism and Nonconformity* (London, 1843), 99–105.

3. Consideration of the book trade is especially important when we recall that as an undergraduate Milton had access to neither his university nor his college library. The booksellers seem also to have been the standard sources of news; see, for example, Joseph Mede's letter to Martin Stuteville of November 29, 1628 (British Library, MS Harley 390, fol. 456r), "I heard at the Booksellers that Felton was arraigned & condemned this week."

4. *Epistolae familiares*, 11 ("Typis donata") = *CPW*, 1:314. Gordon Campbell and Thomas N. Corns, *John Milton: Life, Work, and Thought* (Oxford: Oxford University Press, 2008), 41, propose that these verses were written to be performed by the fellow Robert Gell; they cannot have been "Naturam non pati senium," for which see below. For Cambridge publishing and book trade in the period, see David McKitterick, *A History of Cambridge University Press*, vol. 1, *Printing and the Book*

*Trade in Cambridge, 1534–1698* (Cambridge: Cambridge University Press, 1992), 160–93, esp. 175–76 for student poetry, both printed and manuscript.

5. Hugh Trevor-Roper, "Laudianism and Political Power," in *Catholics, Anglicans and Puritans: Seventeenth-Century Essays* (1987; repr. London: Fontana, 1989), 49; Hoyle, *Reformation and Religious Identity*, 98–102, 166, 185. Bainbridge turned with the political wind and hurriedly de-Laudianized his chapel in early 1641 (215).

6. Jeffrey K. Jue, *Heaven Upon Earth: Joseph Mede (1586–1638) and the Legacy of Millenarianism* (Dordrecht: Springer, 2006), 143. For the survival of millenarianism, see William Poole, *The World Makers: Scientists of the Restoration and the Search for the Origins of the Earth* (Oxford: Peter Lang, 2010), 155–69.

7. Joseph Mede, *The Key of the Revelation*, trans. Richard More (London, 1643), 14–21.

8. Jue, *Heaven Upon Earth*, 28–30.

9. Only a few of the college's fellows actually taught the undergraduates; the most prominent such tutors just before Milton's time were apparently Chappell (whose pupils were nicknamed "Puritans"), William Power ("Powritans"), and Mede ("Medians"), although Robert Gell had replaced Power by Milton's time (Peile, *Christ's College*, 138; Norman Postlethwaite and Gordon Campbell, "Edward King, Milton's 'Lycidas': Poems and Documents," special issue, *Milton Quarterly* 28 (1994): 78.

10. A transcription of King's will is printed in Postlethwaite and Campbell, "Edward King," 95.

11. Thus Peile in the *Register;* his source is Bodleian, MS J. Walker c. 7, fol. 126r, where Alsop's nephew insists that "he was personally, & intimately acquainted w$^{th}$ Des Cartes: & was y$^{e}$ first occasion of introduing that Philosophy into Camb: & occasion'd those many Letters between Cartes & Dr Moor of X$^{ts}$ Coll, w$^{ch}$ are printed in his works, & this I have bin assured of severall times from D$^{r}$ Moor, & D$^{r}$ Cudworth his contemporaries" (Josias Alsop to John Walker, January 18, 1712). No other testimony corroborates this claim, however. For a devastating critique of More and for "the non-existence of 'Cambridge Platonism,'" however, see now Dmitri Levitin, *Ancient Wisdom in the Age of the New Science: Histories of Philosophy in England, c. 1640–1700* (Cambridge: Cambridge University Press, 2015), 126–39.

12. See, for example, John Lightfoot, *The Works of the Reverend and Learned John Lightfoot, D.D.*, 2 vols. (London, 1684), 1:945–46, 1083–84; 2:380–81.

13. John Dryden, *Of Dramatick Poesie: An Essay* (London, 1668), 23.

14. Fletcher, *Intellectual Development*, 2:360–66; T. H. Howard-Hill, "Milton and 'the Rounded Theatre's Pomp,'" in *Of Poetry and Politics: New Essays on Milton and his World*, ed. P. G. Stanwood (Binghamton, NY: Medieval and Renaissance Texts and Studies, 1995), 105–7. A strong case for Stubbe is made in Sarah Knight, "Milton's Student Verses of 1629," *Notes and Queries* 57, no. 1 (2010): 37–39.

15. Roslyn Richek, "Thomas Randolph's 'Salting' (1627), Its Text, and John Milton's Sixth Prolusion as Another Salting," *English Literary Renaissance* 12, no. 1 (1982): 103–31.

16. *Poems* (London, 1645), 72.

17. *An Apology* (London, 1642), 12–13.

18. Morgan, *History,* 325–33.

19. For Keckermann in Milton's *Logica* see *CPW,* 8:330, 374.

20. On Keckermann at Christ's see Fletcher, *Intellectual Development,* 2:147–48, and more generally Skinner, "The Generation of John Milton." For the centrality of Keckermann to the tutorials of Mede see his accounts, now in Christ's College Library, T 11.1–4, being tutorial accounts for 1615 to 1636, arranged by pupil surname.

21. The preface to the *Epistolae familiares* of the publisher, Brabazon Aylmer, explains that he had initially planned to publish, but had been prevented from doing so, Milton's public as well as his familiar correspondence, and so had been forced to go back to Milton for more material to make up the volume; these "juvenilia," "scattered here and there" (*hic illic disjecta*) had been found "by chance" (*forte*) and supplied (sig. A3r–v).

22. For the Cambridge curriculum see William T. Costello, *The Scholastic Curriculum at Early Seventeenth-Century Cambridge* (Cambridge, MA: Harvard University Press, 1958); for the BA requirements, see Skinner, "The Generation of John Milton," 63–66. The fullest study of Milton's writings from this period is John K. Hale, *Milton's Cambridge Latin: Performing in the Genres 1625–1632* (Tempe, AZ: Arizona Center for Medieval and Renaissance Studies, 2005). For the problems we face when seeking to date the *prolusiones* absolutely or to tie them to specific degree exercises, see Campbell and Corns, *Milton,* 35–37.

23. Disputations: IV (held in the college); V (held in the Schools). Act Verses: "Naturam non pati senium," "De idea platonica," printed consecutively in the 1645 *Poemata.* Declamations: I (college); II (Schools), III (Schools), VII (college, specifically in the chapel). Salting: VI, to which probably also belong the English verses, published in the 1673 *Poems,* "At a Vacation Exercise" (college, in the vacation).

24. Knight, "Milton's Student Verses of 1629."

25. *Epistolae familiares,* 115 = *CPW,* 1:267.

26. *Epistolae familiares,* 150–51 = *CPW,* 1:300–301.

27. *Epistolae familiares,* 131–32 = *CPW,* 1:283, and see Ovid, *Metamorphoses,* 12.189–209, and Virgil, *Aeneid,* 6.448–49 for Caeneus.

28. *Epistolae familiares,* 134, resting on Suetonius's account (Nero, 33.1) of Nero punning on *morari* and *mōrari.*

29. *Epistolae familiares,* 71–72 = *CPW,* 1:222–23.

30. Giovanni Boccaccio, *De genealogia deorum* (Basel, 1532), 3–7 (1.2–4), on Chaos, Demogorgon, and Pan (not quite Milton's Phanes). Milton's specific insertion of Phanes into this narrative appears to be original, however: Phanes (also known as Protogonus) is more often figured in Orphic sources as a divinity begotten from an egg (e.g., Orphic Hymn 5, "To Protogonus, or the First-Born"; compare *Orphic Argonautica,* 15–16, where Phanes is the parent of Nux or Night); he is not present in Hesiod. But then compare the Chorus of Birds on their own origin in Aristophanes, *Birds,* 690–702.

31. *Epistolae familiares,* 136–37 = *CPW,* 1:289.

32. Trinity College, Cambridge, MS R. 5. 4 (the "Trinity College Manuscript"), 7 (second draft of letter, with minor emendations).

33. See Nicholas McDowell, "How Laudian Was the Young Milton?," *Milton Studies* 52 (2011): 3–33, especially his conclusion that "Milton's composition of the poems on the Passion and the Circumcision cannot be said confidently to show either his taste or distaste for Laudian values in the early 1630s; rather, the lyrics reflect his efforts to compose in the devotional mode fashionable in his university at the time." Thomas F. Healy, *Richard Crashaw* (Leiden: Brill, 1986), 40–65, also offers some useful perspectives on Cambridge poetical trends in the period and on how potentially misleading it is to equate political or religious convictions with such trends.

34. See Ian Gadd, ed., *History of Oxford University Press,* vol. 1 (Oxford: Oxford University Press, 2013), 561 for details; for book burnings, see Cyndia Susan Clegg, *Press Censorship in Jacobean England* (Cambridge: Cambridge University Press, 2001), chap. 2; and, more diffusely, the same author's *Press Censorship in Caroline England* (Cambridge: Cambridge University Press, 2008).

35. *Decretum Universitatis Oxonienses damnans propositiones neotericorum infra-scriptas* (Oxford, 1622). The offending section may be found in David Pareus, *In divinam ad Romanos S. Pauli Epistolam commentarius* (Heidelberg, 1613), under Romans 13, "De potestate civili," prop. 2, cols. 1350–53.

36. Roger Maynwaring, *Religion and Alegiance* (London, 1627), 8, 11, 26; Vivienne Larminie, "Maynwaring, Roger," in *ODNB.*

37. Samuel Ward to James Ussher, May 16, 1628 (in Elizabethanne Boran, ed., *The Correspondence of James Ussher: 1600–1656,* 3 vols. (Dublin: Irish Manuscripts Commission, 2015), 2:427–29).

38. Margo Todd, "Anti-Calvinists and the Republican Threat in Early Stuart Cambridge," in *Puritanism and Its Discontents,* ed. Laura Lunger Knoppers (Newark, NJ: University of Delaware Press, 2003), 85–105; Ronald Mellor, "Tacitus, Academic Politics, and Regicide in the Reign of Charles I: The Tragedy of Dr. Isaac Dorislaus," *International Journal of the Classical Tradition* 11, no. 2 (2004): 153–93.

39. Francis Peck, *Desiderata Curiosa,* vol. 2 (London, 1735), lib. 11, 9.

40. John Wildman, "A brief discourse concerning the businesse of intelligence and how it may be managed to the best advantage," in C. H. Firth, "Thurloe and the Post Office," *English Historical Review* [hereafter *EHR*] 13 (1898): 529–33.

## NOTES TO CHAPTER FOUR

1. John Aubrey, *Brief Lives,* ed. Kate Bennett, 2 vols. (Oxford: Oxford University Press, 2015), 1:660, 668.

2. See, for example, *Epistolae familiares* (London, 1673), 19, and the "Letter to a Friend," Trinity College Manuscript, 7.

3. Sonnet 7, first published in *Poems* (London, 1645), 49; Trinity College Manuscript, 6.

4. Gordon Campbell, "Shakespeare and the Youth of Milton," *Milton Quarterly* 33, no. 4 (1999): 95–105.

5. Horace, *Odes*, 3.3.0.1–2.

6. W. R. Parker, *Milton: A Biography*, rev. Gordon Campbell, 2 vols. (Oxford: Clarendon Press, 1996), 120.

7. *Poems* (London, 1645), 27.

8. Nicholas Lloyd, *Dictionarium historicum, geographicum, poeticum*, 2nd ed. (London, 1686), s.v. "Sibyllæ." Lloyd's dictionary is a revision of the famous dictionary of Carolus Stephanus; all subsequent references to this useful contemporary reference work are to this second edition.

9. "Il Penseroso," line 42. As Carey's note comments, these all rest on the myth of Niobe, petrified in grief over the loss of her children. See Ovid, *Metamorphoses*, 6.145–310; and Apollodorus, *Bibliotheca*, 3.5.6.

10. Note, for instance, that in the "Ideas for Dramas" drafts, Milton skipped the Old Testament narrative of Jephtha, perhaps because Buchanan's neo-Latin drama had effectively monopolized the story, whereas in his jottings for "Scotch" dramas he happily envisages revisiting the tragedy of Macbeth. This is not to deny that Milton was a careful reader of the Folio: in *Eikonoklastes*, for instance, Milton accuses Charles I of plagiarizing not only Sidney but also Shakespeare's *Richard III* ([London, 1650], 10–11).

11. Ben Jonson, "To the Memory of My Beloved the Author, Mr. William Shakespeare." See T. W. Baldwin, *William Shakspere's Small Latine & Lesse Greeke*, 1:27–29. Baldwin also shrewdly noted that the pyramid points to a star because of Ovid's "Parte tamen meliore mei super alta perennis / Astra ferar" (*Metamorphoses*, 15.875–76). In turn, I suspect Cowley borrowed from all of these, including Milton, when he wrote " 'Tis not a *Pyramide* of Marble stone / Though high as our ambition, / 'Tis not a Tombe cut out in Brasse, which can / Give life to th'ashes of a man, / But Verses onely" ("On the praise of Poetry," in *Poeticall Blossoms*, 3rd ed. (London, 1637), sig. F4r).

12. He mentions Chaucer and Gower at *CPW*, 1:570, 579, 580, 595, 667 (Chaucer, first four mentions in *Of Reformation*, last in *Animadversions*), 946 (Gower, in *An Apology*). The only other English poets he mentions as such are the primeval Gildas (i.e., Cambrius not Priscus), and that fascinating versifier of Dares Phrygius, the twelfth-century Latin hexameter poet Joseph of Exeter, "the only smooth Poet of those times" (*CPW*, 5:15); the "late court-poet" ' of *The Ready and Easie Way* (*CPW*, 7:426) remains unidentified. Milton was also interested in early stories of English poets: he noted down in his commonplace book the story from Bede of Caedmon, who became a poet by divine inspiration, and likewise King Alfred, *peritissimus* as a poet (Commonplace Book MS, 57).

13. *CPW*, 2:516; 3:390. Talus is ultimately from Apollonius of Rhodes, discussed below.

14. *Eikonoklastes* (London, 1650), 11.

15. For this extremely knotty business, see Neil Harris, "John Milton's Reading of the *Orlando Innamorato*," *La Bibliofilia* 88 (1986): 25–43.

16. These works are, respectively, Jacopo Mazzoni's *Discorso in Difesa della Commedia della Divino Poeta Dante* (Cesena, 1572); Torquato Tasso's *Discorsi del poema eroico* (Naples, 1594); and Lodovico Castelvetro's *Poetica d'Aristotele vulgarizzata e sposita* (Vienna, 1570).

17. *Epistolae familiares*, 20.

18. For some conjectures why, see William Poole, "Milton and the Beard-Hater: Encounters with Julian the Apostate," *Seventeenth Century* 31, no. 2 (2016): 164.

19. G. Brugnoli and F. Stock, eds., *Vitae Vergilianae Antiquae* (Rome: Typis Officinae Polygraphicae, 1997), 23, 86, 150; Gordon Campbell, "Milton and the Lives of the Ancients," *Journal of the Warburg and Courtauld Institutes* 47 (1984): 234–38. The ancient lives of Virgil, however, also state clearly that he was a pederast.

20. This and the following account are more fully discussed in William Poole, "John Milton and Giovanni Boccaccio's *Vita di Dante*," *Milton Quarterly* 48, no. 3 (2014): 139–70.

21. Leo Miller, "The Italian Imprimaturs in Milton's *Areopagitica*," *Papers of the Bibliographical Society of America* 65, no. 4 (1971): 345–55.

22. *Reason*, in *CPW*, 1:811.

23. John Harington, trans., *Orlando Furioso in English Heroical Verse* (London, 1591), 417.

24. Harington, *Orlando Furioso*, 415–16; Jacobus Philippus Thomasinus, *Petrarcha redivivus, Laura comite* (Padua, 1635), 15, cited by Milton in his commonplace book (Commonplace Book MS, 189); Ovid, *Amores*, 1.15.5–6; Milton, "Ad patrem," lines 71–72.

25. Harington, *Orlando Furioso*, 420.

26. The most thorough work on Milton and the Italians is Estelle Haan, *From "Academia" to "Amicitia": Milton's Latin Writings and the Italian Academies* (Philadelphia: American Philosophical Society, 1998). For judicious summaries of Milton's literary experiences in Italy see H. R. Trevor-Roper, "Milton in Politics," in his *Catholics, Anglicans and Puritans: Seventeenth-Century Essays* (London: Secker and Warburg, 1987), 244–46, and Gordon Campbell and Thomas N. Corns, *John Milton: Life, Work, and Thought* (Oxford: Oxford University Press, 2008), 108–25. More detailed studies can be found in Mario Di Cesare, ed., *Milton in Italy: Contexts, Images, Contradictions* (Binghamton, NY: Medieval and Renaissance Texts and Studies, 1991).

27. Giovanni Battista Manso, *Vita di Torquato Tasso* (Venice, 1621), ch. 9.

28. Haan, *From "Academia" to "Amicitia,"* explicit sightings of Milton on 19–21, 36.

29. Davide Messina, " 'La Tina' Regained," *Milton Quarterly* 45, no. 2 (2011): 118–22; Antonio Malatesti, *La Tina: equivoci rusticali*, ed. Davide Messina (London: Modern Humanities Research Association, 2014).

30. *Gerusalemme Conquistata*, cant. 20, in the edition of Rome, 1593, 240. The *Gerusalemme Conquistata* was Tasso's own radical revision of the *Gerusalemme Liberata*. Milton cites the lines on Manso in his headnote to his reply poem for

Manso, "Mansus," and under the form *Gerusalemme Conquistata*, which he must therefore have been reading.

31. *Poemata*, 4, the pun being from Bede, *Historia Ecclesiastica*, 2.1.

32. *Poemata*, 4. Meles is the river associated with Homer; Mincius with Virgil; Sebetus is Neapolitan Sebeto, the river of Tasso.

33. *Poemata*, 4, 10. Ironically, "Selvaggi" was probably an English Benedictine, as first proposed by Edward Chaney in *The Grand Tour and the Great Rebellion: Richard Lassels and "The Voyage of Italy" in the 17th Century* (Geneva: Slatkin, 1985), appendix 3. Dryden's epigram is *"Three Poets, in three distant Ages born, / Greece, Italy, and England did adorn. / The First in loftiness of thought surpass'd; / The Next in Majesty; in both the Last. / The force of Nature cou'd no farther goe: / To make a Third she joynd the former two."*

34. *Poemata*, 8.

35. "Mansus," lines 78–84.

36. Ibid., lines 99–100.

37. Quoted in Haan, *From "Academia" to "Amicitia,"* 21, with her translation. Doni is Nicolo Doni, not Milton's other friend, Giovanni Battista Doni.

38. Pliny the Younger, for example Epistle 7.17 on the reading of all kinds of genres, including tragedy. Pliny frequently mentions literary recitations, perhaps unusually so—for which see William A. Johnson, *Readers and Reading Culture in the High Roman Empire: A Study of Elite Communities* (Oxford: Oxford University Press, 2010), 42–56.

### NOTES TO CHAPTER FIVE

1. For Milton's pupils, both certain and conjectural, see W. R. Parker, *Milton: A Biography*, rev. Gordon Campbell, 2 vols. (Oxford: Clarendon, 1996), 837, 922–25; John T. Shawcross, *Milton: The Self and the World* (Lexington: University Press of Kentucky, 2001), 81.

2. They were Lucretius and Manilius for Latin; Hesiod, Aratus, Dionysius "Afer" (Dionysius Periegetes, as he is better known), Oppian, Apollonius, and Quintus Smyrnaeus ("Calaber") for Greek.

3. For Aubrey's own priorities in education reform see William Poole, *John Aubrey and the Advancement of Learning* (Oxford: Bodleian Library, 2010), 30–31, 47–49.

4. John Aubrey, *Brief Lives*, ed. Kate Bennett, 2 vols. (Oxford: Oxford University Press, 2015), 1:669–70.

5. Timothy Raylor, "Milton, the Hartlib Circle, and the Education of the Aristocracy," in *The Oxford Handbook of Milton*, ed. Nicholas McDowell and Nigel Smith (Oxford: Oxford University Press, 2012), 382–406; William Poole, " 'The Armes of Studious Retirement'?: Milton's Scholarship, 1632–1641," in *Young Milton: The Emerging Author, 1620–1642*, ed. Edward Jones (Oxford: Oxford University Press, 2012), 40.

6. Edited in H. F. Fletcher, *Intellectual Development of John Milton*, 2:623–64. For Holdsworth, Mede, and the Cambridge curriculum, see also David McKitterick,

*A History of Cambridge University Press,* vol. 1, *Printing and the Book Trade in Cambridge, 1534–1698* (Cambridge: Cambridge University Press, 1992), 1:217–34.

7. Seneca, *Epistulae morales,* 1.7.8. Or, as Phillips put it, "Thus by teaching he in some measure increased his own knowledge, having the reading of all these Authors as it were by Proxy" (Helen Darbishire, ed., *The Early Lives of Milton* (London: Constable, 1932), 60). Richard J. DuRocher, *Milton among the Romans: The Pedagogy and Influence of Milton's Latin Curriculum* (Pittsburgh: Duquesne University Press, 2001), promises a more systematic treatment than it delivers.

8. George Abbot, *The Reasons which Doctour Hill hath Brought for the Upholding of Papistry* (Oxford, 1604), 88. For a common complaint about Anglified Latin, see, e.g., under John Evelyn's diary entry for May 13, 1661.

9. *Of Education* (London, 1644), 4.

10. Celsus, 1.1. There were many print editions of this work, but it is striking that the most often printed text (editions of, e.g., Haguenau, 1528; Solingen, 1538; Lyon 1549, 1566, 1587, 1608; Venice, 1566; Geneva, 1625) combined Celsus with Quintus Serenus Sammonicus's *Liber medicinalis,* and (pseudo-)Quintus Remmius Palaemon's *Carmen de ponderibus et mensuris.* A scholarly one-volume edition is that of Baldaeus Ronsseus (Leiden, 1592).

11. It was printed, for instance, at Eton in 1613. Other technical or moral literature in Greek included (pseudo-)Plutarch's *Placita philosophorum,* a summary work of natural philosophy, in which philosophy is helpfully organized in all its branches and schools; as well as (genuine) Plutarch's *On the Education of Children,* another classic schoolroom piece, often paired with the same author's *How the Young Man Should Study Poetry.* To the *Placita* Milton added Diogenes Laertius's *Lives of the Philosophers,* the foundational series of biographies of the major philosophers, doubling as a bibliography and a history of classical philosophy.

12. The major editions were the free-standing Greek edition of Paris, 1555 (based on the Aldine text of 1513), and a uniform-format Latin translation of Paris, 1562; as well as a Greek text with an interpolated Latin translation of Venice, 1555, by Ludovicus Nogarola. But it also appeared in the 1578 Stephanus collection of Platonic texts.

13. Altdorf, 1590, a parallel text, edited by Edo Hildericus. It is possible that Milton employed a collected edition for his astronomers, namely Dionysius Petavius's *Uranologion* (Paris, 1630).

14. Commonplace Book MS, 19.

15. *Of Education,* 4–5. Phillips recalled the use of the textbooks of Christianus Urstitius, a Ramist arithmetician who taught at Basel; Petrus Ryff, a Ramist geometrician, also of Basel; Bartholomäus Pitiscus, a trigonometer, indeed the man who coined the term "trigonometry"; and finally the evergreen Johannes Sacrobosco, the thirteenth-century Ptolemaic astronomer whose *Tractatus de Sphaera* was easily the most popular textbook in traditional astronomy in the Western academe from the thirteenth to the seventeenth centuries; it was last printed as a viable textbook in 1674. The pertinent editions are Christianus Urstitius, *Elementa arithmeticæ* (Basel, 1579, 1595, 1602); Petrus Ryff, *Quæstiones*

*geometricæ,* with an appendix on *Geodæsia* (Frankfurt, 1600, 1602, 1621); Bartholomäus Pitiscus, *Trigonometria* (first published as an appendix to Abraham Scultetus, *Sphæricorum libri tres* [Heidelberg, 1595]; then individually at Augsburg, 1600, 1608; Frankfurt, 1612, 1642; an English translation was published in London in 1614, 1630, 1642). For Sacrobosco, see Olaf Pedersen, "In Quest of Sacrobosco," *Journal for the History of Astronomy* 16, no. 3 (1985): 175–221, esp. 183–84; the best editions of Sacrobosco in Milton's time were those of Melanchthon, Christopher Clavius, and Franco Burgersdijck.

16. Solinus was partially derived from Pomponius Mela, and from Pliny.

17. *Defensio secunda* (London, 1654), 82–83.

18. Commonplace Book MS, 12.

19. Allan H. Gilbert, "Pierre Davity: His 'Geography' and Its Use by Milton," *Geographical Review* 7, no. 5 (1919): 322–38.

20. Pierre Davity, *Les Estats, Empires, et Principautez du Monde* (Paris, 1613), 859. The name "Sericana" is probably an allusion to Ariosto's *Orlando Furioso,* however, where it is frequently mentioned (1.55, etc.).

21. "Phalereus" is perhaps less well known; this is Demetrius of Phalerum, then believed to be the author of a (much later) treatise on eloquence, published under the title *Peri hermeneias / De elocutione.* The most advanced editions available to Milton were those of Piero Vettori, most recently that of Florence, 1594.

22. Milton took notes from the *Institutes* in his commonplace book (e.g., Commonplace Book MS, 113, 179, 182, 190), but it was in the period of the later divorce tracts that he read properly the more advanced parts of the *Corpus Juris Civilis,* as well as later Roman (Byzantine) law in Leunclavius's *Iuris Graeco-Romani tam canonici quam civilis tomi duo* (Frankfurt, 1596). In the next decade, he blew the dust off his civil law texts to attack Salmasius and More.

23. *Of Education,* 5, 6–8.

24. *Of Education,* 2.

25. The targums of Onkelos and Jonathan were presumably studied in parallel Aramaic-Latin editions, such as the 1541 edition of Paulus Fagius; the Syriac New Testament was again usually encountered in the classroom in a parallel Latin-Syriac edition. Milton was likely using the 1621 (reissued 1622) Köthen ("Cotenis Anhaltinorum") edition of Martin Trost, which placed a Latin gloss at the foot of the page.

26. Milton's printed marginal glosses on these point out Hebraisms; for example, in his translation of Psalm 88 in *Poems* (1673), on "Thou break'st upon me all thy waves, / And all thy waves break me" (p. 164) he comments: *"The Hebr. bears both."* Carey's note states this is only true of the first verse, but perhaps Milton is being more sensitive to the possibilities of grammatical ellipsis: Psalm 88:7 is literally "you have set your wrath upon me and [with] all your waves you have afflicted [me]" (my thanks to Joanna Weinberg for this).

27. It is quite possible that Milton and his pupils worked from Lectius's *Poetæ Græci veteres carminis heroici scriptores* (Geneva, 1606), a gravid folio of all the Greek

hexameter poets, with accompanying Latin glosses and an index that could be used to ascertain parallel passages. It was, for instance, an edition owned by Milton's schoolmaster, Alexander Gil the Elder (his copy is now Westminster Abbey P 1.63). In 1614 Lectius followed this with a companion volume for Greek drama and other genres of poems; Milton could easily have used this too. For poets other than Homer, there was also the handy Cambridge imprint, the *Poetæ Minores Græci* (1635), edited by Ralph Winterton, for the popularity of which see McKitterick, *History of Cambridge University Press*, 1:182–83.

28. Deployed by Milton himself in, for example, the first prolusion (*Epistolae familiares*, 78, quoting the Hymn to Dawn). For a variety of contemporary opinions on the antiquity and existence of Orpheus, see the entry in Nicholas Lloyd, *Dictionarium historicum, geographicum, poeticum*, 2nd ed. (London, 1686). What constituted "Orphic" poetry was debatable, the major texts being the *Argonautica*, the *Hymns*, and *On Stones*. There were many editions, but all three could be found, for instance, in Lectius's *Poetæ Græci*. A survey of the editorial tradition to that date may be found in Eschenbach's preface to the reader in his edition of the *Argonautica* (Utrecht, 1689).

29. The Oppian of the *Halieutica* and the Oppian of the *Cynegetica* are now considered to be two separate poets. Early editions of Oppian could be rather spare, taking, for example, the Parisian 1549 edition of the *Cynegeticon*, which presents a bare Greek text. A popular edition of both poems was that of Conrad Rittershusius (Leiden, 1597). The anecdote of the staters is from the *Suda*, and appeared routinely in reference works thereafter, including Lloyd, *Dictionarium*, s.n.

30. As pointed out in Todd's annotation to *PL* 9.510 (from Henry Meen) in Henry John Todd, ed., *Poetical Works of John Milton* (London, 1801), referring to *Theriaca*, 264–70; also Claes Schaar, *The Full-Voic'd Quire Below: Vertical Context Systems in Paradise Lost* (Lund: CWK Gleerup, 1982), 281–82.

31. The two major early modern editions of Nicander were the Cologne 1530 edition with scholia and an appended translation by Johannes Lonicer, and the Parisian parallel editions of the physician Johannes Gorraeus (*Alexipharmaca*, 1549; *Theriaca* and *Alexipharmaca*, 1557). Gorraeus's editions leave one in no doubt that the medical content of these poems was taken quite seriously.

32. "Utrum dies an nox praestantior sit?' [*Prolusio* I], in *Epistolae familiares*, 71–72.

33. More will be said on Apollonius below. The major editions were again sixteenth century: Frankfurt, 1546; Basel, 1572; Geneva, 1574. The major edition in Milton's earlier life was the Leiden 1641 edition of Jeremias Hoelzlinus. It is important to recognize that all of these editions included the ancient scholia on Apollonius, a mine of literary information; the most handy is the 1574 Stephanus edition, which prints the scholia surrounding the text. There is a useful parallel French-Greek indexed modern edition of the scholia, *Scholies à Apollonios de Rhodes*, ed. Guy Lachenaud (Paris: Les Belles Lettres, 2010).

34. As his early modern editor explains, Quintus was called "Calaber" merely because Cardinal Bessarion had found the manuscript in the Monastery of St Nicholas, near Hydrus in Calabria; but "Smyrnaeus" should be preferred, as it was,

following this edition (*Ilias*, ed. Laurentius Rhodomanus (Hanover, 1604), sigs. +7v-+8r). Note, however that Milton, in the reference supplied in the next note, did call him "Smyrnaeus . . . sive Calaber" (Smyrnaeus . . . or Calaber).

35. *Defensio secunda* (1654), 57–58 = *CPW*, 4:595.

36. It achieved both Oxford (1592) and Cambridge (1595) editions, for instance, explicitly for academic use, but both printed as bare Greek texts without any editorial apparatus or gloss. Both survive in such small numbers that they were evidently shaken to pieces by vexed students.

37. See Catalogue of English Literary Manuscripts (henceforth CELM), *MnJ 123 for Milton's copy; for the scholia and their authorship see the discussion in the Loeb edition, 316–18. The best discussion is Harris F. Fletcher and John T. Shawcross, "John Milton's Copy of Lycophron's 'Alexandra' in the Library of the University of Illinois," *Milton Quarterly* 23, no. 4 (1989): 129–58.

38. See the 1604 Hanover edition of Quintus Smyrnaeus, and CELM, *MnJ 119.

39. See CELM, *MnJ 117.

40. John K. Hale, *Milton's Languages: The Impact of Multilingualism on Style* (Cambridge: Cambridge University Press, 1997), 77; William Poole, "John Milton and Giovanni Boccaccio's *Vita di Dante*," *Milton Quarterly* 48, no. 3 (2014): 158.

41. On this see William Poole, "Milton and the Beard-Hater: Encounters with Julian the Apostate," *Seventeenth Century* 31, no. 2 (2016): 166. Milton followed Socrates Scholasticus in attributing 1 Cor. 15:33 to Euripides; by Milton's time most scholars accepted the alternative attribution, originally found in Jerome, to the *comic* writer Menander, a generic shift it seems Milton was not willing to contemplate.

42. See now the superb edition and translation by J. L. Lightfoot, *Dionysius Periegetes: Description of the Known World* (Oxford: Oxford University Press, 2014).

43. There were highly serviceable continental editions for the purpose, often with parallel texts and commentaries (e.g., of Paris, 1559, and Antwerp, 1575). Something of the work's currency in Milton's educational milieu is shown by the existence of an Eton edition of probably 1615, a simple piece of printing evidently for classroom use, followed by a Cambridge edition of 1633 (edited by Ralph Winterton), like the Eton imprint furnishing just a bare Greek text, and indeed printed specifically for use at Eton.

44. A good example is the Wykehamist Richard Zouche, *The Dove: or Passages of Cosmography* (Oxford, 1613).

45. Lightfoot, *Dionysius Periegetes*, 120.

46. It is suggestive that even after he became blind Milton was enquiring about the comparative coverage and quality of the more recent (and in the event too expensive) Blaeu and Janssonius atlases; was this preparation for getting the geographical names in *Paradise Lost* right? (Milton to Peter Heimbach, November 8, 1656, in Milton, *Epistolae familiares*, 48–49, translation in *CPW*, 7:494–95). For the sources of Milton's place names, see Allan H. Gilbert, *A Geographical Dictionary of Milton* (New Haven, CT: Yale University Press, 1919).

47. John Milton, *A Brief History of Moscovia* (London, 1682), 29–36, and compare *PL* 3.437–49 on the "Chineses." Maps in the late sixteenth-century Ortelius-Mercator tradition continued to identify "China" as applying to the southern and coastal regions (compare Milton's "*China* Sayles," *Moscovia,* 31); and "Cathay" as some kingdom in the north, adjacent to the Great Wall (compare Milton's description of the Great Wall, *Moscovia,* 33–35). Davity said likewise; as did Peter Heylyn in his *Microcosmos* (1621, many subsequent editions), and Purchas, whom Milton studied carefully, gave rather mixed signals. For these see Loren Pennington, ed., *The Purchas Handbook,* 2 vols. (London: London Hakluyt Society, 1997), 1:274). The *Atlas Sinensis* (1655) of Martino Martini, which settled the problem, appeared after Milton had gone completely blind.

48. Milton's *Euripides* (Geneva, 1602, 2 vols.) is today in the Bodleian Library; the best analysis is Maurice Kelley and Samuel D. Atkins, "Milton's Annotations to Euripides," *Journal of English and Germanic Philology* 60 (1961): 680–87. For the use to which Milton put the volume see William Riley Parker, *Milton's Debt to Greek Tragedy in "Samson Agonistes"* (Baltimore: Johns Hopkins Press, 1937), esp. 245–47, and Nicholas McDowell, "Milton's Euripides and the Superior Rationality of the Heathen," *Seventeenth Century* 31, no. 2 (2016): 215–37. Parker, *Milton's Debt,* 168n2, provides a table of parallelisms of structure between *Oedipus Coloneus* and *Samson Agonistes*—"so striking one is tempted to infer a certain amount of conscious imitation."

49. Joannes Buchlerus, *Sacrarum profanarumque phrasium poeticarum thesaurus* (London, 1669), 377–88. This is followed by Phillips's *Compendiosa enumeratio poetarum, &c.* (388–402), a survey of modern poets, arranged by nation.

50. Phillips evidently means Nicodemus Frischlinus's essay "De veteri comoedia eiusque partibus," prefaced to his edition of Aristophanes (Frankfurt, 1586), 16–18, which he directly paraphrases here; this is another essay we can tentatively add to the reading done in Milton's classroom. (This essay can be found in other editions too, e.g., Leiden, 1625.) Frischlinus was himself a prominent writer of neo-Latin plays on both sacred and secular themes.

51. See *The Complete Works of John Milton* [hereafter *OM*], gen. ed. Gordon Campbell and Thomas N. Corns, 11 vols. (Oxford: Oxford University Press, 2008–), 3:282–83 and 2:68, respectively, for Milton's remarks on the meters of his Ode to Rouse and the choruses of *Samson Agonistes.*

52. See Steven M. Oberhelman and John Mulryan, "Milton's Use of Classical Meters in the 'Sylvarum Liber,'" *Modern Philology* 81, no. 2 (1983): 137–43, for a metrical analysis of both poems. Again, such virtuosity was encouraged by the Cambridge vogue: Crashaw's "In Apollinem depereuntem Daphnen," for instance, displayed twenty-two different meters in its twenty-two lines; see Thomas F. Healy, *Richard Crashaw* (Leiden: Brill, 1986), 41.

53. For this kind of Alexandrianism see Reviel Netz, *Ludic Proof: Greek Mathematics and the Alexandrian Aesthetic* (Cambridge: Cambridge University Press, 2009), chap. 4, esp. 176–78, 193, 216–18 (on Apollonius), 182–88, 221–23 (Aratus), 189–90, 193 (Nicander), 218–21 (Theocritus), 223–24 (Lycophron).

54. J. C. Scaliger, *Poetices libri septem* (Geneva, 1561), 1.1 (1–3). A prominent example of the influence of "the Prince of all learning, the Iudge of iudgements" on vernacular treatises is Henry Peacham's *The Compleat Gentleman* (London, 1620), chaps. 6, 10 (quotation from p. 91). We can be sure Milton read Scaliger with care: see for example the reference to Scaliger on mimes in *An Apology* (London, 1642), 9.

55. The comment is preserved in Censorinus, *De die natali*, 21.1–6.

56. Scaliger, *Poetices libri septem*, 1.2 (3–6).

57. One barometer is the French critic Rapin, who in his treatise on Aristotle's *Poetics* remarked that Nicander, Aratus, and Lucretius all failed where Virgil succeeded: "It is not enough to exhibit *Nature,* which in certain places is *rude* and unpleasant; he [the successful poet] must . . . discern what to choose, and what to refuse . . . that he may avoid the object that will not *please,* and retain what will." See René Rapin, *Reflections on Aristotle's Treatise of Poesie* (London, 1674), 54.

58. The classic study of the arts degree in the period remains Mordechai Feingold, "The Humanities," in *The History of the University of Oxford IV: The Seventeenth Century*, ed. Nicholas Tyacke (Oxford: Oxford University Press, 1997), 211–357.

59. [James Harrington], *Some Reflexions upon a Treatise Call'd Pietas Romana & Parisiensis Lately Printed at Oxford* (Oxford, 1688), 26.

60. Abraham Cowley, *A Proposition for the Advancement of Experimental Philosophy* (London, 1661), 45–50.

61. Aubrey (*Early Lives,* 3, 4; John Aubrey, *Brief Lives,* 2 vols., ed. Kate Bennett (Oxford: Oxford University Press, 2015), 664, 667) and Skinner (*Early Lives,* 29) both state that the dictionary was commenced after Milton had gone blind; but Edward Phillips, who would know, and in whose keeping the manuscript at one point was, said that "he had long since been Collecting" for the work, and the nature of the authors excerpted would support this (*Early Lives,* 72).

62. Anon., revising Adam Littleton et al., *Linguæ Romanæ Dictionarium Luculentum Novum: A New Dictionary in Five Alphabets* (Cambridge, 1693), sig. A2r. It is on Skinner's authority that Milton, in addition to his Latin thesaurus, commenced a Greek thesaurus (*Early Lives,* 29).

63. Difficult, but not impossible. Of the various dictionaries comprehended in Littleton, Milton's lexicon was used to augment the "Latin classic" dictionary. The general preface to the 1693 edition explains that additions to the previous (1684) edition of this dictionary were generated by (1) a fresh reading of authors, of whom six are named; (2) the second edition of Stephanus's *Thesaurus;* (3) Milton's manuscript; and (4) the word indexes of the popular French Delphin editions. Some dull hero willing to collate the 1684 and 1693 editions, siphoning off additions traceable to 1, 2, and 4 above, will be rewarded with what is quite likely to be a very high percentage of Miltonic material. Spot checks, for instance, do quickly turn up words where Miltonic authors have been added to entries—see, for instance, "Abigo," where 1693 adds to 1684 quotations from Varro and from Livy.

64. See the sections on "Domain" and "Curriculum" in my forthcoming edition of the commonplace book for the *Oxford Milton*.

65. *Of Education,* 5. Milton's commonplace book confirms that Milton himself studied the church historians with particular intensity in the later 1630s, in the parallel Greek-Latin *Historiæ Ecclesiasticæ Scriptores Graeci* (Geneva, 1612); among modern church history he was particularly drawn to accounts of the Vaudois, especially Pierre Gilles's *Histoire Ecclésiastique des Eglises Réformées . . . autrefois appelées Eglises Vaudoises* (Geneva, 1644), which he also cited.

66. *Brief Lives,* 671. Compare Aubrey on Thomas May—translating Lucan "made him in love with the Republique" (*Brief Lives,* 574).

67. *Brief Lives,* 671.

68. *Early Lives,* 60 (Phillips).

### NOTES TO CHAPTER SIX

1. For Moseley's career, see J. C. Reed, "Humphrey Moseley, Publisher," *Oxford Bibliographical Society Proceedings and Papers* 2 (Oxford: Oxford University Press, 1930), 55–142.

2. Jason McElligott, *Royalism, Print and Censorship in Revolutionary England* (Woodbridge, UK: Boydell, 2007), 217–18.

3. *Poems* (1645), sig. a4v.

4. Ibid., 57.

5. For such "conformable puritanism," see Jeffrey Alan Miller, "Milton and the Conformable Puritanism of Richard Stock and Thomas Young," in *Young Milton: The Emerging Author, 1620–1642,* ed. Edward Jones (Oxford: Oxford University Press, 2012).

6. Gordon Campbell and Thomas N. Corns, *John Milton: Life, Work, and Thought* (Oxford: Oxford University Press, 2008), 57–58, remark that elegies on the same woman survive by other hands, and it may be that a university volume was planned but abandoned. This may also explain why a variant manuscript text of the poem circulated (CELM, MnJ 9).

7. Miller, "Milton and the Conformable Puritanism."

8. Nicholas McDowell, "Dante and the Distraction of Lyric in Milton's 'To My Friend Mr. Henry Lawes,'" *Review of English Studies,* 59, no. 239 (2008): 232–54; McDowell, *Poetry and Allegiance in the English Civil Wars: Marvell and the Causes of Wit* (Oxford: Oxford University Press, 2008), 69–90. Another sane reading of the volume is Colin Burrow, "Poems 1645: the future poet," in Dennis Richard Danielson, *The Cambridge Companion to Milton,* 2nd ed. (Cambridge: Cambridge University College, 1999), 54–69.

9. One could always approve the poems and not the poet: see Nicholas von Maltzahn, "An Early Comment on Milton's Poems (1645)," *Milton Quarterly* 48, no. 1 (2014): 15–18 for the fascinating reactions of Milton's contemporaries the royalists Peter Gunning and Christopher Hatton to the volume. This kind of judgment was repeated in some of the earliest responses to *Paradise Lost.*

10. For some sensible warnings about these manuscript titles and the effect on subsequent criticism of Milton's erasures see Annabel Patterson, "Milton's Heroic

Sonnets," in *A Concise Companion to Milton*, ed. Angelica Duran (Oxford: Blackwell, 2007), 78–94.

11. Bodleian Library, MS Ashmole 36 / 37, fol. 22r; CELM, MnJ 21; William Poole, "Milton's Two Poems to be Fixed on Objects," *Notes and Queries* 56, no. 2 (2009): 213–15.

12. British Library, MS Sloane 1446, fols. 37v–38v; CELM, MnJ 9.

13. Milton's second Hobson poem was first published, incompletely, in the prose-and-verse miscellany, *A Banquet of Jests* (London, 1640), 129–31; see also CELM, MnJ 2–5 for traced manuscripts.

14. Trinity College Manuscript, 43.

15. In the early Restoration, Vane's chaplain and biographer George Sykes found it, presumably filed among his late employer's correspondence, and could date it to the day (July 3, 1652); but when publishing it for the first time in his biography, he tactfully accredited it merely to "a learned Gentleman" (George Sykes, *The Life and Death of Sir Henry Vane, Kt.* ([London], 1662), 93–94).

16. Henry and William Lawes, *Choice Psalmes* (London, 1648), sig. a1r.

17. For Lawes see the study of Ian Spink, *Henry Lawes: Cavalier Songwriter* (Oxford: Oxford University Press, 2000), esp. 55–62. A sense of how Lawes functioned as a nexus of poetic activity can be gleaned through the Folger Union First Line Index of English Verse (http://firstlines.folger.edu/), by searching for poems with "Lawes" in the title.

18. In the phrase of David Pinto in *ODNB*.

19. Lawes, *Choice Psalmes*, sig. [A4]r.

20. McDowell, "Dante and the Distraction of Lyric," 240.

21. *Ayres and Dialogues* (London, 1653); sig. A1v; Spink, *Henry Lawes*, 62. Note that Edward refers to "Marenzo" in his poem, that is, Luca Marenzio, one of the composers whose sheet music Milton shipped back from Italy.

22. *Purgatorio*, 2.106–17.

23. *Purgatorio*, 2.118–23; 1.39.

24. For Lucan see especially *Pharsalia*, 2.380–83.

25. Sallust, *Catiline*, 54. It is of course the running ethical comparison of the *Pharsalia* too.

26. *Satires*, 1.10.74.

27. The number is arrived at thus: Milton first presented his prose works to 1645, eleven in number (Arch. G e.44). He presented the 1645 *Poems*, twice (first copy lost; second is 8° M 168 Art, moved to Arch. G f.17; the accompanying poem, in the hand of Milton's nephew John Phillips with one correction by Milton, is now MS Lat. misc. d. 77). In probably 1651 Milton sent the library a large-paper copy of his *Defensio prima* (E 2.20 Art). In 1656 his nephew Edward Phillips presented a couple of his own books as well as his uncle's *Eikonoklastes* and *The Tenure of Kings and Magistrates*, both in 1650 imprints (4° Rawl. 408). This volume is annotated as *ex dono authoris* in the hand of Rouse's successor, Thomas Barlow. (Why this is

among the Rawlinson books is something of a puzzle—it was perhaps hidden in the library in the Restoration and reshelved much later among the Rawlinson books, acquired in the 1750s. But it may genuinely have left the library for a period.) As Nicholas von Maltzahn observes, Anthony Wood when researching Milton's life had access to lost presentation copies of Milton's *Defensio secunda* and *Defensio pro se* too—thus seventeen titles in total, one presented twice; see von Maltzahn, "Wood, Allam, and the Oxford Milton," *Milton Studies* 31 (1994): 172n15, from Wood's notes on Milton, Bodleian, MS Wood F 51, fol. 34v.

28. A bill dated June 20, 1645 from Thomas Robinson to Rouse for twenty-six books includes Milton's *Areopagitica* and *Doctrine and Discipline of Divorce*—the former costing 10*d*, the latter 2*s* (Bodleian, Lib. recs. b 36, fol. 30r, on which see Gwen Hampshire, "An Unusual Bodleian Purchase in 1645," *Bodleian Library Record* 10, no. 6 (1982): 339–48.

29. For Milton and "the people" compare Paul Hammond, *Milton and the People* (Oxford: Oxford University Press, 2014). A seminal piece on Milton's self-presentation in the prose works of the 1640s is Thomas N. Corns, "Milton's Quest for Respectability," *Modern Language Review* 77, no. 4 (1982): 769–79, which poured some tactful but necessary cold water on Christopher Hill's *Milton and the English Revolution* (London: Faber and Faber, 1977).

### NOTES TO CHAPTER SEVEN

1. The standard study of Milton's professional life is Robert Thomas Fallon, *Milton in Government* (University Park: Pennsylvania State University Press, 1993); see more briefly W. R. Parker, *Milton: A Biography*, rev. Gordon Campbell, 2 vols. (Oxford: Clarendon, 1996), 352–56, for Milton's initial duties. A convenient digest of orders involving Milton from the Order Book of the Council of State can be found in Henry John Todd, *Some Account of the Life and Writings of John Milton* (London, 1826), 107n; a better-referenced resource is Gordon Campbell's *A Milton Chronology* (Basingstoke, UK: Houndmills, 1997), from March 13, 1649, the day Milton was invited to become Secretary for Foreign Tongues.

2. *Documents relating to the University and Colleges of Cambridge*, vol. 3 (London, 1852), 198–99 (Statutes of Christ's College, cap. 32); there were twenty shillings to the pound, and twelve pence a shilling. This applied to fellows in orders but without yet having higher degrees; BDs received 15*s*, and DDs 16*s* 8*d*. It is hard to calculate dons' incomes as they could supplement their stipends with fees from teaching or by taking other college offices. A comparison from Oxford is the new foundation of Wadham College, Oxford (1610), where the fellows were waged by statute at £10 *per annum*. See Thomas Graham Jackson, *Wadham College, Oxford* (Oxford: Oxford University Press, 1893), 63.

3. "On the late Massacre in Piedmont," first published in the 1673 *Poems*. On this see Joad Raymond, "The Daily Muse: Or, Seventeenth-Century Poets Read the News," *Seventeenth Century* 10, no. 2 (1995): 203–11.

4. Society of Antiquaries Library, MS 138, mostly published by John Nickolls in 1743 as *Original Letters and Papers of State, Addressed to Oliver Cromwell*. The realization that these must have been supplied to Milton for some purpose is that of Hugh

Trevor-Roper; see H. R. Trevor-Roper, "Milton in Politics," in his *Catholics, Anglicans and Puritans: Seventeenth-Century Essays* (London: Secker and Warburg, 1987), 271 and note.

5. John Lilburne, *As You Were; or, the Lord General Cromwel and the Grand Officers of the Armie their Remembrancer* ([Amsterdam?], 1652), 16.

6. Gordon Campbell and Thomas N. Corns, *John Milton: Life, Work, and Thought* (Oxford: Oxford University Press, 2008), 247.

7. The Hartlib Papers, 28 / 1 / 61B.

8. This is the interesting suggestion of Parker, *Milton*, 354.

9. Alastair Hamilton and Francis Richard, *André Du Ryer and Oriental Studies in Seventeenth-Century France* (Oxford: Oxford University Press, 2004), 54–55.

10. *The Alcoran of Mahomet* (London, 1649), esp. sigs. Ee1v–Ee2r for Ross's "Areopagiticanism." G. J. Toomer, *Eastern Wisedome and Learning: The Study of Arabic in Seventeenth-Century England* (Oxford: Clarendon Press, 1996), 200–201; Noel Malcolm, "The 1649 English Translation of the Koran: Its Origins and Significance," *Journal of the Warburg and Courtauld Institutes* 75 (2012): 261–95; Mordechai Feingold, " 'The Turkish Alcoran': New Light on the 1649 English Translation of the Koran," *Huntington Library Quarterly* 75, no. 4 (2012): 475–501, and subsequent ripostes.

11. Noel Malcolm, "The Study of Islam in Early Modern Europe: Obstacles and Missed Opportunities," in *Antiquarianism and Intellectual Life in Europe and China, 1500–1800*, ed. Peter N. Miller and François Louis (Ann Arbor: University of Michigan Press, 2012), 268.

12. Ross, "A needful Caveat," in *The Alcoran of Mahomet*, sig. Ee1r.

13. *The Alcoran of Mahomet*, 22. Compare chap. 65, "The Chapter of Divorce" (i.e., Surat at-Talaq), 353–54.

14. The watershed of three marriages might have reminded Milton of a comment he had written down in his commonplace book, namely that the Emperor Leo VI "the Philosopher" (866–912) married three times (albeit following the natural deaths of his wives), but on his fourth marriage he was excommunicated by the Patriarch Nicolaus. See Commonplace Book MS, 109.

15. Samuel Johnson, "Milton," in *Lives of the Poets*, ed. Roger H. Lonsdale, 4 vols. (Oxford: Clarendon, 2006), 1:276. For the claim that "Mohammed was a good familist," see William Bedwell, *Mohammedis Imposturæ* (London, 1615), secs. 69–71, including comments on the Surat al-Baqarah. For this work see Toomer, *Eastern Wisedome*, 61–62. It clearly influenced the translator of the English Quran, as the latter's preface has some unacknowledged debts to it.

16. Theodorus Bibliander, ed., *Machumetis Saracenorum principis, eiusque successorum vitae, doctrina, ac ipse Alcoran* (Basel, 1543), 9.

17. *The Alcoran of Mahomet*, 3–4.

18. Gerald MacLean, "Milton, Islam and the Ottomans," in *Milton and Toleration*, ed. Sharon Achinstein and Elizabeth Sauer (Oxford: Oxford University Press, 2007), 294.

19. Bedwell, *Mohammedis Imposturæ*, sec. 19, 36–38.

20. The best account is Martin Dzelzainis, "Milton and Antitrinitarianism," in *Milton and Toleration*, 171–85, esp. 177–84.

21. Dzelzainis, "Milton and Antitrinitarianism," 183, and the commentary on this interpretation by Blair Worden, *Literature and Politics in Cromwellian England: John Milton, Andrew Marvell, Marchamont Nedham* (Oxford: Oxford University Press, 2007), 239–40.

22. Joseph Milton French, ed., *The Life Records of John Milton*, 5 vols. (New Brunswick, NJ: Rutgers University Press, 1949–58), 2:321, 3:206, 212–13; Leo Miller, "New Milton Texts and Data from the Aitzema Mission, 1652," *Notes and Queries* 37, no. 3 (1990): 281. The anecdote comes from a report in Dutch: "Milton gevraegt seyde ja ende dat hy een bouckien op dat stuck hadde uyt gegeven, dat men geen boucken behoorde te verbieden: dat hy in't approbeeren van dat bouck nit meer gedaen had als wat syn opinie was" (Milton, asked, said yes, and that he had published a book on that subject, that people ought not to forbid any books: that he in approving that book had done no more than what his opinion was) (French, *Life Records*, 3:206).

### NOTES TO CHAPTER EIGHT

1. *De doctrina*, 1.5 = *OM*, 8:146–49. Milton was, however, buried in St Giles Cripplegate, where his father was, and so Milton at his death evidently identified neither strongly with dissent nor strongly against the established church, at least for the purposes of burial. Parts of this chapter revise sections of my own "Milton's Theology," in *Milton in Context,* ed. Stephen B. Dobranski (Cambridge: Cambridge University Press, 2010), 475–86.

2. John Locke, "An Essay for the Understanding of St Paul's Epistles by Consulting St Paul Himself" (London, 1707); it is edited in *Locke: Writings on Religion,* ed. Victor Nuovo (Oxford: Clarendon, 2002), 51–66.

3. Martin Dzelzainis, "Authors 'Not Unknown' in Milton's *Tetrachordon,*" *Notes and Queries* 45, no. 1 (1998): 44–47.

4. *The Doctrine and Discipline of Divorce* (London, 1644), sig. A4v; *Areopagitica* (London, 1644), 27.

5. *De doctrina*, 1.1 = *OM*, 8:18–21.

6. Helen Darbishire, ed., *The Early Lives of Milton* (London: Constable, 1932), 61.

7. For the genre, structure, and sources of Milton's treatise, see chiefly Maurice Kelley, *This Great Argument: A Study of Milton's "De Doctrina Christiana" as a Gloss upon "Paradise Lost"* (Princeton, NJ: Princeton University Press, 1941), building on the same author's "Milton's Debt to Wolleb's Compendium Theologiae Christianae," *PMLA* 50, no. 1 (1935): 156–65, and Kelley's superb commentary in the sixth volume of *CPW*; Gordon Campbell, "The Theology of the Manuscript," in *Milton and the Manuscript of* "De Doctrina Christiana," by Gordon Campbell, Thomas N. Corns, John K. Hale, and Fiona J. Tweedie (Oxford: Oxford University Press, 2007), 89–120, largely reprised in *OM*, 8:55–57. See also the case study by

John K. Hale, "Points of Departure: Studies in Milton's Use of Wollebius," *Reformation* 19 (2014): 69–82.

8. The reason is this: Barclay published initially in Amsterdam with the radical printer Jacob Claus, who advertised the book as on sale in three further European cities; whereas Skinner approached the famous Elzeviers, who proved unwilling to proceed without a second opinion. Barclay's work is framed as an elaborate commentary on fifteen theses which he had initially published in 1674, and includes a scriptural index.

9. William Ames, *Medulla S.S. Theologiae* (London, 1630), 4 (1.2.1); Johannes Wolleb, *Christianae Theologiae Compendium* (Cambridge, 1642), 8.

10. *De doctrina*, 1.2 = OM, 8:24–51.

11. Thus Ames, *Medulla*, 2.2–5.

12. *De doctrina*, 1.2 = OM, 8:31.

13. *De doctrina*, 1.4 = OM, 8:79.

14. *De doctrina*, 1.5 = OM, 8:203.

15. John Rumrich, "Milton's Arianism: Why It Matters," in *Milton and Heresy*, ed. Stephen B. Dobranski and John Rumrich (Cambridge, 1998), 75–92.

16. *De doctrina*, 1.5 = OM, 8:149.

17. *De doctrina*, 1.5 = OM, 8:143.

18. Jonathan D. Spence, *Emperor of China: Self-Portrait of K'ang-Hsi* (New York: Vintage, 1988), 84.

19. Anselm of Canterbury, *Cur Deus Homo*, notably 2.6, where it is affirmed that no being, except the God-man, can make an atonement adequate to save man.

20. See generally Klaus Scholder, *The Birth of Modern Critical Theology: Origins and Problems of Biblical Criticism in the Seventeenth Century* (London: SCM, 1990), chap. 2, and the essays in Martin Mulsow and Jan Rohls, eds., *Socinianism and Arminianism: Antitrinitarians, Calvinists and Cultural Exchange in Seventeenth-Century Europe* (Leiden: Brill, 2005); and for the English context see John Marshall, "Locke, Socinianism, "Socinianism," and Unitarianism," in *English Philosophy in the Age of Locke*, ed. M. A. Stewart (Oxford: Clarendon, 2000), chap. 5, and Sarah Mortimer, *Reason and Religion in the English Revolution: The Challenge of Socinianism* (Cambridge: Cambridge University Press, 2010).

21. *De doctrina*, 1.14 = OM, 8 :477.

22. *De doctrina*, 1.14 = OM, 8:481. Milton made other statements about the limits of human reason especially in *De doctrina*, 1.5 = OM, 8: e.g., 136–37, 138–39, 148–49.

23. *De doctrina*, 1.16 = OM, 8:521.

24. Thus Milton did not hold a "governmental" view of Atonement either, namely that God through the punishment of Christ demonstrated his displeasure with sin, a theory traditionally traced to Hugo Grotius's *Defensio Fidei Catholicae de Satisfactione Christi adversus F. Socinum* (Leiden, 1617; there was an Oxford printing in 1636). Compare Gregory Chaplin, "Beyond Sacrifice: Milton and the Atonement," *PMLA* 125, no. 2 (2010): 364–65, more sympathetic to the Grotian comparison.

25. *De doctrina*, 1.11 = *OM*, 8:418–19. Compare the citation of Homer at 1.4 (116–17). Nicholas McDowell has collected passages where Milton appears to prefer pagan to sacred texts (McDowell, "Euripides and the Superior Rationality of the Heathen," *Seventeenth Century* 31, no. 2 (2016): 215–37). But such occasions are very rare, and in general I adhere to the view that Milton thought he must privilege revelation and generally believed that he did so, despite some remarkable contortions of traditional exegesis throughout his oeuvre. Compare too Richard Strier, *The Unrepentant Renaissance: From Petrarch to Shakespeare to Milton* (Chicago: University of Chicago Press, 2011), 256–93, on dignity versus humility, arguing that classical dignity overpowers Christian humility in Milton; and see further Chapter 20 on "contamination" for the larger problem of the profane and the sacred.

26. Time and space, in Ames's typical formulation, are only "concreated, or annexed, knit to the things created: because they have not an absolute, but only a relative entitie or being." Ames, *Medulla*, 40 (1.8.25), in the translation of William Ames, *The Marrow of Sacred Divinity* (London, 1643), 33.

27. Arnold Williams, *The Common Expositor: Commentaries on Genesis, 1527–1633* (Chapel Hill: University of North Carolina Press, 1948), 45; G. N. Conklin, *Biblical Criticism and Heresy in Milton* (New York: Columbia University Press, 1949), 68.

28. *De doctrina*, 1.5 = *OM*, 8:134–37.

29. Campbell, "The Theology of the Manuscript," 108, from *De doctrina*, 1.7.

30. Justin Martyr, *First Apology*, sec. 10 ("ἐξ ἀμόρφου ὕλης"). See the editorial note in Justin Martyr, *Apologia Prōtē*, ed. Joannes Ernestus Grabe (Oxford, 1700[ / 1]), 17, for earlier attempts to declare this clause an interpolation or to explain it as referring to an intermediary process after the initial creation *ex nihilo*.

31. Edward Stillingfleet, *Origines Sacræ* (London, 1662), 437; Hugh MacCallum, *Milton and the Sons of God: The Divine Image in Milton's Epic Poetry* (Toronto: University of Toronto Press, 1986), 51.

32. Ames, *Medulla*, 41–3 (1.8.29–46), in the translation of Ames, *Marrow*, 34–35; cp. Johannes Wolleb, *Compendium*, 29–35.

33. For contemporary angelology, see Robert Hunter West, *Milton and the Angels* (Athens: University of Georgia Press, 1955), chaps. 2–4; Joad Raymond, *Milton's Angels: The Early-Modern Imagination* (Oxford: Oxford University Press, 2010), 48–88.

34. *PL* 1, Arg.; *De doctrina*, 1.7 = *OM*, 8:298–99; West, *Milton and the Angels*, 125. The *locus classicus* on the problem that Genesis does not explicitly mention the angelic creation is Augustine, *City of God*, book 11, chap. 9. The necessary patristic personalities could be generated from even vernacular commentaries: Raymond, *Milton's Angels*, 65–67.

35. P[atrick] H[ume], *Annotations on Milton's Paradise Lost* (London, 1695), 6.

36. *De doctrina*, 1.9 = *OM*, 8:351.

37. Commentators since Thomas Newton in his 1749 edition have derived Milton's emphasis on angelic materiality from the dialogue *On the Operation of Demons* of

the eleventh-century Byzantine writer Michael Psellus; and indeed Psellus's dialogue had a strong publication record in the period, most recently the parallel edition of Paris, 1615. In Psellus's dialogue, the interlocutor Thrax argues that demons are (1) material; (2) can change shape at will and assume either sex; (3) consume and excrete; (4) can enter the bodies of people and animals; and (5) be struck with a weapon and feel pain, but with their parted substance soon reuniting. Nevertheless he treats these attributes as if they apply to demons only, excluding the unfallen angels from such materiality (see the 1615 Parisian edition, 32–35), whereas Milton extended these attributes, other than possession and passability, to *all* angels, a problem not properly addressed by what is otherwise the fullest direct discussion, Robert H. West, "Milton and Michael Psellus," *Philological Quarterly* 28 (1949), 477–89. It is possible, as Henry John Todd shrewdly observed in his 1801 edition of Milton (see his note to *PL* 1.423), that Milton encountered Psellus through discussions of the issue in Johann Weyer's *De praestigiis daemonum* (Basel, 1563) or Robert Burton's "Digression of the Nature of Spirits" in *The Anatomy of Melancholy* (Oxford, 1621). Indeed there survives in private hands today a copy of the former text (in the edition of Basel, 1577), with a purchase inscription attributable to Milton (dated to 1629, with the price 3s 6d). And the relevant passage in Burton is particularly rich when reading from a Miltonic point of view: "*Psellus* . . . a great observer of the nature of Devils, holds they are corporeall, and have *aeriall bodies, that they are mortall, live and dye*, (which *Martianus Capella* likewise maintains, but our Christian Philosophers explode) *that they are nourished and have excrements, they feele pain if they be hurt . . . or stroken*: and if their bodyes be cut, with admirable celerity they come together agayne" (Robert Burton, *The Anatomy of Melancholy*, 5th ed. (Oxford, 1638), 40 = part. 1, sect. 2, memb. 1, subsect. 2).

38. Ames, *Medulla*, 178–85 (1.34.1–36); translation from Ames, *Marrow*, 148–53.

39. *De doctrina*, 1.30 = *OM*, 8:794–805.

40. *De doctrina*, 1.30 = *OM*, 8:810–15.

41. *De doctrina*, 1.30 = *OM*, 8:815.

42. Dennis Danielson, *Milton's Good God: A Study in Literary Theodicy* (Cambridge: Cambridge University Press, 1982); Michael Bauman, *Milton's Arianism* (Frankfurt: Lang, 1987).

43. J.-P. Pittion, "Milton, La Place, and Socinianism," *Review of English Studies* 23, no. 90 (1972): 138–46; Michael Lieb, "Milton and the Socinian Heresy" in *Milton and the Grounds of Contention*, ed. Mark R. Kelley, Michael Lieb, and John T. Shawcross (Pittsburgh: Duquesne University Press, 2003), 234–83.

44. For a handy if polemical compendium, see George Ashwell, *De Socino et socinianismo dissertatio* (Oxford, 1683), 108–16 (God and his attributes); 116–21 (the Trinity).

45. *The Racovian Catechisme* ([London], 1652), 33–34.

46. *De doctrina*, 1.30 = *OM*, 8:814–17; Ashwell, *De Socino et socinianismo dissertatio*, 102–7.

47. Gordon Campbell, "Milton's Theological and Literary Treatments of the Creation," *Journal of Theological Studies* 30, no. 1 (1979): 128–37.

48. Note how close Milton's position is to the remarks quoted earlier from Gil's *Sacred Philosophie.*

49. *Racovian Catechisme,* 28.

50. *Racovian Catechisme,* 59.

51. *CPW,* 8:233.

52. Robert Barclay, *An Apology for the True Christian Divinity* ([London?], 1678), 41.

53. Barclay, *Apology,* sig. [B3]v.

### NOTES TO CHAPTER NINE

1. *Elegia prima,* lines 27–46.

2. Helen Darbishire, *The Early Lives of Milton* (London: Constable, 1932), 21 (Skinner), 38 (Wood), 59 (Phillips), 95 (Toland).

3. Daniel Heinsius, *On Plot in Tragedy,* trans. Paul R. Sellin and John J. McManmon (Northridge, CA: San Fernando Valley State College, 1971), 37.

4. John Foxe, *Christus triumphans, comoedia apocalyptica,* 3.1.1–7, quoted from the Nuremberg 1590 edition, sigs. a5v–a6r.

5. There is a modern parallel edition: *George Buchanan: Tragedies,* ed. Peter Sharratt and Patrick Gerard Walsh (Edinburgh: Scottish Academic Press, 1983).

6. For an intricate discussion of *Jephthes,* see Deborah Kuller Shuger, *The Renaissance Bible: Scholarship, Sacrifice, and Subjectivity* (Berkeley: University of California Press, 1998), 134–60; the quoted phrase is hers (137). A different argument about the origins of *Samson,* as a "Simple Pathetic Tragedy" on the model of Sophocles's *Ajax,* and so not necessarily requiring *peripeteia* or *anagnorisis* in its plotting, is presented in Blair Hoxby, *What Was Tragedy?: Theory and the Early Modern Canon* (Oxford: Oxford University Press, 2015), 137–45.

7. Commonplace Book MS, 241.

8. *Of Reformation* (London, 1641), 39.

9. *Areopagitica* (London, 1644), 10.

10. Robert Cooke, *Censura quorundam scriptorum* (London, 1614), 18–19.

11. Commonplace Book MS, 57, from Bede, *Ecclesiastical History,* 4.24.

12. Milton discusses both in *The Reason of Church Government* (*CPW,* 1:815); and David Paraeus on Revelation again in *OM,* 2:66–67, from the preface to *Samson Agonistes.*

13. *Preparation for the Gospel,* 9.22 (Theodotus on Dinah), 9.28 (Ezekiel on Exodus). See William Poole, "Milton, Dinah, and Theodotus," *Milton Quarterly* 47, no. 2 (2013): 65–71. For a modern edition with a translation, see Howard Jacobson, *The Exagoge of Ezekiel* (Cambridge: Cambridge University Press, 1983).

14. I differ from three other plausible attempts. In 1740 Peck suggested (expressed in my manner of subdivision): Act I a–c, II d–f, III g–i, IV j, V k–n. The great Milton scholar J. H. Hanford disagreed, proposing instead in his *A Milton Handbook* (1926, 4th ed. New York: F. S. Crofts and co., 1961): Act I a–b, II c, III d–f, IV g–i, V j–n. But he later changed his mind (see *CPW,* 8:595–96): Act I a–c, II d–f, III g–i, IV j,

V k–n. Fowler's edition of *Paradise Lost*, 1–4, offers some excellent remarks on the four drafts.

15. *PL* 5.760 (actually a place name), 7.131, 10.425 (again partially deflected into a place name).

### NOTES TO CHAPTER TEN

1. William Davenant, *Madagascar: with Other Poems* (London, 1638), 54–65. For another Cavalier epyllion, see Edmund Waller's quirky "Battell of the Summer Islands," in three cantos, in *Poems* (1645), 95–108.

2. This exists under the variant titles of *Preface* and *Discourse* (see English Short Title Catalogue R10896 and R8934); the typeface of the latter looks suspiciously English. *Gondibert* itself appeared in quarto and then octavo London editions in 1651; Davenant personally corrected and inscribed many of the quartos, such as Bodleian, 4° D 8 Art.Seld., presented to John Selden. The printing of the quarto was uneven (hence Davenant's extensive pen-and-ink corrections), and occasionally unintentionally ironic: "posting upon *Pegasus*," for instance, was unfortunately botched to "boasting upon *Pegasus*" (31–32). A *Seventh and Last Canto* appeared posthumously in 1685. *ODNB* garbles the publication history of this poem.

3. Colin Burrow, *Epic Romance: Homer to Milton* (Oxford: Clarendon Press, 1993).

4. See the edition of David F. Gladish (Oxford: Clarendon Press, 1971); Simon Andrew Stirling, *Shakespeare's Bastard: The Life of Sir William Davenant* (Stroud, UK: History Press, 2016), 96–105; and, for a notable adversarially annotated copy, Niall Allsopp, " 'Lett none our Lombard author rudely blame for's righteous paine': An Annotated Copy of Sir William Davenant's *Gondibert* (London, 1651)," *The Library* 16, no. 1 (2015): 24–50. We might also note that William Davenant, second son of the poet, read Greek and Latin authors with Milton after the Restoration; see Helen Darbishire, ed., *The Manuscript of Milton's Paradise Lost, Book 1* (Oxford: Clarendon Press, 1931), xv, and W. R. Parker, *Milton: A Biography*, rev. Gordon Campbell, 2 vols. (Oxford: Clarendon, 1996), 1129–30.

5. See *PL* 7.126–30 and Fowler's note there to *Gondibert*, 2.7.22.

6. William Davenant, *Gondibert: A Heroick Poem* (London, 1651), quarto edition, "Preface," 2–7.

7. Davenant, as his editor has noted, even integrates some specifically Shakespearean plotting into *Gondibert* (Gladish, xv–xvi, from *Much Ado*).

8. Thus Thomas Rymer in his preface to his translation of René Rapin, *Reflections on Aristotle's Treatise of Poesie* (London, 1674), sig. [A7]v.

9. *Of Education* (London, 1644), 6.

10. Torquato Tasso, *Discourses on the Heroic Poem*, trans. Mariella Cavalchini and Irene Samuel (Oxford: Clarendon Press, 1973), bk. 2, esp. 34–51.

11. *Gondibert* (London, 1651), quarto edition, 17 (I.i.80).

12. Hobbes's response (72–73) sets up four parallel triads:

| 1. realms: | Celestial | Aerial | Terrestrial |
|---|---|---|---|
| 2. locations: | Court | City | Country |
| 3. modes: | Heroic | Scommatic | Pastoral |
| 4. genres: | Epic / Tragedy | Satire / Comedy | Pastoral / Comedy |

13. *Gondibert*, 76–78, 81.

14. For example, "I honor Antiquity, but that which is commonly called *old time,* is *young time*" (86) is an obvious allusion to Bacon's *antiquitas saeculi juventus mundi.*

15. *Gondibert*, 87–88. On these devices and their influence on Hobbes, see Noel Malcolm, "The Title Page of *Leviathan,* Seen in a Curious Perspective," in his *Aspects of Hobbes* (Oxford: Clarendon, 2002).

16. *Gondibert*, 2.5.39. This passage evidently influenced Thomas Heyrick's peculiar 1691 Pindaric ode "The Submarine Voyage."

17. In the preface to his 1656 *Poems* Cowley explained he would not republish such juvenilia, his rejection subtly advertising once again his own precocity: "all those which I wrote at *School* from the age of ten years, till after fifteen" (sig. [(a)3]v).

18. *Poems*, 12, the headnote to Milton's paraphrases of Psalms 114 and 136. Milton prefaced eight of his Latin poems with expressions of his age, ranging from his sixteenth to twentieth year. In the 1673 edition of his poems he added two more such headings, but to English texts, marked as written in his seventeenth ("On the Death of a Fair Infant") and nineteenth ("At a Vacation Exercise") years respectively, demonstration that he excluded certain youthful poems from his 1645 volume.

19. *An Apology* (London, 1642), 14.

20. Cowley, *Poems* (London, 1656), sig. [(a)4]r–v.

21. David Norbrook, *Writing the English Republic: Poetry, Rhetoric and Politics, 1627–1660* (Cambridge: Cambridge University Press, 1999), 84.

22. Abraham Cowley, *The Late Civil War* (London, 1679), 13.

23. Cowley, *Poems* (London, 1656), sigs. (b2)r–v, [(b3)]r.

24. Giles Fletcher, *Christs Victorie, and Triumph in Heaven and Earth, Over and After Death* (Cambridge, 1610), "To the Reader."

25. Quarles published versified biblical paraphrases from 1620 at the rate of about one a year, collected along with his devotional sonnets and elegies in 1630 as *Divine Poems.* He had attended Christ's College but left in 1609. His poetry bears much more sharply than does Milton's the stamp of Ramist Cambridge.

26. Thomas Heywood, *The Hierarchie of the Blessed Angells: Their Names, Orders and Offices, the Fall of Lucifer with His Angells* (London, 1635), a huge, ragbag biblicophilosophical poem in nine books and 622 pages of folio, replete with digressions and prose commentaries. Ironically, it was a different work of Heywood's which probably assisted Milton with his Mulciber: see Ernest Schanzer, "Milton's Fall of Mulciber and 'Troia Britannica,'" *Notes and Queries* 202 (1957): 379–80; but note, too, the scattered recycling of the Mulciber passage in Heywood's *Hierarchie,* 504–5.

27. Bodleian Library, C 2.21 Art. Cowley, in *The Late Civil War,* 21, misrepresented the Parliamentarians as having sacked the Bodleian. Unlike Milton, Cowley continued to present books to the Bodleian after the Restoration: see 8° A 13 Med.BS (his 1662 *Plantarum libri duo*).

28. Cowley's fifth note to his first book in the English version suggests (but does not finally confirm) that Cowley wrote the English version first, then started drafting the Latin, and later finalized the notes to the English text; but these three processes may have overlapped.

29. See no. 360 in the prospectus of "Books Printed for Humphrey Moseley," of which there is a copy at the end of Bodleian, Don. f. 144, an exemplar of Waller's *Poems* (London, 1645). The discussion of Philip Hardie, "Abraham Cowley *Davideis. Sacri poematis operis impertecti liber unus*" in *Neo-Latin Poetry in the British Isles,* ed. Luke Houghton and Gesine Manuwald (London: Bristol Classical Press, 2012), chap. 5, would seem to confirm the priority of the English to the Latin version.

30. For Barnes see Kristine Haugen in *ODNB,* and for some pertinent vernacular work of his see Christopher Burlinson, "Joshua Barnes's *Kosmopoiia* and *Man's Fall* (1668 / 9): A New Context for John Milton's *Paradise Lost* in a Cambridge Manuscript," *Transactions of the Cambridge Bibliographical Society* 14, no. 3 (2010): 218–82, although it seems very unlikely to me that these poems were influenced by Milton.

31. Samuel Johnson, "Cowley," in *Lives of the Poets,* ed. Roger H. Lonsdale, 4 vols. (Oxford: Clarendon Press, 2006), 1:229.

32. The entire Hell section in the *Davideis* is lifted with almost no revision from *Civil War,* 2.365–96, and "The parted head hung downe on either side" of Stane at Newbury (3.404) is reused for one of Saul's opponents; see Abraham Cowley, *The Civil War,* ed. Allan Pritchard (Toronto, University of Toronto Press, 1973), 52–55. Is this "parted head" the hint for Milton's Moloc, "Down clov'n to the waste, with shatterd Armes" (*PL* 6.361)?

33. Johnson, "Cowley," 227.

34. *Davideis,* 4.232–33.

35. Cowley, *Poems* (London, 1678): *Davideis,* 149.

36. Joseph Milton French, ed., *The Life Records of John Milton* (New Brunswick, NJ: Rutgers University Press, 1949–1958), 5:322–23, explicitly excluding Dryden.

37. Timothy Dykstal, "The Epic Reticence of Abraham Cowley," *Studies in English Literature, 1500–1900* 31, no. 1 (1991): 95–115.

38. Cowley, *Poems* (1678): *Davideis,* 72, 153.

39. Ibid., 43.

40. See, for example, Rymer in René Rapin, *Reflections on Aristotle's Treatise of Poesie,* sigs. [A6]v–a4v. By Dryden's "A Discourse Concerning the Original and Progress of Satire" prefaced to Dryden, et al., *The Satires of Decimus Junius Juvenalis* (London, 1693) Milton had joined them.

## NOTES TO CHAPTER ELEVEN

1. Bodleian, MS Ashmole 436, part 1, fol. 119r. As Milton is there described solely as the author of *Eikonoklastes*, it is tempting to date the chart from just after the publication of that book in late 1649, but perhaps before the *Defensio prima* of 1651. It may simply be that Milton was better known to vernacular readers for his vernacular book. There are nativities in the same hand in this manuscript of the Earl of Peterborough, b. October 18, 1623 (66r), and also Oliver Plunket, the Roman Catholic archbishop of Armagh, b. November 1, 1625 (fol. 119r, so sharing the page with Milton's nativity).

2. Harry Rusche, "A Reading of John Milton's Horoscope," *Milton Quarterly* 13, no. 1 (1979): 8–9. Rusche cites William Lilly, *Christian Astrology Modestly Treated of in Three Books* (London, 1647), 581–82.

3. Gordon Campbell, *A Milton Chronology* (Basingstoke, UK: Houndmills, 1997), 135–36; Gordon Campbell and Thomas N. Corns, *John Milton: Life, Work, and Thought* (Oxford: Oxford University Press, 2008), 212.

4. *Defensio secunda* (London, 1654), 42; *PL* 3.25.

5. Celsus 6.6; for *suffusio* see 6.6.35; Aristotle, *On the Generation of Animals*, 780a17. The former was certainly and the latter possibly a classroom text for Milton; see Chapter 5. For an accessible vernacular reference work, see Lazarus Rivierius, *The Practice of Physick in Seventeen Several Books*, trans. and ed. Nicholas Culpeper et al. (London, 1655), 3.1 (on the *gutta serena*, "when the sight is gone, and no fault appears in the Eyes"), 3.3 (on *glaucoma*, affecting the "Crystalline Humor," or lens, and which is incurable), 3.4 (on suffusion, "called in Greek ὑπόχυμα, in Latin *Suffusio*, by the Arabians, Water, vulgarly a *Cataract*," and which is curable). Another useful contemporary source is Walter Baley, *Two Treatises Concerning the Preservation of Eie-Sight* (Oxford, 1612), especially the second book, gathered from the French physicians Jean Fernel and Jean Riolan.

6. Michael Hunter, *Boyle: Between God and Science* (New Haven, CT: Yale University Press, 2009), 91–92.

7. Helen Darbishire, ed., *The Early Lives of Milton* (London: Constable, 1932), 61.

8. CELM, MnJ 1.

9. *Eikonoklastes* (London, 1650), Canterbury Cathedral, shelfmark Elham 732, also noted in Campbell, *Milton Chronology*, 139. This copy itself was a gift from the printer, Thomas Newcomb, on August 12, 1651.

10. David Lloyd, *Eikon Basilike* (London, 1660), 65. On these Restoration taunts, compare Campbell and Corns, *Milton*, 311–13.

11. *The Out-Cry of the London Prentices* (London, 1659[ / 60]), 6.

12. I. T., *The Traytors Perspective-Glass* (London, 1662), 21–22.

13. John Heydon, *The Idea of the Law: Charactered from Moses to King Charles* (London, 1660), sigs. N4v–N5r.

14. *The Picture of the Good Old Cause Drawn to Life in the Effigies of Master Prais-God Barebone* (London, 1660), single sheet.

15. Bodleian, MS Rawl. E 69, fol. 12r (sermon of Robert South before the king at Whitehall, January 30, 1662).

16. *A Guild-Hall Elegie upon the Funerals of That Infernal Saint, John Bradshaw* (London, [1659]), single sheet.

17. Roger L'Estrange, *No Blinde Guides* (London, 1660).

18. British Library, MS Sloane 2896, fol. 143r, orthography adjusted (commonplace books of Abraham Hill).

19. R. A. Beddard, "Of the Duty of Subjects: A Proposed Fortieth Article of Religion," *Bodleian Library Record* 10 (1978–1982), 229–36.

20. Milton, *Pro se defensio* (London, 1654), 8 = *CPW*, 4:703, where "court of inquisitions" is however too strong for "ab eo mox consessu qui quaestionibus tum praefuit."

21. [Alexander More and Peter Du Moulin], *Regii sanguinis clamor ad coelum adversus parracidas Anglicanos* (The Hague, 1652), sig. [A8]v, quoting Virgil, *Aeneid,* 3.658.

22. Plutarch, *Life of Timoleon*, 37.7–38.7. But see Campbell, *Milton Chronology,* 209–10.

23. Livy, *Ab urbe condita,* 9.29.6–11. Livy comments, however, that he was struck blind by the gods for disturbing the established order of religious ceremonies.

24. The standard accounts are Cicero, *Pro Scauro,* sec. 23 (=Loeb Cicero, vol. 14, 302–3), and Ovid, *Fasti,* 6.437–54. But the detail on his blindness, not mentioned by Cicero or Ovid, probably comes from Pliny, *Natural History,* 7.43.141 (=Loeb Pliny, vol. 2, 600–601).

25. *CPW*, 4:585–87.

26. *Early Lives,* 73 (Edward Phillips). For a summary see John S. Diekhoff, "The Trinity MS and the Dictation of Paradise Lost," *Philological Quarterly* 28 (1949): 44–52.

27. *Early Lives,* 33.

28. John Aubrey, *Brief Lives,* ed. Kate Bennett, 2 vols. (Oxford: Clarendon Press, 2015), 661. Aubrey's plural may be optimistic; after saying that Milton "taught her Latin," he adds that she "read [i.e. read aloud, but not necessarily with comprehension] Greeke and Hebrew to him," and then crossed out "Hebrew," commenting "quære," i.e. inquire whether true.

29. Milton to Peter Heimbach, August 15, 1666, in *Epistolarum familiarum liber unus,* 66.

30. *Brief Lives,* 1:670, *Early Lives,* 13 (Aubrey, but from Edward Phillips); *Early Lives,* 73 (Phillips himself).

31. *Early Lives,* 73 (Phillips).

32. *Early Lives,* 291; *Vita Virgili,* sec. 22 (Donatus, speaking specifically of the *Georgics;* sec. 23 contains the notorious claim that the *Aeneid* itself was drafted in prose!), in *Vitae Vergilianae Antiquae,* 28–29; Campbell and Corns, *Milton,* 345–46.

33. Bodleian, MS Smith 13, 95. On this see William Poole, "Praise and Plagiarism: Charleton / Posthius on Milton / Falconetus," *Milton Quarterly* 47, no. 4 (2013): 230–34.

34. LSJ, s.n. Ὅμηρος. Milton will have read an associated story, that the poet Stesichorus, following Homer's account of Helen, was struck blind by her as a liar and recovered his sight only on recanting: Dio Chrysostom, 11.40 ("That Troy Was Not Captured"); Milton owned a copy of Dio (CELM, *MnJ 119). For an extraordinary early modern fictionalizing of blind Homer from just after Milton's death see Joshua Barnes, *Gerania* (London, 1675), 54–65. For more on this Miltonic passage, see Noam Reisner, *Milton and the Ineffable* (Oxford: Oxford University Press, 2009), 184–85.

35. Homer, *Iliad*, 2.594–600, in the translation of Richmond Lattimore (Chicago: University of Chicago Press, 1951).

36. William Whallon, "Blind Thamyris and Blind Maeonides," *Phoenix* 18, no. 1 (1964): 9–12. Milton's exact point of entry into this tradition cannot be known, but he can scarcely have avoided the assumption in Propertius, 2.22 and Apollodorus, 1.3.3.

37. Thence the entry in Stephanus's *Dictionarium*, from which Fowler's note is derived.

38. Patrick Hume, *Annotations upon Milton's Paradise Lost* (London, 1695), 99. See (pseudo-)Plutarch, *Of Music*, in the *Morals*, in the Philemon Holland translation (London, 1603), 1249, where the text is already recognized as pseudepigraphic.

39. Pausanias, 4.33.7. Pausanias mentions the *Minyas* several times and quotes it once; this is almost the only evidence we have for the poem, which evidently featured extended passages on Hades. See Martin L. West, *Greek Epic Fragments* (Cambridge, MA: Harvard University Press, 2003), 268–75.

40. Lycophron, *Alexandra*, 681–83. Milton also mentions Tiresias in "De Idea Platonica," 25–26, and "Elegia sexta," 68.

41. *Reason of Church Government Urg'd against Prelaty, in Two Books* (London, 1641), 34.

42. *Defensio secunda* (London, 1654), 43–44, in the translation of *CPW*, 4:584–85. Milton himself quoted first in Greek and then in Latin translation.

43. *Epistolae familiares*, 41, translation adjusted from *CPW*, 4:869, quotation from Apollonius of Rhodes, *Argonautica*, 2.205.

44. Apollonius of Rhodes, *Argonautica*, 2.181–82, in the prose translation of Richard Hunter (Oxford: Clarendon Press, 1993).

45. Scholion to Apollonius of Rhodes, *Argonautica*. 2.178–82, as printed in, for example, the Geneva 1574 edition, 77 = Loeb edition of Hesiod (ed. H. G. Evelyn-White), 177. John Selden, for one, heavily annotated his copy of the 1574 edition, including this passage (Bodleian, 4° A 54 Art.Seld). The existence of Varro's poem was known from a famous passage in Ovid on poetic legacy (*Amores*, 1.15.21–22).

46. Valerius Flaccus, 4.474, 481.

47. Sophocles, *Antigone*, 968–76; also available through the scholion to Apollonius of Rhodes, 2.177.

48. *Orphic Argonautica*, 669–74, in the edition of A. C. Eschenbachius (Utrecht, 1689).

## NOTES TO CHAPTER TWELVE

1. Andrew Laird, "Re-inventing Virgil's Wheel" in *Classical Literary Careers and their Reception*, ed. Philip Hardie and Helen Moore (Cambridge: Cambridge University Press, 2010), 138. The editors' introduction and the chapter by Michael C. J. Putnam, "Some Virgilian Unities" (17–38), are also pertinent.

2. Associated with Ovid, whose genuine tragedy *Medea*, said to have preceded the *Metamorphoses*, is lost; the loss of this work was often lamented, as well as that of the six last books of the *Fasti*, and a (now considered spurious) *Halieutica* on fishing, surviving in fragmentary form (see, e.g., the entry in Nicholas Lloyd's *Dictionarium*).

3. See for example the 1570 London edition of Virgil's *Opera*, 119.

4. As appended to a chapter of Eusebius's *Vita Constantini* (4.32) and common through Augustine (*De civitate Dei*, 10.27). Lactantius (*Divinæ Institutiones*, 7.24) assumed Sybilline influence on Virgil, but gave a millennial interpretation of the prophecy. In Dante (*Purgatorio*, canto 22), Statius tells Virgil that it was his prediction that converted him to Christianity. Milton later excerpted from all four of these texts in his commonplace book. For the sources, see Ella Bourne, "The Messianic Prophecy in Vergil's Fourth Eclogue," *Classical Journal* 11, no. 9 (1916): 390–400.

5. "Elegia prima," lines 21–22; Maggie Kilgour, "New Spins on Old Rotas: Virgil, Ovid, Milton," in *Classical Literary Careers*, 183–84.

6. See Ann Baines Coiro, "Fable and Old Song: *Samson Agonistes* and the Idea of a Poetic Career," *Milton Studies* 36 (1998): 123–52.

7. *Defensio secunda* (London, 1654), 90, translation from Milton, *Areopagitica and Other Writings*, ed. William Poole (London: Penguin Books, 2014), 308–9.

8. See the commentary in John Semple Smart, ed. *The Sonnets of Milton* (Oxford: Clarendon Press, 1966).

9. Phillips, "The Life of Mr. John Milton," xxxvii, in John Milton, *Letters of State* (London, 1694).

## NOTES TO CHAPTER THIRTEEN

1. G. E. B. Eyre and C. R. Rivington, eds., *A Transcript of the Registers of the Worshipful Company of Stationers: from 1640 to 1708*, 3 vols. (London, 1913–1914), 2:381. The scribe, anticipating, originally wrote "in" after "Paradise lost" and then erased it.

2. Anthony Wood, *Life and Times of Anthony Wood, Antiquary, of Oxford 1623–1695*, ed. Andrew Clark, 5 vols. (Oxford: Oxford Historical Society, 1891–1900), 1:445, 465.

3. Thomas Tomkins, *The Inconveniencies of Toleration* (London, 1667), 2, 37.

4. Wood, *Life and Times*, 2:242.

5. Eyre and Rivington, *Transcript*, 2:369–91.

6. For Tomkins see Anthony Wood, *Athenæ Oxonienses*, ed. Philip Bliss, 4 vols. (London, 1813), vol. 3, cols. 1046–48; *ODNB*; ESTC; Nicholas von Maltzahn, "The First Reception of *Paradise Lost*," *Review of English Studies* 47, no. 188 (1996):

479–99, esp. 481–87. For Tomkins and Davis see David Mateer, "Hugh Davis's Commonplace Book: A New Source of Seventeenth-century Song," *Royal Musical Association Research Chronicle* 32 (1999): 67; and for the *Paradise Regained / Samson Agonistes* volume, see Eyre and Rivington, *Transcript*, 2:415, under September 10, 1670.

7. Hugh Davis, *De jure uniformitatis ecclesiasticæ* (London, 1668), sig. e2r, 46, 47, 48. Davis twice refers to the "late" Milton—it is uncertain whether he means "recent" or whether he indeed thought Milton had recently died, or enjoyed pretending so.

8. There is a modern edition by Harriet Spanierman Blumenthal, *Pordage's "Mundorum explicatio"* (New York: Garland, 1991), and see William Poole, *Milton and the Idea of the Fall* (Cambridge: Cambridge University Press, 2005), 107–13. The work, however, attracted almost no notice at the time, and the identification of the author "S. P. Armig." with Samuel Pordage was not made by contemporary bibliographers, such as Anthony Wood. Its reappearance in 1663 was merely a reissue of unsold stock.

9. Helen Darbishire, ed., *The Early Lives of John Milton* (London: Constable, 1932), 239. The earliest example in the epic is *PL* 1.19–22, where Milton addresses (what we assume is) the Holy Ghost in terms that would not make a Trinitarian blink; and yet it is clear from the *De doctrina* (e.g., *OM*, 8:244–47, 252–53, 270–71); that Milton thought quite otherwise of both the name and the range of beings to which it might apply.

10. For Milton's contract, see Peter Lindenbaum, "Milton's Contract," *Cardozo Arts & Entertainment Law Journal* 10 (1992): 439–54, esp. 446–49, and Kerry MacLennan, "John Milton's Contract for 'Paradise Lost': A Commercial Reading," *Milton Quarterly* 44, no. 4 (2010): 221–30.

11. D. F. McKenzie, "Milton's Printers: Matthew, Mary and Samuel Simmons," *Milton Quarterly* 14, no. 3 (1980): 87–91. Thomas Corns comments privately to me that Simmons's downfall—for if he were trying to launch himself as a printer-bookseller then he soon failed—was probably caused by his obsession with publishing Joseph Caryl's commentaries on Job.

12. The original is British Library, MS Add. 18861 (CELM, MnJ 111); a convenient facsimile with commentary can be found in Robert Woof, Howard J. M. Hanley, and Stephen Hebron, *Paradise Lost: The Poem and Its Illustrators* (Grasmere, UK: Wordsworth Trust, 2004), 84–85. A receipt for one of the installments of £5 survives, dated April 26, 1669, now in Christ's College, Cambridge (CELM, MnJ 112); there is a facsimile in Samuel Leigh Sotheby, *Ramblings in the Elucidation of the Autograph of Milton* (London, 1861), between 136, 137. This document calls the original contract a "covenant." For earlier agreements consider, for instance, the Stationer Richard Royston, who in April 1651 was reported as being the first stationer to pay a royalty to Henry Hammond for his *Annotations on the New Testament* (see *ODNB*). Still earlier, a detailed agreement of 1624 survives between the Oxonian geographer Nathanael Carpenter and specific Oxford printers and booksellers, whereby Carpenter agreed to pay the printers for the entire production costs of an edition of 1,500 copies of his *Geographie Delineated*, published in 1625, and then to sell the whole edition to a bookseller for a little over twice the

cost of production; the bookseller is then assumed to have retailed the books for around three times the unit cost of production. See I. G. Philip, "A Seventeenth Century Agreement between Author and Printer," *Bodleian Library Record* 10, no. 1 (1978): 68–73.

13. Lindenbaum, "Milton's Contract," 443.

14. The contract uses the language of "impression," not "edition," but the fact that Simmons settled with Milton's widow in 1680 for £8 suggests that "impression" here means "edition" in the modern bibliographical sense; this is confirmed by the notional legal maximum in the period (by an order of the Stationers' Company of December 4, 1587) of 1,500 copies per edition.

15. Henry Spelman, *Glossarium Archaiologicum* (London, 1687), sig. b2r. As the same passage admits, Bill still had the greater part of the edition on his hands in 1637, so his may have been a sensible decision.

16. John Philips, *Cyder,* ed. John Goodridge and J. C. Pellicer (Cheltenham, UK: Cyder Press, 2001), xviii.

17. Thomas Ellwood, *The History of the Life of Thomas Ellwood,* 2nd ed. (London, 1714), 246.

18. For Royston, see *ODNB;* for Tokefield see Cyprian Blagden, *The Stationers' Company: A History, 1403–1959* (London: Allen and Unwin, 1960), 161, 215–16; Andrew Marvell, *The Prose Works of Andrew Marvell, 1676–1678,* ed. Martin Dzelzainis, Annabel M. Patterson, N. H. Keeble, and Nichols Von Maltzahn, 2 vols. (New Haven, CT: Yale University Press, 2003), 1:28–29.

19. CELM, MnJ 22, most fully described by Darbishire in her edition.

20. Gordon Campbell, Thomas N. Corns, John K. Hale, and Fiona J. Tweedie, *Milton and the Manuscript of "De Doctrina Christiana"* (Oxford: Oxford University Press, 2007), 59.

21. Hugh Amory, "Things Unattempted Yet," *Book Collector* 32, no. 1 (1983): 41–66, the definitive account. Compare Stephen B. Dobranski, *Milton, Authorship, and the Book Trade* (Cambridge: Cambridge University Press, 1999), 33–40, and for an important technical summary of the printing of the first edition see R. G. Moyles, *The Text of* Paradise Lost: *A Study in Editorial Procedure* (Toronto: University of Toronto Press, 1985), 3–21.

22. *Pace* Dobranski, *Milton, Authorship, and the Book Trade,* 38, who maintains "we ought not to infer too much" from such details.

23. *Early Lives,* 295 (Richardson).

24. As shrewdly argued by von Maltzahn, "First Reception," 487.

25. For the four issues, see Amory, "Things Unattempted Yet," 63–66; for a summary of the booksellers, see W. R. Parker, *Milton: A Biography,* rev. Gordon Campbell, 2 vols. (Oxford: Clarendon Press, 1996), 1112–13, and see ESTC for profiles of these booksellers' careers.

26. For an illuminating comparison of the publication of Milton and Dryden, see Tobias Gabel, *Paradise Reframed: Milton, Dryden, and the Politics of Literary Adaptation, 1658–1679* (Heidelberg: University of Heidelberg, 2016), 85–117.

NOTES TO CHAPTER FOURTEEN

1. For a critical survey, see Neil Forsyth, *The Satanic Epic* (Princeton, NJ: Princeton University Press, 2003), 314–28.

2. *Retractationes,* bk. 2, comment printed as part of Joannes Ludovicus Vives's standard commentary in early modern editions of *The City of God,* the English translation of John Healey (London, 1610), sig. [B6]r.

3. For some excellent remarks on Milton and prophetic history see H. R. Trevor-Roper, "Milton in Politics," *Catholics, Anglicans and Puritans: Seventeenth-Century Essays* (London: Secker and Warburg, 1987), 237–41; and for some comparisons not shackled to the historiography of Dissent, see the essays in James E. Force and Richard H. Popkin, eds., *Millenarianism and Messianism in Early Modern European Culture,* vol. 3: *The Millenarian Turn: Millenarian Contexts of Science, Politics and Everyday Anglo-American Life in the Seventeenth and Eighteenth Centuries* (Dordrecht, Netherlands: Kluwer Academic, 2001).

4. David Loewenstein, *Milton and the Drama of History* (Cambridge: Cambridge University Press, 1990), 16–17, 22–23.

5. Dante, from the nineteenth canto of the *Inferno,* translated by Milton thus: "Ah *Constantine,* of how much ill was cause / Not thy Conversion, but those rich demaines / That the first wealthy *Pope* receiv'd of thee" (*Of Reformation* (London, 1641), 30). Milton then quotes from Petrarch's 108th sonnet (138 in modern editions), and then from *Orlando Furioso,* 34.80; compare also 17.78 and 46.84. On these passages see William Poole, "John Milton and Giovanni Boccaccio's *Vita di Dante,*" *Milton Quarterly* 48, no. 3 (2014): 151–53, and Nicholas Havely, " 'Swaggering in the fore-top of the State": Milton, the Prelates and the Protestant Dante, from *Lycidas* to *Of Reformation,*" in *Dante and Milton: Envisioned Visionaries,* ed. Christoph Lehner and Christoph Singer (Newcastle upon Tyne, UK: Cambridge Scholars, 2016).

6. Barnabas 2:1, 4:9. After an abortive attempt by Archbishop Ussher, a successful *editio princeps* of the Epistle of Barnabas was only achieved in 1645 in Paris, an international event, and one perhaps therefore noticed by Milton. See Jean-Louis Quantin, "L'orthodoxie, la censure et la gloire: La difficile édition princeps de l'épître de Barnabé, de Rome à Amsterdam (1549–1646)," in *"Editiones principes" delle opere dei Padri greci e latini,* ed. Mariarosa Cortesi (Florence: SISMEL, 2006), 103–62.

7. Here is the comparison in lengths between the affected books in the 1667 and 1674 editions respectively:

| | | |
|---|---|---|
| Book 7 = 1,290 (second longest) | *becomes* | Book 7 = 640 (now shortest) |
| | | Book 8 = 653 (now third shortest) |
| Book 10 = 1,541 (longest) | *becomes* | Book 11 = 901 |
| | | Book 12 = 649 (now second shortest) |

8. For a survey of problems and suggestions, see John K. Hale, "*Paradise Lost*: A Poem in Twelve Books, or Ten?," *Philological Quarterly* 74, no. 2 (1995): 131–49, notably his comment, "I am haunted by the thought that in a poem of such a dense unity *any* local idea or motif or word can be followed out into a pattern of

the whole." Hale rightly rejects the advanced school of numerological criticism of *Paradise Lost* as fantasy.

9. This was of course an editorial intervention, based on the analogy of the twenty-four letters of the Greek alphabet.

10. It is now suspected these poems were written by different men, but Milton's age did not think so; see the entry in Lloyd's *Dictionarium*.

11. Boiardo wrote three books, whereas Ariosto managed forty-six, so both are members of the $1 \times 2 \times 3 \times 4$ group; only Tasso and Camões struck a decimal note of ten and twenty books respectively, and Davenant's projected five was a modernist imitation of the five acts of drama.

12. For summary and extended accounts see, respectively, Barbara Lewalski, *The Life of John Milton* (Oxford: Blackwell, 2000, rev. 2003), 448, 460–61, and Charles Martindale, *Milton and the Transformation of Ancient Epic*, 2nd ed. (London: Bristol Classical Press, 2002), 197–224. David Quint, *Inside "Paradise Lost": Reading the Designs of Milton's Epic* (Princeton: Princeton University Press, 2014), 204, 210, offers one shrewd local analysis.

13. Lucan, *Pharsalia*, trans. Thomas May (London, 1627), sig. N1r.

14. William Camden, *The Historie of . . . Elizabeth* (London, 1630), 191–92, quoting *Pharsalia*, 1.348. Milton cited from the Latin original of this work in his commonplace book.

15. David Norbrook, *Writing the English Republic: Poetry, Rhetoric and Politics, 1627–1660* (Cambridge: Cambridge University Press, 1999), 44–48.

16. Norbrook, *Writing the English Republic*, 23–62, 83–92.

17. *Pharsalia*, 2.672–77, 5.508f, 9.619–937, 700–33. See variously William Blissett, "Caesar and Satan," *Journal of the History of Ideas* 18, no. 2 (1957): 221–32; Claes Schaar, *Full Voic'd Quire Below: Vertical Context System in* Paradise Lost (Lund: CWK Gleerup, 1982), 163–71; Martindale, *Milton and the Transformation of Ancient Epic*, 221–23; Norbrook, *Writing the English Republic*, as cited in the following note; Quint, *Inside "Paradise Lost*," 210; and most recently Ivana Bičak, "Transmutations of Satan and Caesar: The Grotesque Mode in Milton's *Paradise Lost* and Lucan's *Pharsalia*," *Milton Quarterly* 49, no. 2 (2015): 112–25. Milton had been absorbing Lucan into his poetry since at least "In Quintum Novembris": line 48, for instance, is based on *Pharsalia* 1.183.

18. The best attempt is Norbrook, *Writing the English Republic*, 433–67. Norbrook (447, 456) rightly traces the tradition of Lucanic criticism back to the commentary on *Paradise Lost* by Patrick Hume (1695), although investigation in Hume suggests that these are rarely primary or exclusive allusions.

19. Norbrook, *Writing the English Republic*, 445.

20. Hobbes, agreeing with Davenant, has been discussed above; Servius's view comes from his note on *Aeneid* 1.382: "Lucanus namque ideo in numero poetarum esse non meruit, quia videtur historiam composuisse non poema."

21. Adapted from Quint, *Inside "Paradise Lost*," 234.

22. The "two ways" motif once again strongly recalls the Epistle of Barnabas, of which the second half is indeed an exposition of the "Ὁδοὶ δύο" or "Two Ways" (18:1). This section is a close parallel to the opening of the Didache, but that text was only recovered in 1873.

23. As praised by Joseph H. Summers, *The Muse's Method: An Introduction to "Paradise Lost"* (London, 1962), 112–13, and perhaps regretted by Quint, *Inside "Paradise Lost,"* 234–35.

24. Loewenstein, *Milton and the Drama of History,* 92–125, rightly emphasizes the unresolved intermingling of optimism and pessimism in the final two books, mirroring Milton's deep ambivalence about providence in history, notwithstanding individual lives of spiritual heroism.

### NOTES TO CHAPTER FIFTEEN

1. For a survey of critical approaches to Milton's Universe, see John Leonard, *Faithful Labourers: A Reception History of Paradise Lost, 1667–1970,* 2 vols. (Oxford: Oxford University Press, 2013), 705–819, and his summary of his own position now in *The Value of Milton* (Cambridge: Cambridge University Press, 2016), 64–69. Note the young John Wesley's comment in his diary for June 3, 1725: "learned the *geography* of the First Book of Milton," my emphasis, quoted in John Wesley, *Milton for the Methodists: Emphasized Extracts from "Paradise Lost,"* ed. Frank Baker (London: Epworth, 1988), vii.

2. For three other analyses of Milton's readings in Hesiod, see William M. Porter, *Reading the Classics and* Paradise Lost (Lincoln: University of Nebraska Press, 1993), 43–67; Neil Forsyth, *The Satanic Epic* (Princeton, NJ: Princeton University Press, 2003), 30–35; and Stephen Scully, *Hesiod's* Theogony: *From Near Eastern Creation Myths to* Paradise Lost (Oxford: Oxford University Press, 2015), 171–83.

3. *Du Bartas* (London, 1611), 8, 9. Compare Ovid, *Metamorphoses,* 1.15–20.

4. *De rerum natura,* 2.398–425.

5. See *Oxford English Dictionary* (www.oed.com), s.n. "clan," 1a, hence 2.

6. S[amuel] B[arrow], "In Paradisum Amissam," line 12, in Milton, *Paradise Lost* (London, 1674), A2r. For the author, see Nicholas von Maltzahn, "'I admird Thee': Samuel Barrow, Doctor and Poet," *Milton Quarterly* 29, no. 1 (1995): 25–28.

7. John Leonard, "Milton, Lucretius, and "the Void Profound of Unessential Night", in *Living Texts: Interpreting Milton,* ed. Kristin A. Pruitt and Charles W. Durham (Cranbury, NJ: Associated University Presses, 2000), 198–217, largely a reaction to John Rumrich's influential discussion in *Milton Unbound* (Cambridge: Cambridge University Press, 1996), 118–46; Rumrich's reply is printed in Pruitt and Durham, *Living Texts,* 218–227. Leonard restates most of this essay in his excellent introduction to his Penguin edition of *Paradise Lost* (London: Penguin, 2000).

8. Scully, *Hesiod's* Theogony, 116–25. Night also appears fully personified as *pronuba* or "brideswoman" to Proserpina in Claudian's *De raptu Proserpinæ,* 2.362.

9. Irenaeus, *Adversus Haereses,* 1.1. Another text in play here is Boccaccio's encyclopedic *De genealogia deorum,* in which Demogorgon in particular features regularly in the very opening discussions, as the ultimate progenitor of the pagan deities, creator of Earth, and the being who feels a disturbance within the womb of Chaos. There is now an I Tatti parallel edition of Boccaccio's *De genealogia deorum,* ed. Jon Solomon (Harvard, 2011–).

10. The prompt for this strategy had in fact been provided by Irenaeus himself, and none too subtly so (*Adversus Haereses,* 1.11.4).

11. On the deflection in this passage, see Robert M. Myers, "'God Shall Be All In All': The Erasure of Hell in *Paradise Lost,*" *Seventeenth Century* 5 (1990): 47.

12. In the *De doctrina,* the original matter of the universe was "not to be thought of as an evil or worthless thing, but as a good thing, a seed bank of every subsequent good" (*De doctrina,* 1.7 = OM, 8:293).

13. "The Womb of nature and perhaps her Grave," PL 2.911 = *De rerum natura,* 5.259.

14. *De rerum natura,* 5.837–48, and see the discussion below.

15. Leonard, *Faithful Labourers,* 705–9.

16. "De Idea Platonica," lines 16–18.

17. Origen, *Contra Celsum,* 6.22–23; M. J. Edwards, "Porphyry's 'Cave of the Nymphs' and the Gnostic Controversy," *Hermes* 124 (1996): 90–91.

18. See especially Leonard, "Milton, Lucretius, and 'the Void Profound,'" 200–202; Leonard, *Faithful Labourers,* 716–19.

19. *Iliad,* 7.18–27.

20. Hesiod, *Theogony,* 722–25.

21. *Aeneid,* 6.577–79.

22. *Phaenomena,* 96–116.

23. Fowler interprets 3.562–64 as Satan himself standing at the "eastern point / Of Libra" looking toward Aries, but Satan is rather "above" both equally, near the North Pole, where he had been looking at the mystical stairs, as the full parallel grammar shows: "Round he surveys . . . *from* eastern point / Of Libra *to* the fleecy star . . . / then *from* pole *to* pole / He views." But the problem remains how he can see the eastern point of a constellation God has yet to create. Fowler detects several astronomical prolepses or moments of dramatic irony, however (see, e.g., his notes to 3.557–58 and 9.64–6); is this one such?

24. See for example Aristotle, *Meteorologica,* 2.4–6.

25. As in Vitruvius, *De architectura,* 1.6.4–13, who also reports lesser systems of four and eight.

26. For an affirmation of the classicism of Milton's winds, see Gordon Campbell, "Milton's Catalogue of the Winds," *Milton Quarterly* 18, no 4 (1984): 125–28.

27. Martinus Martinius, *Sinicæ historiæ decas prima* (Munich, 1658), 3.

28. *CPW,* 7:492.

29. Hesiod, *Theogony,* 749–54, trans. Hugh G. Evelyn-White (Loeb [1926]).

30. On this and other quasi-mechanical contrivances in *Paradise Lost,* see Stephen B. Dobranski, *Milton's Visual Imagination: Imagery in* Paradise Lost (Cambridge: Cambridge University Press, 2015), 68–77.

31. It was first published in English, in the verse translation of Richard Fanshaw, in 1655, by Milton's publisher Humphrey Moseley. Interestingly, Fanshaw prefaced his work with supplementary translations of Petronius's *Bellum civile* (=*Satyricon,* secs. 119–24), which he considered to have been Camões's classical model, and Tasso's sonnet on Vasco. Fanshaw also translated a portion of *Os Lusíadas* into Latin hexameter.

32. Ludovico Ariosto, *Orlando Furioso,* trans. Guido Waldman (Oxford: Oxford University Press, 1983), 15.21, 22. Harington in his translation added a shoulder note to Sir Francis Drake at this moment.

33. J. Martin Evans, *Milton's Imperial Epic:* Paradise Lost *and the Discourse of Colonialism* (Ithaca, NY: Cornell University Press, 1996).

34. William Poole, *The World Makers: Scientists of the Restoration and the Search for the Origins of the Earth* (Oxford: Peter Lang, 2010), 27–37; *CPW,* 7:491.

35. William Poole, *Milton and the Idea of the Fall* (Cambridge: Cambridge University Press, 2005), 188.

36. The fullest account is now Dennis Danielson, *Paradise Lost and the Cosmological Revolution* (Cambridge: Cambridge University Press, 2014).

37. *Areopagitica* (London, 1644), 8; Leo Miller, "The Italian Imprimaturs in Milton's *Areopagitica,*" *Papers of the Bibliographical Society of America* 65, no. 4 (1971): 345–55.

38. See for instance the letter of the Savilian Professor of Geometry, John Wallis, to Henry Oldenburg, June 22, 1674, on how the individual must decide whether to assent to the ideas of Copernicus and Harvey (A. Rupert Hall and Marie Boas Hall, eds., *The Correspondence of Henry Oldenburg,* 13 vols. (Madison: University of Wisconsin Press et al., 1965–1986), 11:37).

39. For a summary see Poole, *World Makers,* 143–53.

40. The latter passage refers to the sun's "Station" (3.587), as if it were indeed immobile, and this word prompted Milton's first commentator, Hume, to pause. Is this "according to the *Copernican* Opinion?" he wondered. Not necessarily, he replied: "Station, Lat. *Statio,* does not imply a want of Motion, but is referable to the Orb, wherein the Sun is placed, and this very word is used by *Pliny, Statio Syderum,* for the Starry Orbs." To this I might add the usage at 7.563, which confirms Hume's exact ear: "The Planets in thir station list'ning stood."

41. Here I perhaps disagree in emphasis with the most recent treatment of Milton and astronomy, Danielson, *Paradise Lost and the Cosmological Revolution.* He states that Raphael's "What if" "although still properly tentative, is fully authorized" (128). I would reverse this sentiment—"although authorized [in the sense that Milton wrote it into his poem], it is still properly tentative." Milton was stylistically keen on such qualifications, as with, for example, his alchemists, who "can turn, or hold it possible to turn" base metals into gold (5.439–43); for two more important "or" formulations see 5.696–97 and 9.529–30. But on such "incertitude" compare Peter C. Herman, *Destabilizing Milton: "Paradise Lost" and the Poetics of Incertitude*

(Basingstoke, UK: Palgrave Macmillan, 2005), chap. 2, where this "aporetic" Milton is pushed too hard.

42. A general study is Steven J. Dick, *Plurality of Worlds: The Origins of the Extraterrestrial Life Debate from Democritus to Kant* (Cambridge: Cambridge University Press, 1982); see more particularly Francis Godwin, *The Man in the Moone,* ed. William Poole (Peterborough, Ontario: Broadview, 2009), 42–44, and Danielson, *Paradise Lost and the Cosmological Revolution,* 182–85.

43. Patrick Hume, *Annotations on Milton's Paradise Lost* (London, 1695), annotation to *PL* 1.650. This is the second of eight mentions of Galileo by Hume; see also his notes to 1.290, 3.460, 5.262, 5.268, 7.579, 8.145, and 8.149.

44. See, for instance, Augustine's discussion of Varro on the lunary Heroes, Lares, and Genii (Augustine, *City of God,* 7.6).

45. See the English translation and commentary by Edward Rosen: *Kepler's Somnium: The Dream, or Posthumous Work on Lunar Astronomy* (Madison: University of Wisconsin Press, 1967; repr. New York: Minelola, 2003).

### NOTES TO CHAPTER SIXTEEN

1. For a survey of debates on *Paradise Lost* and epic up to 1970, see John Leonard, *Faithful Labourers: A Reception History of Paradise Lost, 1667–1970,* 2 vols. (Oxford: Oxford University Press, 2013), 268–326, esp. 268–80 for the earlier commentators. An essay compatible with my own is Francis C. Blessington, Paradise Lost *and the Classical Epic* (London: Routledge, 1979), although Blessington emphasizes "synthetic" over the "disruptive" elements.

2. For the former see Stella Purce Revard, *The War in Heaven:* Paradise Lost *and the Tradition of Satan's Rebellion* (Ithaca, NY: Cornell University Press, 1980), 213–17, and for some more recent English "Parliaments of Hell" see Sharon Achinstein, *Milton and the Revolutionary Reader* (Princeton, NJ: Princeton University Press, 1994), 182–210; for the latter see Dana F. Sutton, "Milton's *in Quintum Novembris, anno aetatis* 17 (1626): Choices and Intentions," in *Qui Miscuit Utile Dulci: Festschrift Essays for Paul Lachlan MacKendrick,* ed. Gareth L. Schmeling and Jon D. Mikalson (Wauconda, IL: Bolchazy-Carducci, 1998).

3. C. S. Lewis, *Preface to Paradise Lost* (Oxford: Oxford University Press, 1942), 12–50.

4. Alastair Fowler, *Kinds of Literature: An Introduction to the Theory of Genres and Modes* (Oxford: Clarendon Press, 1982), 162–63.

5. Flavius Josephus, *Against Apion,* 1.12–13 (=Loeb Josephus, 1:166–69); Homer, *Ilias* [etc.], ed. Obertus Gifanius (Strasburg, 1572), "Ad lectorem," 15–16; Anthony Grafton, "Prolegomena to Friedrich August Wolf," in his *Defenders of the Text: The Traditions of Scholarship in an Age of Science, 1450–1800* (Cambridge, MA: Harvard University Press, 1991), 214–43.

6. William Poole, *Milton and the Idea of the Fall* (Cambridge: Cambridge University Press, 2005), 146–47.

7. Justus Lipsius, *Syntagma de bibliothecis* (Leiden, 1602), 10–14. A good modern account is Lionel Casson, *Libraries in the Ancient World* (New Haven, CT: Yale University Press, 2001), 31–47.

8. *Of Education* (London, 1644), 6. Milton's age considered the work *On Style* attributed to Demetrius to have been genuine; it is now considered to have been written much later, perhaps in the second century AD.

9. Nicholas Lloyd, *Dictionarium historicum, geographicum, poeticum* (London, 1686), s.v. "Callimachus."

10. Accounts differ, but see, for example, under "Lycophron" in Lloyd, *Dictionarium*.

11. For example, Milton, *Epistolae familiares* (London, 1674), 97, 127.

12. *Argonautica*, 1.2–4.

13. Apollonius, *Argonauticorum Libri IV*, ed. Jeremias Hoelzlinus (Leiden, 1641), Prolegomena, 3: "Neque enim Aeneis Virgiliana esset quod est, si nullus fuisset Apollonius." Parallel-spotting between Apollonius and Virgil had been popularized by J. C. Scaliger, *Poetices libri septem* (Geneva, 1561), 5.6.

14. Claes Schaar, *Full Voic'd Quire Below: Vertical Context System in* Paradise Lost (Lund: CWK Gleerup, 1982), 242–51.

15. *Argonautica*, 4.1541–46.

16. *Argonautica*, 1.503–9. See Lloyd, *Dicitonarium*, s.v. "Ophion," for parallels in Claudian's *De raptu Proserpinæ* and Ovid's *Metamorphoses*, both relevant to Milton's passage too, as they confirm the serpentine reference.

17. The major patristic source on the battle of Ophioneus and "Kronos" is Origen, *Contra Celsum*, 6.42; the whole passage, on the contested priority of pagan versus sacred permutations of similar stories, is pertinent. The other patristic site is Eusebius, *Preparation for the Gospel*, 1.10. For this theomachy see M. L. West, *Early Greek Philosophy and the Orient* (Oxford: Clarendon Press, 1971), 15–23, 40–50; Hermann S. Schibli, *Pherekydes of Syros* (Oxford: Clarendon Press, 1990), 78–103, where Schibli warns that the original account probably featured "not a war that deposes Ophioneus and his clan from supremacy; it should rather be seen as the unsuccessful attempt of a powerful and monstrous earth-god to usurp the rule of Heaven" (96); also Neil Forsyth, *The Old Enemy: Satan and the Combat Myth* (Princeton, NJ: Princeton University Press, 1987), 68–71.

18. J. L. Vives in Augustine, *Of the Citie of God* (London, 1610), 513 (bk. 14, chap. 11). Compare the similar remark in George Sandys, trans., *Ovid's Metamorphoses Englished* (London, 1632), 27, a passage cited by Fowler in his excellent note. Sandys, incidentally, repeated this annotation and identification in his translation and edition of Hugo Grotius, *Christs Passion: A Tragedy. With Annotations* (London, 1640), 111.

19. Tertullian, *De corona*, sec. 7 (= *Opera* (Paris, 1634), 123; this is the edition Milton cited in his commonplace book [Commonplace Book MS, 4]); West, *Early Greek Philosophy*, 23; Schibli, *Pherekydes*, 97.

20. Available to Milton were either the edition of Giovanni Battista Pio (Bologna, 1519), with a continuation to ten books; or that of Louis Carrion (Antwerp, 1565); or the small, fat Leipzig 1630 edition, with very detailed commentary. For Valerius there is now Debra Hershkowitz, *Valerius Flaccus' Argonautica: Abbreviated Voyages in Silver Latin Epic* (Oxford: Clarendon Press, 1998).

21. *Odyssey*, 12.61–72; Theocritus 13, 22; Catullus 64.

22. C. W. Brodribb, "Milton and Valerius Flaccus," *Notes and Queries* (December 3, 1938).

### NOTES TO CHAPTER SEVENTEEN

1. Michel Jeanneret, *A Feast of Words: Banquets and Table Talk in the Renaissance* (Cambridge: Polity, 1991), esp. 112–28.

2. The best accounts are Stella Purce Revard, *The War in Heaven: Paradise Lost and the Tradition of Satan's Rebellion* (Ithaca, NY: Cornell University Press, 1980), and Neil Forsyth, *The Satanic Epic* (Princeton, NJ: Princeton University Press, 2003).

3. [Lucy Hutchinson, formerly attributed to Allen Apsley], *Order and Disorder, or the World Made and Undone, being Meditations upon the Creation and Fall* (London, 1679), 46; William Poole, *Milton and the Idea of the Fall* (Cambridge: Cambridge University Press, 2005), 99.

4. *Aeneid*, 10.360–61; this and the following example appear as early as Hume's 1695 commentary.

5. Spenser, *Faerie Queene*, 3.1.61.

6. *Iliad*, 5.339–42, 899–904. The self-healing spirit may come from the demonological tradition rooted in Psellus: see Fowler's note on the passage, and the note on Psellus in Chapter 8 above on "Systematic Theology."

7. *Faerie Queene*, 1.7.13.1–6.

8. Joseph Mede, *The Key of the Revelation*, trans. Richard More (London, 1643), 116–18; Ludovico Ariosto, *Orlando Furioso*, trans. Guido Waldman (Oxford: Oxford University Press, 1983), 9.28–29, 91. See Revard, *The War in Heaven*, 188–91; for more on this passage of Revelation, see the commentators gathered by Matthew Poole, *Synopsis criticorum*, 4 vols. in 5 (London, 1669–1676), 4: cols. 1804–6.

9. Claudian, *Gigantomachia*, lines 70–71, 85–87; John Leonard, *Faithful Labourers: A Reception History of Paradise Lost, 1667–1970*, 2 vols. (Oxford: Oxford University Press, 2013), 273.

10. A tradition stemming from the pseudepigraphical Enoch 7.19, often associated with Genesis 6:1–4. Neil Forsyth, *The Old Enemy: Satan and the Combat Myth* (Princeton, NJ: Princeton University Press, 1987), 147–91; Poole, *Milton and the Idea of the Fall*, 187–88.

11. *A Narration of the Siege and Taking of the Town of Leicester the Last of May, 1645 by the Kings Forces* (London, 1645), 7, 8; Barbara Donagan, *War in England 1642–1649* (Oxford: Oxford University Press, 2008), 78–79. For the development of English ordnance (used extensively abroad) to 1642 see Mark Charles Fissel, *English Warfare 1511–1642* (London: Routledge, 2001), 181–88.

12. Claudian, *Gigantomachia*, 29.

13. This forced rejection looks forward to the even more difficult rejection of all book learning by Jesus in *Paradise Regained*, 4.322–30.

14. John Harper, " 'One equal music': The Music of Milton's Youth," *Milton Quarterly* 31, no. 1 (1997): 1–10. There is now a recording by Fretwork from reconstructions

by Richard Rastall of Milton Senior's chamber music: *Sublime Discourses: The Complete Instrumental Music of John Milton and Martin Peerson*, Regent Records, B005SRPMJ4, 2012, audio CD.

15. Plato, *Republic*, 399A; Thucydides, 5.70; Gellius, 1.11.1–9. Thucydides's emphasis is more on the use of the pipes to make the soldiers march in step. Gellius next comments that, in contrast, Homeric warriors went to war in silence.

16. George F. Butler, "Nonnos and Milton's 'vast *Typhœan* rage': The *Dionysiaca* and *Paradise Lost*," *Milton Quarterly* 33, no. 3 (1999): 71–76, thinks that this is a specific reference to Nonnus's epic, the first two books of which narrate the war between Zeus and Typhoeus.

17. Charles Leslie, *The History of Sin and Heresie* (London, 1698), sig. A2r-v. Leslie is discussing both Milton's epic and Dryden's dramatic rewrite of it.

18. As Robert H. West, *Milton and the Angels* (Atlanta: University of Georgia Press, 1955), 118, shrewdly observed.

19. Samuel Morland, *The Urim of Conscience, with Three Select Prayers for Private Families* (London, 1695), 13–14.

20. Thomas Heywood, *The Hierarchie of the Blessed Angels* (London, 1635), 341, discussed in Joad Raymond, *Milton's Angels: The Early-Modern Imagination* (Oxford: Oxford University Press, 2010), 216.

### NOTES TO CHAPTER EIGHTEEN

1. *Argonautica*, 1.496–502.

2. Damien Nelis, "Demodocus and the Song of Orpheus: Ap. Rhod. *Arg.* 1.496–511," *Museum Helveticum* 49 (1992): 153–70, at 166.

3. That Uriel's remarks to Satan on Creation ("I saw when at his Word the formless Mass," *PL* 3.708) might be an echo of the Song of Orpheus in Apollonius was shrewdly noted by Benjamin Stillingfleet, reported in Henry John Todd, ed., *Poetical Works of John Milton* (London, 1801), 6:422.

4. Milton read several books that include accounts of this euhemerizing tradition, such as Clement of Alexandria, *Stromateis*, 1.15, and Eusebius, *Preparation for the Gospel*, 9.17. For the sources, see Arthur Stanley Pease, ed., *Publi Vergili Maronis Aeneidos, Liber Quartus* (Cambridge, MA: Harvard University Press, 1935), 254.

5. The best discussion of Iopas is Philip R. Hardie, *Virgil's Aeneid: Cosmos and Imperium* (Oxford: Clarendon Press, 1986), 56–66. For a comment from Milton's time on Iopas and others as teachers of "Naturall and Morall Philosophie," see Henry Peacham, *The Compleat Gentleman* (London, 1622), 79.

6. *Eclogues*, 8.31–44.

7. "Ascraeo . . . seni" (*Eclogues*, 6.70). This eclogue had started out, too, with reference in its first line to Virgil's Theocritan ("Syracusan") origins ("Syracosio . . . uersu").

8. *Georgics*, 2.475–82.

9. A final, ecphrastic example read by Milton: in Claudian, *Proserpina*, just before her rapture, sings as she sews, and the pattern she sews is, indeed, a cosmogony in

tapestry (*De raptu Proserpinæ*, 1.248–51). Her tapestry develops into a map of the world according to classical geography, divided into its five zones—but as she starts to embroider in the surrounding ocean, she is forced to break off, and, "praescia" (provident of the future), she weeps.

10. Hardie, *Cosmos and Imperium*, 62.

11. Pliny, *Natural History*, 18.5.22. See Arnaldo Momigliano, *Alien Wisdom: The Limits of Hellenization* (Cambridge: Cambridge University Press, 1975), 4–6, for Punic lore; Carthaginian culture was in his phrase "murdered by the Romans." But for a more skeptical view of what the (early) Romans really wanted from Punic texts, see now Denis Feeney, *Beyond Greek: The Beginnings of Latin Literature* (Cambridge, MA: Harvard University Press, 2016), 43, 203–4.

12. "At a Vacation Exercise," lines 48–52, and see David Quint, *Inside Paradise Lost: Reading the Designs of Milton's Epic* (Princeton, NJ: Princeton University Press, 2014), 273–74n36.

13. *Theogony*, 295–318.

14. *Areopagitica*, 11.

15. J. C. Scaliger, *Poetices libri septem* (Geneva, 1561), 1.5; John Selden, *Marmora Arundeliana* (London, 1628), 9, 97–98; see Nicholas Lloyd, *Dictionarium* (London, 1686), s.n. "Hesiodus," "Homerus," for conventional lists of available authorities. Thomas Pope Blount's chronological *Censura celebriorum authorum* (London, 1690), commences with Hermes, then Hesiod, then Homer.

16. Joshua Barnes, Αυλικοκάτοπτρον *seu Estheræ historia* (London, 1679), lines 836–46.

17. Milton likens this to *De Rerum Natura*, 1.991–99; see Maurice Kelley and Samuel D. Atkins, "Milton's Annotations of Aratus," *PMLA* 70, no. 5 (1955): 1092.

18. Thus 78–79 (Latin), 364–65 (Greek) of Milton's edition (Basel, 1544) = sec. 69 (73–74) in the modern French / Greek edition of Félix Buffière, *Héraclite: Allégories d'Homère* (Paris: Belles Lettres, 1962). For a discussion with reference to Milton see Kenneth Borris, *Allegory and Epic in English Renaissance Literature: Heroic Form in Sidney, Spencer, and Milton* (Cambridge: Cambridge University Press, 2000), chap. 1, esp. 13–21.

19. Against Sir Walter Ralegh, *The History of the World* (London, 1614), 1.6.7 (93), in Bodleian, K 3.6 Art.

20. G. J. Vossius, *De theologia gentili*, 2 vols. (Amsterdam, 1641, reissued 1642). For an analysis of this tradition and its demise at the hands of David Hume, see R. W. Serjeantson, "Hume's *Natural History of Religion* (1757) and the Demise of Modern Eusebianism," in *The Intellectual Consequences of Religious Heterodoxy 1600–1750*, ed. John Robertson and Sarah Mortimer (Leiden: Brill, 2012), 267–95.

21. Dmitri Levitin, *Ancient Wisdom in the Age of the New Science: Histories of Philosophy in England, c. 1640–1700* (Cambridge: Cambridge University Press, 2015), 146–53 (all of Levitin's chapters 3 and 6 are pertinent here).

22. Eusebius, *Preparation for the Gospel*, 9.20 (Philo), 9.22 (Theodotus), 9.28 (Ezekiel). The Philo fragments quite boggled Eusebius's early modern editor Vigerus, in his edition of Paris, 1628, and they continue to puzzle.

23. Eusebius, *Preparation for the Gospel*, 1.9–10 (Sanchuniathon); 10.5, 6 (Cadmus). Eusebius reported on Punic historians at 10.11.

24. The text as reported, however, despite the pre-Trojan claim (1.9) contains a disapproving reference to "Hesiod and the celebrated Cyclic poets," who "framed theogonies of their own" (1.10), an obvious anachronism.

25. Notably *Preparation for the Gospel*, 9.11 (block quotation from Josephus, on how Berosus also recounted a myth of a flood and an ark), and 10.11 (from Tatian, on Manetho). For a contemporary digest of opinions on the antiquity and status of Berosus and Manetho, see Vossius, *De historicis Graecis* (Leiden, 1601), bk. 1, chaps. 13, 14 (85–91).

26. "De Idea Platonica," lines 29–31. See Eusebius, *Preparation for the Gospel*, 1.9, although, as Carey's note implies, Milton is more likely to have taken these exact details from John Selden's chapter on Baal or Belus in *De diis Syris* (London, 1617), 103–41.

27. Thus if Moses was born in 1571 BC and lived for over a century, and Troy was finally destroyed in 1184 BC, to follow Archbishop Ussher's reckoning (James Ussher, *Annals of the World* [London, 1658], 12, 29), then Sanchuniathon could have lived quite close in time to Moses. The dating of the Trojan War was of course a various affair, the Parian Marble offering what Selden equated to 1209 BC for the conclusion of the war (*Marmora Arundeliana*, 94).

28. Eusebius, *Preparation for the Gospel*, 1.9.

29. See Vigerus's appendiced commentary to his edition of Eusebius, *Praeparatio evangelica* (Paris, 1628), 2, to the text at 33.

30. Eusebius, *Preparation for the Gospel*, 1.10; the comment is Barr's (see note 31). Milton's text will have read *Zophasemin; Zophaim* is the modern emendation. For contemporary views of Sanchuniathon, see, for example, G. J. Vossius, *De historicis Graecis*, 3–4.

31. See Albert I. Baumgarten, *The Phoenician History of Philo of Byblos: A Commentary* (Leiden: Brill, 1981), the culmination of the pioneering James Barr, "Philo of Byblos and his 'Phoenician History,'" *Bulletin of the John Rylands University Library* 57, no. 1 (1974): 17–68.

32. Anthony Grafton, *Joseph Scaliger: A Study in the History of Classical Scholarship. II: Historical Chronology* (Oxford: Clarendon Press, 1993), 435, from J. J. Scaliger, *Opus de emendatione temporum* (Cologne, 1629), Fragmenta, 27.

33. Edward Stillingfleet, *Origines Sacrae, or A Rational Account of the Grounds of Christian Faith* (London, 1662), 26–32, at 32.

34. *CPW*, vol. 5:3.

35. The Oannes myth survived through Georgius Syncellus's quotations in the *Chronographia* from the lost Greek text of Eusebius's *Canones*. Milton may have encountered this material through J. J. Scaliger's reconstruction of Eusebius's *Canones* (*Thesaurus temporum* [Leiden, 1606], Graeca, part 1, 5; see also Grafton, *Joseph Scaliger*, 710). The nearer source is Selden's *De diis syriis* (London, 1617), esp. 171–89 (2.3) on Dagon / Oannes. Translated by author, from Georgius

Syncellus, *Chronographia*, ed. Jacques Goar (Paris, 1652), 28–29. We may deduce that Milton owned this volume of the Corpus Byzantinum, for in a later letter to the French scholar Emeric Bigot, Milton listed the volumes of this series he lacked, and this was not among them (*Epistolae familiares* (London, 1674), 50–51, translation in *CPW*, 7:498).

36. Syncellus, *Chronographia*, 29.

37. Compare the even more disturbing irony at 5.127–28, in an otherwise nice passage a nasty echo of 2 Peter 3:7 on the Day of Judgment (Fowler).

38. Matthew Poole, *Synopsis criticorum*, 4 vols. in 5 (London, 1669–1676), 2, col. 699.

39. Philip Hardie, "The Presence of Lucretius in *Paradise Lost*," *Milton Quarterly* 29, no. 1 (1995): 13–24; William Poole, "Lucretius and Some Seventeenth-Century Theories of Human Origin," in *Lucretius and the Early Modern*, ed. Stephen Harrison, Philip Hardie, and David Norbrook (Oxford: Oxford University Press, 2015), 191–99.

40. Lucretius, *T. Lucretius Carus the Epicurean philosopher, his six books De natura rerum done into English verse, with notes*, trans. Thomas Creech (Oxford, 1682), 164.

41. Thomas Stanley, *History of Philosophy [The Fifth Part: Concerning the Epicurean Sect]* (London, 1660), 172–73.

42. Lucretius, trans. Creech, 165; William Poole, *The World Makers: Scientists of the Restoration and the Search for the Origins of the Earth* (Oxford: Peter Lang, 2010), 124–27.

43. Lucretius, trans. Creech, 165; Stanley, *History of Philosophy*, 172–73.

44. On this word, compare John Rogers, *The Matter of Revolution: Science, Poetry, and Politics in the Age of Milton* (Ithaca, NY: Cornell University Press, 1996), 118–22, although this is not, as he claims, "the most radical of the vitalist discourses of the 1640s," but a commonplace of experimental chymistry as practiced within and without the academe of Milton's day.

### NOTES TO CHAPTER NINETEEN

1. See Gordon Teskey, *The Poetry of John Milton* (Cambridge, MA: Harvard University Press, 2015), 184–88, for Theocritus's presence in "Lycidas." It is no less obvious in the "Epitaphium Damonis," especially the first idyll, in which Thyrsis laments the dying shepherd Daphnis.

2. Also recounted by Hesiod in *Theogony*, 535–70.

3. Milton may also be thinking of Tertullian, *De corona*, sec. 7 (= *Opera* [Paris, 1632], 124), where Tertullian too recalls Hesiod's Pandora and compares her to Eve, remarking that whereas the latter is true, the former is mere myth.

4. See *Eclogue*, 6.1, and the discussion in Chap. 18 on the place of this in Virgil's plans for martial or even cosmological poetry.

5. Elijah Fenton, ed., *Paradise Lost . . . to which is prefixed an Account of [Milton's] Life* (London, 1725), xx.

6. Francis Peck, ed., *New Memoirs of the Life and Poetical Works of Mr. John Milton* (London, 1740), 37.

7. C. S. Lewis, *A Preface to "Paradise Lost"* (Oxford: Oxford University Press, 1967), 139–40; see also Timothy J. Burbery, *Milton the Dramatist* (Pittsburgh: Duquesne University Press, 2007), 80–83, although these need not be acted to be dramatic.

8. Dennis Richard Danielson, *Milton's Good God: A Study in Literary Theodicy* (Cambridge: Cambridge University Press, 1982), 192.

9. In her dream, Eve sees Satan as an angel, whose "dewie locks distill'd / Ambrosia" (5.56–57), and when Satan pretends to be "a stripling Cherube," he sports "flowing haire," which "in curles on either cheek plaid" (3.640–41). In Heaven as on Earth angels have fine hair (3.361, 626); Eden is "hairie" (4.135), and its trees have "locks" (10.1066). For more on Milton and hair see most recently Stephen B. Dobranski, *Milton's Visual Imagination: Imagery in* Paradise Lost (Cambridge: Cambridge University Press, 2015), 153–75.

10. Augustine, *City of God,* 14.13; William Poole, *Milton and the Idea of the Fall* (Cambridge: Cambridge University Press, 2005), 27.

11. John Milton, *Artis Logicæ Plenior Institutio* (London, 1672), 165–66 (2.9, appendix) = *CPW,* 8:356–57.

12. That the Celts worshipped trees came chiefly from Pliny, *Natural History,* 16.95, who also supposed that "druid" derived from the Greek δρῦς, "tree"; Caesar, *Gallic Wars,* 6.14, reported the oddity that the Druids wrote in Greek script. Compare Lucan 1.453–54 on the Druids, "nemora alta remotis / Incolitis lucis" (dwellers in deep forests with sequestered groves). See Thomas Smith, *Syntagma de druidum moribus ac institutis* (London, 1661), 6–12, for a contemporary and skeptical review of the evidence for such an etymology; but the connection between druidism and tree-worship was not doubted.

13. The classic analysis of this system of puns, one among many so explored, is Christopher Ricks, *Milton's Grand Style* (Oxford: Clarendon, 1963), 73–74.

14. The old claim derives from the (as yet unrevised) entry in the Oxford English Dictionary, itself perhaps indebted to the entry in Samuel Johnson's own *Dictionary* (1755). For the use in Meres, see Francis Meres, *Palladis Tamia* (London, 1598), 44, identified by means of the Early English Books Online Text Creation Partnership. Closer to Milton, we might note that his nephew used (or at least printed) the word before him too: see under "Disard" in Edward Phillips's dictionary *The New World of English Words* (London, 1658).

15. R. H. Charles, ed., *The Apocrypha and Pseudepigrapha of the Old Testament in English* (Oxford: Clarendon, 1913), "Vita Adae et Evae," i, 1.

## NOTES TO CHAPTER TWENTY

1. Eusebius, *Preparation for the Gospel,* 1.2. Milton probably used the edition of Franciscus Vigerus, S. J. (Paris, 1628).

2. Palaephatus was at the time most commonly encountered in successive editions of Jacob Moltzer's collection of Hyginus and the mythographers (e.g., Basel, 1549, 1570; Lyon, 1608).

3. Lactantius, *Divinæ Institutiones,* 1.9–15; Augustine, *City of God,* 8.22. These and other passages look back to the suggestive remark in Justin Martyr, *Apologia,*

sec. 5, that "not knowing that these were demons, they [the pagans] called them gods, and gave to each the name which each of the demons chose for himself." This is the ultimate source for *PL* 1.364–75.

4. Terence, *Andria*, Prologue 15–16: "id isti vituperant factum atque in eo disputant / *contaminari* non decere fabulas," my italics.

5. The classic exploration is G. W. Pigman, "Versions of Imitation in the Renaissance," *Renaissance Quarterly* 33, no. 1 (1980): 1–32, especially his comments on "eristic" imitation: "an open struggle with the model for preeminence, a struggle in which the model must be recognized to ensure the text's victory . . . admiration for a model joined with envy and contentiousness" (4).

6. Compare Claes Schaar's "vertical context systems" in his excellent quasi-commentary on Milton's epic, Claes Schaar, *Full Voic'd Quire Below: Vertical Context System in Paradise Lost* (Lund: CWK Gleerup, 1982).

7. Du Bartas, "The Advertisement," in Simon Goulart, *A Learned Summary*, trans. T[homas] L[odge] (London, 1621), sig. a2r–v.

8. J. W. Binns, *Intellectual Culture in Elizabethan and Jacobean England: The Latin Writings of the Age* (Leeds: Francis Cairns, 1990), 84–86.

9. Patrick Hume, *Annotations upon Milton's Paradise Lost* (London, 1695), 150.

10. Ovid, *Metamorphoses*, 3.402–510.

11. Leonard Digges, trans., *The Rape of Proserpine, translated out of Claudian in Latine into English Verse* (London, 1617), sigs. A4r–B2r.

12. Sir Walter Ralegh, *The History of the World* (London, 1614), 1.6.5 (90–91); editors usually cite Ralegh's source text, in Diodorus Siculus (2.5), but Ralegh has already gone some way to imposing a Eusebian interpretation on his sources: "Betweene this tale of the *Lybian Gods,* and the *Ægyptian* fables of *Osiris,* there is a rude resemblance, that may cause them both to be taken for the crooked images of some one true historie" (91). Compare *PL* 9.507–8 on Ammonian Jove too.

13. Samuel Purchas, *Purchas his Pilgrimage* (London, 1626), 743 (bk. 2, sec. 1 "Of the Hill of Amara"), 745 (bk. 2, sec. 3, "Of the Princes of the Blood there kept"); Joseph Ellis Duncan, *Milton's Earthly Paradise: A Historical Study of Eden* (Minneapolis: University of Minnesota Press, 1972), 35, 194–99. The description in Peter Heylyn's *Mikrokosmos* (Oxford, 1621; exp. ed. 1631), 728, derives solely from Purchas.

14. Purchas, *Purchas his Pilgrimage*, 743.

15. In 1626, for instance, the Oxford scholar and chronologist Thomas Lydiat earnestly desired to be allowed diplomatic passage to Amara, "to know the truth of what hath bene reported touching the Librarie there; and therabouts to studie Diuinitie, Historie, and Astronomie," Bodleian, MS Bodl. 313, fol. 35v; modernized text in J. O. Halliwell, ed., *A Collection of Letters Illustrative of the Progress of Science in England* (London, 1841), 55. Even more strikingly, when the Oxford don Daniel Vivian visited Rome in 1637, months before Milton arrived there, he met a "Habbashinian" who claimed to have been the librarian of Amara, and offered

him safe passage there and back! (Oxford, New College MS 349, 175, unpublished account of "A Voyage begun from Bristow December the first 1636").

16. Compare, for instance, *PL* 9.439–43, for another simile on gardens, concluding with an implicit reference, again, to Amara ("where the Sapient King / Held dalliance with his faire *Egyptian* Spouse").

17. Commonplace Book MS, 4.

18. Milton, *Poems* (London, 1645), 104.

19. Cedric C. Brown, *Milton's Aristocratic Entertainments* (Cambridge: Cambridge University Press, 1985).

20. In Ignatius, *Quæ extant omnia*, ed. Nicolaus Vedelius (Geneva, 1623), sec. 7 [sec. 6 in modern editions, translation from the Ante-Nicene Christian Library (ANCL)]. Milton had already cited from this edition in his commonplace book, 109, before he made this entry from Tertullian. Compare Comus, his mother Circe, and their cups in *A Maske*, lines 50–53, 150–53, 252–55, 520–30.

21. Maureen Quilligan, *Milton's Spenser: The Politics of Reading* (Ithaca, NY: Cornell University Press, 1983) offers the most extended treatment.

22. *Areopagitica* (London, 1644), 12–13.

23. Peter Herman, *Squitter-Wits and Muse Haters: Sidney, Spencer, Milton and Renaissance Anti-Poetic Sentiment* (Detroit: Wayne State University Press, 1996), 194–97; Zoe Hawkins, "Spenser, Circe, and the Civil War: The Contexts of Milton's "Captain or Colonel,'" *Review of English Studies* 66, no. 277 (2015): 876–94.

24. *Aeneid*, 6.126, 128–29; see also William M. Porter, *Reading the Classics and Paradise Lost* (Lincoln: University of Nebraska Press, 1993), 100–105.

25. For the development of Milton's "animist materialism," reading it as a reaction against mechanism, see Stephen M. Fallon, *Milton among the Philosophers: Poetry and Materialism in Seventeenth-Century England* (Ithaca, NY: Cornell University Press, 1991), 79–110.

26. Giovanni Pico della Mirandola, "Oratio quaedam elegantissima," in *Opera Omnia* (Reggio Emilia, Italy, 1506), sig. [Svi]r, with expansions and some emendations. Pico appears as a character several times in a satirical text Milton admired, Traiano Boccalini's *De Ragguagli di Parnasso* (Venice, 1612), cited several times in his commonplace book.

27. Ovid, *Metamorphoses*, 8.42.

28. Ovid, *Metamorphoses*, 8.41.

29. Compare Anthony D. Nuttall, *The Alternative Trinity: Gnostic Heresy in Marlowe, Milton, and Blake* (Oxford: Clarendon Press, 1998), esp. chap. 3.

30. We might note that Milton, who was in his prose writings interested in the word "parl(i)ament" and the origins of that institution, excised the word in any form from *Paradise Lost*; "assembly" is preferred. See Hannah Crawforth, *Etymology and the Invention of English in Early Modern Literature* (Cambridge: Cambridge University Press, 2013), 160–67.

31. On this see most recently Diana Treviño Benet, "The Fall of the Angels: Theology and Narrative," *Milton Quarterly* 50, no. 1 (2016): 1–13. Benet treats this incompatibility as a sign that Milton "could not bring the theological issues and the requirements of narrative into one harmonious consistency" (10).

32. Augustine, *City of God*, 12.7; William Poole, *Milton and the Idea of the Fall* (Cambridge: Cambridge University Press, 2005), 28–30.

33. Hesiod, *Theogony*, 924–29.

34. Porphyry, *De antro nympharum*, secs. 2–5. See M. J. Edwards, "Porphyry's "Cave of the Nymphs" and the Gnostic Controversy," *Hermes* 124 (1996): 88–100.

35. As memorably analyzed by Christine Froula, "When Eve Reads Milton: Undoing the Canonical Economy," *Critical Inquiry* 10, no. 2 (1983): 321–47.

### NOTES TO CHAPTER TWENTY-ONE

1. This is the central question of Milton criticism. The brilliantly perverse William Empson, *Milton's God* (London: Chatto and Windus, 1961; repr. Cambridge: Cambridge University Press, 1981) was most fully answered by Dennis Richard Danielson, *Milton's Good God: A Study in Literacy Theodicy* (1982; repr. Cambridge: Cambridge University Press, repr. 2009), from which gentler readings of Milton may take their start.

2. *The Judgement of the Synode holden at Dort, concerning the Five Articles* (London, 1619). Notice that the five articles were arranged differently and covered slightly different territory from the subsequent way theologians have expressed them (namely: total depravity, unconditional election, limited atonement, irresistible grace, and perseverance of the elect, hence the acronym "TULIP" of modern enthusiasts).

3. The two classic studies are Nicholas Tyacke, *Anti-Calvinists: The Rise of English Arminianism c.1590–1640* (Oxford: Oxford University Press, 1987) and Anthony Milton, *Catholic and Reformed: The Roman and Protestant Churches in English Protestant Thought, 1600–1640* (Cambridge: Cambridge University Press, 1995).

4. Danielson, *Milton's Good God*, 172–77.

5. *Of True Religion, Hresie, Schism, Toleration, and What Best Means May Be Us'd against the Growth of Popery* (London, 1673), 7–8.

6. Stephen M. Fallon, *Milton's Peculiar Grace: Self-Representation and Authority* (Ithaca, NY: Cornell University Press, 2007), esp. 182–202 (chap. 7).

7. For instance, Danielson, *Milton's Good God*, 83, comments that Milton does recognize the category in *De doctrina*, citing his remark on the kind of election "whereby a choice is made [*elegitur*] for any task" (1.4 = *OM*, vol. 6, part 1, 74–75); Danielson cites the older Yale translation "by which he [God] chooses an individual for some employment" (*CPW*, 6:172).

8. For the long tradition from *Gilgamesh* to Augustine, see Neil Forsyth's splendid *The Old Enemy: Satan and the Combat Myth* (Princeton, NJ: Princeton University Press, 1987), and with respect to Milton's Satan, his *The Satanic Epic* (Princeton, NJ: Princeton University Press, 2003), 167–87.

9. *De doctrina*, 1.2 = *OM*, vol. 8, part 1, 34–37. The invocation to the third book bears instructive comparison with its model, the invocation to Tasso's *Le sette giornate del mondo creato* (1607).

10. Albert C. Labriola, "The Son as an Angel in *Paradise Lost*," in *Milton in the Age of Fish: Essays on Authorship, Text, and Terrorism*, ed. Michael Lieb and Albert C. Labriola (Pittsburgh, PA: Duquesne University Press, 2006), 105–18. This striking essay also concludes that the Son-as-Angel does not know everything that the Father knows, and the Son-as-Man still less so, an excellent way into reading Milton's final poem, *Paradise Regained*.

11. *De doctrina*, 1.10 = *OM*, vol. 8, part 1, 358–59.

12. John Peter Rumrich, *Matter of Glory: A New Preface to* Paradise Lost (Pittsburgh, PA: University of Pittsburg Press, 1987), 155–66.

13. Peter C. Herman, "'Whose Fault, Whose but His Own?': *Paradise Lost*, Contributory Negligence, and the Problem of Cause," in *The New Milton Criticism*, ed. Peter C. Herman and Elizabeth Sauer (Cambridge: Cambridge University Press, 2012). He adds the example of Uriel, unable to see through Satan's disguise, but Milton's angelology can cope with that.

14. *Areopagitica* (1644), 12.

## NOTES TO CHAPTER TWENTY-TWO

1. W. R. Parker, *Milton: A Biography*, rev. Gordon Campbell, 2 vols. (Oxford: Clarendon, 1996), 676–77; Aubrey, *Brief Lives*, ed. Kate Bennett (Oxford: Oxford University Press, 2015), 1:660–72; commentary 2:1616–33; checked against the manuscript, MS Aubrey 8, fols. 634–86v, reordered by Bennett to reflect order of composition.

2. For the Phillips brothers see William Godwin, *The Lives of Edward and John Phillips, Nephews and Pupils of Milton* (London, 1815).

3. Joannes Buchlerus, *Sacrarum profanarumque phrasium poeticarum thesaurus*, 17th ed. (London, 1669), 399 ("poema ut præ se fert Heroicum, Grande quidem Inceptum fuit, at qui talia aggreditur, oportet eum Oeconomiam & Decorum poetarum optimorum observare"; "poema Heroicum Inscriptum, idque non male si modo Legitimam Inventionem & Decoram in eo ubique observari constet").

4. Ibid., correcting the misprint "saffragiis."

5. Edward Phillips, *Theatrum Poetarum* (London, 1675), 114.

6. Ibid., 114–15.

7. The letters, among the Tanner MSS in the Bodleian (Tanner 45, fol. 258r; Tanner 45*, fol. 271r), were first printed by James M. Rosenheim, "An Early Appreciation of 'Paradise Lost,'" *Modern Philology* 75, no. 3 (1978): 280–82; see further Nicholas von Maltzahn, "The First Reception of Paradise Lost (1667)," *Review of English Studies* 47, no. 188 (1996): 490–94.

8. Ants Oras, *Milton's Editors and Commentators from Patrick Hume to John Henry Todd (1695–1801): A Study in Critical Views and Methods* (Tartu, Estonia: Mattiesen, 1930).

9. Marcus Walsh, "Literary Annotation and Biblical Commentary: The Case of Patrick Hume's *Annotations* on *Paradise Lost*," *Milton Quarterly* 22, no. 4 (1988): 109–14; John Leonard, *Faithful Labourers: A Reception History of Paradise Lost, 1667–1970*, 2 vols. (Oxford: Oxford University Press, 2013), 12–14.

10. This edition has been done to death, but the three major reference points are J. H. Monk, *Life of Richard Bentley, D.D.*, 2nd ed. (London, 1833), 309–23; J. M. Levine, "Bentley's Milton: Philology and Criticism in Eighteenth-Century England," *Journal of the History of Ideas* 50, no. 4 (1989): 549–68; and Kristine Louise Haugen, *Richard Bentley: Poetry and Enlightenment* (Cambridge, MA: Harvard University Press, 2011), 211–12, 219–29.

11. Haugen, *Bentley*, 220.

12. I provide more documentation for this hypothesis in my forthcoming Oxford edition of Milton's "Ideas for Dramas" manuscript, part of the Trinity papers.

13. Chronological lists of translations may be found in Henry John Todd, ed., *Poetical Works of John Milton*, 5th ed. (London, 1852), 4:532–39; and under "Translations, Poetic," in William B. Hunter, ed., *A Milton Encyclopedia* (Lewisburg, PA: Bucknell University Press, 1978–1983), 8:78–86.

14. Haak's text was first published by Pamela Barnett in *Theodore Haak, F.R.S. (1605–1690): The First German Translator of "Paradise Lost"* (The Hague: Moulton, 1962); see also Poole, "A Fragment of the Library of Theodore Haak (1605–1690)," *Electronic British Library Journal* (2007), http://www.bl.uk/eblj/2007articles/article6.html; and most recently Nigel Smith, "Haak's Milton," in *Milton and the Long Restoration*, ed. Ann Baynes Coiro and Blair Hoxby (Oxford: Oxford University Press, 2016), 379–96.

15. W. E. Knowles Middleton, ed. and trans., *Lorenzo Magalotti at the Court of Charles II: His "Relazione d'Inghilterra" of 1668* (Waterloo, Ontario: Wilfrid Laurier University Press, 1980), 148.

16. Thomas Birch, *History of the Royal Society of London for Improving of Natural Knowledge*, 4 vols. (London, 1756), 2:250–54, 256.

17. "Nemora Florentina," an elegy on the advocate Stephen Waller, in Henry Newton, *Epistolæ, Orationes, et Carmina* (Lucca, 1710), "Carmina," 31. Newton had just mentioned his translation of *Cyder*.

18. British Library, MS Lansdowne 845, fol. 15r (to fol. 20r, this contains a translation of *PL* 1.1–241). My thanks to Will Bowers for help with the Italian. There is a text in MS Lansdowne 928 as well, among Basil Kennett's collections; he became chaplain to Henry Newton. The fragments were published by Franceso Viglione, "Lorenzo Magalotti primo traduttore del 'Paradise lost' di John Milton," *Studi di filologia moderna* 6 (1913): 74–84; see also George E. Dorris, *Paolo Rolli and the Italian Circle in London, 1715–1744* (The Hague: Mouton, 1967), 149.

19. See, for example, Sir Francis Kynaston's Chaucerian *Amorum Troili et Creseidæ libri duo priores Anglico-Latini* (Oxford, 1635), and William Bathurst's Spenserian *Carmen pastorale* (London, 1653).

20. John Nichols, *Literary Anecdotes*, 9 vols. (London, 1812–1816), 2:138; for some further remarks on the translation see William M. Porter, *Reading the Classics and*

Paradise Lost (Lincoln: University of Nebraska Press, 1993), 136–40. For Benson himself on *Paradise Lost,* see John T. Shawcross, ed., *John Milton: The Critical Heritage,* 2 vols. (London: Routledge, 1995), 2:104–7.

21. A good study of the earlier period is Dustin H. Griffin, *Regaining Paradise: Milton and the Eighteenth Century* (Cambridge: Cambridge University Press, 1986). A helpful collection of primary documents is Shawcross, *John Milton: The Critical Heritage;* there is also Shawcross's revised database, *Milton: A Bibliography for 1624 to 1799* (Medieval and Renaissance Texts and Studies online, 2016). See also now the essays in Blair Hoxby and Ann Baynes Coiro, eds., *Milton in the Long Restoration.*

22. John Hopkins, *Milton's Paradise Lost Imitated in Rhyme, in the Fourth, Sixth and Ninth Books* (London, 1699), sig. A4r.

23. See Dustin Griffin, "The Bard of Cyder-Land: John Philips and Miltonic Imitation," *Studies in English Literature, 1500–1900* 24, no. 3 (1984): 441–60, and the essay by J. C. Pellicer prefaced to his and John Goodridge's edition of the poem, *Cyder: A Poem in Two Books (1708)* (Cheltenham, UK: Cyder Press, 2001).

24. [Elijah Fenton], *Cerealia, An Imitation of Milton* (London, 1706), 2.

25. For a fine defense of Whig imitations of Miltonic blank verse, see Dustin D. Stewart, "Angel Bodies to Whig Souls: Blank Verse after Blenham," in *Milton in the Long Restoration,* chap. 11.

26. John Philips, *Cyder, A Poem in Two Books* (London, 1708), 47–48 (1.784–91 in the 2001 Goodridge and Pellicer edition). The final line is, rhetorically, an *anacoluthon,* and thus recalls *PL* 1.84, a particularly sad echo.

27. Wentworth Dillon Roscommon, *An Essay on Translated Verse* (London, 1685), 24–26.

28. It is usually attributed to the clergyman Abel Evans, but that is most unlikely, as the article on him in *ONDB* remarks.

29. Pope, *Rape of the Lock,* 3.151–52.

30. Alexander Gilchrist, *The Life of William Blake* (London, 1863), 115.

31. Dorothy Wordsworth, *The Grasmere Journals,* ed. Pamela Woof (Oxford: Clarendon, 1991), 62 (February 2, 1802); William Wordsworth, *The Prelude,* 3.293–302. For more on Romantic readings of the poem aloud, see Angelica Duran, " 'Join Thy Voice': Oral Readings of 'Paradise Lost,' " *Milton Quarterly* 44, no. 4 (2010): 255–60.

32. South Bucks Standard, Friday, August 30, 1901, 5.

33. T. S. Eliot, "Notes on the Blank Verse of Christopher Marlowe," in *The Sacred Wood* (London: Methuen, 1920); see Leonard, *Faithful Labourers,* 1:175, and discussion there.

34. John Wesley, ed. *Milton for the Methodists: Emphasized Extracts from "Paradise Lost"* (London: Epworth, 1988); Marcus Walsh, *Shakespeare, Milton, and Eighteenth-Century Literary Editing: The Beginnings of Interpretive Scholarship* (Cambridge: Cambridge University Press, 1997), 56. Wesley's acts of censorship are instructive, such as the cutting of Milton's lines celebrating prelapsarian sex (*Milton for the Methodists,* 39).

# Index